Lee Parrott

Leslie Parrott

THE ONE YEAR®

LOVE
TALK
Devotional
FOR COUPLES

DRS. LES & LESLIE
PARROTT

TYNDALE HOUSE PUBLISHERS, INC.
CAROL STREAM, ILLINOIS

Visit Tyndale online at www.tyndale.com.

Visit Les and Leslie's website at www.realrelationships.com.

TYNDALE and Tyndale's quill logo are registered trademarks of Tyndale House Publishers, Inc.

The One Year is a registered trademark of Tyndale House Publishers, Inc.

The One Year Love Talk Devotional for Couples

Copyright © 2011 by Les and Leslie Parrott. All rights reserved.

Cover photographs copyright © by Image Source Photography/Veer. All rights reserved.

Designed by Daniel Farrell

Published in association with Yates & Yates (www.yates2.com).

Unless otherwise indicated, all Scripture quotations are taken from the Holy Bible, New Living Translation, copyright © 1996, 2004, 2007 by Tyndale House Foundation. Used by permission of Tyndale House Publishers, Inc., Carol Stream, Illinois 60188. All rights reserved.

Scripture quotations marked NIV are taken from the Holy Bible, New International Version,® NIV.® Copyright © 1973, 1978, 1984 by Biblica, Inc.™ Used by permission of Zondervan. All rights reserved worldwide. www.zondervan.com.

Scripture quotations marked NASB are taken from the New American Standard Bible,® copyright © 1960, 1962, 1963, 1968, 1971, 1972, 1973, 1975, 1977, 1995 by The Lockman Foundation. Used by permission.

Scripture quotations marked ESV are taken from The Holy Bible, English Standard Version® (ESV®), copyright © 2001 by Crossway, a publishing ministry of Good News Publishers. Used by permission. All rights reserved.

Scripture quotations marked NKJV are taken from the New King James Version.® Copyright © 1982 by Thomas Nelson, Inc. Used by permission. All rights reserved. NKJV is a trademark of Thomas Nelson, Inc.

Scripture quotations marked KJV are taken from the Holy Bible, King James Version.

Scripture quotations marked NCV are taken from the New Century Version.® Copyright © 2005 by Thomas Nelson, Inc. Used by permission. All rights reserved. NCV is a trademark of Thomas Nelson, Inc.

Scripture quotations marked The Message are taken from The Message by Eugene H. Peterson, copyright © 1993, 1994, 1995, 1996, 2000, 2001, 2002. Used by permission of NavPress Publishing Group. All rights reserved.

ISBN 978-1-4143-3739-5

Printed in the United States of America

17 16 15 14 13 12 11
7   6   5   4   3   2   1

INTRODUCTION

Most people fail in the starting. —**MAUREEN FALCONE**

WE'VE GOT A CONFESSION to make right at the start. The two of us are busy. Sometimes hurried and harried. We live in a busy household in the city of Seattle with two little boys and a jam-packed schedule. We feel the press of impending deadlines. We don't always have the luxury of time to talk like we want. But that's not our confession—that's life!

The confession is that we wrote this One Year devotional for ourselves as much as we did for you. It's not a hard-hitting, roll-up-your-sleeves kind of book with challenging techniques, tips, and tests. We've written plenty of those kinds of books, but this is not one of them. This is more contemplative, reflective. Not so much a study in "how-tos" as it is an experience in having time to talk about what matters most as you walk together with God.

Along the way we've found something to be true for us that may become true for you as you read these daily meditations together. Sometimes we feel as though we are shoehorning into our lives these four or five minutes of reading and talking and sometimes praying. On occasion, we feel as though we are even forcing it. "There, we've had our 'time together,'" kind of idea. "Now we can check that off our list and get back to the real tasks at hand." You might feel the same way occasionally as you go through these pages.

That's okay. Some days you'll have more time than others. What we have also found is that the daily effort, even if it was very little, seemed to make a big difference. In fact, we've come to call these little meditations our "penny moments." Why? Well, because pennies are a dime a dozen, so to speak. Without much effort, one could find a penny on the floor or in a parking lot. And without much effort you can spend five minutes at some point in your day on a meditation from this book. No big deal.

Or so it seems.

In truth, these penny moments seem to add up when a husband and wife begin to collect them, just like actual pennies do, and even compound. For example, did you know that a one-cent-per-case increase of Coca-Cola would bring the company an additional $45 million a year? Or that if Krispy Kreme increased the cost of each donut by one penny, the company would increase profits by $27 million?

It's hard to believe, but it's true. And it may seem hard to believe that the few minutes you'll spend each day, over the course of using this book for a year, could have a huge payoff, but we are confident that it will.

It says a great deal about you and your marriage that you have decided to start this process. We wish you every success as you join your spirits together in this daily routine.

Les and Leslie Parrott
Seattle, Washington

SETTING YOUR SAIL FOR THE COMING YEAR

Trust in the LORD with all your heart; do not depend on your own understanding. Seek his will in all you do, and he will show you which path to take. PROVERBS 3:5-6

YOU'RE DRIVING TO A NEW location when the following takes place:

"Does this seem right to you?" she asks.

"I'm not sure, but let's see what's up the road a bit," he replies.

"Why don't we ask for directions," she urges.

That's when you know you have arrived at one of those prototypical marriage moments. And that's when your husband begins to drive faster, right? "I know where I'm going," he will say, as if he's suddenly tuned into an internal gyroscope that only he can read.

We all know an experience like this. And more than likely we will repeat it many times. But when it comes to setting out on the metaphorical journey of marriage each year, we can't afford to wander without a clear sense of direction. So we dedicate this first meditation to helping you set your sail for the coming year.

What does it mean to set your sail? It means being proactive about where you'd like to be as a couple twelve months from now. Rather than simply reacting to outside forces, it means taking charge and sitting in the driver's seat. Far too many couples ride like passengers on a bumpy bus, watching the scenery flash by their window as life passes by.

We'll be honest. Setting your sail for the coming year is not easy. It requires initiative. It will ask that you take responsibility for the condition of your marriage. It will then demand that you make the sacrifices to make your dreams a reality. In other words, the kind of marriage you want will be forged by your efforts. You will never achieve your ideal marriage as a mere passenger; you and your spouse must have a hand on the wheel. It is as George Bernard Shaw concluded, in his play *Man and Superman*: "Hell is to drift, heaven is to steer."

Some couples look for any reason to avoid charting their courses; they go through life piling one excuse on top of another for the state of their marriage: fate, in-laws, lack of money, temperament, the government, or even their church. Setting your sail does away with the blame game and puts an end to excuses. It gives you the opportunity to make your marriage everything you want it to be.

Take a moment here at the beginning of a new year to talk with each other about where you want your marriage to be in twelve months. Be as concrete as you can: What awaits your relationship out on the horizon in a year's time, and what can you do to ensure that you will get to the destination you desire?

Love does not consist in gazing at each other but in looking together in the same direction. —ANTOINE DE SAINT-EXUPÉRY

THE MISSION OF YOUR MARRIAGE

The LORD says, "I will guide you along the best pathway for your life. I will advise you and watch over you. Do not be like a senseless horse or mule that needs a bit and bridle to keep it under control." Many sorrows come to the wicked, but unfailing love surrounds those who trust the LORD. PSALM 32:8-10

FEW OBSTACLES CAN deter a person who has a passionate mission. It's what propelled William Tyndale to work for years in translating the Bible into English for a lay readership of the sixteenth century. It's what emboldened John Adams to envision a new nation, the Wright brothers to build the first successful airplane, and NASA to land a man on the moon. Obstacles abounded in every case, but it was a mission that kept them going.

If you don't see the value of having a mission or purpose, you need to know about Ramchandra Das, who lives in Bihar, India. In order to access nearby fields for food and work, Das and his fellow villagers had to take a 4.3-mile trek around a mountain. In time, he and the villagers grew weary of this obstacle, and Das became a man on a mission. With just a hammer and chisel, he cut a 33-foot-long, 13-foot-wide tunnel through a narrow area of the mountain. It took him fourteen years.

But Das wasn't the first person to embody such a mission. He was inspired by another villager, who cut a 393-foot-long, 33-foot-wide, 26-foot-high passage through another mountain so that villagers could reach a local hospital. That man landed on his mission when his wife died because he was unable to get her to the hospital.

Few obstacles can deter a person with a passionate mission. That's why, on this second day of the new year, we want to challenge you to explore your mission as a couple in your marriage. It goes right along with setting your sail for the coming year. In fact, what we are proposing is nothing short of building a compass for your relationship— a compass in the form of a marital mission statement.

We know this may sound intimidating—or corporate—but it's easier than you think. Simply begin with the words: "Our purpose as a married couple is . . ." We know that could lead in a hundred different directions, but how would you two finish that sentence? What comes to mind first? Take a stab at it. There are no right or wrong answers. This is simply a start in the process of articulating the mission of your marriage. So draft some ideas and don't get hung up on making this the perfect and ultimate statement. You're not writing it in stone. You're just setting a measure for yourself to gauge in the coming months. Try it today.

 Intimate relationships cannot substitute for a life plan. But to have any meaning or viability at all, a life plan must include intimate relationships. —HARRIET LERNER

IN GOD WE TRUST?

You are God, O Sovereign LORD. Your words are truth, and you have promised these good things to your servant. 2 SAMUEL 7:28

IN HIS BOOK *RUTHLESS TRUST,* Brennan Manning tells a poignant story about the brilliant ethicist John Kavanaugh, who worked for three months at "the house of the dying" in Calcutta. Kavanaugh was seeking clear direction on how best to spend the rest of his life. On the first morning there he met Mother Teresa, who asked what she could do for him. When Kavanaugh asked her to pray for him, she asked what she could pray for. He said, "Pray that I have clarity."

She said firmly, "No, I will not do that. Clarity is the last thing you are clinging to and must let go of." When Kavanaugh commented that she always seemed to have the clarity he longed for, she laughed and said, "I have never had clarity; what I have always had is trust. So I will pray that you trust God."

How does that strike you? If you're like us, it's a bit jolting. After all, we all want clarity to know what God wants us to do! But once we feel we have the clarity we're looking for, we are far less likely to depend on God's continuing guidance. In the last two days you have given some thought to the direction you want for your marriage in this coming year. You have begun to "set the sail." And you've also considered your marital mission, viewing it as a kind of compass for where you are heading. And if you've done this with any sincerity and effort, you are likely feeling somewhat secure in knowing where you're going and what you need to do. But we would be remiss if we didn't point out that no matter how mission-minded you are, and no matter how clearly you see your goals, you are certain to stumble along the way. You are certain to encounter a jolt or experience dark clouds that seem to linger too long. In these times, it's your trust in God that will see you through.

Read Deuteronomy 1:30-33 together as though it were written specifically for the two of you. Think about its imagery and how it can apply to your marriage journey.

This is our prayer for you as you're setting your sail for the coming year of married life: that in the times when you have clarity and in the times when you don't, that you would always trust God to go ahead of you and to care for you.

Courage, brother, do not stumble, though thy path be dark as night: There's a star to guide the humble: Trust in God and do the right. Let the road be rough and dreary, and its end far out of sight, foot it bravely; strong or weary, . . . trust in God, and do the right.
—NORMAN MACLEOD

YOUR PERSONAL TIME CAPSULE

In his presence, a scroll of remembrance was written to record the names of those who feared him and always thought about the honor of his name. MALACHI 3:16

TUCKED AWAY IN THE corner of the basement of our house is a tightly wrapped box labeled, "For John Parrott—to be opened on his sixteenth birthday." There's a similar box earmarked for John's little brother, Jackson.

What does each of these homemade time capsules contain? A copy of the newspaper on the day the boy was born, his birth announcement, a letter from Mom and Dad, and about a half dozen trinkets, photos, and memorabilia that are sure to generate conversation for a sixteen-year-old boy when he opens it on his birthday.

Time capsules aren't just for kids, of course. Instant archaeology has long been created by civic groups, schools, churches, and businesses. The first such capsule of note in America was the dream of a Civil War widow, Mrs. Charles Deihm. At the Philadelphia Centennial Exhibition of 1876, Mrs. Deihm closed up some commemorative items in a "century safe" to be opened in 1976. President Ford had it duly unsealed, revealing several items of historic Americana.

Iphigene Ochs Sulzberger, daughter of the publisher of the *New York Times*, buried a time capsule in the Times Tower in 1904 and was on hand to open it in 1964. In 1977 a two-disc gold record set titled *Sounds of Earth* was mounted on the *Voyager 2* spacecraft before its launch. The set includes recordings of Chuck Berry, Mozart, and a human kiss, as well as instructions for playing them.

There's something intriguing to the human spirit about leaving messages and artifacts for future delivery. And it's a pretty good exercise to consider what you might put in a personal time capsule—especially at the start of a new year. That's why we want to suggest you consider a time capsule for your marriage. Whether you actually build one or not, consider what you might put into your time capsule. If it were to be opened in one hundred years by your grandchildren and great-grandchildren and you wanted them to know about your relationship specifically, what would you include? What artifacts would you want them to see and talk about as they relate to your marriage? It's a useful exercise, one that may help you be more intentional about your marital legacy.

While you're at it, what would you place in a time capsule to be opened on your fiftieth wedding anniversary? Do any artifacts come to mind? How about a simple letter from each of you to the other that won't be read until that day?

One of the truths about time capsules is that they are as much for the here and now as they are for the future. —CATHLEEN O'CONNELL

DOING GOOD TOGETHER

Whenever we have the opportunity, we should do good to everyone—especially to those in the family of faith. GALATIANS 6:10

THE FILM *PEARL HARBOR* tells the story of two friends, Rafe and Danny, who survive the attack on Pearl Harbor and enter into World War II as fighter pilots.

In response to the Japanese attack, the Americans plan a risky, top-secret strike on Japan called the Doolittle Raid, and Rafe and Danny are recruited for the mission. Because of the tremendous risk, Colonel Jimmy Doolittle gives every pilot the choice to back out, but they all choose to go.

On the aircraft carrier en route to Japan, Rafe and Danny are painting logos on their airplanes when Danny quips, "Hey, Red, you think they picked us because we're young and dumb?"

"No, Goose. We're the tip of the sword," says Rafe.

Colonel Doolittle, off in the shadows, looks at his two key pilots and tells his fellow commander, "We may lose this battle, but we're going to win this war. You know how I know?"

Doolittle points at Rafe and Danny. "Them—because they are rare. At times like these you see them stepping forward." After a long pause, he adds, "There's nothing stronger than the heart of a volunteer."

And he's right. A volunteer is a person who is working on behalf of others or a particular cause without payment for his or her time or services. Like Rafe and Danny, volunteers feel the mission deep in their hearts. It compels them.

Chances are, at some point you have each volunteered for something or someone. But have you considered volunteering for something together as a couple? Does that fit into your mission for the year? We raise the question because volunteering as a husband-and-wife team is sure to strengthen your relationship—but not only that, it's sure to help you leave a legacy as well. As writer Albert Pike has said, "What we have done for ourselves alone dies with us; what we have done for others and the world remains and is immortal."

So what act of kindness for others can you do together? What is the need around you? Is it mentoring a younger, less experienced couple? Maybe it's caring for an elderly shut-in who has few visitors. Or helping out in your church's youth program. Whatever the activity, we urge you to build it into your own mission for the year. It is these acts that will be the most radiant pages of your love story.

Unselfish and noble actions are the most radiant pages in the biography of souls.
—DAVID THOMAS

PASSING THE PEACE

You will experience God's peace, which exceeds anything we can understand. His peace will guard your hearts and minds as you live in Christ Jesus. PHILIPPIANS 4:7

EVERY SERIOUS GOLFER knows the name *Paul Azinger*. Azinger, also known as "Zinger," won eleven tournaments on the PGA Tour. In 1993 he was on top of his game, but he was also diagnosed with non-Hodgkin's lymphoma at the end of the season. His treatment included six months of chemotherapy and five weeks of radiation. Paul and his wife, Toni, have been married since 1982, and they battled his cancer together. But both say they could not have made it without their Christian faith.

"I can honestly say I never said, 'Why me?' he has said. "There are two ways you can react to something like this. You can say, 'Why me, God? Why me?' Or you can do an about-face and run to God and cling to him for your security and your hope. That's what I did."[1]

Azinger's faith was evident to many, including PGA colleague Payne Stewart. Payne himself made a passionate commitment to Christ later in life; during those latter years he often spoke of his Christian fellowship group and wore a WWJD bracelet that his son gave him.

Shortly after winning the US Open in 1999, Stewart was up early in the morning fixing pancakes for the family. After breakfast, he kissed his wife, Tracey, and their children good-bye. Later that morning he boarded a private plane headed for Texas that mysteriously veered off course and ended up crashing in South Dakota. Though the force of the crash obliterated the plane and much else, the National Transportation Safety Board found several items intact. These included Payne's wedding ring, a gold pendant he had worn on a chain around his neck since his engagement in 1981, and amazingly, the WWJD bracelet.

A close friend of Payne's, Paul Azinger spoke at the funeral to the three thousand people and the millions watching on television: "Payne Stewart has finished the race, he has kept the faith, and now the crown of righteousness is his. Payne Stewart loved life and loved people. . . . During this past year, everyone who knew Payne Stewart saw this dramatic change in his life. They saw in Payne what the Bible calls a 'peace which passes all understanding.' Only God can do that, because only God can change a heart."

And only God can sustain your marriage through trials like cancer, the loss of a loved one, or whatever else you may face. Take a moment to review the early and recent years of your marriage, and relive times when you experienced a deep peace in the midst of unsettling circumstances. If you find that you can't relate to such a peace, reflect on why that might be.

The peace I have now is so wonderful. I don't understand how I lived so long without it.
—PAYNE STEWART

THE VALUE OF YOUR TIME

There is a time for everything, and a season for every activity under heaven.

ECCLESIASTES 3:1, NIV

EVER HEARD OF HOROLOGY? It's the science of measuring time, and it has been around, well, a long time. It started back in the days of the Babylonians, who came up with the idea for the sixty-second minutes and the sixty-minute hours we use now.

The first time-keeping device was probably a primitive, stick-in-the-ground version of the sundial, with the stick's shadow moving as the sun moved. Other devices involved bowls of water filled or emptied within a certain period of time, bowls of watermarked candles, oil lamps that would burn a measured amount of oil, or sticks of incense that burned at a measured rate and would drop a thread-suspended metal ball onto a bell. These days, horology is in the hands of scientists who go to great lengths to accurately measure minuscule moments in time: it's now measured literally in billionths of a second by atomic clocks. Horology has come a long way.

When it comes to measuring time in your marriage, we want to suggest you use a different device. Consider measuring time in terms of its value. In other words, how valuable is the time you spend together? After all, each of us places a different value on the increments of time, as the following popular illustration reveals:

To know the value of *one year* . . . ask the student who failed the final exam.
To know the value of *one month* . . . ask the mother of a premature baby.
To know the value of *one week* . . . ask the editor of a weekly newsmagazine.
To know the value of *one day* . . . ask the wage earner with six children.
To know the value of *one hour* . . . ask the lovers waiting to meet.
To know the value of *one minute* . . . ask the person who missed the plane.
To know the value of *one second* . . . ask the accident survivor.
To know the value of *one millisecond* . . . ask the Olympic silver medalist.

When you begin to measure time in terms of its value, rather than how many minutes or hours have passed, it helps you put it into perspective. Rather than thinking about where you can carve out an hour together in your schedules, you can begin to think in terms of what you'd like that hour to accomplish for you. Maybe what you really want is time to share a good laugh, or time to be known, or time to solve a particular problem. And any one of these may take more or less than an hour.

Get the point? Rather than measuring time in increments, try measuring your time in terms of its purpose. You'll be amazed to find you have more time than you thought.

I learned to tell time and now I'm always late. —**LILY TOMLIN**

UNION AND COMMUNION

If I only touch his cloak, I will be healed. MATTHEW 9:21, NIV

A WOMAN NAMED BRIGITTE GERNEY was trapped beneath a thirty-five-ton collapsed construction crane in New York City for six hours. Throughout her ordeal, she held the hand of one of three police officers, who stayed by her side as heavy machinery moved the tons of twisted steel from her crushed legs. A stranger's touch gave her hope and the will to live.

Think about that. A simple act of holding another person's hand—even as a stranger—can be a lifesaver. Scientists have studied the value of human touch and have found amazing results from such a simple display of care. It turns out that human touch is one of the most powerful communication tools. From a mother's cradling embrace to a friend's comforting hug or a spouse's caress, touch has the special power to send messages of union and communion. Even a momentary and seemingly incidental touch on your partner's shoulder or hand can strengthen the marital bond by conveying affirmation, comfort, and security.

By the way, both the "toucher" and the "touchee" receive emotional and physiological benefits, scientists say. Stacks of research, for example, have shown that a gentle touch or hug can cause a speeding heart to quiet, soaring blood pressure to drop, and severe pain to ease. A study at UCLA estimated that if some "type-A driven" men would hug their wives several times each day, it would increase their life spans by almost two years, not to mention the way it would improve their marriages. That same study reported that eight to ten meaningful touches each day help us maintain emotional and physical health.

Of course, this isn't earth-shattering news if you're a student of Scripture. Early on, the Bible shows the value of physical touch as a communication of a blessing (see Genesis 27:26; 48:9-14). In the Old Testament, the people laid their hands on the Levites to demonstrate that they were setting them apart for their priestly duties (Numbers 8:10). Moses laid his hands on Joshua to symbolize that he was giving Joshua authority over the people (Numbers 27:18). And Jesus, of course, was a master of communicating love through touch: "Then he took the children in his arms and placed his hands on their heads and blessed them" (Mark 10:16).

So consider the value of meaningful touch to your marriage. When was the last time you enjoyed the simple pleasure of holding hands? After all, if a stranger's touch meant life to Brigitte Gerney, think of what a meaningful touch from you can do for your spouse.

Do not try to get the jar off my head, because it hurts when you pull. Please simply sit next to me and hold my hand, and the jar will come off itself. —WINNIE THE POOH

INSTANT EMPATHY

Don't just pretend to love others. Really love them. . . . Be happy with those who are happy, and weep with those who weep. ROMANS 12:9, 15

HAVE YOU EVER HAD your luggage lost? What a frustration that is! Even if you've experienced waiting in increasing anxiety for your luggage to wind its way past you on the carousel, it's because you can easily imagine how big a problem lost luggage can be for a passenger. Well, in the 1930s, lost luggage was a big problem for an entire airline: American Airways, which later became American Airlines. Passenger complaints kept coming even after the company tried their best to get their station managers to overcome the problem. But the problem persisted.

Finally, LaMotte Cohn, general manager of the airline at the time, came up with an idea. Cohn set up a meeting at the airline's corporate headquarters that every station manager across the country was asked to attend. Then he made sure that every manager's luggage was lost in transit.

The result? You guessed it: the airline suddenly had a huge leap of progress in curtailing the problem of lost luggage. Because the airline's personnel instantly saw the problem from the customer's point of view, they were suddenly more motivated to solve that problem.

This true problem-solving story is a great model for solving certain problems in relationships. When you are able to clearly see any situation from another's point of view, when you can experience it like he or she does, you instantly take a different approach to it. We titled this day's thoughts "Instant Empathy," and we know that the word "instant" carries a strong promise—but it's true. Should we hedge our bets by aiming for "almost instant" empathy? We don't think so. Empathy can actually change everything in a moment. The moment you see a predicament from your spouse's angle, once you have put yourself thoroughly in his or her shoes, you change—that very instant.

Once that happens, just like the station managers for American Airways, you won't have to be goaded and pressured to make changes. You'll make the changes without further prodding because you feel the need for change that the other feels. That's the promise of instant empathy. Take a few minutes to think about a problem, large or small, that has plagued your marriage. Is there some way you can try to look at the problem from another angle—the one from which your spouse is looking at it? Look at it that way for a while. Then make a change.

True contentment comes with empathy. —TIM FINN

NOT SO QUICK

You know that the rulers in this world lord it over their people, and officials flaunt their authority over those under them. But among you it will be different. Whoever wants to be a leader among you must be your servant, and whoever wants to be first among you must become your slave. MATTHEW 20:25-27

BUSYNESS IS A PROBLEM for just about every couple—in fact, for just about every person these days! Sometimes busy seasons can't be avoided. But have you ever known people who actually feel complimented when you tell them they look tired? "Been pushing hard," they'll say with the pride of the achiever—or with the false humility of the martyr. They wear *Busy* as a badge of honor. Why?

From a psychological point of view, the reason has to do with something we call secondary gains. When you consider the state of busyness, its primary gain appears to be productivity. But just under the surface lies a secondary gain, which has little to do with being productive; in fact, it's closer to license to being *unproductive*.

Busyness can keep us from having a conversation that's long overdue. It can be a means of avoiding an issue that begs to be addressed. Maybe it's your mounting financial debt or the lack of passion you feel in the bedroom. Maybe it's the feeling of just drifting through life without real meaning or presence. You get the idea.

You see, what we also gain from running in high gear is the excuse to keep from reflecting on the deeper issues of our lives or our relationships. Those issues could be thoughts that we are afraid to face, or they could take the form of feelings and even people we dread. In short, busyness gives us license to arrive late, slip out early, or be absent altogether—whether physically or mentally. And in a relationship like the marital one, busyness can keep us from emotionally connecting at an intimate and vulnerable level.

Don't be so quick to let yourself be busy. If the two of you are ever going to be successful in wrestling your chronic busyness to the ground, you need to slow down and take a serious look at any potential secondary gains you may be getting from it. You need to ask yourself what exactly your busyness is getting you besides the belief that you're getting more done. Be honest, brutally honest, with yourself as you explore your answers together.

When we get too caught up in the busyness of the world we lose connection with one another—and ourselves. —JACK KORNFIELD

MARRIAGE MENTORING

Wisdom and money can get you almost anything, but only wisdom can save your life.

ECCLESIASTES 7:12

YEARS AGO WE BEGAN USING the term "Marriage Mentors" in relationship to a program we developed called Saving Your Marriage Before It Starts. Through a seminar we launched in Seattle, we were beginning to help hundreds of newlyweds get started on the right foot. But soon we began to wonder whether the information we were teaching was actually sticking. We began to wonder how we could build in some accountability for these couples who went through our program, how we could help ensure they were actually putting the information into practice.

There were too many newlyweds for us to follow up on personally, so we began recruiting older, more experienced couples to meet with these newlyweds. At first we asked these mentors to simply check in with their assigned couple every so often to see how things were going. It didn't take long for us to realize that something exciting was happening because of this fledgling program. We were beginning to hear remarkable stories convincing us that even without much training, the time-honored concept of a mentor is more than apt as applied to marriages in all stages.

We have a dream that one day a massive network of a million marriage mentors will undergird marriages across North America and around the world. Serving as a relational safety net, these mentors would lift up and support couples at crucial crossroads—those just starting out, about to have a baby, in crisis, blending a family, raising teenagers, and so on. Just as mentoring in general can be beneficial at various times during a person's life, marriage mentoring applies to every stage and phase of married life.

A mentor is simply someone who will walk alongside you, offering the wisdom of his or her own experience and helping you live through yours. Couples are crying out for this kind of relationship. In a recent survey, 62 percent of respondents said they would like to find a mentor couple in their church, and 92 percent said they would especially like to have a mentor to help them through tough times.

So what about the two of you? Could you benefit from finding a marriage mentor couple who would walk alongside you? Or maybe you're in a place to mentor another couple? Either way, consider the possibility of getting involved in marriage mentoring.

People are not very good at taking orders, but they are great at imitating.
—WAYMAN MITCHELL

DREAM "VENTI"

Always continue to fear the LORD. You will be rewarded for this; your hope will not be disappointed. PROVERBS 23:17-18

WE LIVE IN SEATTLE and so perhaps it follows naturally that I (Leslie) love coffee. Les doesn't drink it, but he tells me I drink enough for both of us: "Venti," still the largest cup for hot drinks, is not an uncommon order for me. Many of my thoughts about life, and even my prayers, have been scribbled on a napkin in the white space that forms the margins around the green-and-white Starbucks logo. That's where I once wrote these words:

> *In these quiet moments*
> *That form the margins of my life,*
> *Sitting, sipping, breathing*
> *My land-locked soul,*
> *Freeing it to dive*
> *Into the mysteries of the deep*
> *Though I, like T.S. Eliot,*
> > *doubt the mermaids*
> > *will sing for me.*
> *When ideas bubble up to the surface*
> *Like the white rings from a scuba diver's tank,*
> *My heart is energized.*
> *I dare*
> *To dream Venti.*

And I do. If there's one thing I've learned about making a difference with my life, it's that my difference-making is only limited by the size of my dreams.

And so is yours. That's why we hope you dream big. We hope you talk to each other about your dreams—for your two lives but also the dreams you have for your relationship together. We hope you pray about them often. And when you do, we encourage you to dream Venti.

Dreams are the touchstones of our characters. . . . Our truest life is when we are in dreams awake. —HENRY DAVID THOREAU

SAFE AT HOME

The Lord is my shepherd; I have all that I need. PSALM 23:1

WOULDN'T YOU LIKE to provide comfort—truly abiding comfort—to each other? Truth is, you can. The key is found in focusing on what makes each of you feel emotionally safe. This is the secret to emotional connection and comfort, and here's how it works.

Wives, say your spouse feels most safe when he is gaining control of his time. This means that he's going to feel most threatened when his time is being wasted. And if the two of you are trying to solve a problem together, look out: he's going to be an aggressive problem solver, because he wants to be efficient in his conversations. He wants to get to the bottom line. And when you understand that this is how he's hardwired, that this is how God designed him, you'll have more understanding, grace, and empathy for his bold and sometimes blunt approach.

We know this from personal experience. Gaining control of his time makes Les feel most safe. I, on the other hand, would place time at the bottom of my emotional-safety needs list. So guess what? This makes me a passive problem solver. I'm far more inclined to just "give it time." I'm more accommodating than assertive. For his part, Les is more decisive than docile.

So do my passive approach and Les's aggressive approach to problem solving impact our conversations? Only on a daily basis! It was the greatest source of miscommunication we ever had—until we recognized how we were hardwired differently because of our differing needs for emotional safety. Once I saw how much Les feared losing control of his time, I almost instantly had more grace and understanding of his aggressive style. And once he knew I understood how much he valued his time, he began to relax and loosen up when it came to solving problems together.

Of course, it goes both ways. Once Les understood how I am hardwired for approval, he now gives me more grace when I become impulsive or unrealistic in a conversation. You get the idea. An emotional safe room is built in your relationship whenever you both understand and accept each other's unique safety needs. That's when you enjoy the inexpressible comfort of speaking each other's language fluently.

Oh, the comfort—the inexpressible comfort of feeling safe with a person—having neither to weigh thoughts nor measure words. —DINAH CRAIK

SPREADING THE GOOD NEWS—ABOUT YOUR SPOUSE

Let everything you say be good and helpful, so that your words will be an encouragement to those who hear them. EPHESIANS 4:29

"YOUR WIFE WAS BRAGGING on you last week," Marissa told me in the church foyer.

"What are you talking about?" I asked.

"We were having our usual Monday morning coffee together with a few other moms after we dropped off our kids at school," Marissa continued, "and Leslie told all of us how you masterfully got your little boy to quit fussing about what he was wearing to school."

"Oh, that's right," I remembered. "Jackson was really headstrong about wearing the same hooded sweatshirt every day for some reason, and Leslie was at her wits' end."

"Whatever you did," Marissa said, "it impressed your wife. She was going on and on about you being a great dad. Way to go!"

Have you ever heard a secondhand compliment from your spouse like this? If so, you know just how much it can do for your spirit—and for your marriage. Knowing that your spouse is saying good things about you when you're not around is almost as important as hearing these good things directly. In fact, in some ways, it makes even more of an impact. Why? Because it's said without any assurance that you will ever even hear it.

In media circles this is called positive press or good press, and it typically requires the work of a top-notch publicity agent. Public figures pay significant sums to obtain such services to secure testimonial compliments. Why? Because good press always benefits a person's public image. In the same way, "good press" can benefit your spouse's personal image too. Few things can boost a man's self-esteem more than hearing that his wife has been putting him in a positive light in front of others—and the principle works that way for women, too. When two people are doing that for each other mutually, they reap a double dose of love.

Don't overlook an opportunity to serve as positive press for one another. Speaking lovingly of others pleases God, and it will do wonders for pleasing your spouse.

What kills a skunk is the publicity it gives itself. —ABRAHAM LINCOLN

THE HAPPIEST HUMAN BEINGS

Give, and you will receive. Your gift will return to you in full—pressed down, shaken together to make room for more, running over, and poured into your lap. The amount you give will determine the amount you get back. LUKE 6:38

RUNNING BACK Tony Richardson has made a career out of helping other players. Over the span of seventeen pro football seasons, teams have often paired Richardson with some of the best backs in pro football. But his mission to help his peers goes beyond blocking for them. He talks to them constantly, giving advice, encouragement, and inspiration. In a *Sports Illustrated* interview, Richardson said, "I can't explain it, but it just means more to me to help someone else achieve glory. There's something about it that feels right to me."[2]

Whether he knew it or not, Richardson had a lock on a fundamental psychological law: When you help other people, you immediately receive a payoff yourself. George Burton Adams, an American educator and historian, said it nicely: "Note how good you feel after you have encouraged someone else. No other argument is necessary to suggest that you should never miss the opportunity to give encouragement." Ralph Waldo Emerson put it this way: "You cannot sincerely help another without helping yourself." And he could not have been more right. When we empty ourselves of our self-centered desires, when we surrender our desires to get our way, we are filled with grace. Each act of kindness, each act of self-giving love, expands our lives.

Numerous studies find that the ability to practice appreciation and love is the defining mark of the most happy of human beings. When people engage in self-giving love by doing something extraordinarily positive, they use higher-level brain functions and set off a series of neurochemical reactions that shower their systems in positive emotions.

Perhaps you are wondering if this kind of happiness is triggered just as readily by having fun as it is by an act of self-giving love. Martin Seligman, of the University of Pennsylvania, wondered the same thing. He gave his students an assignment: to engage in one pleasurable activity and one philanthropic activity and then to write about both. Turns out, the "pleasurable" activity paled in comparison with the effects of the loving action. Seligman states that "when our philanthropic acts were spontaneous . . . the whole day went better."[3]

Of course, this was God's design: "Give, and you will receive." And as a couple, you and your spouse have an opportunity to have your gift "return to you in full" together. Those who engage in shared service are the happiest and most satisfied couples around.

No man can sincerely try to help another without helping himself.
—RALPH WALDO EMERSON

ACCEPTING OURSELVES

Christ has truly set us free. Now make sure that you stay free, and don't get tied up again in slavery to the law. GALATIANS 5:1

DESPITE HER MANY accomplishments in the world of writing, it's a little strange that journalist and novelist Joie Davidow founded the regional magazine *L.A. Style.* After all, it chronicled the Los Angeles lifestyle, with all the fashion and parties and inclusion in the "in crowd" that went with it, but the irony is that Joie herself never felt like an insider. She was born with a large birthmark that covered nearly half of her face, which made her an object of ridicule. When she was growing up other children called her "monster girl." In her memoir *Marked for Life*, Davidow recounts how for years she saw herself as abnormal and unattractive, and how joining a support group helped change her perspective. Meeting with others led to greater self-acceptance. Davidow writes, she realizes that she is "no more strange and no less strange than anyone."[4]

Of course, you don't have to be born with a birthmark to struggle to accept yourself just as you are. Many of us continually compare ourselves to others: *She plays tennis better than I do. . . . I'm not smart enough. . . . I'm the worst singer in the choir.* If we let them, opportunities for comparison could go on and on. The underlying assumption for us in these situations is that our worth is questionable—with each experience, each conversation, each look giving a clue to our worth and value. This is a false assumption, since our worth is intrinsic to our creation in God's image. When we are healthy, we are able to accept ourselves.

But as Christians, should we really *accept* ourselves? We have a fallen human nature—how can we accept that? The answer is found in truly understanding acceptance. Accepting the self does not imply belief that everything within one's inner experience is good, valuable, or right, but only that it exists. Realism, not narcissism, is the goal. The healthy person recognizes shortcomings, accepts them as his or her particular shortcomings, and realistically evaluates how they can be changed. Unless you accept yourself—the good as well as the bad—you cannot hope to be set free from the slavery of sin.

How might you need to accept yourself today? And how can you serve as a support for your spouse on his or her own journey of self-acceptance?

 God loves each of us as if there were only one of us. —ST. AUGUSTINE

A FEW GOOD QUESTIONS

Keep on asking, and you will receive what you ask for. Keep on seeking, and you will find. Keep on knocking, and the door will be opened to you. For everyone who asks, receives. Everyone who seeks, finds. And to everyone who knocks, the door will be opened.

MATTHEW 7:7-8

TODAY'S VERSE IS ABOUT addressing questions to our Father in heaven—but it's also a good model for us as we think about making sure we keep in touch with our spouses. Every teacher knows that asking good questions opens the door to knowledge and understanding wider than simply imparting information does. And every marriage counselor knows that asking good questions opens the door to your partner's heart.

No matter what stage your marriage is in, you could probably benefit from showing some genuine interest in what's in your spouse's heart. If you're both ready to go beneath the surface and explore each other's hearts, we want to suggest a few good questions to get you started:

"What do you dream about?" We're talking about dreams for the future—not dreams from last night. To understand the mind you can look at what we have already achieved; to understand the heart you'll want to look at what we dream about. And of course this may change over time, whether because as we grow and change so might our dreams, or because life can intervene and disillusion us. Do you know what your partner dreams most about these days? If that has changed from when you first met, do you know why?

"What do you cry about?" When we know where people carry their pain, what makes them hurt, we naturally start to understand their hearts at a deeper level. What pain is your spouse carrying right now? If you know the issues, dig a little deeper. Do you know why that painful experience is difficult for your spouse to get over? Is there something you can do to alleviate the pain that you haven't thought of yet?

"What do you sing about?" When you know what brings joy to your partner, you know the source of his or her strength. What is your partner singing about this week? What's bringing him or her the most joy? Or, if joy is scarce these days, what used to bring joy to your spouse—and how might you help start a new burst of "singing"?

These three questions are probably enough to get you going. Of course, you'll likely come up with other good questions on your own. The point is to continually ask good questions. Why? Asking one another questions on a regular basis is essential to the growth of your relationship.

You can tell whether a man is clever by his answers. You can tell whether a man is wise by his questions. —NAGUIB MAHFOUZ

THE NICEST THING YOU COULD SAY ABOUT EACH OTHER

Do not withhold good from those who deserve it when it's in your power to help them.

PROVERBS 3:27

YOU MAY HAVE READ the true story of Sister Helen Mrosla that became an e-mail chain letter.[5] Sister Helen taught third grade at Saint Mary's School in Morris, Minnesota. That's where she met Mark Eklund, who talked incessantly and needed regular reminders that talking without permission was not acceptable. Each time, Mark would respond sincerely, "Thank you for correcting me, Sister."

But one morning Sister Mrosla's patience was growing thin, and she made a novice teacher's mistake when she said, "If you say one more word, I am going to tape your mouth shut!" Sure enough, before the next minute was up, Mark was talking. Without saying a word, the nun proceeded to Mark's desk and made a big X with tape over his mouth. She said that, as she returned to the front of the room, she glanced at Mark to see how he was doing, and he winked at her. That's all it took and she started laughing. The class cheered as she removed the tape and shrugged her shoulders. Despite the regular correction, at the end of every day, Mark would go up to the teacher's desk and say, "Good night, Sister. Thank you for teaching me."

Sister Mrosla encountered Mark again some years later, when he was a student in her junior-high math class. On one occasion, the class had worked hard and needed a break, so she asked them to write the nicest thing they could about each of the other students and hand it in. She compiled individual results for each student, adding her own compliment at the end of each list, and handed them out the next school day.

Several years later, Mark was killed in Vietnam. After the funeral, some of his former classmates gathered at Mark's parents' luncheon. Sister Mrosla was there too. Mark's father took a wallet out of his pocket, which he said had been found on Mark after he was killed. He carefully removed a folded, refolded, and taped paper—the list of Mark's classmates' compliments. His mother talked about how he treasured it.

Some of Mark's classmates then admitted that they, too, still had their lists—one in his wedding album, one in her diary, and one, like Mark, on his person.

This true story about the impact of Sister Mrosla's unplanned classroom exercise underscores just how valuable a note of encouragement and affirmation can be to the human spirit. If you were to be called upon to write a note like this, what would you say about your partner?

 If you haven't any charity in your heart, you have the worst kind of heart trouble.
—BOB HOPE

THE RACE TO BE SLOW?

Love each other with genuine affection, and take delight in honoring each other.

ROMANS 12:10

HUSBAND: "I didn't know what you meant."

Wife: "You didn't ask me."

Husband: "Why would I ask when it seemed so obvious?"

Wife: "Well, it wasn't obvious to me."

It could be about anything: picking up dry cleaning, scheduling a dinner, meeting at a designated place, whatever. The list is painfully endless. But the crux of the matter is clear: misunderstanding. One person sees a situation one way while the other sees it differently. Neither knows there is a difference until it's too late. So the misunderstanding turns into friction, and the relationship is suddenly fraught with tension.

We heard about a strange bicycle race in India that underscores the point. The object of the race is to go the shortest distance possible within a specified time. At the start of the race, everyone cues up at the line, and when the gun sounds, all the bicycles, as best they can, stay put. Racers are disqualified if they tip over or if one of their feet touches the ground, so they inch forward just enough to keep the bike balanced. When the time is up and another gun sounds, the person who has gone the farthest is the loser and the person closest to the starting line is the winner!

Imagine coming upon the race just before it begins, assuming you know the drill based on American races, and managing to join the race. At the first gunshot, you pedal as hard and fast as you possibly can. You're out of breath. You're sweating. You glance back—and it looks like you're going to break the record!

When you hear the second gunshot, you look to either side of you and realize you are unquestionably the winner—except that you are unquestionably the loser. Why? Because you misunderstood how the race is run. In that moment, you might feel cheated. "Why didn't someone tell me?" But of course, you didn't bother to ask.

That's the exasperation of a misunderstanding. Both sides see it from their angle. But in most small misunderstandings, all it takes is one person putting his or her perspective on hold to resolve the misunderstanding and to ease the tension.

It only takes one person to turn around a misunderstanding by honoring the other perspective. Think about a recent misunderstanding or disagreement with your spouse and take the time to understand it from your spouse's perspective. And next time you are about to reach a standstill—or an argument—picture yourself in that race in India. Ask whatever you need to ask in order to ensure you're not pedaling like crazy toward the wrong goal.

Constant kindness can accomplish much. As the sun makes ice melt, kindness causes misunderstanding, mistrust and hostility to evaporate. —**ALBERT SCHWEITZER**

TAKE CARE

God blesses those who are merciful, for they will be shown mercy. MATTHEW 5:7

DURING THE LEBANON HOSTAGE CRISIS from 1986 to 1990, Frank Reed, director of the American Lebanese International School, was held hostage in Lebanon. For months at a time Reed was blindfolded, living in complete darkness, or chained to a wall and kept in absolute silence for his captivity. On one occasion, he was moved to another location where, though blindfolded, he could sense others in the room. Yet it was three weeks before he dared peek out to discover he was chained next to fellow captives Terry Anderson and Tom Sutherland.

Although he was beaten, made ill, and tormented, Reed felt most keenly the lack of caring. He said in an interview with *Time*, "Nothing I did mattered to anyone. I began to realize how withering it is to exist with not a single expression of caring around you. . . . I learned one overriding fact: caring is a powerful force. If no one cares, you are truly alone."[6]

Care is so germane, so essential to our relationships, yet so basic that it often goes unnoticed. Ask any couple what matters most in their relationship and care is not likely to make the list. But when you put this quality on a list of traits and ask people to rate its importance, you'll see it rise near the top. Why? Because without care, as Frank Reed can vividly attest, we wither.

It seems strange that we toss this vital force around so haphazardly. "Take care," we might say to the grocery clerk who rings up our items. "Take care," we say at the end of a phone conversation with a near stranger. Saying "I care about you" can make a real difference in a relationship, and so can saying the opposite: "I don't care" is like a deadly bullet in the heart of any relationship.

The word *care* comes from the Germanic *karo*, which originally meant "sad." It alludes to the idea that a caring person feels sad when you feel sad. In other words, care is a kind of compassion that allows someone else to enter your world and feel your pain. Care means that whatever happens to you happens to me; when sadness hits you it hits me, too. Of course, care also means that when something terrific happens to you I rejoice too, because your life makes a genuine difference to my own. That's the essence of caring.

As you go about your day, be mindful of the power seemingly small acts of kindness have to impact your spouse.

} *It was "at home"—in one's family or in one's community with those closest—that the genuineness of love is easily tested and proved.* —MOTHER TERESA

THE GOOD NAME

God saved you by his grace when you believed. And you can't take credit for this; it is a gift from God. EPHESIANS 2:8

BILL AND GLORIA GAITHER had been married a couple of years when they began looking for some land where they might one day build a house. They were both school teachers in Alexandria, Indiana, where Bill had grown up. They had their eye on a parcel south of town where cattle grazed, and they learned it belonged to a ninety-two-year-old retired banker named Mr. Yule. They asked around and learned that he owned quite a bit of land in the area but he would not sell any of it. He gave the same speech to everyone who inquired: "I promised the farmers they could use it for their cattle."

Bill and Gloria, long before they won Grammy awards and sold millions of gospel albums, visited Mr. Yule at the bank. Although he was retired, he spent a couple of hours each morning in his office. He looked at them over the top of his bifocals.

Bill introduced himself and told him they were interested in a piece of his land. "Not selling," he said pleasantly. "Promised it to a farmer for grazing."

"I know," said Bill, "but we teach school here and thought maybe you'd be interested in selling it to someone planning to settle in the area."

He pursed his lips and stared at Bill. "What'd you say your name was?"

"Gaither. Bill Gaither."

"Hmmm. Any relation to Grover Gaither?"

"Yes, sir. He was my granddad."

Mr. Yule put down his paper and removed his glasses. "Interesting. Grover Gaither was the best worker I ever had on my farm. Full day's work for a day's pay. So honest. What'd you say you wanted?"

Bill told him again.

"Let me do some thinking on it, and then come back and see me."

Bill came back within the week, and Mr. Yule told Bill he had had the property appraised. Bill held his breath. "How does $3,800 sound? Would that be okay?"

"$3,800?" Bill repeated.

"Yup. Fifteen acres for $3,800."

Bill knew it had to be worth at least three times that. He readily accepted.

Nearly three decades later, Bill and his son strolled that beautiful, lush property that had once been pasture land. "Benjy," he said, "you've had this wonderful place to grow up through nothing that you've done, but because of the good name of a great-granddad you never met."[7]

We are all the beneficiaries of a gift because of the good name of Jesus: "God saved you by his grace when you believed. And you can't take credit for this; it is a gift from God." And by that grace, live out your marriage in such a way that you might leave a good name behind you.

Regard your good name as the richest jewel you can possibly be possessed of. —SOCRATES

THE MEANING OF MAKING A DIFFERENCE

What do people get for all their hard work under the sun? ECCLESIASTES 1:3

THE CHARACTER WARREN SCHMIDT, played by Jack Nicholson in the film *About Schmidt*, is a man leading a life of quiet desperation. He retires from his vice-president position at an insurance company, looking back on a meaningless life and ahead to a meaningless retirement.

One day while watching television, Warren sees an opportunity to give money and write letters to an underprivileged child in Tanzania. Warren responds to the appeal, and throughout the movie he faithfully sends the twenty-two dollars a month and writes poignant letters to a child named Ndugu.

On one occasion after a long road trip, Warren comes home to an empty house—a metaphor for his empty life. He walks in with an armload of impersonal junk mail, ambles up the stairs, and looks disappointedly at the disheveled state of his bedroom. Throughout this scene, the audience hears Warren's voice-over narration of a letter he recently composed to Ndugu. He pours out his intense feeling of emptiness:

> *I know we're all pretty small in the scheme of things, and I guess the best you can hope for is to make some kind of difference. What difference have I made? What in the world is better because of me? I am weak, and I am a failure. There's just no getting around it. Real soon I will die. Maybe twenty years—maybe tomorrow— it doesn't matter. Once I am dead and everyone who knew me dies, it is as though I never existed. What difference has my life made to anyone? None that I can think of. Hope things are fine with you.*
>
> *Yours truly,*
>
> *Warren Schmidt*

At the end of the narration, the depression on Warren's face gives way to wonder as he stares down at a letter from Tanzania. It is a letter from a nun who works in the orphanage where six-year-old Ndugu lives. She tells Warren that Ndugu thinks of him every day and hopes he is happy. Enclosed is a picture drawn by Ndugu for Warren—two stick people smiling and holding hands. Warren is overcome by the realization that he has finally made a difference. He lifts his hands to his tired face and cries.

Let's never forget that our meaning on this earth becomes most clear when we are making a difference in other people's lives—when we are meeting each other's needs, especially the needs of our spouses.

Our obligation is to give meaning to life and in doing so to overcome the passive, indifferent life. —ELIE WIESEL

BELIEVING IN EACH OTHER

Get up, for it is your duty to tell us how to proceed in setting things straight. We are behind you, so be strong and take action. EZRA 10:4

YOU PROBABLY KNOW THAT Nathaniel Hawthorne is among the great American writers. You may not know that he owes his acclaim in part to his inspiring wife, Sophia. Nathaniel went home from his job as a weigher and gauger at the Boston Custom House one day with a heavy heart because he had been fired. But when he told his wife of his failure, she exclaimed with joy, not disappointment. "*Now*," she said, "you can write your book!"

Nathaniel didn't share her joy. "And what shall we live on while I am writing it?"

To his amazement, she opened a drawer and pulled out a substantial amount of money—enough for them to live on for an entire year. "Where on earth did you get that?" he exclaimed.

Sophia explained that she recognized in her husband the genius to write a masterpiece. Because of this, every week she saved a little money out of what had been allotted for housekeeping, and she had amassed enough to buy her husband one year's worth of writing time.[8] It was during that year that Nathaniel Hawthorne wrote one of the greatest novels of American literature, *The Scarlet Letter*.

The Hawthornes, by all accounts, enjoyed a long and happy marriage, and that is surely in part due to the mutual regard they had. Nathaniel referred to his wife as his Dove, saying that she "is, in the strictest sense, my sole companion; and I need no other—there is no vacancy in my mind, any more than in my heart. . . . Thank God that I suffice for her boundless heart!"[9]

Sophia believed in her husband Nathaniel because she entered his world. Because she knew his dreams, she understood his passion for writing. Because she knew his talents, she believed in his possibilities. Empathy does that in a marriage. It helps us realize each other's dreams. You see, once you understand what energizes your spouse's vision for his or her life—as well as your life together—you're far more likely to do whatever you can to make those dreams a reality. And he or she is far more likely to do the same for you.

How many marriages would be better if the husband and the wife clearly understood that they're on the same side? —ZIG ZIGLAR

UNCHAINING THE ELEPHANT

This means that anyone who belongs to Christ has become a new person. The old life is gone; a new life has begun! 2 CORINTHIANS 5:17

IN HIS BOOK *Teaching the Elephant to Dance*, James Belasco describes how young elephants are trained. Shackled by heavy chains to stakes embedded deep within the ground, an elephant learns to stay in its place. When the trained elephant is older, even though it is amply strong enough to uproot such a stake, it will never even attempt it—which is especially ironic given that once an elephant is trained it is no longer even staked. Its conditioning has so limited its sphere of movement that now, with only a small metal bracelet around its foot attached to nothing, it stands in place.

This lesson from the elephant has powerful application to our own lives. Like mighty elephants, many people are bound by earlier conditioned restraints. Just as the unattached bracelets around the elephants' feet keep them from moving, so some people allow the reminders of past "conditioning" to needlessly limit their personal progress.

Don't let this happen to you as a couple. We've seen it happen all too often. It occurs when a rocky relationship gets to a stalemate because of one partner's resistance to change. "If you don't go with me to see a counselor, I'm out of here." That's when the couple enters a very scary space, when the resistant person's deep need for loyalty is threatened to its very core—when that person feels that he or she may lose the other person's loyalty and commitment altogether.

There's no need for any couple to let things get so destructive. Even the conditioned elephant will change at this point: when the circus tent catches on fire and the elephant sees the flames and smells the smoke, it forgets its conditioning and runs for its life. And get this: forty-five percent of Americans report that they would change a bad habit if they could.[10] The truth is, we *can* change. Think of a time when you felt stuck but were finally able to make a change. Can you apply the same effort to something that has your marriage stuck, bound by the past? Renew your hope and courage together as a couple and ask God to help you tackle anything that has seemed insurmountable.

When we are no longer able to change a situation . . . we are challenged to change ourselves. —VIKTOR FRANKL

A FUNNY WAY TO COPE

You will grieve, but your grief will suddenly turn to wonderful joy. JOHN 16:20

JANET, THE CONSUMMATE HOSTESS, wanted to impress the new pastor's family with an elaborate dinner. She cooked all day and even had her teenage son help to serve the meal. All went well until the main course. As the young server was bringing in the crown roast, the kitchen door hit him from behind and the platter flew across the room. The hostess froze, regained her composure, then commanded, "Dear, don't just stand there. Pick up the roast, go in the kitchen, and get the other one!"

Humor helps us cope—not just with the trivial but even with the tragic. Psychoanalyst Martin Grotjahn, author of *Beyond Laughter*, notes that "to have a sense of humor is to have an understanding of human suffering." Charlie Chaplin could have said the same thing. Chaplin grew up in the poorest section of London. His mother suffered from serious mental illness, and his father died of alcoholism when Charlie was just five. Laughter was Chaplin's tool for coping with life's losses. Eating a boiled leather shoe for dinner in his classic film, *Gold Rush*, is more than a humorous scene. It is an act of human triumph, a monument to the coping power of humor.

One does not need to be a professional comedian, however, to benefit from comedy. Viktor Frankl gives another example of how humor can empower a person to cope with life, even amid horrendous circumstances. In Frankl's book *Man's Search for Meaning*, he speaks of using humor to survive imprisonment during World War II. Frankl and another inmate would invent at least one amusing story daily to help them cope with their horrors.

According to Bill Cosby, "If you can find humor in anything, you can survive it." Researchers agree. Studies reveal that individuals who have a strong sense of humor are less likely to experience burnout and depression and are more likely to enjoy life in general—even when carrying heavy burdens.

No matter what kind of time your marriage is in, be intentional in the near future about sharing a point of laughter with your spouse. Study your spouse's funny bone and cater to it! It will make you laugh together, and that will help you cope together.

[The human] race has unquestionably one really effective weapon —laughter.
—MARK TWAIN

ACROSS THE KITCHEN TABLE

Spouting off before listening to the facts is both shameful and foolish. PROVERBS 18:13

I (LES) TALKED WITH A MAN recently who was at a meeting in New York where the Toshiba computer people were demonstrating a remarkable new product, a universal translation computer that can translate words from one language to another at a rate of one thousand words per minute.

The demonstration involved two couples conversing long distance. One couple from Africa spoke Swahili. The other, in Alaska standing by their igloo, spoke Tlingit. As the Swahili couple talked to the couple in Alaska, they smiled in understanding and appreciation as their words were instantly translated near the bottom of a life-size split screen that showed both couples.

The only problem came when the Swahili man, trying to use an idiomatic expression to compliment the wife of the Tlingit gentleman, said that she looked like a bird. This was the highest compliment in Swahili. However, when it was translated, it came through as "Your wife looks like a pigeon."

The Tlingit man scowled at what the African had said to him about his wife until the machine straightened out the translation, and he understood that his wife was beautiful, like the most lovely bird they have on the African continent. It was at that point, my friend told me, that the couples' expressions began to glow. They understood each other.

Understanding, whether it be across continents with different languages or across the kitchen table with different perspectives, is the bridge we build from our hearts, and it cannot be constructed quickly—not even with a high-powered computer. Of course, that's the temptation, especially in marriage. We want to take a shortcut through our partner's pain, or happiness, as the case may be. But understanding can never be rushed. Martin Luther King Jr. once said, "Shallow understanding from people of good will is more frustrating than absolute misunderstanding from people of ill will." King would know. And so, I suppose, would we.

How many times have you heard your partner describe a predicament—a mishap at work, a problem with the kids, a misunderstanding with a friend—and proceeded to prematurely solve his or her problem? You laid out three easy steps to improve the whole mess, checked it off your evening's to-do list, and went on to the next thing. Husbands, in particular, seem compelled to fix their partner's problems, but the truth is men and women are equally guilty of this marital mishap.

So the next time you are tempted to fix, solve, or explain your spouse's problem, remember the words of today's proverb. Or think of it this way: listen to your partner as if you were from two different continents.

} *The single biggest problem in communication is the illusion that it has taken place.*
—GEORGE BERNARD SHAW

ARE YOU UP FOR A DARE?

Common sense and success belong to me. Insight and strength are mine. PROVERBS 8:14

ON THIS DAY IN 2008 a surprise box-office hit debuted in movie theaters across the country. The film, written and produced by brothers Alex and Stephen Kendrick, was shot on location in the small town of Albany, Georgia. Upon the film's release, we conducted a marriage seminar at Sherwood Baptist Church in Albany, the church at which the Kendrick brothers are on staff. That's where we learned that with the exception of Kirk Cameron, none of the actors were professionals. They were volunteers from the congregation. Who could have predicted that a film like this, about marriage and made by church folks in a small town, would become the highest-grossing independent film of the year—and that it would touch the lives of countless couples? Maybe you were among them.

If so, you know that *Fireproof* is the story of Caleb and Catherine Holt, a couple considering divorce after seven years of marriage. In one last attempt to salvage their marriage, Caleb tries a forty-day experiment his father calls The Love Dare. In one scene Caleb (Kirk Cameron), a firefighter, is working out at the gym with one of his co-workers, Michael (Ken Bevel). Caleb is upset about a fight between himself and Catherine the night before, and he's considering quitting The Love Dare. Michael offers the sympathy of one who has been there before and has moved past the kind of crisis Caleb is in. Asked how, Michael explains, pointing to a corner of the gym:

"That treadmill is not broken, but if you don't know how to run it, it ain't gonna work for you."

"Are you saying I need counseling?" Caleb asks with a sneer.

"Well, I think everybody needs counseling," Michael replies.

"Look, man," Caleb says, "I am not about to go talk to somebody I don't even know about something that's none of their business!"

It's a threatening subject, we know. We've seen that up close and personal throughout our professional lives. Some people get hung up on the idea of counseling for various reasons, but it's a topic worth discussion by every married couple from time to time. So while we're still in the first month of a new year, this is as good a time as any to raise the issue: How do you feel about seeking professional help for something in your marriage if and when an important issue needs to be addressed? Do you tend to be a bit like Caleb in your stance? Why or why not?

If it's free, it's advice; if you pay for it, it's counseling; if you can use either one, it's a miracle. —JACK ADAMS

SHOW ME THE MARRIAGE

He will pour out his anger and wrath on those who live for themselves, who refuse to obey the truth and instead live lives of wickedness. ROMANS 2:8

"YOU'LL VACUUM BEFORE they get here, right?" Leslie asked anxiously as we pulled in to the garage.

"I've got it under control," I mumbled.

The tension was rising because in less than an hour, two other couples would be at our doorstep expecting a dinner party. We jumped out of the car, grabbed an armful of groceries, and hurried inside. "I'll take care of these groceries so you can vacuum," Leslie said. As she hollered two more reminders from the kitchen, I walked into my study to look through some "urgent" mail. A few minutes later Leslie walked by and asked, exasperated, "What are you doing?"

"Reading my mail," I said, with the best look of confusion I could put on my face. She didn't buy it. "Don't worry," I said, "I'll take care of the other stuff." Leslie sighed and left the room. Five minutes later I heard the sound of the vacuum cleaner.

I'm almost done here; I'll go in and help her next, I said to myself. Ten minutes later, when the vacuum stopped, I bolted from my chair into the living room. "I thought I was going to do this," I said.

"So did I," she replied.

We've all weaseled our way out of the to-do list at one time or another, haven't we? After all, we've worked hard; we're tired, busy, preoccupied, maxed-out, whatever. There are dozens of reasons we might use to justify one of the deadliest saboteurs of a healthy marriage: selfishness. It lurks just beneath the surface and pounces whenever we are tired and there's a household chore to be done or an errand to be run. That's when we pretend we don't notice the chore or we "forget" about the errand, hoping the other person will take over so we don't have to.

Selfishness seeps into our marriage in a myriad of ways. I (Leslie) am the first to admit I can whine and complain to Les about his busy schedule without considering adjusting my own calendar for the sake of his. Or I might spend extravagantly on a luncheon with a friend but later snipe at Les for buying a gadget he "doesn't need." Let's face it: in big and small ways we all squirrel away money, energy, and time to our own advantage, not realizing that we are squandering countless acts of potential kindness and generosity sure to bring us to a deeper level of intimacy and connectedness with our partners.

When we rationalize our selfishness, we are missing the point of partnership. Selfishness is guaranteed to leave every married couple feeling more like roommates than soul mates. Worse, it always brings conflict: God will "pour out anger and wrath," today's Scripture says, "on those who live for themselves."

 Self-interest is the enemy of all true affection. —FRANKLIN D. ROOSEVELT

WHAT ARE YOU SAYING?

I pray that your love will overflow more and more, and that you will keep on growing in knowledge and understanding. For I want you to understand what really matters, so that you may live pure and blameless lives until the day of Christ's return. PHILIPPIANS 1:9-10

THE WORLD'S LONGEST MARRIAGE was just recently celebrated. According to Guinness World Records, Lee, ninety-one, and Kim, ninety-five, from South Korea celebrated their eighty-second wedding anniversary at a festive event in the house of their eldest son, age seventy-five. Lee and Kim have five sons, three daughters, and 105 grandchildren and great-grandchildren. On their anniversary, the world's longest-married couple was given special gifts, including eighty-two roses . . . and two pairs of hearing aids.

After more than eight decades of marriage they were getting hearing aids! Guess they still wanted to be sure they wouldn't miss a word. Can you imagine the number of conversations this couple has had? In all that time, they must have touched on every conceivable topic a husband and wife could discuss. But this record-breaking marriage got us to thinking. Did Lee and Kim ever pay conscious attention to a particular "conversation" that most couples rarely even recognize?

There's a quiet conversation that takes place every day in your marriage and that almost always goes unnoticed, yet it's the most important discussion you will ever have. Its words linger longer, are felt more deeply, and determine the closeness or distance you feel. We're talking about the conversation you have with *yourself* when your partner isn't listening. We're talking about your relational self-talk.

Each of us, every minute of every hour, holds an unending internal dialogue, which colors every experience in our marriages. Self-talk occurs without any prior reflection or reasoning. The brain instantly reads this information as plausible and valid. Now, self-talk need not be accurate—in fact, for many of us, it rarely is—but this never hinders the mind from acting as if it were. While this dialogue is rarely noticed, it continually shapes our attitudes, emotions, and outlooks. So what are you saying to yourself about your relationship? What does your inner dialogue about your spouse sound like?

Tune in to your self-talk related to marriage. Is it supportive of your spouse and productive to your marriage? Why or why not?

The more faithfully you listen to the voices within you, the better you will hear what is sounding outside. —DAG HAMMARSKJÖLD

SEEING OUR BLESSINGS

When Jesus heard this, he was amazed. Turning to the crowd that was following him, he said, "I tell you, I haven't seen faith like this in all Israel!" LUKE 7:9

HAVE YOU HEARD THIS ONE?
An old man lay dying. His wife of many years was sitting close by his bed, and suddenly he opened his eyes and saw her. "There you are, Agnes," he said, "at my side again."

"Yes, dear," his wife said.

"Now that I am dying, Agnes," the old man said, "I am looking back over my life, and I remember all the times you were at my side. You were there when I got my draft notice and had to go off to fight in the war. You were with me when our first house burned to the ground. When I had the accident that destroyed our car, you were there. And you were at my side when my business went bankrupt and I lost every cent I had."

"Yes, dear," his wife said.

The old man sighed, "I tell you, Agnes," he said, "you've been a real jinx."

This joke pokes fun at marriage, but it also makes an unintentionally helpful point about marriage: it's easy to see your spouse in the most negative light possible. As ridiculous as it seems when you think about it, the person whom you love the most is also the person you can most easily take for granted or even worse—read negative motives where they don't exist and make assumptions that aren't true. It's a good idea to attribute to your spouse the best possible motive, not the worst. When you don't, like the man in this old joke, you choose to ignore the blessing your partner truly is.

So here's a suggestion. Take just a couple of minutes right now to list as many blessings your partner brings into your life as you can—especially those blessings you haven't acknowledged to him or her. Thank God for blessing you through your spouse. Then give your spouse the gift of your appreciation for his or her faithful presence in daily things like meal preparation, childcare, car maintenance, commitment to excellence at a job that provides for your family, or service to others.

We tend to forget that happiness doesn't come as a result of getting something we don't have, but rather of recognizing and appreciating what we do have.
—FREIDRICH KOENIG

RECHARGING OUR BATTERIES

Come to me, all of you who are weary and carry heavy burdens, and I will give you rest. Take my yoke upon you. Let me teach you, because I am humble and gentle at heart, and you will find rest for your souls. For my yoke is easy to bear, and the burden I give you is light. MATTHEW 11:28-30

A FEW YEARS AGO, we traveled through Europe with two other couples. One of our most enjoyable cities together was Milan, Italy, where food was scrumptious, the culture was rich, and our hotel couldn't have been better. It looked over the Duomo—the cathedral—famous for the many treasures stored there including ivories, sacred vases in gold and silver, vestments, and tapestries, not to mention the gorgeous architecture itself. Our little group of six spent the better part of an afternoon there, literally sitting on the floor, backs against the wall, in the vestibule, relaxing in the cool breeze and sometimes talking for a moment about the sights and sounds we were taking in, but mostly sitting in silence.

At one point, as we sat studying the magnificent stained glass windows around us, a cleaning man who had noticed us lingering comfortably for quite some time spoke up. "Recharga your batteries?" he asked. We laughed in agreement, knowing we weren't the first tired tourists to take respite in his cathedral. But we had misunderstood. "No, no," he said, pointing to the electrical outlet near us. He proceeded to tell us about a young man and woman from South America he'd met some months earlier. They entered the Duomo each day for about a month and sat before a statue of Christ. The priests assumed they were just like any other devoted Catholics, coming for prayer. Day after day they came, sat for an hour or so, and left. One day the cleaning man noticed an unusual electrical cord leading from the plug used to provide electricity to light up the statue. Upon further examination, it turned out the young couple had been coming to church to charge up their cell phone battery.

Our new friend was checking to see if we were doing the same thing. "No," said Les, "we're just recharging our physical and spiritual batteries."

The cleaning man smiled, pressed the tips of his fingers together, and with a slight bow said, "As you should. Very good."

It is good, very good, for a couple to recharge their spiritual batteries. So many times we forget that an important part of marital communication is done in silence—giving our souls time to catch up with each other simply by being present and at peace. Surely this is what Scottish historian and essayist Thomas Carlyle was getting at in today's quotation.

Take time to pause in the midst of your daily fray and simply tune in to the present moment together.

Silence is deep as Eternity; speech is shallow as Time. —THOMAS CARLYLE

TIME WELL SPENT

You will always harvest what you plant. GALATIANS 6:7

RECENTLY A 1943 WRISTWATCH giving the time in forty-two cities around the world was sold at auction for 6.6 million Swiss francs. That's over five million US dollars! The eighteen-karat gold wristwatch, made by Geneva watchmaker Patek Philippe, was sold to an unidentified buyer.

Can you imagine spending five million dollars on a watch? How about five thousand dollars? Five hundred? Okay, fifty? We all know that the Timex you spent a few bucks on is going to keep nearly as good a time as the Patek Philippe model—maybe not in forty-two different cities around the world, but it will keep decent time. So why would someone spend that kind of cash on such an exotic watch? Obviously, it's not about keeping time. It's about appreciating quality. It's about the fine art of time keeping. It's about an investment. A significant investment.

The news of this extraordinary purchase got us to thinking about the value of our time as a couple and how we invest it. We began to wonder aloud about the time in our life, and it didn't take us long to realize that the time that is most precious to us is the time we have together. Certainly the time we spend at work is important and often fulfilling. The time we spend at church in worship with others is deeply meaningful. We thoroughly enjoy the time we have with friends. But the most valuable of all our time is the time we devote to our marriage and family. It's priceless.

What gives the time a husband and wife have together such extraordinary value? It's the return on the investment: love, the most valuable resource in the universe. Love is the *summum bonum*—the supreme good, the most excellent way. Love lifts us outside ourselves and allows us to see beyond the normal range of human vision. It inspires us to transcend who we are tempted to settle for in this life. It defines us and shapes us into the persons we were designed to be. No financial investment in the world can pay that kind of a dividend. And no marriage can ever reap the bountiful rewards of this love without the investment of time. To love and be loved you must spend time with the one you love; as you do, love has the chance to compound.

Nothing, not even a five-million-dollar timepiece, can come close to what a husband and wife get from the investment of time together. So as you meditate on the readings in this book, do so together. Consider each one an investment in your love fund. And consider this question: What's one specific difference in your relationship you observe between days when you have time to connect versus those days when time is in short supply?

} *The way you spend your hours and your days is the way you spend your life.*
—JOHN BOYKIN

READING EACH OTHER'S HEADLINES

The words of the godly encourage many, but fools are destroyed by their lack of common sense. PROVERBS 10:21

"I DIDN'T KNOW YOU and Gary planned a ski trip for next month," Leslie said as I hung up the cell phone with my friend Gary.

"Sure you did," I responded. "You were at dinner that night when I told him it would be great to meet in Colorado this winter. Don't you remember?"

"I remember being at dinner with you and Gary, but I don't recall any plans for a ski trip."

Ever had one of those conversations? Or how about this one:

"What do you mean we're going to the Campbell's tomorrow night? You never told me about this."

"Sure I did. Suzy and I planned this ages ago."

Or how about this:

"Honey, did I hear you telling your dad on the phone that you landed an important contract yesterday at work?"

"Yes, I meant to tell you about that. . . ."

It seems most couples, traveling at the speed of life, don't always have a chance to update each other on the happenings of their lives. In fact, one recent study reported that couples with kids spend less than five minutes alone together each day when they are not emotionally tuned into the television, the computer, or a smartphone. We move so quickly that when we get home and begin to wind down, our minds shift into neutral or plug into some technology that keeps us from debriefing with our spouses. It's why you sometimes hear separating couples who have lost all sense of intimacy say, "We've just grown apart."

One of the best ways to counter this experience is with a simple question we've been asking each other for years. At some point in the evening, after the kids are tucked in, we'll say something like this: "What are the headlines of your life I didn't read today?" We both know what that means. It's our way of saying, "Bring me up to speed with anything I don't know about you and your day." And it's when we report on the good and the bad, the things we accomplished and the places where we failed.

Give it a try. This simple exercise, practiced routinely, will nourish the heart of your marriage by keeping you in the know. For as E. Stanley Jones has said, "If either withholds the self, love cannot exist."

For a marriage relationship to flourish, there must be intimacy. It takes an enormous amount of courage to say to your spouse, "This is me. I'm not proud of it—in fact, I'm a little embarrassed by it—but this is who I am." —BILL HYBELS

TAKING YOUR VOW SERIOUSLY

This is my beloved and this is my friend. SONG OF SONGS 5:16, NASB

TO HAVE AND TO HOLD . . . for better or for worse . . . till death us do part. . . .
You remember your wedding vows, don't you? That formal litany of words that marries you and gives meaning to everything else that happens during the wedding day, not to mention your relationship. But there's a surprising trend noticed in the wedding industry that's happening these days.

In a May 2010 article titled "Couples Take Their Vows in a New Direction," *USA Today* reported the following: "The Bible is losing ground on the wedding aisle, and *forever* may follow *obey* into oblivion, particularly for those who marry in civil or nondenominational ceremonies." The piece goes on to interview the editor of *Brides* magazine who says that "many couples prefer to start their lives together with 'guidelines, not a straitjacket of rules.'" The Reverend Ema Drouillard, who is also quoted in the article, says 50 percent of couples now refuse the word *forever* "because 'they really don't believe in it.'"[1]

It's sad, don't you think?

Author Fred Smith tells the story of an experience he had in a doughnut shop in Grand Saline, Texas, several years ago. There was a young farm couple sitting at the table next to his, the young man dressed in overalls, his wife in a gingham dress. After they finished their doughnuts, the man got up to pay the bill, but his wife didn't get up to follow him. When he had paid the check, the man came back and stood in front of his wife. She put her arms around his neck, and he lifted her up—and that's when it became apparent that she was wearing a full-body brace. He lifted her out of her chair, and they backed out the front door to the pickup truck together, a man with a woman hanging from his neck.

Everyone watched the man gently put his wife into the truck and drive away. No one said anything for a while, until a waitress remarked, almost reverently, "He took his vows seriously."[2]

Take a moment to reflect on your vows. They may have included promises to love, comfort, honor, and keep each other; in sickness and in health, for richer, for poorer; for better, for worse; in sadness as well as joy; forsaking all others—as long as you both shall live. Renew your commitment to embody those vows today.

 One vow made and kept after the tempest, is worth one thousand promised in the same. —**THOMAS FULLER**

THIS IS YOUR LIFE

My purpose is to give them a rich and satisfying life. I am the good shepherd. The good shepherd sacrifices his life for the sheep. JOHN 10:10

WHEN WE WERE IN graduate school, we heard a speaker named Tim Hansel. Tim had a remarkable life story, and after hearing him talk, we came to admire his ministry as well as his books. In his book Holy Sweat, Tim tells the apocryphal story of a man who never really understood what it meant to live a fulfilled life. The man thought he could live his life best by avoiding any encounters that could lead to hurt and hardship. While the man saw people being loving toward one another, he also saw that they had to exert a lot of effort and that love put strenuous demands on them. He witnessed arguments between people who were trying to love each other. He saw that love required sacrifice and self-denial. He saw it bring disappointment, pain, and even death. The man decided that loving others was simply not worth all the disappointment and pain that doing so entailed. Love cost too much.

He decided that serving others and giving money to the poor and helpless made little sense because all the giving and serving didn't seem to eliminate the need. Not only that, but some people were not appreciative. So serving others was not for him. He didn't want his life contaminated and dirtied by such efforts. When the man died, he came to God and presented him with his life. Undiminished, unmarred, and unsoiled, it was clean from the filth of the world, and he presented it proudly to the mighty God, saying, "This is my life." And God said, "What life?"[3]

Too often we come to reason that if we are living really good lives, we won't encounter pain and hurt. We think our relationships and our lives shouldn't be so demanding and sacrificial. We think we shouldn't have to deny our own needs so often through compromise. This kind of thinking lays us open to the disillusionment experienced by the man in the story above. But when we realize that pain is the risk we run—and all too often the price we pay—along the way to the truly abundant life of love, what we should also realize is that the reward is worth the risk.

Take a moment to thank your spouse for the sacrifices he or she has made for you and for your marriage. And what about what you've given? Are you holding back in any area because of fear? Reflect on a time when you received great "gain" as a result of a little "pain," and think about how you might do that again today.

We want to live forever for the same reason that we want to live tomorrow. Why do we want to live tomorrow? It is because there is someone who loves you, and whom you want to see tomorrow, and be with, and love back. —HENRY DRUMMOND

BECOMING A NEW CREATION

Anyone who belongs to Christ has become a new person. The old life is gone; a new life has begun! 2 CORINTHIANS 5:17

THE MUSICAL, OR PLAY WITHIN A PLAY, called *Man of La Mancha* tells the story of the character Miguel de Cervantes, a writer, among other things. Cervantes is imprisoned and forced by his fellow inmates to mount a mock defense, and he does so in the form of a play based on his unfinished manuscript, *Don Quixote de la Mancha*. He transforms himself into Alonso Quijana, an old gentleman who has lost his mind. Quijana renames himself Don Quixote and sets out to find adventures.

Among the people he meets is a part-time prostitute at an inn. Don Quixote believes she is the lady Dulcinea, to whom he has sworn eternal loyalty. Everyone is surprised and annoyed by his strangely kind treatment of a woman no one else respects.

In his own romantic, twisted way, Don Quixote sees in her what no one else does—beauty and virtue. "I see heaven when I see thee," he says to her. "Thy name is like a prayer an angel whispers." He creates an affirmation of her that essentially says, "I see you speaking gently and tenderly and behaving as a grand lady in spite of the derision and vulgarity around you."

Then, in his ultimate attempt to change her paradigm, he bestows upon her a new name: "Now I've found thee and the world shall know thy glory, Dulcinea, my lady!"

At first Dulcinea rejects Don Quixote's attempts to change her. "I'm not your lady," she retorts. "I'm not any kind of a lady."

But Don Quixote persists. "Never deny that you are Dulcinea," he tells her. "Now and forever, you are my lady, Dulcinea."

Eventually, Dulcinea wants to believe the beautiful tale Quixote is telling her, but her old scripts almost overpower her. She cries out in anguish, "You have shown me the sky. But what good is the sky to a creature who'll never do better than crawl?"

Quixote patiently persists until his affirmations gradually begin to convince Dulcinea to believe in herself. Eventually she comes to believe in her soul and see in her mind what Don Quixote has told her about herself. She begins to live from a new script, a new self-identity. At Don Quixote's deathbed, she thanks him.

As far-fetched as the plot of this play (or the novel that inspired it) may be, it nevertheless has something important to say to you in regard to your marriage. Don't underestimate the power you hold to gently shape the way your spouse views himself or herself. Harness that power as you affirm your spouse, and be careful to do so in a way that brings a God-honoring new script into your lives.

Often, it's not about becoming a new person, but becoming the person you were meant to be, and already are, but don't know how to be. —HEATH L. BUCKMASTER

A HOLY PLACE OF LOVE

You cannot become my disciple without giving up everything you own. LUKE 14:33

A WELL-KNOWN JEWISH LEGEND tells of two brothers who shared a field and a mill long ago, when the world was young. One brother lived alone, and the other had a wife and family. Each day the brothers would work the land and grind the grain together, and each night they would divide the grain.

One day, the single brother thought, "It really isn't fair that we divide the grain evenly, for I have only myself to care for, while my brother has children to feed." So each night the single one secretly took some of his grain to his brother's granary, to ensure that he would never be without.

But the married brother said to himself one day, "It really isn't fair that we divide the grain evenly, because I have children to provide for me in my old age, but my brother has no one. What will he do when he is old?" So every night the married one secretly took some of his grain to his brother's granary, to ensure that he would never be without. As a result, both of them always found their supply of grain mysteriously replenished each morning.

Then one night they met each other halfway between their two houses. They suddenly realized what had been happening and embraced each other in love. The legend is that God witnessed their meeting and proclaimed, "This is a holy place—a place of love—and here it is that my temple shall be built."[4]

A place of love is holy whenever mutual kindness overflows. We like to think it creates a bit of heaven on earth. And that's exactly what happens when a husband and wife continually look out for one another's needs within their home. When a man and a woman find reason to extend more for the other than for themselves, they create a heavenly and holy place together—a place where, as in a temple, God is honored.

Have you given up "everything you own" for your spouse's happiness? How can you create a little heaven on earth for him or her today?

Love is when the other person's happiness is more important than your own.
—H. JACKSON BROWN JR.

A KISS ON THE LIPS

An honest answer is like a kiss on the lips. PROVERBS 24:26, NIV

AT A CHURCH NEAR OUR home in Seattle, a Japanese couple, recently arrived in the States, were getting married. Despite their limited exposure to Western customs, their American-style wedding went well. But when the minister invited the couple to kiss, nothing happened. Surprised, the minister turned to the bride and said, "How about a little kiss?" Not wanting to offend, she shyly leaned forward and kissed the minister!

She's not the first bride to be confused by kissing. A kiss can mean different things at different times—*good morning, good-bye, I missed you, I'm sorry, I love you, I'm in the mood*, and so on. But perhaps the sweetest of all kisses is the good night kiss that says *I'm going to be missing you even while I sleep*. Remember when you were dating each other how difficult it was to say good night after a date? You'd say good night countless times, with just as many kisses.

Poets and lyricists have done their best to capture the magic and mystery of a kiss. Here's how Edmund Vance Cooke put it:

> *Kisses kept are wasted;*
> *Love is to be tasted.*
> *There are some you love, I know;*
> *Be not loath to tell them so.*
> *Lips go dry and eyes grow wet*
> *Waiting to be warmly met.*
> *Keep them not in waiting yet;*
> *Kisses kept are wasted.*

Not bad. But we think a brief line from the book of Proverbs says it best: "An honest answer is like a kiss on the lips." Solomon, in all his wisdom, equated a kiss on the lips to an honest answer. When we are kissing our spouse on the lips, especially to say good night, we are conveying our honest feelings. It's a kind of lover's shorthand to the questions we rarely articulate but deeply feel: *Do you still love me, in spite of all the mistakes I make? Do you still want to be with me when I burn the toast, leave my clothes on the floor, and all the rest?* A kiss on the lips is a way of honestly answering in the affirmative these unspoken questions.

As you're edging toward this Valentine's season, give kissing some special consideration. Don't take it for granted. "Soul meets soul on lovers' lips," says poet Percy Bysshe Shelley. So don't kiss flippantly. Give one another a really good kiss and then enjoy the intimacy of a couple whose love is as honest as their hearts.

> *How did it happen that their lips came together? How does it happen that birds sing, that snow melts, that the rose unfolds, that the dawn whitens behind the stark shapes of trees on the quivering summit of the hill? A kiss, and all was said.*
> —VICTOR HUGO

SLOWING DOWN, NATURALLY

It is useless for you to work so hard from early morning until late at night, anxiously working for food to eat; for God gives rest to his loved ones. PSALM 127:2

IN HIS BOOK *STRESS FRACTURES*, Charles Swindoll writes about a time when he was in the undertow of too many commitments in too few days. "It wasn't long before I was snapping at my wife and our children," he says, "choking down my food at mealtimes, and feeling irritated at those unexpected interruptions through the day." Before long, the whole Swindoll family was suffering from Chuck's hurry-up style, and it was becoming unbearable. He recalls that one night after supper the Swindolls' younger daughter, Colleen, blurted out these words as quickly as she could: "Daddy-I-wanna-tell-you-somethin'-and-I'll-tell-you-really-fast." Suddenly realizing her frustration, Chuck answered, "Honey, you can tell me . . . and you don't have to tell me really fast. Say it slowly."

"I'll never forget her answer," he says: "Then listen slowly."

Have you ever been infected with hurry sickness? I know we have. And most couples we know have combated it as well. That's one of the reasons pillow talk can be so important in the life of a married couple. Bedtime forces you to slow down. Even as you get under the covers, you begin to breathe more deeply and slowly. Your body temperature drops slightly, and your heart rate and blood pressure go down. Muscles relax. Your metabolic rate (the overall pace of your body processes) slows down too. Falling asleep is God's plan for helping you conserve energy and refuel your tank.

So as you hit the hay tonight, take a moment to savor the change in your pace. Notice your body's desire to submit to this antidote to stress and hurry. Talk to each other about your busy day and listen to each other slowly. If you're looking for something to talk about, explore what the two of you might do to schedule a downshift in your schedules. This is a perfect topic for pillow talk. Considering what you can do to live a more balanced life is more productive when you are relaxing. Making specific plans and working on schedules is better left to the early, more productive times of the day, but as you're edging toward sleep, explore how you might like to change the pace.

Slow down and enjoy life. It's not the scenery you miss by going too fast—you also miss the sense of where you are going and why. —EDDIE CANTOR

HOW ABOUT A SET OF SATIN SHEETS?

The LORD God made a woman from the rib, and he brought her to the man. "At last!" the man exclaimed. "This one is bone from my bone, and flesh from my flesh! She will be called 'woman,' because she was taken from 'man.'" This explains why a man leaves his father and mother and is joined to his wife, and the two are united into one.

GENESIS 2:22-24

SHINY. SMOOTH. LUSTROUS. Even the words describing them sound sensual. Satin sheets evoke the epitome of a bed that is ready for lovemaking. To slide between these silky sheets and cozy up to your husband or wife is bound to get most couples in the mood. Truth be told, however, you may sleep on cotton jersey, flannel, or crisp linen; the kind of sheets on your bed says little about your love life. Far more telling is the status of your relationship outside the bedroom.

Of course, that's not the cultural message this month. Do you feel the pressure? Just five more days until couples everywhere are celebrating Valentine's Day. So let's take a moment to look at the sensual pleasures (and sometimes pressures) this season conjures up for married couples.

What do we know helps a husband and wife have success in the bedroom? Although biology, especially the neurochemistry that determines each person's hormonal levels, is a significant factor in sexual motivation, it has long been established that couples who are simply intentional about their sex lives enjoy more fulfillment between the sheets—satin or otherwise. What does this mean? First, these couples aren't afraid to schedule times of physical intimacy. This may sound like it takes all the spontaneity out of it, but you won't hear these couples complaining. Second, these couples talk to each other about what they like and don't like when it comes to sex, and they respect each other's desires.

The point is that if you want your sex life to be tuned up for Valentine's Day, you don't have to purchase an expensive set of sheets. As a married couple you have the opportunity to enjoy something especially wonderful, since married people have better sex lives than single people. Get this: married people are about twice as likely as unmarried people to make love at least two or three times a week. And that's not all: married sex is more fun. Forty-eight percent of husbands say sex with their wives is extremely satisfying, compared to just 37 percent of men cohabiting with their unmarried partners.

So take a moment to inventory your sex life this week and, if need be, get intentional about how to make it better.

} *The sexual part of us is simple, yet complex. It is predictable, yet changeable, diverse, unknowable, mysterious, and forever beyond our full understanding. If this sounds confusing and contradictory—it is.* —**CLIFFORD AND JOYCE PENNER**

THE HUGS HAVE IT

Give freely and become more wealthy; be stingy and lose everything. PROVERBS 11:24

SEVERAL YEARS AGO as graduate students living in Pasadena, California, we attended a lecture on Valentine's Day by the acclaimed Leo Buscaglia, affectionately known as The Love Doctor. A professor at the University of Southern California, Dr. Buscaglia was wildly popular at the time with several bestselling books, a PBS series, and a national speaking schedule. We enjoyed his inspiring and lively lecture, but what amazed us the most was the huge line of people that formed at the conclusion of his talk. It wound around the entire auditorium. "What are they lining up for?" we asked a fellow attendee. He looked startled that we didn't know and simply said, "A hug." And he was right. Several hundred people queued up for a quick hug from "the hug doctor." We hadn't seen anything like it before, and we haven't seen anything like it since. It certainly made an impression.

Some weeks later, by coincidence, I (Les) happened to cross paths with Dr. Buscaglia in a gourmet grocery store. I couldn't help but ask him, "Why do all those people line up to be hugged by you?" He laughed and then got serious. This is what he told me: "A hug helps people make it through tough times and lifts the spirit of anyone who is already flying high."

It was a question he'd obviously been asked before. As I was about to say thanks, he leaned toward me and gave me a hug—right there in the frozen food section! I'm not making this up. I was startled. He was happy.

Truth is, I'm not the huggy type. And I didn't really need a hug from the famous doctor, but I'll take a hug from my wife any day. As the saying goes, sometimes a hug can say what words can't.

Would you believe there is a World Hug Week? It's true. The sponsoring group believes the world would be a better place if there was a massive movement to embrace our loved ones for five seconds at some point during this week. Silly as it sounds, they are probably right. A five-second hug goes a long way—especially when it comes to getting your daily requirement of touch in marriage. Have you made hugging a habit? If not, we offer a simple suggestion: ask for one. "May I have a hug?" is all it takes. Say thanks, hello, or good-bye with a hug. Soon you'll have the hug habit.

Millions and millions of years would still not give me half enough time to describe that tiny instant of all eternity when you put your arms around me and I put my arms around you. —JACQUES PRÉVERT

ONE FOR THE GUYS

In the same way, you husbands must give honor to your wives. Treat your wife with understanding as you live together. She may be weaker than you are, but she is your equal partner in God's gift of new life. Treat her as you should so your prayers will not be hindered. 1 PETER 3:7

OKAY, WE'RE JUST three days from Valentine's Day, and I (Les) have to tell you that in my counseling and speaking I often hear how much pressure this day creates for men. So I want to devote this meditation specifically to the guys. In fact, I want to give you a little nugget that is about as time tested as they come. You've heard it before, but it's always a good reminder.

You see, in marriage, men typically don't feel the need to seduce or to build anticipation—that's an effort we think we no longer need to do now that we have officially wooed our partners. We come to believe that if we're in the mood, they should be too. Of course, that's not the case. You must elicit your wife's desire; too often we make the mistake of simply monitoring it. We wait. We observe. We look for signs, a glimmer of an indication that she might be in the mood. That's not the way to approach it! You need to cultivate your wife's desire. You need to woo her.

Because of what I do for a living, every year around this time of the year I receive dozens of requests for interviews with the media. They all want an "expert" to talk about how men can make the most of this day. After doing countless call-in shows on the subject, I can tell you that most men hate this holiday. They don't like the pressure. They feel coerced into having to buy something or do something for their wives just because it's on the calendar. They'd rather cultivate romance and passion on their own schedules.

Well, that's what wooing a woman is all about. So here's what I suggest: make up your own Valentine's Day. Write her a little note, buy her a little treat, deliver a cup of coffee to her work, let her sleep late, leave her a loving voice message. Do whatever you'd like to do—just be sure you woo her. Seduce her. This builds the anticipation for a great night of sex, whatever date is on the calendar. Now, I realize you can't do this all the time. The point, in fact, is that this kind of wooing is to be special and surprising. But if you're wise, you won't just wait for Valentine's Day to woo your wife!

 Passion, though a bad regulator, is a powerful spring. —RALPH WALDO EMERSON

TANGIBLE AFFIRMATION

In the beginning the Word already existed. The Word was with God, and the Word was God. . . . The Word gave life to everything that was created, and his life brought light to everyone. JOHN 1:1, 4

CONSIDERING THE VAST array of exhibits at the Smithsonian Institution, you might easily miss the display of the personal effects found on Abraham Lincoln the night he was shot. These include an embroidered handkerchief, a penknife, a spectacle case repaired with cotton string, and a Confederate five-dollar bill. But the real treasure was the final item found on Lincoln: a worn newspaper clipping extolling his accomplishments as president. It begins, "Abe Lincoln is one of the greatest statesmen of all time."

Does it seem odd to you that Lincoln would so obviously cherish these words of affirmation? Of course, we think of our nation's sixteenth president as a great man, a great president, indeed as one of the greatest statesmen of all time. But when Lincoln was president, he wasn't as popular as he became after his death. The nation was bitterly divided, and Lincoln's leadership was constantly threatened. He was the object of a critical press. He was viciously criticized for refusing to compromise on the slavery issue. At the same time, he was strongly criticized for not moving quickly enough in abolishing slavery. So in the midst of this barrage of criticism, Abraham Lincoln needed something in his pocket to remind himself that his critics were not his only observers. He carried with him a tangible manifestation of affirmation, a physical reminder that someone believed in him.

Just think, if a tangible reminder like this was valuable to our powerful president, how much more valuable would it be to your own husband or wife to receive a note or symbolic object from you? Maybe he or she already has such a thing from you—and vice versa. What is it, and why is it meaningful in your relationship to have these kinds of tangible affirmations? Or if not, what sort of thing could you tuck away for your spouse to find and be reminded of your loving support? Most important of all, how can your relationship be strengthened by God's own icon of affirmation, his Holy Word?

I am not at all concerned about [whether God is on our side], for I know that the Lord is always on the side of the right. But it is my constant anxiety and prayer that I and this nation should be on the Lord's side. **—ABRAHAM LINCOLN**

NO TIME FOR SEX? REALLY?

Let your wife be a fountain of blessing for you. Rejoice in the wife of your youth. She is a loving deer, a graceful doe. Let her breasts satisfy you always. May you always be captivated by her love. PROVERBS 5:18-19

OUR FRIENDS DAVID AND CLAUDIA ARP once wrote a book for married couples called *No Time for Sex*. "It's a complaint we are hearing from more and more couples," Claudia told us. "They are so busy running the rat race that when they fall into bed, that's about all they can do."

And she's right. We hear the same complaint at our marriage seminars around the country. Strange, isn't it? After all, making love is something that most couples rank very high on their list of favorite activities. According to one survey reported in *USA Today*, the top of women's favorite home activities is "spending time with family," chosen by 65 percent of respondents. Next was listening to music (47 percent) but next in line was making love (46 percent). It may not surprise you to know that men, on the other hand, ranked "making love" as their very first favorite home pursuit (64 percent). Spending time with family was second (56 percent).[5]

So why aren't couples finding the time for one of the activities they enjoy the most? Perhaps German philosopher Søren Kierkegaard hinted at the answer when he said, "Most [people] pursue pleasure with such breathless haste that they hurry past it." Could it be? In our fast pace, could we be failing to savor the scintillating pleasure of making love as husband and wife? Could we be cutting the corners on this delectable delight?

The answer is yes. At the end of a long day, most couples are too worn out for sex. Working fewer hours is one way to free up energy and time for sex, which is why couples make love more on vacation. But fatigue and time pressure are not the only reasons for having a sex-starved marriage. According to Carl Honoré, author of *In Praise of Slowness*, "Our hurry-up culture teaches that reaching the destination is more important than the journey itself—and sex is affected by the same finishing line mentality."[6]

We can hear some of you saying that speed has its place between the sheets. Long live "the quickie." Sure. But making love slowly can be a profound experience. Some soft music, a few candles, and plenty of time for gentle caresses are sure to join your spirits and slow down your souls. Not to mention that it will extend your pleasure.

So if you've been rushing through the bliss of married sex, slow down. There's no need to hurry. Taking your time to make love to each other is some of the most important time that a husband and wife ever spend. Make it last.

When you're deeply absorbed in what you're doing, time gives itself to you like a warm and willing lover. **—BRENDAN FRANCIS**

BE MY WHO?

Many waters cannot quench love, nor can rivers drown it. If a man tried to buy love with all his wealth, his offer would be utterly scorned. SONG OF SONGS 8:7

HIS NAME WAS VALENTINE, and he lived in Rome during the third century. At that time Rome was ruled by an emperor named Claudius. Valentine didn't like Claudius. Few did. Claudius, you see, wanted to have a big army and he expected men to volunteer to join. But as is the case today, many men did not want to fight in wars because they did not want to leave their wives and families.

Claudius, who became furious when the men of Rome did not sign up for his army, reasoned that if men were not married, they would not mind joining the army. So the emperor decided not to allow any more marriages. Young people thought his new law was cruel, but Valentine thought it was preposterous. As a priest, he wasn't about to support a law forbidding one of his priestly duties: performing marriages.

Even after the marriage ban was passed, Valentine kept performing marriage ceremonies—in secret. No wedding bells tolled those weddings, and no guests celebrated them either. Just the bride and groom and the priest would be present, and the ceremony would be conducted under utmost secrecy. But during one ceremony, Valentine was discovered. He was able to give the newly married couple time to escape, but he was thrown in jail and sentenced to death. As the story goes, he remained cheerful. Young people came to see him in jail, throwing flowers and notes up to his window. They wanted him to know that they, too, believed in love.

One of these young people was the daughter of a prison guard. Her father allowed her to visit Valentine. They struck up a serious friendship, talking for hours. On the day Valentine was to die, he left his friend a little note thanking her for her friendship and loyalty. He signed it, "Love from your Valentine."

That note, written on the day he died—February 14, AD 269—started a custom of exchanging love messages that continues to this day. It is because of Valentine the priest that every year on this day people think about love. And when they think of Emperor Claudius, if they think of him, they remember how he tried to stand in the way of love, and they laugh—because they know that love cannot be stopped.

Oh, if it be to choose and call thee mine, love, thou art every day my Valentine!
—**THOMAS HOOD**

IT'S YOUR CHOICE

Today I have given you the choice between life and death, between blessings and curses. Now I call on heaven and earth to witness the choice you make. Oh, that you would choose life, so that you and your descendants might live! DEUTERONOMY 30:19

"I NEVER KNEW I HAD A CHOICE." It's the saddest sentence we ever hear in our counseling offices. Many things in life are beyond our control—our eye color, our race, hurricanes. But there is a vast, unclaimed territory of actions over which we have a major say.

In a very simple experiment, psychologists Ellen Langer of Harvard and Judith Rodin of Yale clearly demonstrated the beneficial effects of making choices for oneself.[7] They gave a group of nursing home residents potted plants to care for. In addition to taking responsibility for the little plants, they were also offered suggestions on doing more for themselves, making their own decisions, instead of letting the staff do that for them. A second group, matched with the first in terms of degree of ill health or disability, received the usual nursing home treatment with the staff announcing that they would be responsible for the residents' care, making all the decisions for them.

Within three weeks, the first group showed significant improvement in physical and emotional health and the amount of activity engaged in. Even more dramatic were the results after eighteen months. The death rate of the group encouraged to make their own decisions was only half that of the other group.

So what decision—what choices—are calling you? More specifically, what choice can the two of you make, starting today, that will positively impact your relationship? In fact, let's get even more specific. What choice to do something you wouldn't have done otherwise can the two of you make that will benefit your relationship within the next four days? Why four? you wonder. Because it's measurable and can quickly demonstrate the powerful impact of making a choice together.

You may choose to take a walk together after dinner each night for the next four nights. You may choose to have a long-overdue date night together. You may choose to help a needy neighbor. You get the idea. The point is simply to choose to do something that helps you become the kind of couple you want to be.

Someone once said that there are always two choices, two paths to take. One is easy and that is its only reward. More often than not, that easy path is to make no choice at all. Make a positive choice for the life of your relationship today.

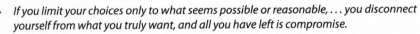

If you limit your choices only to what seems possible or reasonable, . . . you disconnect yourself from what you truly want, and all you have left is compromise.
—ROBERT FRITZ

A NOT-SO-SECRET SECRET

In the beginning was the Word, and the Word was with God, and the Word was God.

JOHN 1:1

WE DO A LOT OF marriage seminars around the country, which means we often fly into a city on Friday evening and fly home on Saturday after the seminar ends. Because we've been doing this for quite a few years, we've come to know most major airports pretty well. We know where we're going to eat, for example, on a layover in Denver or Chicago. We know where we can get some good pasta in Orlando or a deli sandwich at Reagan National.

But if we fly in to California, we almost never eat in the airport. Nope. We save our appetites for a little fast-food chain that is typically open late at night: In-N-Out Burger.

If you've eaten at an In-N-Out, you know it's nothing fancy. Far from it. Just a clean place, with quality burgers, thick shakes, and real fries—and always tasty. This regional chain was started in 1948 by Harry and Esther Snyder. According to the company's website, the Snyders had a simple plan that is still in use today: "Give customers the freshest, highest quality foods you can buy and provide them with friendly service in a sparkling clean environment." It wasn't until the 1970s that they began to expand. The chain had eighteen restaurants when Harry died in 1976. Today the chain has about 250 restaurants, mostly in California.

The menu is simple. They have the usual French fries and milkshakes, plus three burgers: hamburger, cheeseburger, and "Double-Double" (double meat/double cheese). That's it . . . unless you know the secret. Customers in the know often order by name items that are not on the menu but available at every In-N-Out. The "secret menu" includes items like the "3 x 3" or a burger or fries "animal style."

But there's another subtle secret for In-N-Out Burger customers. Harry and Esther placed a Scripture reference on everything they sold—and the company still does that to this day. Somewhere on the wrapper of every burger is Revelation 3:20: "Look! I stand at the door and knock. If you hear my voice and open the door, I will come in, and we will share a meal together as friends." On every beverage you'll find John 3:16: "For God loved the world so much that he gave his one and only Son, so that everyone who believes in him will not perish but have eternal life." We say "subtle" because the references are very small. But almost everyone knows they're there.

It was just one couple's way of getting God's Word into their customers' hands, literally. But like the "secret" 3 x 3 burger, they're not really keeping God's Word a secret, either. Hide it under a bushel? No. Not Harry and Esther Snyder.

Take a moment to consider how you and your spouse can be a shining light together through your shared lives.

Let God's promises shine. —CORRIE TEN BOOM

YOUR BEGINNINGS AS A COUPLE

God created human beings in his own image. In the image of God he created them; male and female he created them. GENESIS 1:27

CHAIM POTOK, BORN IN THE Bronx on February 17, 1929 to Jewish immigrants from Poland, started writing at the age of 16. He submitted his first article to the *Atlantic Monthly* but was rejected. The editor complimented his work, though, and that was enough to keep him going. Potok eventually became a rabbi and later a bestselling author with his 1967 novel, *The Chosen*. It stayed on the *New York Times* bestseller list for thirty-nine weeks and sold more than three million copies.

Potok went on to write other award-winning stories, mostly about aspects of Jewish life. The first sentence of Potok's novel *In the Beginning* reads, "All beginnings are hard." In the book, the main character, David, describes how one evening when he was nine years old, he burst into tears because a passage of a Bible commentary had proved too difficult for him to understand. David's mentor welcomed him warmly to his apartment and spoke in a gentle voice: "Be patient, David, beginnings are hard; you cannot swallow all the world at one time."

Have you ever felt like David? It's only natural when beginning something new—marriage included—to want instant maturity. But seasoned maturity takes time, and growing pains are inevitable. Look back on your own beginnings as a couple today. Maybe those years weren't so long ago; maybe they're hard to remember! Think about what you have gone through together as a couple since your wedding day. Do you see ways God has helped you grow, not only in spite of, but as a result of difficult times? If you're in those difficult times now, take courage—God can use this to grow you as a result.

As you reflect on the beginning of your own marriage, consider another beginning—your own birth. Remember that God made you in his image. This great gift should be affirmed and celebrated. The same God who created you in the image of himself at the beginning of your life is with you as you live out the vows you made at the beginning of your marriage. Thank God for bringing you through the difficult times behind you—and commit to turning to him in any difficult times that may be ahead.

 From small beginnings come great things. —**FOLK PROVERB**

WAIT FOR IT . . . WAIT FOR IT . . .

I always thank my God for you. 1 CORINTHIANS 1:4

YOU MAY FIND THIS hard to believe, but I bought Leslie a birthday gift and waited twenty years to give it to her. I bought it just before we got married. Small enough to fit in one hand, the gift was wrapped in two sheets of simple notebook paper and taped securely at both ends. On the top, I had printed in red ink, "This gift is not to be opened by Leslie until I say so."

Shortly after we were married, we moved from Chicago to Los Angeles, and Leslie came across the gift. "What's in this box?" she asked.

"That's a secret," I said slyly as I took it from her hands.

"Aren't you going to give me a hint?" she asked playfully.

"You'll find out soon enough," I said, tucking it into a drawer under some sweaters.

I'll be honest; I didn't have a time frame in mind. I had thought the gift might be something I'd give during that first married year. But it slipped my mind—until February 18, 2007. That's when I threw a birthday bash for Leslie's fortieth!

With a couple dozen friends filling our kitchen and family room that evening at the party, Leslie spied the familiar package among her other presents and went straight for it. "Hey, everybody!" she exclaimed. "I've been waiting half my life—literally—to open this little box." The anticipation in the room was palpable. She carefully slid the box from the wrapping to reveal a cheap keychain with a tiny Precious Moments figurine dangling on one end.

Leslie started laughing so hard she couldn't speak as she held it over her head to show the eager group. The others were mildly amused, but mostly they were confused. *He kept a keychain in a box for twenty years and gave it to her on her fortieth birthday?*

It didn't really matter what our friends thought. I couldn't contain my own laughter as I watched Leslie reveling in the absurdity of the moment.

"I thought it might be something really meaningful," she laughed, "like a letter you wrote to me twenty years ago or something. But it's a keychain—a Precious Moments keychain!"

"The cashier told me it might be worth something someday," I said with a straight face.

Leslie burst into laughter again.

"The real gift is finally getting to uncover the secret." Leslie told me later. "I'm going to keep this keychain in the box on my desk to remind me of this feeling."

It's been said that pleasures are greatest in anticipation. Now, we wouldn't recommend building up anticipation for a cheap gift that's overhyped. But we do recommend having something to look forward to as a couple. What are you anticipating together?

Marriage is the alliance of two people, one of whom never remembers birthdays and the other never forgets. —OGDEN NASH

IT'S UP TO YOU

If you refuse to serve the LORD, then choose today whom you will serve. Would you prefer the gods your ancestors served beyond the Euphrates? Or will it be the gods of the Amorites in whose land you now live? But as for me and my family, we will serve the LORD. JOSHUA 24:15

DO YOU RECALL WHAT we suggested you do four days ago on February 15? We asked you to make a choice. We asked you to exert your personal freedom and choose to do something that would positively impact your relationship together. We told you about a little experiment that underscored the value and power that comes when we don't leave so much of our lives to chance. In case you need a reminder while you conduct your own experiment, here's another example.

This study was conducted not far from our home in Seattle, at the University of Washington. The researchers divided into two groups students who were going through multiple life changes. One group was led to believe they had no control over what happened to them, and the other group believed they had a considerable amount of control. Depression and anxiety were significantly higher for the students who believed they had no control.[8] Those who perceived themselves as in charge of their lives showed little to no depression or anxiety despite high stress.

Again, we are simply underscoring the fact that if we do not leverage the personal freedom, self-responsibility, and choice we all have as God-given tools in our lives, we miss out on countless blessings that he has waiting for us. In the professional literature on the subject it's called "self-efficacy" and "internal locus of control." But the Bible simply calls this "choice," as in, "choose today whom you will serve." However you label it, you can be certain this quality is being exercised by every healthy and happy individual and couple on the planet.

With the Holy Spirit in our lives we can choose our attitudes about what happens to us and how other people treat us. That includes your spouse. Choose today how you will think about your spouse and about whatever situations you are facing together.

> *God gave us a free choice because there is no significance to love that knows no alternative.* —JAMES C. DOBSON

THE WHISPER TEST

To all who believed him and accepted him, he gave the right to become children of God.

JOHN 1:12

ONE OF THE MOST INSPIRATIONAL stories we have ever read comes from Mary Ann Bird's "The Whisper Test." It's the story of a little girl who was hated for her differences and one day was given the gift of unmerited acceptance.

Mary Ann was born with a cleft palate, and when she started school her classmates made it clear to her how she looked: "a little girl with a misshapen lip, crooked nose, lopsided teeth, and garbled speech."

She was convinced that no one outside her family could love her. When her classmates asked, "What happened to your lip?" she would say that she had fallen and cut it on a piece of glass. It seemed more acceptable, she admits, to have suffered an accident than to have been born that way. An accident might befall anyone, so there was some equalizing power in the story.

Still, school was a difficult place for Mary Ann because she felt so different. There was, however, a caring teacher in the second grade whom all the students adored. Mrs. Leonard was short, round, and happy, "a sparkling lady." She was to administer the annual hearing test to Mary Ann's class that year. Mary Ann knew the drill: one by one each student would stand against the classroom door and cover one ear, waiting for the teacher to whisper something into the other ear. The student was to repeat it back just as he or she heard it. Mary Ann knew to expect "things like 'the sky is blue' or 'Do you have new shoes?'"

Mrs. Leonard gave the test to everyone in the class, and finally it was Mary Ann's turn. She waited, and these were the words she heard Mrs. Leonard whisper: "I wish you were my little girl."

Mary Ann writes about what a difference these words of acceptance made in her life, empowering her to be her own person, regardless of the criticism she felt from the other children and the shame she felt over her physical challenges.

We are all "spiritually challenged" by our sins, yet our God whispers the same thing to us: "Remain in my love" (John 15:9).

As you revel in God's love for you, allow it to shape your own expressions of love for your spouse. You have a powerful opportunity to make a difference in the life of your own husband or wife by remaining in God's love and creating a space for your spouse to do the same.

God loves each of us as if there were only one of us. —ST. AUGUSTINE

KIDNEY SAVES MARRIAGE

Dear brothers and sisters, I plead with you to give your bodies to God because of all he has done for you. Let them be a living and holy sacrifice—the kind he will find acceptable. This is truly the way to worship him. ROMANS 12:1

AFTER TEN YEARS OF MARRIAGE, Cindy and Chip Altemos were in the long process of getting a divorce. The proverbial baggage they had brought from previous marriages seemed too great to overcome, so they separated and even agreed to date other people.

Five years into the painful separation, Chip was in the hospital with kidney failure as a result of juvenile diabetes. With his health deteriorating rapidly, his soon-to-be ex-wife came to his aid—in spite of Chip's being in another relationship at the time. "He was still my husband. There was no way I could walk around with two kidneys, and he had none," Cindy told the press. "It was the right thing to do." Knowing long ago that with his condition he would need a transplant, she had always said she would donate one of hers, and under their current circumstances she added a promise to the donation: she told Chip there were no strings attached, no written agreement concerning a better share in divorce court.

But the transplant took place on February 21, 2007, and a funny thing happened as they both recovered in the hospital. The married and estranged couple fell back in love. As Chip tells it, "I guess just being around each other, we slowly fell back in love again." The ordeal put an end to Chip's other relationship and also to the divorce proceedings.[9]

This is a dramatic story of sacrificial love, no doubt. It shows the power of love to restore even a troubled marriage such as the Altemoses once had. But no matter what state your marriage is in, their story is a reminder that to keep love alive and well in our relationships we are called to give up a part of ourselves on a daily basis. Maybe not something as dramatic as an organ, as Cindy gave, but just as vital a "transplant"—a living sacrifice. How will you put Romans 12:1 into practice today with your spouse? What will you give of yourself so that he or she might live in Christ more abundantly?

> *Peace demands the most heroic labor and the most difficult sacrifice. It demands greater heroism than war. It demands greater fidelity to the truth and a much more perfect purity of conscience.* —THOMAS MERTON

MAKING TIME TO TALK

I appeal to you, dear brothers and sisters, by the authority of our Lord Jesus Christ, to live in harmony with each other. Let there be no divisions in the church. Rather, be of one mind, united in thought and purpose. 1 CORINTHIANS 1:10

A TRADITIONAL NAVAJO WEDDING took place outside of Seattle a few years ago. As is customary, tribal couples crowded into the newlyweds' hogan to offer counsel. One man cleared his throat as if to speak, but at that very moment his wife kneed him in the back. So he kept silent, and others spoke up. Later he tried again, clearing his throat, but again he felt his wife's restraining knee. This happened a third time, so the man gave up.

As the guests filed out, the wife in question asked her husband, "Why did you say nothing?"

"I was going to, but each time I was about to speak I thought you didn't want me to."

"I nudged you three times to get you to speak," she protested. "What would you have said?"

"I would have spoken of the importance of communication in marriage."[10]

You've probably had a few moments of frustrated communication like that, haven't you? And you've probably heard this before, but it's nearly impossible to overstate the importance of communication in marriage—as well as the difficulty it presents for most couples. If you consider how much of the day we spend communicating in general you'd think we'd find it easier. After all, experts estimate that 70 percent of our waking hours are spent either taking information in or giving it out. Thirty-three percent of that time is devoted to talking and 42 percent to listening. We participate in communication more than just about any other human activity. Yet when it comes to marriage, it seems our biggest communication hurdle is simply finding the time to talk.

A friend of ours recently told us that in managing their household of four children, he and his wife feel more like air-traffic controllers than husband and wife. We know the feeling. Most couples do. In a national survey of married couples, researchers found that, on average, we spend less than three minutes of meaningful conversation together in a typical day.

Yikes! Can you believe it? We are so busy that after we coordinate schedules and deal with the business of the day, we don't seem to have enough time to genuinely check in with each other on how we're really doing. Busyness deludes us into thinking that we're conversing when we are actually just trying to hold on to the hectic speed of our days.

Take a few minutes to check in with one another. As you debrief your day (or prepare for the day ahead) ask your spouse to share a high and low as a quick way to connect at a deeper level.

The reason most major goals are not achieved is that we spend our time doing second things first. —ROBERT J. MCKAIN

A WHALE OF A LESSON

God blesses those who work for peace, for they will be called the children of God.

MATTHEW 5:9

WRITER AMY SUTHERLAND learned an important relationship lesson in a very unlikely place. She wrote about it for the *New York Times* in an article called, "What Shamu Taught Me About a Happy Marriage."

Sutherland begins by explaining that after twelve years of marriage, she had become dismayed that her husband Scott still exhibited several irritating habits. Sound familiar? "These minor annoyances are not the stuff of separation and divorce," she writes, "but in sum they began to dull my love for Scott. . . . So, like many wives before me, I ignored a library of advice books and set about improving him. By nagging, of course, which only made his behavior worse." She goes on to describe how in response to this "improvement" her husband would drive faster instead of slower; shave less frequently, not more; and leave his smelly workout clothes on the bedroom floor longer than ever.

The breakthrough came for Amy while researching a book. She attended a school in California for exotic animal trainers where she saw them teach animals to do things you might never expect them to do: elephants to paint, hyenas to turn a pirouette. And that's when it clicked. She wasn't seeing the nagging from her husband's point of view. She wasn't thinking how it would feel to be nagged.

If she were in her husband's shoes, she would be far more motivated to improve her behaviors if she were rewarded for the good than if she were punished for the bad. "After all," she reasoned, "you don't get a sea lion to balance a ball on the end of its nose by nagging." Back in her home state of Maine, she began thanking Scott if he threw one dirty shirt into the hamper. "If he threw in two," she says, "I'd kiss him. Meanwhile, I would step over any soiled clothes on the floor without one sharp word, though I did sometimes kick them under the bed. But as he basked in my appreciation, the piles became smaller."

You get the point. In those pesky marital matters that can become big sources of conflict but that really are small, when we focus on the positive, the negatives seem to take care of themselves. See if you can shift your focus from correction to appreciation and enjoy the results of this change in your marriage!

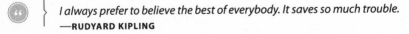

I always prefer to believe the best of everybody. It saves so much trouble.
—**RUDYARD KIPLING**

HAVE YOU FOUND WHAT YOU'RE NOT LOOKING FOR?

"You have eyes—can't you see? You have ears—can't you hear?" Don't you remember anything at all? MARK 8:18

THERE IS A SAYING IN INDIA, "When a pickpocket meets a saint, all he sees are the pockets." Our motives shape what we see—and don't see—around us.

Consider the fabled story of the man from Colorado who moved to Texas and built a house with a large picture window looking out on hundreds of miles of rangeland. "The only problem is," he said, "there's nothing to see." About the same time, a man from Texas moved to Colorado and built a house with a large picture window overlooking the Rockies. "The only problem is I can't see anything," he said. "The mountains are in the way." Each was blind to what the other saw clearly.

Of course, we are all prone to this problem. In varying degrees, we all share a tendency toward denial, an emotionally comfortable strategy that protects us from the distress that recognizing the harsh truth would bring. So we might resort to filtering out information, rationalizing mistakes, avoiding responsibility. Some of us will do just about anything to steer clear of the truth if it might hurt. To make the matter of getting to the truth worse, we even have ways of ensuring that people around us collude with our denial. That's especially true of our spouses. At an almost unconscious level, we can manipulate events in our relationships so that not only we but others also avoid honest, constructive feedback, acting as though everything is fine when in fact it is not. If we are not intentional about staying clear of this tendency, we buy the illusion of harmony at the cost of the truth. And we miss the path that could take us to emotional maturity and spiritual health.

So what illusion might be standing in the pathway to your well-being? Or to look at it from another angle, what is God trying to show you? How is he revealing himself to you? What are you not seeing? Of course, you can't answer that question now. It's an answer that comes only with contemplation and time—as long as you are looking for it. Ask God to give you the eyes to see yourself as you are, so that you may see others as they are.

The truth, as the light, makes blind. —ALBERT CAMUS

THE RETURN FROM HANDS-ON HELPING

Be generous: Invest in acts of charity. Charity yields high returns.

ECCLESIASTES 11:1, THE MESSAGE

HOW MUCH MONEY WOULD you need to improve your life? Go ahead, think about this. Talk it over with each other. After all, nearly everyone, no matter how much money he or she has, would like more. The month of April, when we pay our taxes, is bound to make you consider this question. So how much would it take to really make a difference in your life?

When asked how much money it would take to make a real difference in their lives, 33 percent of people say that an extra $100,000 in the bank would improve their lot, and 14 percent would want up to $500,000. An even million would shake things up, say 16 percent, and 24 percent calculate it would take up to $10 million.

Seems we're all over the map when it comes to feeling financially fit, which makes sense because the value of money, as of time, is relative. Kenneth Behring is a good example. He seemed to have everything. He was affluent and generous. But something transformed him during a trip to Vietnam in 2000. The retired real estate developer was helping a relief organization bring food and medicine to a village, and there he delivered a wheelchair to a six-year-old polio victim. The girl's reaction changed his life—so much so that he created the Wheelchair Foundation, which today delivers 10,000 wheelchairs a month worldwide.

You don't have to be a wealthy benefactor to give with a hands-on approach. In fact, it doesn't matter how much money you have. Giving is good for your marriage. We know that agreeing on financial matters in marriage is not always easy. We certainly don't always see eye-to-eye on finances in our home. But a fundamental shift of attitude toward giving took place when we changed the question we were asking each other. Rather than "How much of our money should we give to God?" we learned to ask, "How much of God's money should we spend on ourselves?" The difference between these two questions was monumental for us. With the understanding that our income is all God's as a starting point, we eliminated much of the legalistic thinking and guilt related to giving based on a set percentage of income.

Only 13 percent of the population believes money can buy happiness. But almost everyone believes that giving generously to others brings great joy. And it does. So consider how the two of you might spend some time doing a little hands-on helping. It may be one of the most important investments you ever make in your marriage.

 } *Time is the coin of your life. It is the only coin you have, and only you can determine how it will be spent. Be careful lest you let other people spend it for you.* —CARL SANDBURG

WHO CAN BE AGAINST US?

What, then, shall we say in response to this? If God is for us, who can be against us?

ROMANS 8:31, NIV

WE WERE VISITING with John and Margaret Maxwell in their Atlanta home when I (Les) asked to see John's study. I'm always eager to see where another writer does his thinking, dreaming, and creating. I also knew that John was an avid collector of memorabilia from John Wesley's life. In fact, he may have one of the most important privately held historical collections of its kind. When I asked him about his most prized piece in his collection, John didn't hesitate. He pointed to a letter that was signed by John Wesley, founder of the Methodist movement in England, with a postscript by his brother Charles, remembered for the many hymns he wrote.

"On February 26, in 1791," John told me, "William Wilberforce was facing yet another discouraging defeat in his attempt to abolish Britain's slave trade, when he received a letter from John Wesley." Very carefully, John was revealing the document as he talked. "That now-famous letter would prove to be a continuing source of strength for the rest of his life." It read:

> *Dear Sir:*
>
> *Unless the divine power has raised you up . . . I see not how you can go through your glorious enterprise, in opposing that execrable villainy, which is the scandal of religion, of England, and of human nature. Unless God has raised you up for this very thing, you will be worn out by the opposition of men and devils. But, "if God be for you, who can be against you?" Are all of them stronger than God? O "be not weary in well doing!" Go on, in the name of God and in the power of His might, till even American slavery (the vilest that ever saw the sun) shall vanish away before it.*
>
> *. . . That He who has guided you from your youth up, may continue to strengthen you in this and all things, is the prayer of,*
>
>

Your affectionate servant,
J. Wesley
>

Four days after writing that letter, Wesley was dead and once again Wilberforce was defeated when the vote was taken in Parliament. He would ultimately prevail in his just and holy cause. During the intervening years, however, he faced innumerable disappointments and was tempted to give up the fight more than once. He was vilified in published articles and victimized in vicious whispering campaigns. His opponents arranged for him to be challenged to a duel and even attempted to kill him, but he would not be deterred.

And every time he became discouraged, he returned to Wesley's letter. Each time he read it, it was like the first time. Never did it fail to encourage and strengthen him.

Think of the encouraging power we can give one another through a written note.

When life knocks you down you should always try to land on your back because if you can look up, you can get up! —LES BROWN

A GOOD LAUGH

A glad heart makes a happy face. PROVERBS 15:13

"DO YOU TWO NEED A TISSUE?" a voice gently whispered from behind us. We were sitting in a quiet theater watching a somber play when—at the saddest moment—something struck us as being funny. Hysterically funny.

At just that moment, Les had found a withered old banana in his coat pocket. Who knows how long it had been there, but he set this surprising discovery on my knee. Caught off guard by the incongruity of the banana and the scene, I developed one of the worst cases of the giggles I've ever had. Les quickly caught the same disease. We tried desperately to stifle our laughter in the hushed theater, but as we bowed our heads to hide our faces, we couldn't keep our shoulders from shuddering. An older woman behind us, thinking we were moved by what was happening on stage, offered us a tissue for our tears, which made us want to laugh all the more. When Les accepted her kind offer, I really lost it and had to leave the theater.

Just another day in the marriage of Les and Leslie? Not quite, but we do laugh a lot together. As you can tell, the tiniest of things can sometimes set us off—a slight inflection or a knowing glance, for example. We can quote a funny line from a movie or sitcom for weeks. Better still are the unplanned faux pas in front of others that bring embarrassment. We have the same funny bone and can't keep from using it. No wonder we enjoy our marriage.

Laughter does that. Any good friend will tell you that laughter is the shortest distance between two people—and that's especially true in marriage. No matter what your personalities are like, if you're living together, making decisions together, and spending time together, you should naturally have your own inside jokes and meaningful lines. Using them is actually healthy for a number of reasons, one of which is that shared laughter strengthens a bond. Don't overlook an opportunity to share a laugh with your spouse today. Be intentional and bring home a story from the day or a joke you know will cause the two of you to revel in a moment of shared laughter.

The most thoroughly wasted of all days is that on which one has not laughed.
—NICOLAS CHAMFORT

PRAYING LIKE NEVER BEFORE

Pray in the Spirit at all times and on every occasion. Stay alert and be persistent in your prayers for all believers everywhere. EPHESIANS 6:18

AS ANY COUPLE WHO has experienced a tumultuous pregnancy or a crisis with an infant or child knows, the vulnerability you feel as a parent is almost beyond description. Without the gift of prayer we cannot imagine how we could have sustained our strength.

You see, our son John was born three months ahead of schedule, weighing just a pound and fighting against all odds to survive. And in our moments of crisis with baby John we prayed with hearts on our sleeves. You might be interested to know that our prayers together sometimes felt awkward or uncomfortable—especially when one or both of us may not have felt much like praying. But our deep need for prayer overcame all the resistance and kept us praying our imperfect prayers. There were moments so intense that they literally drove us to our knees.

So many points in our crisis could not have been survived without shared prayer: the day Leslie was wheeled directly from the doctor's office to the hospital for what was to be the remainder of the pregnancy; the doctor's announcement that the decision to deliver at 28 weeks was unavoidable; the phone call in the early morning hours summoning us to the hospital for John's emergency surgery; the dreaded news of a brain bleed, a collapsed lung, a serious eye disease. Each of these moments required a focused strength not possible without God's presence.

There were also the moments of gratitude so rich that we understood how Christ felt when he said, "If these people don't praise God, the very rocks will cry out in praise" (see Luke 19:40). It was 11:30 p.m., Sunday evening, February 28, 1998, when John's postoperative body finally pulled out of severe shock and the monitors fell to safer levels while he lapsed into sleep after five days of terrifying pain and fragility. And July 11, 1998, was the day an intricate eye exam revealed John's deteriorating eyesight was stabilizing and had actually begun a healing process that would reverse the current damage. The immensity of gratitude that filled our marriage in those moments and the prayers of simple thanksgiving we shared obliterated any remnant of feeling that prayer was a duty for us to perform rather than a power that enables us to live in God's presence. What do you need to pray together about today? Have you tried and felt strange doing so? Keep trying. Keep praying.

Trouble and perplexity drive me to prayer, and prayer drives away perplexity and trouble.
—PHILIPP MELANCHTHON

DON'T JUST TALK ABOUT IT— DO SOMETHING

Faith by itself isn't enough. Unless it produces good deeds, it is dead and useless. . . . I will show you my faith by my good deeds. JAMES 2:17-18

THE MOVIE *THE PATRIOT* starring Mel Gibson reminds us that some things are worth fighting for.

It's 1776 in South Carolina when Gabriel Martin opens the door of the church where a memorial service is in progress. Gabriel addresses Reverend Oliver, asking his permission to make an announcement that the South Carolina militia is being called up. "I'm here to enlist every man willing."

Oliver descends the stairs toward Gabriel. "Son, we are here to pray for the souls of those men hanging outside."

"Yes, pray for them," Gabriel says, "but honor them by taking up arms with us."

A man in the congregation stands to speak. "And bring more suffering to this town?"

Another man adds, "If King George can hang those men, our friends, he can hang any one of us."

Anne Patricia Howard stands up and addresses the protesters and other men in the congregation, reminding various ones of them of the support of the common cause they had voiced at some point in time. "Will you now, when you are needed most, stop only at words? Is that the sort of men you are? I ask only that you act upon the beliefs of which you have so strongly spoken and in which you so strongly believe."

"Who's with us?" Gabriel asks.

One by one, the men and their sons stand in response to Anne Howard's challenge.

It's what we call a "stop the clock" moment. Time stands still as the human spirit ponders not what to say but what to do. It's a moment when words are put into action and we summon the courage and the will to do what we believe is right.

Rhetoric, after all, comes easily, but not action. It's true in our marriages as well. Think of the words we utter in our wedding vows. We can say them with great conviction, but it's not until we truly love each other "in sickness and in health, for richer or poorer" that the words mean much.

What have you been talking about together that you haven't put into action? Installing a weekly date night or planning a getaway for just the two of you? Starting a group for other couples or mentoring just one other couple? Learning a new hobby together or simply prioritizing a shared meal time? It could be anything. Don't wait for a "stop the clock" moment to get you into action. Act upon your beliefs, as Anne Howard urged, and fight for your marriage. Don't just talk about it; do what you know will make it stronger.

 Remember, people will judge you by your actions, not your intentions. You may have a heart of gold—but so does a hard-boiled egg. —AUTHOR UNKNOWN

BEING ANGRY THE "RIGHT WAY"

Stay away from fools, for you won't find knowledge on their lips. PROVERBS 14:7

ON A TRIP TO LONDON we visited the Winston Churchill "war rooms," where we learned that the bombs dropped during World War II are still killing people in Europe. They turn up—and sometimes blow up—at construction sites, in fishing nets, or on beaches more than half a century after the war.

What is true of undetonated bombs is also true of unresolved anger. Buried anger explodes when we least expect it, especially in marriage. Ever feel like you stepped on a buried bomb? It's not uncommon for most couples. In fact, anger can become quite contagious and cause people to be irrational.

Consider the story Billy Martin, former New York Yankees manager, tells in his autobiography, *Number One*, about hunting with Mickey Mantle at his friend's ranch. When they reached the ranch, Mantle told Martin to wait in the car while he asked if they could hunt. Mantle's friend gave his permission but asked for a favor. He had a pet mule that was going blind, and he didn't have the heart to put it out of its misery, so he asked Mantle to do it for him. Mantle agreed, but he went back to the car pretending to be angry, slamming the door and saying his friend wouldn't let them hunt. "I'm so mad at that guy," Mantle said, "I'm going out to his barn and shoot one of his mules!" Mantle drove like a maniac to the barn. Martin tried to stop him, but Mantle was adamant. "Just watch me!"

When they got to the barn, Mantle jumped out of the car with his rifle, ran inside, and shot the mule. Suddenly hearing two more shots, he ran back to the car. Martin had taken out his rifle too, and he shouted, "We'll show him! I just killed two of his cows!"

Does anger ever have its place? Well, anger is a human emotion, so on the one hand, it does have its place. But here's how Aristotle put it: "Anybody can become angry—that is easy; but to be angry with the right person, and to the right degree, and at the right time, and for the right purpose, and in the right way—that is not within everybody's power and is not easy."

The key to being angry the "right way" is to ensure that you are not using your anger to inflict pain or pay back evil with evil (Romans 12:17). In other words, you are not seeking revenge but leaving that up to God. When you allow this principle to keep your anger in check, you are far more likely to reclaim countless moments in your marriage that would otherwise be given over to the ravages of rage and resentment. How might you better handle an angry situation with your spouse in the future?

Anger blows out the lamp of the mind. —ROBERT GREEN INGERSOLL

THE PERFECT TREAT

Yes indeed, it is good when you obey the royal law as found in the Scriptures: "Love your neighbor as yourself." JAMES 2:8

GEORGE BERNARD SHAW gives the ancient Greek story of Pygmalion a twentieth-century twist. In the legend, Pygmalion creates a wonderful statue of a maiden and begs the gods to give the statue life, which they do. Shaw's *Pygmalion*, further adapted for the silver screen as *My Fair Lady*, has a phonetics professor bring gentility to a London "guttersnipe."

Professor Henry Higgins prides himself on being able to identify any Londoner's residence within a few blocks just by listening to his or her dialect. The professor's friend Colonel Pickering bets Higgins that he cannot take a Cockney flower girl and pass her off as a lady after just three months of instruction. This challenge is too much to resist for the haughty professor, and he chooses Eliza Doolittle as the object of his experiment.

Higgins drives Eliza like a slave master. Pickering tries to soften the professor's treatment of Eliza, but to Higgins she is nothing but an experiment. The great day arrives, and Higgins unveils his masterpiece at a royal reception. Eliza enters wearing jewels and a gown. She walks gracefully, demonstrates impeccable manners, and dances divinely. Her diction is pure; her conversation refined. No one suspects Eliza's origins, and she becomes the toast of London. Later, Higgins touts his own genius: "I created this thing out of squashed cabbage leaves."

Eliza eventually confronts the prideful professor: yes, she says, he may have changed her dialect, but the kindness of Colonel Pickering changed her heart. Pickering's gentle affirmation through the months of criticism and toil made the difference.

Eliza says to Colonel Pickering, "I owe so much to you. . . . It was from you that I learned really nice manners, and that's what makes one a lady, isn't it?"

Pickering bashfully responds, "No doubt. Still, he taught you to speak, you know, and I couldn't have done that."

Eliza continues, "Of course. That was his profession. It's just like learning to dance in the fashionable way, nothing more than that in it. You know what began my real education? Your calling me 'Miss Doolittle' that day when I first came to [the professor's study]. That was the beginning of self-respect for me. You see, the difference between a lady and a flower girl isn't how she behaves. It's how she is treated. I know that I shall always be a flower girl to Professor Higgins because he always treats me as a flower girl and always will. But I know that I can be a lady to you because you always treat me as a lady and always will."

How we treat each other has great power to help us become what we were meant to be.

> *Treat people as if they were what they ought to be, and you help them to become what they are capable of being.* —JOHANN WOLFGANG VON GOETHE

WHAT DID YOU EXPECT?

Listen to my voice in the morning, LORD. Each morning I bring my requests to you and wait expectantly. PSALM 5:3

ONE OF THE CLASSIC EARLY studies in psychology and learning was conducted by Robert Rosenthal, professor emeritus at Harvard. He told elementary school teachers that some of the students had been identified as "intellectual bloomers" by a test they took. The teachers were told the names of those students and were led to expect that those students would do particularly well over the course of the coming academic year.

In fact, the information given to the teachers was bogus. The students identified as bloomers were not necessarily any different academically from the other students: their names were selected at random. Only their teachers' expectations for them differed. Yet, sure enough, the students who were expected to bloom really did do better, significantly better, than the others by the end of the school year.

Some years later, another research team performed a similar experiment, but this time focusing on the students' expectations of the teacher. One group of students was told their teacher was "quite effective," and another group was told their teacher was "incompetent." This time the teachers knew nothing about it. The results? Students with a negative expectation rated the lessons as being "more difficult, less interesting, and less effective." They also scored lower on their exams than the other group. Students with a positive expectation leaned forward more in their chairs and had better eye contact with the teacher, in addition to earning higher test scores.

It's difficult to dispute: expectations are a powerful influence on learning outcomes. But the research on expectations goes far beyond education. These studies were conducted decades ago. By now, the power of expectations has been clearly demonstrated not just in classrooms, but also in workplaces, courtrooms, the military, doctors' offices, parent-child interactions, counseling, consumer transactions, and more. In short, expectations are a powerful influence in all relationships—including yours.

A fundamental shift takes place in the life of every couple when they expect the best from each other. You may think this sounds silly, but research backs it up. When we expect our spouses to behave in positive ways toward us, we are likely to see such behavior. The bottom line is that our expectations impact our reality and create self-fulfilling prophecies as a result. So what are you expecting from each other these days?

High achievement always takes place in the framework of high expectation.
—CHARLES F. KETTERING

KEEPING THE COVENANT STRONG

Guard your heart; do not be unfaithful to your wife. MALACHI 2:16

LIKE MOST COUPLES DEEPLY IN LOVE, we longed to find ways to make our love endure even before we were married. Part of the impetus for our vision came from reading *A Severe Mercy*, the real-life love story of Sheldon and Davy Vanauken, two people who not only dreamed about building a soulful union but actually devised a concrete strategy for doing so called their "Shining Barrier." Its goal: to make their love invulnerable. Its plan: to share everything. Everything! If one of them liked something, they decided, there must be something to like in it—and the other must find it. Whether it be poetry, strawberries, or an interest in ships, Sheldon and Davy committed to share everything. That way they would create a thousand strands, great and small, that would link them together. They reasoned that by sharing everything they would create a glue to hold their covenant of marriage together forever.

Well, as romantic and noble as this goal seems, it became impractical for us. Like most other couples moving at the speed of life, we soon struggled to just keep abreast of one another's days. And if you know the story of Sheldon and Davy, you know it didn't exactly work for them either. To keep our covenant strong, we realized eventually that we would need something far more practical to serve as the superglue of our connection. That's when we asked a simple question: what makes a marriage endure?

Ask most people this question and you'll undoubtedly hear something about love. Ask people who have given serious thought to the subject, dedicating themselves to study and research on it, and you will probably hear a different answer. Better yet, ask this question of couples who have a long-lasting and good marriage in spite of the bad things they've encountered, and you'll hear the answer that matters most. That's what we did, and here's what they told us: a good, enduring marriage is built by two people's capacity to adjust to things beyond their control, even bad things. Couples who hone this ability through the inevitable jolts of life develop what has been called "the habit of happiness," which is simply the capacity to choose the right attitude in spite of the circumstances.

What areas of life require resilience from one or both of you to protect your marriage? Today's verse is set in the context of a warning against divorce, but guarding your heart against other calamities is just as important to your marriage. How can you cultivate the habit of happiness in your own heart in a way that strengthens your marriage?

 A covenant made with God is not restrictive, but protective. —RUSSELL M. NELSON

WALKING ON HOLY GROUND?

"Do not come any closer," the LORD warned. "Take off your sandals, for you are standing on holy ground." EXODUS 3:5

ELIZABETH BARRETT BROWNING was born on this day, March 6, 1806, in a small English village. She was the eldest of twelve children, and she is said to have begun writing poetry at the age of six. Eventually her poems became world famous and even led to her marriage. In 1844 Robert Browning wrote to her, telling her how much he loved her poems. They met five years later, began one of the most famous courtships, and wrote numerous love sonnets. But it's a sentence she penned about shoes that has caught our attention this day:

"Earth's crammed with heaven, and every common bush afire with God," said Elizabeth Barrett Browning. "But only he who sees, takes off his shoes—the rest sit round it and pluck blackberries." Isn't it true? Don't you feel that you're sometimes missing out on God's voice, on God's dramatic movement, because you aren't attuned to the holy ground you're walking on? Oblivious to what God could be doing, probably we often miss the spectacular signs of his activity because we're overly focused on the details and complications of our own lives.

Seeing and hearing God in the common places is not always easy; our myopic, egocentric vision sees to that. Relaxing our minds enough to let God be God is unquestionably challenging. That's why even as a sincere God-follower you unknowingly end up walking on holy ground on your way to pick blackberries, never realizing what could have happened if you had taken off your proverbial shoes.

The only thing that makes these efforts easier is wisdom. Of course, that's a tall order. Thomas Carlyle said wisdom is the highest achievement of humankind. So don't expect it to come overnight—but you can expect it. Wisdom is the by-product of routinely, over time, clearing your head of your concerns and giving God space to fill it with his. And the holy moments you experience with God are moments of wisdom. The more you experience, the more wisdom you acquire. Soon you'll have a history of sacred moments with God, and you'll be proficient at hearing his whispers (see Proverbs 1:5).

Try this as a couple. Ask God for wisdom. Sounds too simple, we know. But we urge you to ask. In fact, ask boldly without a second thought. And make it a habit. The invitation is as clear as day: "If you need wisdom, ask our generous God, and he will give it to you" (James 1:5).

Look around you, and see the holy ground on which you walk. —NICK HARRISON

TILL DEATH DO US PART

Let's not get tired of doing what is good. At just the right time we will reap a harvest of blessing if we don't give up. GALATIANS 6:9

IN MARCH 1990, Dr. Robertson McQuilkin announced his resignation as president of Columbia Bible College in order to care for his wife, Muriel, who was suffering from the advanced stages of Alzheimer's disease. In his resignation letter he wrote about Muriel's failing health and his conviction that it was his next task in life to care for her himself.

"Muriel now, in the last couple of months, seems to be almost happy when with me, and almost never happy when not with me. In fact, she seems to feel trapped, becomes very fearful—sometimes almost terror—and when she can't get to me there can be anger; she's in distress. But when I'm with her she's happy and contented, and so I must be with her at all times. And you see, it's not only that I promised in sickness and in health, till death do us part, and I'm a man of my word. But as I have said . . . it's the only fair thing. She sacrificed for me for forty years to make my life possible, so if I cared for her for forty years I'd still be in her debt. However, there's much more. It's not that I *have* to. It's that I *get* to. . . . It's a great honor to care for such a wonderful person."[1]

Robertson relied on God to give him the strength to meet his wife's needs week after week, month after month, for thirteen years. Muriel's last day on this earth was September 19, 2003.

In a culture in which people prize their individual freedoms above all else, this simple story of a man who loved and served his wife has touched people in a way that he never anticipated. The story of Robertson's act of love spread across the country. Pastors mentioned it from the pulpit, leading couples to renew their wedding vows. *Christianity Today* printed two articles by Robertson, and in 1998 he expanded that material into a book, *A Promise Kept*. Robertson couldn't understand why so many people were inspired by his choice. Then an oncologist who worked with dying patients told him, "Almost all women stand by their men; very few men stand by their women."[2]

Consider how you can reveal continuing faithful love to your spouse today, and take a moment to express your thanks for the gift of his or her continued caring presence in your life.

> *Most baby boomers and their offspring have an internalized therapist in our heads— the internalized voice of the consumer culture—to encourage us to stop working so hard or to get out of a marriage that is not meeting our current emotional needs.*
> —WILLIAM J. DOHERTY

SLEEPING WELL

Finally, I confessed all my sins to you and stopped trying to hide my guilt. I said to myself, "I will confess my rebellion to the LORD." And you forgave me! All my guilt is gone. PSALM 32:5

WHEN I (LES) WAS WORKING on my doctoral dissertation, I was immersed in heady studies on guilt and remorse. I spent countless hours in the library researching the subject. And the research librarian who was assisting me not only knew the library inside and out, but she also came to know me and my research topic well. Most days, when I came into the library and headed for my usual study, Carol, the librarian, would stop by with a few more articles or research leads for me. On one occasion, however, she dropped off a paper with an inscription saying, "Thought this was funny." The page contained this story: A shoplifter writes to a department store and says, "I've just become a Christian, and I can't sleep at night because I feel guilty. So here's $100 that I owe you." The "former" shoplifter signed his name, and in a little postscript at the bottom added, "If I still can't sleep, I'll send you the rest."

Few things prohibit a good night's sleep more than a nagging conscience. What about in our marriages? Who among us hasn't tossed and turned into the wee hours because of an unkind word or behavior that was more selfish than usual toward a spouse? Guilt has robbed countless couples of a good night's rest, but of course it doesn't have to. There is a simple remedy to this late-night torment, and it involves making a clean start.

Consider anything that might be nagging your conscience. Maybe it was the way you brushed off your spouse's request for a favor earlier in the week. Maybe you barked an order when you were under pressure or made a critical or snide remark you regret. Maybe there's something even heavier weighing on your conscience. Most of us have little difficulty recalling something we later regretted having said or done. Whatever might be tugging at your conscience, why don't the two of you go to bed tonight with clean sheets, a fresh start. How? Saying a simple "I'm sorry" may be the ticket. A good old-fashioned apology may be just what the doctor ordered for allaying anything that's pestering your principles. A clean confession accompanied by heartfelt sorrow could give both of you the best night's sleep you've had in months.

There is no pillow so soft as a clear conscience. —FRENCH PROVERB

WHAT ARE YOU SAYING?

Don't use foul or abusive language. Let everything you say be good and helpful, so that your words will be an encouragement to those who hear them. EPHESIANS 4:29

A WOMAN WORE A WOOL JACKET to work one day and decided to get her car washed on the way home. Since it had warmed up outside, she slipped her jacket off while she waited for the car to be cleaned. The next morning, her jacket was nowhere to be found. *Maybe I left it at the car wash*, she thought, and she called the number. "Did I leave a burgundy blazer there yesterday?" she asked the young man who answered. A minute later he returned from checking. "I'm sorry, Ma'am. There's no burgundy Blazer here, just a gray Bronco."

It's just another in a long string of examples of how easy it is for miscommunication to occur. It happens all the time, especially in marriage. Men and women, as has been pointed out in numerous bestsellers, can communicate very differently—sometimes as if they were from different planets. A survey of more than a thousand married couples reported in *U.S. News and World Report* that in general, we don't even talk about the same topics. The leading discussion subject reported for men was news events (talked about in the previous week by 71 percent of respondents), followed by work (68 percent). The study found that women, on the other hand, talked about food (76 percent) and health (72 percent). Men were more likely to have talked about sports (65 percent to women's 42 percent); women were more likely to have discussed personal matters (52 percent to men's 40 percent). Different conversational priorities can often lead to difficult communication.

Whatever the topic, however, we have one thing in common: both men and women depend on communication to keep their marital relationships running. It is the lifeblood of every marriage. Couples who can't communicate well, who don't speak clearly and listen carefully, soon fall apart.

So when was the last time the two of you talked about talking? Sounds strange, we know. But it's important to monitor our communication status now and then, so consider how well you are doing at this important task. If you were to rate your effectiveness on a scale of one to ten, how well do you communicate as a couple? And why do you rank it at that level?

Another important question: how would you rate yourself when it comes to listening to your partner? Be honest and not defensive as you talk to each other about this. What seems to distract you most (your cell phone, for example) while you're trying to have a conversation, and why? More importantly, what will you do to minimize the distraction? As Voltaire said, the road to the heart is the ear. Carefully listening to your partner is the quickest path to intimacy.

Good communication is stimulating as black coffee. —ANNE MORROW LINDBERGH

A DIFFERENT KIND OF MARCH MADNESS

Short-tempered people do foolish things, and schemers are hated. PROVERBS 14:17

ANYONE WHO HAS EVER had an airport hassle might be able to identify with Neil Melly's frustration. Melly tried to get from Los Angeles International Airport to Australia, but he couldn't get a ticket because he lacked a valid credit card. From that small humiliation Melly went on to greater matters of shame: hours later, he stripped off his clothes in angry protest of his situation and made a dash for the airport runway. Baggage handlers watched as Melly scaled a fence topped with three strands of barbed wire, without fear or injury—or clothing. Eventually reaching a jumbo jet, he crawled inside the wheel well of a plane bound for Australia.

Obviously, the dangers were great. As an airport spokeswoman pointed out, had the plane taken off, the stowaway could have been sucked into an engine, frozen to death in flight, or crushed by the landing gear. But pilots were able to stop the plane quickly,[3] and Melly was coaxed from his hiding place and arrested on charges of trespassing. Apparently there's no law against poor problem solving.

How we solve problems when things aren't going our way says a lot about us. Some of us are quick to give up. Others of us enjoy a challenge. A lot of us, like Melly, are prone to lose our cool under pressure. We might yell or point fingers or smolder with fury. Of course, this doesn't match stripping in public and climbing barbed wire, but it's just about as useful. Melly can attest to the truth of today's verse—but so can the rest of us. When we are faced with circumstances that aren't going our way, it's easy to become impatient. Our urgency can lead us to do stupid things.

What a shame! Think of all the time we waste when we let urgency get the better of us and how rarely we do our best thinking when we feel frustrated and pressured. That's why one of the kindest things we can do for each other as husband or wife is to ease each other's urgency. How? By lending a listening ear and serving as a solid sounding board. Let's face it, supposing Melly was married, had his wife been on hand when he was contemplating how to get to Australia, do you think he would have streaked into the news that fateful day at LAX? Doubtful.

Sure, it's an extreme example, but it makes the point. Marriage provides a built-in mechanism for keeping us sane, if we let it. Think of a time when you were feeling under pressure and made a quick decision or behaved rashly. Wouldn't you have benefited from the objective ears of your spouse? Never take your spouse for granted. He or she may save you a lot of time, not to mention a lot of shame.

A stitch in time would have confused Einstein. —AUTHOR UNKNOWN

SWEET DREAMS

I will pour out my Spirit upon all people. Your sons and daughters will prophesy. Your young men will see visions, and your old men will dream dreams. ACTS 2:17

"COPY ... SHEETS ... COPY."

"What?" I asked Leslie, who was obviously dreaming as we lay in bed.

"The sheets must be copied, please," she replied sternly with eyes still closed as she tossed and turned.

"You're dreaming," I said softly.

Her eyes flashed open, and she looked around the room for a moment. "What a weird dream."

"You were probably dreaming about getting a copy of our manuscript made," I suggested.

"No," Leslie said, still rubbing the sleep from her eyes. "I dreamed you had painted a beautiful scene on our bedroom sheets, and I wanted copies made so we wouldn't lose it."

Strange, indeed. Especially since I don't paint—on sheets or anything else.

Dreams, those mystical fantasies of slumber, are often bizarre, and we can't always make much sense of them. Though we may not all remember our dreams in the morning, everybody dreams. A normal night's sleep always includes not one but several periods of dreaming. This has been established by research studies beyond any doubt; the question has been, what is the purpose of these dreams? Today's experts are finding answers. Like the hard drive on your computer getting cleaned up, during dream sleep the brain consolidates memory, clears our unresolved issues, and helps us forget things we don't need to remember.

Here's the key to a good night's dream: you have to get enough dream sleep to achieve the benefits. If you sleep only six hours, you will be missing out on several major periods of dreaming and will not be getting enough dream sleep. So you should do what you can to get the sleep you need, not just for your body but for your mind, too.

But equally important to dreaming while you sleep is the dreaming you do—together—when you are awake. Why? Because a couple who holds on to dreams they both share is a couple who hopes, and hope is at the heart of a joyful marriage. Hope engenders an optimistic spirit you share as you look toward the horizon together, uplifted by imaginings that you both support and strive to achieve.

When did the two of you last talk about your dreams together—the ones you have as individuals as well as the dreams you have for your relationship and your family? If it has been a while, why not explore them right now? You can start with short-term dreams—maybe to experience something or go somewhere within a year's time. Or you might talk about more long-term dreams, like what you'd like to do or achieve in your marriage over the next decade. Just make sure to dream your sweet dreams together.

> *Dreams are ... illustrations from the book your soul is writing about you.*
> —MARSHA NORMAN

I CAN'T READ YOUR MIND

As he thinketh in his heart, so is he. PROVERBS 23:7, KJV

IT WEIGHS JUST THREE POUNDS and is composed of mostly water, yet the human brain has been called the most sophisticated information system on earth. To call it amazing is an understatement. That's why various organizations in nearly sixty countries dedicate a few days in March each year to highlighting the immeasurable importance of the human brain during Brain Awareness Week.

Consider what your brain is doing right now while you are reading these words. Your occipital lobes, near the back of your head, are processing how you see this sentence. The frontal lobes of your cerebral cortex are engaged in thinking through the meaning of these words, helping you see how the content might apply to you. Meanwhile, you just blinked because of the motor area of your brain. And it is because of your cerebellum, in the lower portion of your brain, that you are able to hold this book in your hands, as well as anything else you're doing right now that calls for balance and coordination—like sitting.

All the while, your metabolism and hormonal functions like the ones that control various levels in your body are being controlled by your pituitary gland, deep inside your brain. And if you are sitting outside on a park bench on a cold, early spring day right now, your hypothalamus is responsible for warning you to go inside by causing you to shiver. By the way, you'll remember what you're reading here due to your hippocampus, whose job it is to transfer short-term to long-term memory. It also enables you to remember that the point of this elaborate example is to underscore how complex and marvelous your brain is.

We usually take the brain for granted, yet it is amazing. Complete understanding of the brain will be a long time coming. Even so, the human brain is child's play compared to the intangible human mind. "The mind is its own place," said English poet John Milton, "and in itself, can make heaven of Hell, and a hell of Heaven." Scientists have pretty well mapped out the terrain of the brain, but they are far from understanding the complexities of the mind. After all, you can't x-ray the mind. It's beyond physical location.

Yet how often do we couples run into trouble because we expect our spouses to read our minds? "You should have known what I was thinking," we might say in exasperation. French philosopher René Descartes gave us one of history's most memorable sound bites: "I think, therefore I am." We want to amend this for couples: "You think, therefore I want to know what's on your mind."

The next time you catch yourself wanting your spouse to read your mind, make it easy and just say what you have on it.

The brain is like a muscle. When it is in use we feel very good. Understanding is joyous.
—CARL SAGAN

DO YOU PROMISE NOT TO TELL?

Whatever you have said in the dark will be heard in the light, and what you have whispered behind closed doors will be shouted from the housetops for all to hear!

LUKE 12:3

A JEWISH PUBLICATION RAN an advertisement dominated by a drawing of a very stern-looking, bearded rabbi of the nineteenth century, Yisrael Meir Kagan, otherwise known by the name of his famous book on the Jewish laws of speech, the Chofetz Chaim, adapted as *Guard Your Tongue.* The ad included a hotline number to call anonymously if you had information about someone's potential marriage, business dealings, or whatever. A rabbi at the other end would tell you whether your gossip is important enough to pass along. If not, you would be counseled to guard your tongue.

Interesting, isn't it? The advertisement reveals as much about the state of our relationships as it does about our propensity for gossip. Who among us hasn't been hurt by a broken confidence? It usually begins when someone says to you, "You have to promise you won't tell so-and-so I told you this because she made me swear not to tell anyone. . . ." It sounds very confidential, but then why is that person telling you the secret? There is the appearance of keeping a secret but not the reality. Or then there are the things we say that don't qualify as secrets at all because they're simply our own ugly opinions, which shouldn't be let out in the open, either. Jesus understood all this when he said, "Whatever you have said in the dark will be heard in the light, and what you have whispered behind closed doors will be shouted from the housetops for all to hear."

We've all shared private and personal information with a trusted friend only to learn later that our friend has blabbed it to the world. But does this mean we should never confide in anyone again? No. We actually need to tell our secrets. Doing so helps us explore what is troubling us and sometimes leads to helpful feedback. Sharing our secrets lets us test the reaction to what we've been holding in our hearts. Not only that, it's a relief not to be the only person who has experienced something, whether a temptation or a tragedy. It makes us feel less alone to unburden our souls and hear "Me, too" or "I understand."

Sharing secrets with your spouse—and keeping them—can bring you closer together and deepen your relationship. Take time to be vulnerable with your spouse, and protect his or her vulnerability with you.

 *If a is success in life, then the formula is a = x + y + z. Work is x, play is y and z is keeping your mouth shut.* —ALBERT EINSTEIN

KEEPING HOPE ALIVE

Hope does not disappoint us, because God has poured out his love into our hearts by the Holy Spirit, whom he has given us. ROMANS 5:5, NIV

THE WORD *DISAPPOINTMENT* has French origins going back to the days when a monarch would appoint or "dis-appoint" an officer—it originally meant "to remove from office." Though to be disappointed once meant to lose one's post, these days it means to lose one's hope.

We're familiar with that definition. Disappointments range from getting a dire diagnosis to getting stuck in traffic, but big or small, they are a common part of life. We cannot altogether avoid disappointments, but as long as hope is alive we can learn to rise above them. Given the inevitability of disappointment, how can there possibly be a hope that "does not disappoint," as today's verse says? This is possible when that hope is sustained by faith in what is promised—that is, in the love God pours into our hearts. It is faith that changes everything.

In the words of the apostle Paul, "Faith is the confidence that what we hope for will actually happen" (Hebrews 11:1). It moves worry backstage and hope to center stage. Faith emboldens our beliefs and expectations with confidence. Faith can make us fearless. "Hope is hearing the melody of the future," said Brazilian philosopher Rubem Alves. "Faith is to dance to it."

How does faith do this mystical work? By giving us an eternal perspective. People of faith look at life differently because we know it is not the only one we will have. Hope is more than just optimism about our future; when bolstered by faith, hope moderates our anxiety about the present. We look at life through a bigger lens. Viewing life's problems through the big lens of the ultimate future helps put in perspective today's aggravations—car troubles, family quarrels, delayed flights. So many things that rile us up can be seen in the context of eternity for what they are: temporary irritants.

But faith goes deeper than helping us cope with trivialities. The true power of faith is seen most clearly in pain. Faith turns hope into a certainty that suffering will make sense even when our earthly perspective can only see it as senseless. In other words, when pain cuts you to the core and hardships punch you in the solar plexus, faith is responsible for keeping your hope alive.

As a couple, you have the privilege of bolstering each other's faith. Are you using it? Can you identify one or two specific ways you've done this for each other in the past—or perhaps how you will in the future?

The antidote to frustration is a calm faith, not in your own cleverness, or in hard toil, but in God's guidance. —NORMAN VINCENT PEALE

TWO ESSENTIAL WORDS

When you are praying, first forgive anyone you are holding a grudge against, so that your Father in heaven will forgive your sins, too. MARK 11:25

IN *LOVE IN THE TIME OF CHOLERA*, Nobel laureate Gabriel García Márquez portrays a marriage that disintegrates over a bar of soap. In that culture, it was the wife's job to keep the house in order, including the towels, toilet paper, and soap in the bathroom. One day Fermina forgets to replace the soap. Her husband, Juvenal, exaggerates the oversight: "I've been bathing for almost a week without any soap." She vigorously denies forgetting to replace the soap, and she continues to do so for years. Although she indeed forgot, her pride is at stake, and she won't back down. For the next seven months the two sleep in separate rooms and eat in silence. Their marriage had suffered a heart attack.

"Even when they were old and placid," writes Márquez, "they were very careful about bringing it up, for the barely healed wounds could begin to bleed again as if they had been inflicted only yesterday." How can a bar of soap ruin a marriage? The answer is actually simple: because neither partner would say, "Forgive me." In fact, Fermina never admitted her lapse, and they only returned to a semblance of peace after Juvenal finally decided to confess that the soap had been there all along and that it was he who had never wanted to admit his error—even though they both knew this wasn't the truth.

Honesty and forgiveness are essential to a successful partnership. Of course we try to avoid hurting each other, but we will still do so because we are sinful people. So these "fault" lines in our relationship must be continually sealed in forgiveness. Why? Because without forgiveness our foundational connection would crack under the unbearable weight of blame and pain.

What do you need to ask or offer forgiveness for today? Make it one of your top priorities.

He who is devoid of the power to forgive is devoid of the power to love.
—MARTIN LUTHER KING JR.

A STOREHOUSE OF HAPPINESS

It is a sin to belittle one's neighbor; blessed are those who help the poor. PROVERBS 14:21

HAPPINESS IS THE THEME of a wonderful fable about a young girl and a butterfly. The girl was walking through a meadow one day when she saw a butterfly impaled on a thorn. She gently freed the butterfly from its snare, and it flew off a short distance. Suddenly, the butterfly changed into a beautiful fairy. "For your kindness," said the fairy to the little girl, "I will grant your fondest wish." The little girl thought about this carefully. After a moment she replied, "I want to be happy," for this little girl had been alone and unloved. The fairy leaned toward her, whispered in her ear, and vanished.

True to the fairy's word, as the girl grew up, no one in the land was happier than she. But whenever anyone asked her the secret of her great happiness, she would only smile and say, "I listened to a good fairy."

As she grew old, the neighbors were afraid the marvelous secret might die with her. "Tell us, please," they begged, "tell us what the fairy said to make you so happy." The girl, a lovely old lady by then, smiled and said, "She told me that everyone, no matter how secure they seem, has need of me."

It's true. When we embrace the fact that we can be helpful to everyone—especially to the loves of our lives—life gets easier. Of course, some will argue that this is not the secret to happiness but to misery. These people have never experienced the joy of being needed.

If you're not inclined to hear this message from an ancient fairy tale, take it from science. Dr. Hans Selye, a world-renowned endocrinologist, stands on a mountain of research when he proclaims that the happiest people are those who win the gratitude of people around them. Selye adapted the biblical principle to "Love thy neighbor as thyself" as "Earn thy neighbor's love." Rather than trying to accumulate more money or power, he suggested we acquire goodwill by helping others. "Hoard goodwill," Dr. Selye advised, "and your house will be a storehouse of happiness."[4]

How can you earn the goodwill of your spouse today?

If you want to live a long life, focus on making contributions. —HANS SELYE

HOT THOUGHTS

We destroy every proud obstacle that keeps people from knowing God. We capture their rebellious thoughts and teach them to obey Christ. 2 CORINTHIANS 10:5

DID YOU KNOW THAT conjuring a mental image can actually determine your body's temperature? Specialists in biofeedback refer to "hot thoughts"—images of hot scenes, such as being in the desert or on a beach on a sunny day. These mental images literally increase blood flow and warmth to cold hands and feet.[5]

Mental imagery is a practice that today's top athletes are using. Studies on everything from golf to basketball to swimming to playing darts have revealed that those who use positive mental imagery of successful performance before an athletic event consistently improve their actual performance. They have an arguable edge over athletes who do not first conjure an image of themselves successfully competing.[6]

If you are training for a marathon, for example, and you mentally rehearse running the race, you are likely to effect muscular changes before you even cross the start line. Your blood pressure will go up, your brain waves will be altered, your sweat glands will even become active—all in the absence of physical activity.

Equally amazing, if not more so, is the power of mental imagery on more general life. The level of joy and fulfillment we experience every day is due to a great extent to our self-image. And that self-image is created by our attitudes and self-talk—what we tell ourselves is true about ourselves, others we interact with, and our circumstances. For this reason, the very best kind of self-talk is the kind that gives us freedom to choose our attitudes, that says, "I choose my responses; they don't choose me." It says, "No thought can dwell in my mind without my permission." After all, our thoughts, especially those about ourselves, ought to obey Christ.

As you consider how you might "take captive every thought," be sure to reflect on your relationship with your spouse and the thinking that relates to that relationship. What thoughts can you choose to dwell on that will strengthen and protect your marriage—and what thoughts need to be captured and taught to obey Christ?

> *She that fails to command her thoughts will soon lose command of her actions.*
> —ANONYMOUS

TOTAL COMMITMENT

No, dear brothers and sisters, I have not achieved it, but I focus on this one thing: Forgetting the past and looking forward to what lies ahead, I press on to reach the end of the race and receive the heavenly prize for which God, through Christ Jesus, is calling us. PHILIPPIANS 3:13-14

ACCORDING TO A HAITIAN PARABLE, a man wanted to sell his house. Another man wanted very badly to buy it but couldn't afford the full price. After much bargaining, the owner agreed to sell the house for half the original price with just one stipulation: he would retain ownership of one small nail protruding from just over the door. The request seemed harmless to the buyer, and the deal was struck. After several years, the original owner wanted the house back, but the new owner was unwilling to sell. So the first owner hung the carcass of a dead dog from the nail he still owned. Soon the house became unlivable, and the family was forced to sell the house to the owner of the nail.

The point of the parable is simple. If we leave the devil one small area in our lives, he will return to hang his rotting garbage there, making it unfit for Christ's indwelling. True commitment, whether it be to Christ, to each other, or to any other person or cause, requires us to dedicate every aspect of our beings to the goal we have set.

The apostle Paul understood this when he wrote to the Philippians encouraging them by example to "[forget] the past . . . press on . . . and receive the heavenly prize."

If you were to symbolically identify the "small nail" over the doorframe of your life that needs your attention right now, what would it be and why? What about on the frame of your marriage relationship? If there is anything that needs to be pulled out, talk it over with your spouse today.

Guidance means I can count on God. Commitment means God can count on me.
—ANONYMOUS

MAKE A GUILT-FREE DROP

Now there is no condemnation for those who belong to Christ Jesus. ROMANS 8:1

"THIS MORNING WE are going to learn to juggle. Each of you should be holding three brightly colored scarves."

More than a thousand of us had gathered in the ballroom of a hotel for a conference on laughter. This morning we were listening to Dr. Steve Allen Jr., the son of the famous comedian.

"I'm going to lead you through a dozen steps to teach you the fine art of juggling," he told us. "First, take one of your scarves, hold it out at arm's length, and drop it."

We couldn't believe our ears. "Drop it?" people murmured. You could feel the resistance. We expected to learn how to keep our scarves up in the air, not on the ground. Nobody wanted to be the one called out for dropping a scarf on the first try. Not a scarf around me was dropped. And I certainly wasn't going to fall for that trick.

"C'mon, now, drop it!" Dr. Allen commanded. One by one, we reluctantly released our scarves, and they fluttered to the carpeted ballroom floor. "There now, doesn't that feel better?" asked Dr. Allen. "You have gotten your mistake over with. This is the first step in learning to juggle. We call it the guilt-free drop."

I could feel the tension roll off my shoulders. *I'm allowed to make mistakes*, I thought. I *don't have to be a great juggler right away.* More importantly, this silly exercise reminded me that no one—myself included—is expected to be perfect.

How many times have you been caught in the guilt trap, trying to ease your conscience from self-inflicted accusations? How many times have you felt guilty for not being perfect? We're not talking about sins you need to confess but imperfections you need to accept. Maybe you didn't hit a home run in some way, and you're still punishing yourself. Whatever its source, we are all victims of guilt we don't deserve—and we've got to let it go, or it will eat us up. Why? Because it does no good to us or to our relationships. False feelings of guilt, in fact, cause us to be more self-focused and less loving. So the next time you are falsely accusing yourself of being less than perfect, make a guilt-free drop and move on.

The greatest mistake you can make in life is to be continually fearing you will make one. —ELBERT HUBBARD

LOOKING FOR A GOOD EXCUSE?

Plans go wrong for lack of advice; many advisers bring success. PROVERBS 15:22

ONE OF THE GREATEST saboteurs of reaching our dreams and goals is a sentence that begins with one word: *Someday.* This word denotes idle thinking that is rarely backed up by action. And most well-intentioned people utter it on a regular basis. It is an easy way to invoke an excuse for putting off what would bring us closer to our goals. And almost everyone loves to have a good excuse.

Zig Ziglar, known worldwide for his upbeat motivational messages, tells the story of the fellow who went next door to borrow his neighbor's lawnmower. The neighbor explained that he could not let him use the mower because all the flights had been canceled from New York to Los Angeles. The borrower asked him what canceled flights from New York to Los Angeles had to do with borrowing his lawnmower. "It doesn't have anything to do with it, but if I don't want to let you use my lawnmower, one excuse is as good as another."

Pretty good reasoning, actually! Well, the same wacky logic is at work anytime we put off something that brings us closer to reaching our goals—even goals regarding our relationships. "Someday when we have the money." "Someday when we have more time." "Someday after the kids have moved out." "Someday. . . ." Some people go through life, day after day, piling one excuse on top of the other for not doing what they plan on doing "someday."

So if you catch yourself wondering why you aren't closer to reaching your dreams and goals as a couple, if you wonder why you're still at the same place you were last year, you may want to tune in to the frequency of your use of "someday." Do you really want to achieve your goals? If you're just struggling to get out of the excuse cycle, consider seeking help. Maybe there's a book or class or conversation you could seek out to help you and your spouse make a good plan—and stick to it.

Procrastination is the fear of success. . . . People procrastinate because they are afraid of the success that they know will result if they move ahead now. Because success is heavy, carries a responsibility with it, . . . it is much easier to procrastinate and live on the "someday I'll" philosophy. —DENIS WAITLEY

STEPPING OFF THE HAMSTER WHEEL

"My dear Martha, you are worried and upset over all these details! There is only one thing worth being concerned about. Mary has discovered it, and it will not be taken away from her." LUKE 10:41-42

THERE IS A GREAT LINE IN the classic novel *Moby Dick*. Sailors are rowing furiously while the whaler is racing frantically to catch the great whale. But there is one person in the boat who is not doing anything. He is just sitting there, quiet and still. It's the harpooner, ready to take aim and throw his deadly dart. Melville writes: "To ensure the greatest efficiency in the dark, the harpoonists of this world must start to their feet out of idleness and not out of toil."

Our culture has a problem with idle harpoonists—people who appear to be unproductive. We are more impressed with the dazzling display of the whirring hamster wheel: the busier the better. Many of us who might be excellent "harpoonists," like Mary in today's verse, get caught up in the relentless pace of Martha and so are never ready to use our gifts when needed most.

Why do we overcommit? It's because of what we don't want to face. We fear boredom—and running in high gear keeps us from being contemplative. We want to avoid certain thoughts and feelings—and being constantly on the go helps us do that. Being busy seems to give us license to slip out early or be absent altogether. But the great sin of busyness is its disruption of our relationships with each other and with God. As Eugene Peterson has said, "Busyness is the enemy of spirituality. It is essentially laziness. It is doing the easy thing instead of the hard thing. It is filling our time with our own actions instead of paying attention to God's actions. It is taking charge."[7]

Set aside a bit of time for quiet and stillness alone or together and enjoy the quiet connection that you experience as a result. Encourage each other to do the same with God—sitting in his presence, rather than taking charge of even the "task" of spending time with him.

Life is what happens to you while you're busy making other plans.
—ALLEN SAUNDERS

A VALID CRITICISM?

To one who listens, valid criticism is like a gold earring or other gold jewelry.

PROVERBS 25:12

WALT DISNEY WAS bankrupt when he took his "Steamboat Willie" cartoon concept around Hollywood in the late 1920s. Can you imagine Disney trying to sell a falsetto-voiced talking mouse in the days of silent movies? Disney's dreams were big, and he had plenty of critics. People closest to him, however, believe Disney thrived on criticism. As the saying would go, if Disney asked ten people what they thought of a new idea, and if they were unanimous in their rejection of it, he would begin work on it immediately.[8]

Few among us actually thrive on criticism like Walt did. In fact, for many, a single critical comment is enough to shut down all sources of creativity and create a social stalemate. Many people stymie all progress for fear of someone saying something critical. Sir Isaac Newton is said to have been so sensitive to criticism that he withheld the publication of a paper on optics for fifteen years, until his main critic died. Now that's a serious case of wanting to avoid criticism.

Truth be told, nobody can ever truly avoid criticism; it comes with the territory of being human. No matter how hard you work, how great your ideas, or how wonderful your talent, at some point you will be the object of criticism. Even the perfect motives of Jesus were often misunderstood, resulting in malicious criticism.

Of course, no critic cuts deeper than one's spouse. When we are criticized on the home front, we feel it to the core. Why? It's because we expect home to be safe and free from verbal critique. And it should be. The exception is when the critique is valid and respectfully put—that's the key. We are far more likely to receive constructive criticism when our spouse gently makes clear how valid the critique is, that is, when he or she gives a concrete example with a loving spirit. Of course, the same is true when the roles are reversed, too—and we do well to remember it.

We are not trying to entertain the critics. I'll take my chances with the public.
—WALT DISNEY

SUNDIALS IN THE SHADE

Whatever is good and perfect comes down to us from God our Father, who created all the lights in the heavens. He never changes or casts a shifting shadow. JAMES 1:17

PEOPLE WHO THRIVE, who excel to the highest levels—personally and professionally—have at least one thing in common: they know what they do best. Take an easy example from the professional world: Warren Buffett, "the world's greatest investor." From outward appearances, this down-home, slightly disheveled financial titan from Nebraska may not seem like one of the wealthiest men ever, but he certainly knows how to sniff out a good investment. His patient and practical mind makes investment his signature strength. What makes him special, according to Marcus Buckingham and Donald Clifton of the Gallup International Research and Education Center, is that "he became aware of it."[9] Buffett knows what he's not so good at (so he leaves that to others), and he knows what he does best. And he loves doing it every day he wakes up.

Authors of a landmark study and book, *Now, Discover Your Strengths*, Buckingham and Clifton have revealed that most people do not know what their strengths are. Business guru Peter Drucker reinforces their point in his endorsement of the book: "When you ask [people about their strengths] they look at you with a blank stare, or they respond in terms of subject knowledge, which is the wrong answer."

The tragedy of life for many people is not that they don't have enough strengths; it's that they are unaware of the ones they have. Benjamin Franklin aptly called these wasted strengths "sundials in the shade." It's especially tragic for a married couple to be unaware of their strengths, because that means they haven't been seeking out those strengths in one another. One of our greatest gifts to our loved ones is our believing in them and helping them to see the best in themselves.

So here's an assignment for you and your spouse today. Take a moment right now, each of you, to identify a personal strength in the other person that you don't think he or she fully recognizes. Exchange observations, and take note. This is not a mere compliment; it goes deeper. Help your spouse see a God-given personality strength, and thank God together for this good gift to you both.

God makes three requests of his children: Do the best you can, where you are, with what you have, now. —AFRICAN-AMERICAN PROVERB

IT'S TIME TO CHOOSE

Today I have given you the choice between life and death, between blessings and curses. Now I call on heaven and earth to witness the choice you make. Oh, that you would choose life, so that you and your descendants might live! DEUTERONOMY 30:19

A MINISTER, A BOY SCOUT, and a computer executive were flying to a meeting in a small private plane. About halfway to their destination, the pilot came back and announced that the plane was going to crash and that there were only three parachutes and four people.

The pilot said, "I am going to use one of the parachutes because I have a wife and four small children," and he jumped.

The computer executive said, "I should have one of the parachutes because I am the smartest man in the world and my company needs me," and he jumped.

The minister turned to the boy scout and, smiling sadly, said, "You are young, and I have lived a good, long life. You take the last parachute, and I'll go down with the plane."

The boy scout said, "Relax, Reverend, the smartest man in the world just strapped on my backpack and jumped out of the plane!"

A high IQ has never guaranteed good decisions. No matter how superior one's intelligence, even a genius may not recognize the obvious. You may be quick witted, clever, and intellectually brilliant, but these enviable traits don't ensure wise judgments. Especially when it comes to saving time.

Most people, no matter how intelligent, neglect their top time-saving device. They wander through their days allowing their schedules to swallow their time—as if they don't have a choice. You see, making a choice is your secret weapon in combating time stealers. Once you realize that you are in charge of your time, you can begin to do something about it.

"You can't do anything about the length of your life," said Evan Esar, "but you can do something about its width and depth." You can choose how you spend the days you have, and you alone are responsible for your choice. If you are feeling like your time is wall to wall, don't look to blame anyone else. Make a new choice.

We shape our lives, not to mention our schedules, by the choices we make. What choice can you make right now to create the pace you long for? What activity can you choose to lop off your schedule? What day or time can you choose to reserve and protect just for the two of you? "When you have to make a choice and you don't make it," said William James, "that is in itself a choice." So the question is not whether you, individually and as a couple, have a choice—each one of us has this inherent time-saving device within our reach—but what your choice will be.

"Time management" is really a misnomer—the challenge is not to manage time, but to manage ourselves. —STEPHEN R. COVEY

WHAT'S IN YOUR BAGGAGE?

You desire honesty from the womb, teaching me wisdom even there. PSALM 51:6

WE'VE GOT A PECULIAR QUESTION for you today, but there's a reason for it, so go with us.

Have you ever thought about what's in the luggage that makes the rounds at the baggage claim area in the airport? As you are waiting for your own bags to arrive, you think to yourself or say to each other, "That monogrammed Louis Vuitton piece must surely contain valuables. . . . That hot pink Samsonite number with the stickers on it looks intriguing. . . . Wonder who has that cardboard box held together with duct tape and string. . . . How about that sleek silver case with the sturdy lock?"

Allow us to further ask what may seem even a bit more peculiar to you: If your psychological baggage were traveling on that same conveyor belt at the airport, what kind of shape would it be in? How would it look? Scuffed up? Tightly locked? Nondescript? We ask such a question because your answer would reveal a bit about how you consider your past. It provides a quick glimpse into your feelings about your personal history. It is those feelings that we psychologists are getting at when we talk about your proverbial "baggage."

History is what has happened in our lives; baggage is how we feel about it. Your psychological perspective on your past determines, to a great extent, your personal health and vitality—not to mention how you and your spouse interact with each other. By the way, you need not suffer a traumatic accident or something dreadful to have "baggage"; we all have it. Even the most adjusted and healthy people have baggage. No one is exempt. You may have childhood angst over parental divorce, conflicts with friends and family, or remorse over missteps and lost opportunities. Everyone has a history and an emotional response to it.

When it comes to being a healthy, thriving human being in a loving relationship, what matters is not whether you have baggage at all but whether you have explored or even unpacked your baggage together. Have you ever taken the time to do that? Or have you let your spouse think your baggage is a bit nicer than it really is? God desires honesty from the very beginning of our lives to the end, and we are wise when we practice it with our spouses. Think about what baggage you might unpack together today.

> *Simplicity is making the journey of this life with just baggage enough.*
> —CHARLES DUDLEY WARNER

LOVE LIKE YOU MEAN IT

No one has ever seen God. But if we love each other, God lives in us, and his love is brought to full expression in us. 1 JOHN 4:12

ANGELA TEETERED AS she walked across a medical conference room, thighs chafing, sweat glands sweating. She tried to squeeze into a regular-size chair, but her lumpy hips snagged on the arms. She moved to an extra-wide armless chair, but then she couldn't cross her legs.

A dietitian helped her climb aboard a stationary bicycle that had been fitted with an oversize seat. But when Angela tried to pedal, thick rolls of abdominal tissue pressed against her fleshy thighs, impeding movement.

"Every move I made was an effort," Angela admitted not long afterward. By then, however, she was back down to her actual weight of 110 pounds.

Angela had been zipped into a bulky beige "empathy suit" designed to help medical personnel better understand the plight of their obese patients. The suit weighs only thirty pounds, but it feels heavier and effectively extends the size of small, low-weight people like Angela. Its heft and bulk is intended to give them a new, deepened understanding of the workaday world of the obese.[10]

Does it work? You bet. As Angela saw firsthand, even a simple movement such as walking may be challenging for the obese. Having worn the suit "makes me feel more respectful, more aware" of other people's feelings, she says.

That's the power of putting oneself in the skin of another—literally. It's called empathy and it's at the heart of every loving relationship. When we can walk in each other's shoes and see the world from another person's perspective, we are loving like we mean it.

Take the time today to put yourself in one another's shoes. How would you feel waking up to the demands of each other's lives? What would you look forward to? What would you dread? How would life be different for you if you were living it in your spouse's shoes? Allow these new insights to give you a deeper understanding of your spouse's perspective.

You will find as you look back upon your life that the moments that stand out, the moments when you have really lived, are the moments when you have done things in a spirit of love. —HENRY DRUMMOND

SHAKE IT OFF AND STEP UP

Don't let evil conquer you, but conquer evil by doing good. ROMANS 12:21

THE PARABLE IS TOLD OF an old dog that fell into a farmer's well. After assessing the situation, the farmer sympathized with the dog but decided that neither the dog nor the well were worth the trouble of saving. Instead he planned to bury the old dog in the well and put him out of his misery.

When the farmer began shoveling, the old dog was hysterical at first. But as the farmer continued shoveling and the dirt hit his back, a thought struck the dog. It dawned on him that every time a shovelful of dirt landed on his back he could shake it off and step up. This he did blow after blow. *Shake it off and step up, shake it off and step up, shake it off and step up!* he repeated to encourage himself.

No matter how painful the blows or how hopeless the situation seemed, the old dog just kept shaking it off and stepping up. It wasn't long before the dog, battered and exhausted, stepped triumphantly over the wall of that well. What seemed as though it would bury him actually benefited him.

The same is true for us, in a sense. We have a choice in how we handle adversity. We can roll over and let the problem bury us. Or we can do our best to shake it off, refusing to give in to panic, bitterness, or self-pity. Of course, rarely if ever can we see the potential blessing of our problems while we're suffering through them. But more often than not, blessings are exactly what our struggles turn out to be.

Of course, as a couple you have the opportunity to help each other through the tough times. You can help one another to prayerfully "shake it off." Can you recall a time, right now, when you have actually done that for each other? If you are struggling through a dark time these days, commit to "[conquering] evil by doing good" to one another, encouraging one another to step up.

Every trial endured and weathered in the right spirit makes a soul nobler and stronger than it was before. —JAMES BUCKHAM

TAKING TENDER

Take a lesson from the ants, you lazybones. Learn from their ways and become wise! Though they have no prince or governor or ruler to make them work, they labor hard all summer, gathering food for the winter. PROVERBS 6:6-8

"WHY DO YOU ALWAYS make the money decisions?" Leslie asked me.

We were standing in the middle of a department store trying to choose a new couch for our apartment, and it seemed to her that I was controlling the purse strings.

"I don't make the money decisions," I said. "Our bank account does." That remark was followed by a lengthy, whiny discussion—okay, it was a fight—over how we manage, or should manage, our money. Was I in charge or were we in charge? It's an important question for all of us.

I don't know how you would answer that question, but if you are like most people we counsel, you might be saying, "We can talk about almost anything except money." And that's understandable. Money is a touchy subject for most. The topic sometimes brings out the worst in people, causing otherwise loving people to become withdrawn, pushy, or manipulative. But it doesn't have to be that way. With the right attitude and an honest agenda, couples can effectively communicate about getting out of debt, spending and giving, investing, and all the rest.

If you need a fresh start in talking with your spouse about your financial future, start by discussing your spending styles of the past. Here are some ideas to get the conversation going. *How did your childhood shape your beliefs about money? How were financial decisions made in the home where you grew up? Was money discussed openly?*

Thinking through this kind of question will give you empathy for one another's money-management style and help you move into discussing how you each approach money today. Are the two styles in sync with each other? Don't be disturbed if you find your priorities conflict. The goal is to communicate and eventually compromise, not to evaluate and judge. Then, if you need further help, get it. Use the resources widely available today to help you gather "food for the winter."

Money often costs too much. —RALPH WALDO EMERSON

DID YOU SEE THAT?

Know the state of your flocks, and put your heart into caring for your herds.

PROVERBS 27:23

IN HER BOOK *READING PEOPLE*, Jo-Ellan Dimitrius tells the story of a man, whom we'll call Ron, who was hired by an environmental institute dedicated to preserving an endangered species of bighorn sheep that lives in the mountains just above the institute's offices.

When Ron visited the institute, the director took him outside, pointed to the hills, and quietly observed, "There are a lot of them out today." Ron squinted up at the hills, but he couldn't see even one sheep. Tactfully, the director called his attention to one after another, and Ron soon began to see dozens.

As Dimitrius points out, the director's eyesight was no better than Ron's, but he had learned to see the sheep. And what had become automatic to him became that way to Ron, too, once he learned to see the sheep.[11]

The same applies to your relationship. If you give careful attention to your partner's subtleties, you will routinely see what most others never even notice—and what you once failed to see. We're talking about the nonverbal expressions your partner makes.

Researchers believe that about 90 percent of emotional communication is nonverbal. Harvard psychologist Robert Rosenthal developed an assessment of people's ability to read emotional cues called the Profile of Nonverbal Sensitivity (PONS).[12] He shows subjects a film of a young woman who expresses feelings like anger, jealousy, love, gratitude. Unbeknownst to the viewer, one or another nonverbal cue has been edited out of the video. For example, sometimes the woman's face is visible but not her body.

The goal of the video study is to force viewers to judge by subtle cues whatever feeling is being expressed. The better they do, the higher their scores. But the real discovery is this: people with higher PONS scores enjoy more successful relationships. The good news for us is that we can all improve our scores by simply taking the time to study one another. Make a study of your spouse to learn his or her nonverbal expressions better than you know them now. Put your whole heart into caring for this person who shares your life.

What you do speaks so loud that I cannot hear what you say.
—RALPH WALDO EMERSON

INTIMATE WORLDS

I hope all is well with you and that you are as healthy in body as you are strong in spirit.

3 JOHN 1:2

WHEN JOHN HINCKLEY ATTEMPTED to assassinate President Reagan on March 30, 1981, the commentators announced in a tone of wonder and mystification that little was known about Hinckley except that "he comes from a good family." Of course, it is possible for a "bad" adult to come from a "good" family, but what did they mean by a good family, after all? That he had two parents at home, that they were religious, that they were respected in the community? The truth is that families aren't good simply because they have traditional signs of success. On the outside, a family can be filled with high achievers, live in a nice neighborhood, attend church regularly—and be miserable on the inside. So what makes the difference?

Award-winning author Maggie Scarf spent eight years attempting to answer this question, and the result was her extraordinary book, *Intimate Worlds*.[13] She outlines the structural blueprints that characterize most families' patterns of being and relating. On the low end of the continuum of family functioning are "severely disturbed" families. Then moving upward, one encounters the "polarized" and "rule-bound" families; and at the top of the scale are families belonging to the "optimal" group.

According to Scarf, families at this healthier end of the continuum have achieved an ability to be comfortable with both their loving feelings and with their feelings of annoyance and frustration. Family members, in other words, take personal responsibility for their mixed, ambivalent thoughts and emotions and are willing to work through them. Families in this position generally find no conflict that cannot be resolved. According to Scarf, because their fundamental relationships with one another feel so secure, there is always the sense that "we can work it out."

The same holds true for all couples, with or without children. So how's your intimate world? Are you enjoying the benefits of the "optimal" level of family functioning? Why or why not? What can you do to create an environment that is safe enough to allow one another to work through even mixed emotions?

Other things may change us, but we start and end with family. —ANTHONY BRANDT

TAKING OFF OUR BLINDERS

If one blind person guides another, they will both fall into a ditch. MATTHEW 15:14

BLIND SPOTS. We all have them. Research has shown that we don't know ourselves as well as we think we do.[14] Psychological and spiritual blind spots keep us from seeing the truth. They distort our perceptions. They trick our reality, and they feed us misinformation. Like the physical blind spots in automobiles, our personal blind spots steer us into danger if we're not careful.

But when the blinders come off, we see the truth. A new reality sets in, literally. A transforming truth about who we are materializes where before we only saw an illusion. This is why discovering your blind spots is key to getting and staying psychologically healthy. It's not easy work, but the payoffs are certainly sweet. Heightening your self-awareness lowers your stress, revolutionizes your relationships, and frees your spirit for optimal fulfillment and closeness to each other—and to God.

Healthy people know themselves well. They know their strengths and limits, their likes and dislikes. They know what ticks them off and what soothes their spirits. They know their dark sides and how to combat them. They monitor their feelings and learn how to manage them. They are aware of their motivations. They are aware of how they come off to others. Healthy people know, for the most part, what other people know about them. They keep their blind spots to a minimum. And the more they do this as a couple, the healthier their relationship becomes.

Can you be honest, in this very moment, and help one another gain clarity on a potential blind spot?

> *For me, the greatest clarity was always the greatest beauty.*
> —GOTTHOLD EPHRAIM LESSING

WHAT A FOOL BELIEVES

Fools have no interest in understanding; they only want to air their own opinions.

PROVERBS 18:2

IN 1957 THE BBC NEWS announced that, thanks to a very mild winter, Swiss farmers were enjoying a bumper spaghetti crop. It accompanied this announcement with footage of Swiss peasants pulling strands of spaghetti down from trees. Huge numbers of viewers called the BBC wanting to know how they could grow their own spaghetti tree.

National Public Radio's *Talk of the Nation* program announced that Richard Nixon, in a surprise move, was running for President again—in 1992. His new campaign slogan was, "I didn't do anything wrong, and I won't do it again." Listeners responded viscerally to the announcement, flooding the show with calls.

In 1996 the Taco Bell Corporation announced it had bought the Liberty Bell and was renaming it the Taco Liberty Bell. Hundreds of outraged citizens called the National Historic Park in Philadelphia to express their anger. The best line of the day came when White House press secretary Mike McCurry was asked about the sale. Thinking on his feet, he responded that the Lincoln Memorial had also been sold. It would now be known, he said, as the Ford Lincoln Mercury Memorial.

Six years later, Burger King published a full-page advertisement in *USA Today* announcing the introduction of a new item to their menu: a "Left-Handed Whopper" specially designed for the thirty-two million left-handed Americans. According to the advertisement, the new Whopper included the same ingredients as the original Whopper, but all the condiments were rotated 180 degrees for the benefit of their left-handed customers. Thousands of customers went into restaurants to request the new sandwich.

In 2010 Google announced it was changing its name to Topeka. The company spokesperson said it was due to the mayor of Topeka, Kansas, making a convincing argument. So they replaced their standard homepage logo with the word *Topeka*, showed the Google headquarters with a freshly updated sign, and gave suggestions on how to use the new vernacular: "I Topeka'd him." Customers thought the company leaders had lost their minds.

Of course, all of these were pranks played on April 1. The exact origin of the day is unknown, although some believe it could be based on a change to the Gregorian Calendar from the Julian Calendar and the resulting confusion that change created.

Here's the point for couples: April Fools' Day provides ample opportunity for you to have fun. Those who infuse their relationship with humor, finding something to laugh about together, discover the bond between them has grown. In fact, did you know that this day also marks the beginning of National Couple Appreciation Month? It was founded to encourage couples to do something special and celebrate their relationship. And that's no joke.

It is the ability to take a joke, not make one, that proves you have a sense of humor.
—MAX EASTMAN

AVOIDING A WARDROBE MALFUNCTION

He explained to me, "Daniel, I have come here to give you insight and understanding."

DANIEL 9:22

APRIL 2 IS CELEBRATED AS International Children's Book Day. You may not have known that, but you probably know the children's story about the emperor with a major wardrobe malfunction. It was penned by Danish writer Hans Christian Andersen (today is also his birthday), and it bears repeating for the fact that it contains a simple message for couples who want to grow.

It is the story of an emperor who was passionate about clothing. Everyone knew about the emperor's love of clothing, and before long two con men appeared on the scene looking to make a fast buck with a clever idea.

The con men announced that they were the world's best tailors and could make wonderful garments for the emperor—clothing such as had never been seen before. There were two catches, they said. First, the price tag for such royal garments would be exorbitant; and second, stupid men, unfit for their jobs, would not even be able to see the fabric out of which the clothes were made. If fabulous new clothes weren't enticing enough, now the emperor wanted these new clothes so that he could find out who was not fit to be serving him.

After collecting a huge fee, the con men went to work, miming the actions of tailors. The emperor was measured and fitted, refitted and remeasured. The kingdom waited breathlessly for the day when the emperor would appear in his new clothing, for word about the enchanted fabric had spread. Finally the day came and the emperor was dressed in his new clothes. Everyone complimented the emperor on his stunning appearance as he strolled regally through his capital city.

Unbeknownst to his people, however, the emperor was having some doubts about his own fitness for his job. He couldn't see his new clothes. Knowing that he could not allow his people to see his own consternation, he went along with the act. The crowd, struggling with the same doubts, acted more and more enthralled with his new outfit. Then suddenly, from somewhere back in the crowd, a young boy shouted, "The emperor has no clothes!"

The emperor was horrified. The crowd was dismayed. But slowly it began to dawn on everyone present that the child had told the truth. Sure enough, the emperor was wearing only his underwear.

And so was born a lesson for all who seek the truth: without honest feedback we live an illusion. Have you been afraid to admit that you need feedback? If you want to gain a little insight and understanding about yourself today, try asking your spouse the simple question, "What is one thing I could do to be a better husband/wife?" Who knows, your spouse may surprise you with just the insight you need to be your best.

Feedback is the breakfast of champions. —**RICK TATE**

CONFESSION IS GOOD FOR THE MARRIAGE

People who conceal their sins will not prosper, but if they confess and turn from them, they will receive mercy. PROVERBS 28:13

ONE OF ENGLAND'S MAJOR NEWSPAPERS, *The Guardian*, carries a daily confessional column called "Corrections and Clarifications." Once edited by Ian Mayes, the column breaks the stodgy English tradition of rarely admitting error. Sometimes done with humor at the paper's own expense, the column averages about five items per day. Typos range from simple misspellings to substituting "having insight" for "having incited." At some point Mayes sensed that more people read the correction than read the original story, and he was right. He published *Only Correct*, a bestselling compendium of his favorite mishaps.

If a newspaper has learned that confession enlarges readership rather than turning people away, perhaps there is a lesson for husbands and wives here too. Neither newspapers nor spouses can avoid making mistakes; there's nothing unusual about that. It is candor in admitting them, and taking responsibility for them, that is unique.

Sometime today, before you turn down the covers of your bed, why don't you take a moment to turn down the covers of your soul? Just enough to let your spouse know *you* know you're human. Confess a foible or two as a husband or wife. What "corrections and clarifications" on your part of the marriage would you like to make today? Maybe you regret the comment you made at dinner tonight. Maybe you wish you had handled a discipline issue with the kids differently. Or maybe you wish you had affirmed your partner at a certain point today for how he or she handled a tough spot at work, and you didn't do it.

The key is to be specific. As Thomas Brooks said, "An implicit confession is almost as bad as an implicit faith; wicked men commonly confess their sins by wholesale. We are all sinners; but the true penitent confesses his sins by retail."

No one is perfect. We all make mistakes. But when we own up to our mistakes and do our best to correct them, we become better for it—and so do our marriages. Try it. What little correction can you confess right now? Review your last day or so and highlight one thing you wish you had handled differently—especially as it pertains to your marriage. The very act of talking about it will help you do better next time.

There are many persons who think Sunday is a sponge with which to wipe out the sins of the week. —HENRY WARD BEECHER

GETTING UNSTUCK

Work hard so you can present yourself to God and receive his approval. Be a good worker, one who does not need to be ashamed and who correctly explains the word of truth.

2 TIMOTHY 2:15

EVERY SERIOUS GOLFER LOOKS forward to the Masters Tournament about this time of year. It's held in Augusta, Georgia, where the winner is awarded the prestigious green jacket that must be returned to the clubhouse a year later. Tickets for the Masters are very difficult to come by, but it's been televised on CBS every year since 1956. Former winners include Sam Snead, Ben Hogan, Tom Watson, Jack Nicklaus, Tiger Woods, Phil Mickelson, and Arnold Palmer. But one well-known professional golfer has never been a serious contender at the Masters. Why? If you ask him, he'd say it was his putting.

Chi Chi Rodriguez, who was inducted into the World Golf Hall of Fame, has long lamented his poor putting. "If I could putt, you would've never heard of Arnold Palmer," he's been known to say. But Rodriguez wasn't always a poor putter. There was a time in his early career when he was a great putter. What happened?

"I never knew what I did putting," Rodriguez said. "I just knew that there was a hole, there was a ball, there was a putter, I was supposed to knock the ball in the hole. But then a magazine paid me $50 to figure out what I did putting, and I haven't putted good since."[1]

So what happened to Chi Chi's putting? Overthinking happened to it, that's what. Actually, it happened to his mind, and that's what threw his putting out of whack. How do we know? Because a group of scientists who've been studying the "paralysis of analysis" have shown that thinking too much impacts everyone's performance. Golfers are an easy example. Too much analysis makes their game worse. Neuroscientist Michael Anderson of St. Andrews University in Scotland says the loss of performance in nearly any area is due to an effect called verbal overshadowing. This occurs when we activate the language centers of our brain, and in a sense, overload them when we need to be accessing other areas with our brain that give us new perspectives.

So here's our question for you as a couple (whether you golf or not): What are you overthinking? Is something causing paralysis of analysis in your relationship? Whatever the issue, if overthinking is making matters worse, we have a suggestion: next time you catch yourself obsessing about an issue, think simply. Do you really need to run those thoughts through your head? Can you instead just focus on one thing you can do to solve the problem, or one positive truth about your spouse? Simple thinking really does relax the tension and make your relationship easier. In short, it gets you unstuck.

I don't fear death, but I sure don't like those three-footers for par.
—CHI CHI RODRIGUEZ

THE LAST REPORT

I heard a voice from heaven saying, "Write this down: Blessed are those who die in the Lord from now on. Yes, says the Spirit, they are blessed indeed, for they will rest from their hard work; for their good deeds follow them!" REVELATION 14:13

DAVID BLOOM BEGAN his television career in La Crosse, Wisconsin, covering local government stories. From there it was on to a small station in Wichita, Kansas, and then on to Miami, Florida, where his coverage of Hurricane Andrew won him a local Emmy and a Peabody Award. That's when he caught the attention of NBC News and became a correspondent, eventually covering the White House.

But in 2003 he was covering the war in Iraq, where he was imbedded with the US Third Infantry Division. In fact, in the news industry, he is remembered for creating the "Bloom Mobile," an Army tank recovery vehicle retrofitted with live television and satellite transmission equipment so he could continuously broadcast reports as troops made their way toward Baghdad.

The general public knew David Bloom as an energetic and popular NBC News reporter. What most didn't know was that Bloom was a family man whose faith in God had become a significant force in his life. Bloom, 39, died of a pulmonary embolism while covering the war in Iraq.

Bloom, who left a wife, Melanie, and three daughters, was a committed Christian. A friend acknowledged that it was just two years before he died that he began to allow his faith to influence his life.

Bloom's very last report out of Iraq on April 5 was not for publication, because it was an e-mail to his wife, Melanie. The message was read at his memorial service: "I hope and pray all my guys (troops) get out of this in one piece. But I am at peace. Here I am, supposedly at the peak of professional success, but I could, frankly, care less. It's nothing compared to my relationship with you and the girls and Jesus."

He had no idea that he would die within twenty-four hours of writing this e-mail to Melanie. He simply knew that his heart belonged to her, his daughters, and Jesus.

Take a moment to reflect on the significant and meaningful way your spouse impacts you and maybe even jot a note that can serve as a concrete reminder to your spouse of how special he or she is to you.

May the road rise to meet you, may the wind be ever at your back. May the sun shine warm upon your face and the rain fall softly on your fields. And until we meet again, may God hold you in the hollow of his hand. —IRISH BLESSING

DYING TO BE MARRIED

Our present troubles are small and won't last very long. Yet they produce for us a glory that vastly outweighs them and will last forever! So we don't look at the troubles we can see now; rather, we fix our gaze on things that cannot be seen. For the things we see now will soon be gone, but the things we cannot see will last forever. 2 CORINTHIANS 4:17-18

WHEN M. CRAIG BARNES SERVED as pastor of National Presbyterian Church in Washington, DC, he was conducting a series of premarital counseling sessions with a young couple. As they came to their last meeting just a few weeks before the wedding, the young man suddenly confessed, "I just have to say that I am so scared of this!" Seeing his fiancée's concern, he quickly added, "It isn't that I'm afraid of being married to you. I'm afraid of losing you. When my mother died, the grief was just overwhelming, and I love you even more. I just don't know how I can ever survive if something happens to you." Then he looked at Pastor Barnes.

"I could tell from his pleading eyes," says Barnes, "that he wanted me to reassure him that they were both young and healthy, and that he needn't worry about such things." But having buried too many young people, he couldn't do that. So he said the following:

> *In my experience, 100 percent of all marriages come to an end—some tragically through divorce or early death; others last for over 60 years. If your marriage is long and filled with intimacy, then when death comes, you're going to be even more in love than you are now. Then it will hurt even more to say goodbye when the time finally comes. And that's the best scenario you've got! So why do you want to go through marriage wondering if this is the day you'll lose your beloved? Give her up today. Get the grieving over with. Die to your right to have her, die to your fear of losing her, and die to the myth that you can keep her. Until you do, you'll be too afraid to enjoy her.*[2]

This may not have been the message the young groom wanted to hear, but as Barnes says, "On this side of Easter, it's the only thing a pastor can say." Why? Because it's only in dying that we can finally live.

Has the fear of loss caused you to hold back from deeper intimacy with your spouse? Take a moment to acknowledge that your spouse is a gift from God, and thank him for each and every day you share together. Then choose to accept whatever God has for your future.

The sum which two married people owe to one another defies calculation. It is an infinite debt, which can only be discharged through all eternity.
—JOHANN WOLFGANG VON GOETHE

STANDING STRONG

We are pressed on every side by troubles, but we are not crushed. We are perplexed, but not driven to despair. We are hunted down, but never abandoned by God. We get knocked down, but we are not destroyed. 2 CORINTHIANS 4:8-9

IT ENDED IN 1994, but for two years, scientists sequestered themselves in an artificial environment in Arizona called Biosphere 2. Inside their self-sustaining community—about the size of 2½ football fields—the Biospherians created a number of mini-environments, including a desert, rain forest, even an ocean. Nearly every weather condition could be simulated, the one exception being naturally occurring wind. Over time, the effects of their windless environment became apparent. A number of trees bent over and even snapped. Without the stress of wind to strengthen the wood, the trunks grew weak and could not hold up their own weight.

Another team of researchers at the University of California at Berkeley did an experiment some time ago that involved introducing an amoeba into a perfectly stress-free environment: ideal temperature, optimal concentration of moisture, constant food supply. The amoeba had an environment to which it had to make no adjustment whatsoever. Oddly enough, it died.

Apparently there is something about all living creatures, even amoebas, and especially humans, that demands the challenge of adversity in order for healthy survival. And this is true even within our treasured relationships. Adversity makes us stronger. Without it, our inner character would literally shrivel up and die. Of course, no one would ever choose any kind of trauma or adversity, but when it blows into your life, recognize that it will make you and your relationship stronger. No matter what kind of troubles you face together, you will never be abandoned by God, never be destroyed. He knows exactly what your "marriage-sphere" needs in order to survive.

Adversity is like a strong wind. . . . It also tears away from us all but the things that cannot be torn, so that afterward we see ourselves as we really are. —ARTHUR GOLDEN

LISTEN TO YOURSELF

We destroy every proud obstacle that keeps people from knowing God. We capture their rebellious thoughts and teach them to obey Christ. 2 CORINTHIANS 10:5

IT WAS FRIDAY NIGHT and Donna wanted her husband, Tim, to suggest a fun restaurant for dinner. *After all,* she thought, *we've both had a tough week at work. He'll realize that I shouldn't make dinner tonight. We can take it easy and spend some time together.* "But I didn't say anything to him," Donna confesses, "because I thought, *He should initiate it. He should know.*" Tim obviously didn't know, because he didn't suggest going out to eat. When Tim didn't, Donna angrily grabbed leftovers and heated those, while thinking, *He doesn't want to spend time with me. He doesn't care about me.*

During the meal Donna sulked, and it only got worse when Tim didn't talk to her about her day. The rest of the evening she avoided him. Why? Because "a woman shouldn't have to ask her man to talk to her." On top of that, she said to herself, *If he really cared about me he'd want to find out how I'm doing.* She threw a pity party, and he didn't even notice. "I sat there feeling rejected and depressed. And I thought, *He's so selfish.*"

If Donna monitored her self-talk, she would have realized she was being her marriage's own worst enemy. While her goal was to connect with her mate, she ended up trying to punish him for not initiating a conversation or asking her out for dinner. Think how her mood—and the evening—would have changed if she'd countered her negative self-talk with positive, more rational self-talk: *I can't expect him to read my mind—he doesn't know I'd like to eat out.* Or *Just because he doesn't initiate a conversation in this moment, that doesn't mean he's not interested in me.* Sure, it may take some mental muscle to conjure these thoughts whenever you're tempted to think opposite ones, but aren't they more accurate? We are to capture rebellious thoughts and teach them to obey Christ—and this goes for all thoughts, self-talk about your spouse included.

What about you? Replay your recent self-talk as it related to your marriage, and see if you can adjust your thoughts in a more positive way.[3]

Change your thoughts and you can change the world. —NORMAN VINCENT PEALE

THE ULTIMATE EMBRACE

He personally carried our sins in his body on the cross so that we can be dead to sin and live for what is right. By his wounds you are healed. 1 PETER 2:24

YEARS AGO, MARK GALLI, senior managing editor of *Christianity Today*, was having an intense conversation with his wife, and he was becoming increasingly agitated. In anger, he yelled at her and punched his fist into their dining room wall. "Unfortunately," Mark says, "the Holy Spirit failed to guide my hand between the studs," and he ended up breaking a knuckle.

Mark grew up in a family where nothing got done until someone yelled, whereas his wife, Barb, came from a family for whom yelling was not comfortable at all. So after this eruption of anger, Mark was sure that Barb was not going to speak to him for weeks. As he writhed in physical pain, he also cringed in emotional pain. He felt like a complete moral failure as a husband.

As he was awkwardly trying to sweep up with one hand the bits of Sheetrock strewn on his dining room floor, he felt a hand on his arm. He turned around, and it was Barb. She said something apologetic. He did the same. And then, he said, "She embraced me for a long time."

Mark goes on to say that Barb had every right to condemn his behavior and distance herself from her husband. "Instead, she embraced the angry sinner, and rather than teaching me a lesson," Mark says, "she helped heal me."[4]

During this time of year, we Christians celebrate a similar event. Good Friday is an example of the righteous embracing the sinner on a cosmic scale. Jesus did not distance himself from our sin. He, the sinless one, came down to embrace us in spite of—in fact, because of—our sin. By this embrace, Jesus made redemption possible.

We all have an opportunity to allow the amazing grace of Jesus to flow through not only ourselves, but out through us to others as well. Allow this grace to flow through you to your spouse today.

God led Jesus to a cross, not a crown, and yet that cross ultimately proved to be the gateway to freedom and forgiveness for every sinner in the world. God also asks us, as Jesus' followers, to carry a cross. Paradoxically, in carrying that cross, we find liberty and joy and fulfillment. —BILL HYBELS

THE GREAT ASCENT

Don't be selfish; don't try to impress others. Be humble, thinking of others as better than yourselves. PHILIPPIANS 2:3

IN SEATTLE, WASHINGTON, where we live, on a glorious sunny day you'll often hear someone say: "The mountain is out." Every Seattleite understands the meaning of this declaration, because we all know that the majesty of snow-capped Mt. Rainier is dominating the southern skyline. Of course, some among us do more than admire it from afar. They climb it. They take on the highest volcano and largest glaciated mountain in the contiguous United States for an up-close look at this alpine giant famous for its pristine wilderness. It's a challenge for even veteran climbers.

Few people know it better than Lou Whittaker. He's climbed it countless times and led numerous expeditions to the summit for most of his life. Lou also led the first all-American team to the summit of Mt. Everest in 1984, and this experience provides a useful lesson for all of us.

After months of grueling effort, the lesson occurred when five members of the team reached the final campsite at 27,000 feet. With 2,000 feet to go, they met in the crowded tent. Whittaker had a tough decision to make: he knew how highly motivated all five climbers were to stand on the highest point on earth. But two would have to go back to the previous camp, load up with food, water, and oxygen, and return to the camp where they now met.

After completing this support assignment, these two climbers would be in no condition to go for the summit. Two others would stay in the tent that day, eat, drink, breathe oxygen, rest, and go for the summit the next day. Whittaker decided he'd better stay at the camp to coordinate the team's activities. When asked why he didn't assign himself the summit run, his answer reflected true character, "My job was to put other people on top."

How did he pick the others' roles? He decided the tougher of the two assignments—returning to the previous camp and ferrying supplies to the final camp—should go to the stronger climbers. The two weaker climbers would rest, renew their strength, and receive the glory of the summit.

That's not a bad lesson for couples. When was the last time you went out of your way to make sure your partner got to the proverbial "summit" before you did? That's love.

 } *It is not the mountain we conquer, but ourselves.* —SIR EDMUND HILLARY

A BOOST OF CONFIDENCE

I am certain that God, who began the good work within you, will continue his work until it is finally finished on the day when Christ Jesus returns. PHILIPPIANS 1:6

"DILBERT IS NOT GETTING MARRIED." That's the announcement Scott Adams made in 2006 when he revealed that at 49 he, in real life, was getting married for the first time. You know Adams's work from his wildly successful cartoon strip that began in the 1990s. What you may not know is how, after years in the workaday world, Scott Adams got his start. Adams tells the story:

"You don't have to be a 'person of influence' to be influential. In fact, the most influential people in my life probably are not even aware of the things they've taught me. When I was trying to become a syndicated cartoonist, I sent my portfolio to one cartoon editor after another—and received one rejection after another. One editor even called and suggested that I take art classes."

But not long after that, Adams received a call from Sarah Gillespie, an editor at United Media and a true expert in the field. She called to offer Adams a contract. "At first, I didn't believe her. I asked if I'd have to change my style, get a partner—or learn how to draw," he said.

But Gillespie believed Scott Adams was already good enough to be a nationally syndicated cartoonist. Her confidence in Scott completely changed his frame of reference and altered how he thought about his own abilities. "This may sound bizarre," he said, "but from the minute I got off the phone with her, I could draw better. You can see a marked improvement in the quality of the cartoons I drew after that conversation."[5]

It's truly remarkable what a boost of confidence can do for the human spirit. And we have the opportunity every week to boost the spirits of our spouses. Often all it takes is an encouraging word or affirmation to infuse a bit of confidence. Where can you be a source of encouragement and confidence for your spouse today?

The greatest barrier to success is the fear of failure. —SVEN-GÖRAN ERIKSSON

ARE YOU SERVING LEFTOVERS?

Seek the Kingdom of God above all else, and he will give you everything you need.

LUKE 12:31

HERE'S SOMETHING WE'VE learned in our many years of marriage: busy people rarely give their best to the ones they love. They serve leftovers. We're not talking about the kind that come from your fridge. We're talking about emotional and relational leftovers—the ones that remain after the prime energy and attention has already been given to someone or something else.

This is sometimes known as sunset fatigue. It's when we are too drained, too tired, or too preoccupied to be fully present with the ones we love the most, so they get what's left over. No relationship can survive on leftovers forever. So what's the solution? Well, there are many, but one of the most important is contained in a little, two-letter word: no.

For some of us, one of the most difficult things we can ever do is say no. Yet this little word is one of our strongest weapons in the war against busyness. If you don't believe us, we've got to tell you that we've seen people literally collapse from fatigue, drown in depression, and develop debilitating illnesses because they never said no.

Some physicians even call cancer "the disease of nice people." Surgeon Bernie Siegel tells about one of his cancer patients who never said no. She began to improve, however, after she finally told her boss that she could no longer work extra hours whenever he asked. She began to reclaim her time.

Siegel said, "People who neglect their own needs are the ones who are most likely to become ill. For them the main problem often is learning to say no without feeling guilty." If you suffer from the disease to please, treat it seriously and assert yourself. Begin by making a list of things you have on your plate right now that it might be healthier to say no to. Discuss them with each other right now. As you do, you'll help each other wield the mighty power of this little word and begin to save the best of yourself to share with one another.

Life lived amidst tension and busyness needs leisure. Leisure that recreates and renews. Leisure should be a time to think new thoughts, not ponder old ills.
—C. NEIL STRAIT

HOW ABOUT A MILLION BUCKS?

My child, listen to what I say, and treasure my commands. . . . Search for [wisdom and insight] as you would for silver; seek them like hidden treasures. Then you will . . . gain knowledge of God. PROVERBS 2:1, 4-5

GLEN AND GLORIA SIMS of Sewell, New Jersey, won a drawing sponsored by tax-preparation company H&R Block, but they didn't believe it when they heard the news. After several attempts to contact them by mail and phone, the Sims still thought it was a scam, dismissing the special notices.

Some time later, H&R Block called one more time, this time to let the Sims know that their deadline for accepting the prize was nearing—and that the story of their refusal to accept the prize would appear on an upcoming episode of NBC's *Today Show*. That got their attention. Mr. Sims finally decided to look into the matter. A few days later he appeared on the *Today Show* himself to tell America that he and his wife had finally gone to H&R Block to claim their rightful prize.

Amazing, isn't it? A million-dollar prize waiting for them to claim, and they almost lost it to their skepticism. Truth is, any of us could have done the same thing. If you've been around long enough you know how easy it can be to be snookered by a sales gimmick. And if you've been married long enough, sadly, you may have fallen into the same mind-set trap with your spouse.

Knowingly or not, we sometimes put our partners in boxes. *He's been like that for years*, we think. *She'll never change.* But he or she can and will make positive changes, if you let it happen. If you refuse to see something good, small increments of improvement in some area, it is you who make the change impossible. It's like not claiming a million-dollar prize when it's there for the asking. So quit rolling your eyes and set aside your skepticism to discover the good changes that may be taking place right beside you.

What treasure in your marriage might you be missing out on by refusing to believe that change is possible? We know this can be a soul-searching question, so you may need some time to think about it. But once you identify a place where you're potentially keeping your spouse from making positive change (because you refuse to believe it will ever happen), see if you can take a step back and accept the possibility that change could happen. You and your marriage will be the richer for it.

Faith is an excitement and an enthusiasm: it is a condition of intellectual magnificence to which we must cling as to a treasure, and not squander on our way through life in the small coin of empty words, or in exact and priggish argument. —GEORGE SAND

OUR SINKING SELF-PRIDE

Those who exalt themselves will be humbled, and those who humble themselves will be exalted. LUKE 18:14

SHE WAS THE LARGEST passenger steamship in the world when she set off on her maiden voyage from Southampton, England, to New York City. The British shipping company that built the passenger liner *Titanic* spared no expense to make sure it would be unsinkable. The ship's officers were unconcerned by their inability to get accurate information on possible hazards that might lie in its course. "Not even God could sink the *Titanic*," was the boast of those who put their confidence in the vessel.

The luxury ship had two lookouts on her masts, but the lookouts had no binoculars. The crew couldn't see far enough ahead to react to danger, and they had no way to get their information to the captain if they did see a problem approaching.

We all know what happened. Four days into the crossing, on April 14, 1912, the "unsinkable" ocean liner sank to her death, along with most of her passengers, on her maiden voyage from England to America, the victim of a disastrous collision with an iceberg. As the King James translation of the proverb says, "Pride goeth before . . . a fall."

Isn't it true? Our self-confidence can sometimes get the better of us. When we put our full weight behind our own judgment, ability, or power, we inevitably push humility out of our hearts. Self-satisfaction and unhealthy pride become visible on the surface, but their danger is submerged in our unconscious. All the while we begin to feel pretty good about ourselves, as if we are actually better than others.

Let's make this clear. Healthy pride, the pleasant emotion of being pleased by our work, is quite different than unhealthy pride where our egos are bloated by arrogance and conceit. And you don't have to be an egomaniac to suffer from unhealthy pride. It has a way of secretly seeping into the crevices of our lives even when we are consciously inclined to avoid it. Ironically, our very efforts to be humble can be tinged with a tendency to look down on other people whom we believe are not.

So here's the challenge as a couple: help each other maintain a healthy sense of pride and dignity while avoiding the unhealthy price of a bloated ego. This can be one of the great ways that "iron sharpens iron" in a relationship.

 A man is never so proud as when striking an attitude of humility. —C. S. LEWIS

CLAIMING OUR DEPENDENCY

Don't love money; be satisfied with what you have. For God has said, "I will never fail you. I will never abandon you." HEBREWS 13:5

IN THEIR BOOK *FREAKONOMICS,* Steven D. Levitt and Stephen J. Dubner explain how a simple change to US tax rules in 1987 exposed the depth of the public's willingness to deceive for financial gain.

In the 1980s, an IRS research officer in Washington named John Szilagyi realized that many taxpayers were incorrectly claiming dependents for the sake of exemption. Sometimes it was an honest mistake, such as a divorced couple each laying claim to their children; sometimes not so honest, such as dependents' names that had to have belonged to family pets.

Szilagyi's idea for solving the problem—requiring taxpayers to submit their dependents' Social Security numbers—gave off a Big-Brother feel at the time, and it was dismissed. Just a few years later, however, the idea was dug up in an effort to gain tax revenue, and the returns that following April were shocking. According to Szilagyi, seven million dependents had vanished from the tax rolls. His simple idea had captured $3 billion in revenues that first year alone.[6]

Some people will do just about anything to cut corners and shave off the truth if it means saving some money—even inventing some children. But on this day, April 15, when every American's taxes are due, it's good to remember that in truth, we are the dependents. We may not be listed that way on a tax form, but we are in the book of heaven. We are children of God. And we depend on him for peace (Isaiah 26:3), for strength and protection (2 Thessalonians 3:3), for victory (Deuteronomy 20:4), and everything else. According to today's verse, he "will never fail you," "never abandon you." Make a point of acknowledging this truth with your spouse today. Have you been satisfied with what you have, or do you need to commit to improving in that area together?

God is looking for imperfect men and women who have learned to walk in moment-by-moment dependence on the Holy Spirit. Christians who have come to terms with their inadequacies, fears, and failures. —CHARLES STANLEY

COUNTING YOUR BLESSINGS

That is why I can never stop praising you; I declare your glory all day long. PSALM 71:8

A FRIEND OF OURS TOLD us about her three-year-old son, Justin, and his creative tactics for staying awake past his bedtime. Asking for the traditional glass of water was child's play for this youngster. He was known to request the slight dimming of a light in his room, or even a minor adjustment on his humidifier. On one particular night, the bedtime rituals had extended longer than the allotted time, and Justin's requests had gone beyond the second drink of water and more stories. But our friend and her husband were soon caught off guard when Justin yelled from his room, "Can three people fit in a big bed?" When they answered yes, he said, "Okay, I'll be right over."

Children can be our greatest cause of annoyance and yet our greatest source of blessing. If you have little ones at your home, like we do, you know just what we mean. But whether you have children or not, you know how easy it is to focus on our annoyances, whatever they might be, rather than our blessings. That's why we love the suggestion somebody recently gave us for falling asleep. Instead of counting sheep, they suggested counting your blessings. Talk about sweet dreams! Isn't that a great idea? We've found it to be a helpful bedtime practice whether it's designed to prevent insomnia or not.

So as you slide between the sheets tonight, take a moment to note the things you are grateful for. Take a moment to count your blessings. In fact, just consider the last forty-eight hours and what you've encountered in your life that you've probably taken for granted, even though it was a great blessing. Share with your spouse, in specific terms, what these things might be. Perhaps it's the gift of living in a free country, using mind-boggling technology, enjoying the simple beauty of your garden, listening to beautiful music, or the comfort of a home-cooked meal. Take a moment to note as many blessings as you can from your last two days, and thank the God who gave you those blessings. Counting your blessings will go a long way in helping you enjoy the blessing of a good night's rest.

The hardest arithmetic to master is that which enables us to count our blessings.
—ERIC HOFFER

CURBING YOUR CRITICISM

Most important of all, continue to show deep love for each other, for love covers a multitude of sins. 1 PETER 4:8

CONSIDER THE FOLLOWING couple we recently saw in our counseling office:

The husband: "Tina just doesn't get it. While I'm working my tail off to close a deal at work, she thinks I just go out for long lunches and talk on the phone all day—and then doesn't understand why I might be tired when I get home. Meanwhile, she's watching the tube and taking the kids to the park—then complaining about how tough her day was. You do the math."

The wife: "Ron has no idea how much work keeping track of two toddlers is. He thinks I'm out with my girlfriends when I take the kids to a park or that I'm home eating chocolates when I'm actually doing the laundry or preparing dinner. I mean, he thinks I have it so easy and that I'm so lazy. Truth is, I miss having a career, but we both decided we didn't want our kids in day care. Ron never seems to remember that."

Can you feel the tension in this relationship? It's palpable. In social situations (whether it be in a counseling office or at a restaurant with a friend) it's often all too easy to tell loving couples from warring ones. Almost everyone has been at a party where one half of a couple has taken a public jab at the other. Perhaps it was along the lines of, "I keep wishing John would get out of his recliner, turn off the television, and help me out in the yard like he promised!" Most would agree that it's a bad idea to use the cover of an audience to say something you might not say in private. Couples who can't contain their anger in public are in serious trouble.

Loving couples, on the other hand, use every opportunity to boost each other in front of other people and to cast each other in the best light—much as they did in their dating days, when they wanted their friends and family to appreciate and like their new love. They say things like, "She has a heart of gold. I still can't get over how she gives herself to others," or "He is one of the most patient men I've ever known." Loving couples— those that go the distance—praise one another in private and in public.

Any fool can criticize, condemn and complain—and most fools do.
—DALE CARNEGIE

SMELLING THE ROSES

Cheerfully share your home with those who need a meal or a place to stay. 1 PETER 4:9

ARCHITECT FRANK LLOYD WRIGHT once told of an incident from his childhood that he saw as having had a profound influence on his life. The winter he was nine, he walked with his uncle across a snowy field. His uncle was a no-nonsense kind of man, and as the two of them reached the far end of the field, he stopped young Frank. He pointed to his own tracks in the snow, running straight along, and then at Frank's tracks, meandering all over the field. "Notice how your tracks wander aimlessly from the fence to the cattle to the woods and back again," his uncle said. "And see how my tracks aim directly to my goal. There is an important lesson in that." Years later the world-famous architect acknowledged that he had indeed taken a lesson from the event: "I determined right then not to miss most things in life, as my uncle had."[7]

It's a good lesson. In an age when we often feel compelled to check our e-mail or instant messages just for the sake of staying on top of our to-do lists, we can miss out on the spontaneity of a moment that offers far more than mere task completion. This is nowhere more true than in our relationships with one another as husband and wife. In fact, we have a friend who frequently made a pact with his wife to no longer touch his BlackBerry or iPad at the table. It had gotten out of hand and he knew it. He was missing out on connecting, always thinking he'd do just one more task before engaging with her. Of course, all of us who do this run the risk of spending our entire lives indefinitely preparing to live—but never actually doing it.

Take the time today to meander off your beeline path to smell the proverbial roses with your spouse.

> *One of the most tragic things I know about human nature is that all of us tend to put off living. We are all dreaming of some magical rose garden over the horizon—instead of enjoying the roses that are blooming outside our windows today.*
> —DALE CARNEGIE

COPING WITH ATMOSPHERIC CONDITIONS

Christ has truly set us free. Now make sure that you stay free, and don't get tied up again in slavery to the law. GALATIANS 5:1

WE HAD JUST FINISHED speaking at a camp in the San Juan Islands when a small plane buzzed overhead and landed on a nearby airstrip. A few minutes later the pilot was flying us over the islands of Puget Sound, and we were approaching the lights of a local airport. At this point, the pilot shared a tip with us. "The most important thing about landing is the attitude of the plane," he said.

"You mean altitude, don't you?" we asked.

"No," the pilot explained, "the *attitude* has to do with the nose of the plane. If the attitude is too high, the plane will come down with a severe bounce. And if the attitude is too low, the plane may go out of control because of excessive landing speed."

Then the pilot said something that got my attention: "The trick is to get the right attitude in spite of atmospheric conditions." Without knowing it, our pilot had given us a perfect analogy for creating happiness in life, and particularly in marriage—developing the right attitude in spite of the circumstances we find ourselves in.

It is no accident that some couples who encounter marital turbulence navigate it successfully while others in similar circumstances are dominated by frustration, disappointment, and eventual despair. Nor is it an accident that some couples are radiant, positive, and happy while other couples are beaten down, defeated, and anxiety ridden.

Researchers who have searched for the difference between the two have come up with all kinds of correlates to marital success: long courtships, similar backgrounds, supportive families, good communication, extensive education, and so on. But the bottom line is that happy couples decide to be happy. In spite of whatever life deals them, they learn to get the right attitude regardless of the circumstances. You can too.

What's your attitude like today? Are you about to hit the ground too hard, or go out of control, because of your attitude? Do you need a little adjustment? If "Christ has truly set us free," you can expect his help in keeping you free from attitude problems, if you ask. So make that choice today, and watch it get you through that turbulence.

Most people are about as happy as they make up their minds to be.
—**ABRAHAM LINCOLN**

I'M ONLY JOKING

Just as damaging as a madman shooting a deadly weapon is someone who lies to a friend and then says, "I was only joking." PROVERBS 26:18-19

LESLIE AND I WERE IN the middle of a joint project and had just resolved a small tiff with the conclusion that I needed to be more patient with her differing work style. She is process oriented, relational, and unruffled, while I am far more task oriented, sequential, and time conscious in tackling a project. And because I push myself hard most of the time, I can, admittedly, push others (including my wife) and become irritatingly impatient.

Well, as I said, we had just resolved this squabble (or so we thought) when only a few minutes later the following words tumbled out of my mouth: "Can't you pick up the pace a little here; we're never going to meet our deadline at this rate?"

Leslie looked at me in sheer amazement, made a quick study of my facial expression, determined that I was serious, and burst into tears.

I would have done anything to rewind the clock thirty seconds at that point, but it was too late. I winced, but I could not deny that my true feelings had seeped out, and I could do nothing to retract them. Or could I? In a vain attempt to do just that, I resorted to a knee-jerk response invented for just such an occasion. With as much sincerity as I could muster, I uttered the infamous: "I was only joking!"

Yeah, right. Leslie and I both knew I wasn't joking. It's one of the oldest tricks in the book—literally. Solomon must have used it himself or heard it used plenty to have written the proverb that is today's verse.

Somehow, if we can convince another person that a harmful statement was made as a joke, we think we'll be off the hook. But this is just another sneaking way of avoiding responsibility. When we cover over a hurtful remark with the "I-was-only-joking" line, it does nothing but add insult to injury in the relationship. It's downright deceitful. And according to Solomon, it's like shooting a deadly weapon. Don't fall victim to the temptation to use humor as a cover for a sharp word—especially one aimed at your spouse.

A word rashly spoken cannot be brought back by a chariot and four horses.
—CHINESE PROVERB

YOUR RELATIONSHIP IS ONE OF A KIND

The very hairs on your head are all numbered. MATTHEW 10:30

SOME CALL IT YOUR TEMPERAMENT. Some call it your nature or your character. Mystics call it your spirit. Whatever you call it, we all have one, and like a fingerprint, each one is totally and completely one of a kind. In spite of all the similarities we share as human beings, that tiny 0.1 percent difference in our genes makes each of us unique. How? Because we inherit three billion pairs of nucleotides, or chemical bases of genetic information, from our mom and our dad. So even a 0.1 percent difference is still three million chemical distinctions. And that's a lot!

It's tough to comprehend. Think of it this way: there are more than three million differences between your genome and anyone else's, and it's these three million different sources of genetic information that make your personality exceptional.

Of course, the same holds true for your spouse. Your marriage brings together two completely unique and special personalities. There has never been a combination like you two before. In all of human history, marriage has never witnessed your inimitable combinations of personalities. Your relationship is unprecedented. It is unmatched.

That's why you may have found that what seems to work wonders for another couple doesn't seem to help the two of you much at all. We have some friends who married about the same time we did, almost twenty-five years ago. If you ask them what keeps their marriage strong, they'll tell you that they have learned to never fight.

"We have frank discussions, but we never raise our voices," one of them will say. "We've learned to discipline ourselves, and we always count to ten when that starts to happen."

"You've got to be kidding!" Les counters. "Is that humanly possible in married life?"

"It works for us," they say with a smile.

And it does. They're a very happy couple. But Les and I will be the first to tell you that doesn't jibe with our own married life. Not that we have frequent yelling matches, not at all. We're grateful that we've learned to curb much of our conflict over the years, but that has had little to do with counting to ten.

The point is that every couple is unique. It's what caused German poet Heinrich Heine to liken marriage to "the high sea for which no compass has yet been invented!" So what would you two say makes you the most unique as a couple? In other words, when you consider how God hardwired your personalities and how the two of you come together, what makes your relationship matchless?

A long marriage is two people trying to dance a duet and two solos at the same time.
—ANNE TAYLOR FLEMING

WORKING AS A TEAM

Two people are better off than one, for they can help each other succeed.

ECCLESIASTES 4:9

ANDREW AND LOUISE CARNEGIE'S life was a whirlwind. They were married on April 22, 1887. As a captain of industry in the nineteenth century, Andrew was building a formidable American steel company that gave the couple more money and prestige than they could have ever imagined. And they didn't take it for granted. Andrew's father was a weaver in Scotland, but when steam-powered looms put him out of business, Andrew's mother went to work to support the family, opening a small grocery shop and mending shoes.

"I began to learn what poverty meant," Andrew would later write. "It was burnt into my heart then that my father had to beg for work. And then and there came the resolve that I would cure that when I got to be a man." Resolve, indeed. When his mother, fearing for her family's survival, moved the family to America, settling with her two sisters in Pittsburgh, then a sooty city that was the iron-manufacturing center of the country, Andrew caught a vision and eventually built a steel empire that became unstoppable, not to mention unimaginably lucrative.

Fond of saying that "the man who dies rich dies disgraced," Carnegie turned his attention in his later years to giving away his fortune. On one occasion, Andrew Carnegie was approached by the New York Philharmonic Society for financial support. It was one of Carnegie's favorite charities, and he was about to write a check to wipe out the Society's entire deficit. Suddenly he stopped: "Surely, there must be other rich, generous music lovers in this town who could help out. Why don't you raise half this amount, and come back to me for the other half," said the great philanthropist, thus inventing the matching gift.

The next day, the treasurer came back and told Carnegie that he had raised $30,000 and would like now to get Carnegie's check. The patron of the arts was immensely pleased at this show of enterprise and immediately handed it over. But he was curious. "Who, may I ask, contributed the other half?"

"Mrs. Carnegie," came the reply.

Evidently, the two were well known as having a common vision. What about you and your spouse? Do you share a common vision, common goals? Are you known for working as a team? Think about ways you could be more united in spirit and in outlook.

> *Teamwork is the ability to work together toward a common vision.*
> —ANDREW CARNEGIE

THE TORTOISE OR THE HARE?

I run with purpose in every step. 1 CORINTHIANS 9:26

ON THE THIRD MONDAY OF every April since 1897, the world's oldest annual marathon takes place in Boston, Massachusetts. That day an average of twenty thousand registered participants wind through the 26.2 miles of streets to the finish line at Copley Square. And it's there that you'll find, year round, a bronze statue of two animals: a tortoise and a hare.

Of course, they are there to remind everyone of the legendary fable attributed to Aesop. One day a hare saw a tortoise walking slowly along and began to laugh and mock him. The tortoise challenged the hare to a race, and the hare accepted. They agreed on a route and started the race. The hare shot ahead and ran briskly for some time. Then, seeing that he was far ahead of the tortoise, he decided he'd sit under a tree and relax before continuing the race. The hare soon fell asleep. When he awoke, however, he found that his competitor, crawling slowly but steadily, had already won the race.

The moral of the story? It depends on who you identify with most. If it's the tortoise, you'll say, "Slow and steady wins the race." But if it's the hare, you'll counter, "You snooze, you lose."

We stood in Copley Square together recently and thought about the fable and who we both identified with. For Les, it was the rabbit. For Leslie, it was the tortoise. Does it make a difference in our relationship? You bet. The difference in our personal pace can work either against us or for us. And to fall into the latter category, it takes mutual attention and compromise.

Which one are you? The tortoise or the hare? Do you approach your day like a long marathon, slow and steady? Or do you jump into the rat race of your day like it's a sprint to the finish? How about your spouse? And how do the combinations of your styles shape your relationship?

Love seems the swiftest but is the slowest of all growths. No man and woman really know what perfect love is until they have been married a quarter of a century. —**MARK TWAIN**

BECOMING TRUSTWORTHY

Don't lie to each other, for you have stripped off your old sinful nature and all its wicked deeds. Put on your new nature, and be renewed as you learn to know your Creator and become like him. COLOSSIANS 3:9-10

JENNIFER IS MARRIED TO a penny-pinching spouse who likes an immediate account-ing of their finances. Whenever Jennifer comes home from nearly any kind of shopping, her husband asks how much things cost, and she doesn't like it.

"You went to that gourmet grocery? How much were these tomatoes?" he'll prod.

"I think they were on sale," Jennifer replies—while craftily avoiding an answer. "Aren't they gorgeous?"

Knowing his wife's predilection to hide the truth in moments like these, he quickly combs through the grocery bags to find the receipt. "You paid almost ten dollars for a pound of tomatoes!" he exclaims.

Although the price may very well be disconcerting to him, it's the fact that Jennifer didn't shoot straight with him on how much she spent that really irritates him. And it's these little deceptions that diminish his trust in her and cause him to question her—which in turn causes her to feel encroached on and to evade him.

This may not be a common scene in your marriage, but it illustrates what is common to every marriage: the need for trust. This involves far more than just money, of course. We show love to our partners better when we shoot straight, especially when we are at fault. "One of the hardest things in this world is to admit you are wrong," said Benjamin Disraeli. "And nothing is more helpful in resolving a situation than its frank admission." So true. Don't be afraid of 'fessing up to your foibles. Whether it's penny-pinching or hiding the truth or any other sin, though you may think it will drive your spouse away, confession will actually bring him or her closer to you because you're becoming more trustworthy.

You can like somebody, you could even love somebody, but you have to work at trusting somebody and you've got to earn that trust. —TONY ORLANDO

MOVING PAST YOUR PAST

When you are praying, first forgive anyone you are holding a grudge against, so that your Father in heaven will forgive your sins, too. MARK 11:25

A MONTH AGO (MARCH 25) we made a suggestion for you to examine your proverbial "baggage" together. Why? Because the way you think about your past is bound to impact your present—especially when it comes to your marriage relationship. That's why we now want to help you circle back to the topic once more.

Consider this study. Participants were asked to write for just fifteen minutes a day about a disturbing experience. They did this for three or four days in a row. Forget polish and politeness. The point was not to craft a wonderful essay but to dig deeply into one's emotional junkyard, then translate the experience onto the page. James Pennebaker, a psychology professor at the University of Texas at Austin and author of the study, then compared a group of college students who wrote about trauma with a group who wrote about trivial things (how they named their pet or the kinds of clothes they like). Before the study, the forty-six students in the study had visited the campus health clinic at similar rates. But after the exercise, the trauma writers' visits dropped by 50 percent relative to the others.[8] Other studies have found that identifying one's feelings about past events increased the level of disease-fighting lymphocytes circulating in the bloodstream. It also lowered blood pressure.

Notice an important distinction. Spending time with your past, coming to terms with it, putting it in perspective, is very different than wallowing in your past and using it as a scapegoat. In order to get beyond your past, you sometimes need to get into your past. That's why it's often helpful to explore it together.

The point is that the emotional response you have to your history needs to be talked about, identified, and owned. It is what will allow you to move past your past. One person's dysfunctional family background is another's entertaining tale or comedy routine. Healthy people are not blessed with an unblemished history. They suffer the same struggles, but they carry their negative history with little ill effect because they understand it to be part of their story. They have come to grips with the hurtful emotions a family member engenders, for example, and they acknowledge when those emotions arise. Because they have traced back the source of their hurt and looked at it from different angles, they are able to forgive and prayerfully set it aside. Their emotional baggage no longer pulls them down.

This can be true of you as well.

One problem with gazing too frequently into the past is that we may turn around to find the future has run out on us. —MICHAEL CIBENKO

THE POISON OF CRITICAL COMMENTS

No one can tame the tongue. It is restless and evil, full of deadly poison. JAMES 3:8

SHORTLY AFTER MIDNIGHT on Saturday, April 26, 1986, routine maintenance was in progress at the Chernobyl nuclear power plant in the northeast corner of the Ukraine when an uncontrolled power surge raced through reactor No. 4, producing steam and hydrogen, which culminated in a massive explosion. A mile-high nuclear cloud hovered for ten days, releasing its nuclear rain.

In the summer of 1993 I (Les) witnessed firsthand the devastation this accident brought to this region and its people, and it's stayed with me to this day. On a humanitarian assignment for World Vision International, I was sent to Chernobyl to help those whose wounds had not been amenable to physical healing. I walked around in an abused landscape that will require many thousands of years of healing. I talked with suffering children. I listened to their desperate parents. I met with courageous doctors, and I saw what life was like in Chernobyl's "Dead Zone." Things will never be simple and uncomplicated again for two million residents of Belarus.

Reflecting upon my experience in Chernobyl's contaminated region, I have come to a fresh realization: as soil and air are poisoned by radiation, so the human heart and mind are poisoned by critical comments. Today's verse says that the human tongue is "full of deadly poison."

Verbal toxicity, however, is often dispensed in subtle forms. We sometimes camouflage our criticism, for example, in humor. We've already discussed trying to wriggle out of cruel statements we've made by saying, "I was only joking." Or we shoot a poisonous dart with "helpful" advice that is actually meant as an artful put-down. Sometimes we withhold our attention to express our disapproval. As a Yiddish proverb says, "If you're out to beat a dog, you're sure to find a stick." Regardless of its form, criticism poisons the human spirit much like a nuclear disaster poisons a landscape.

The next time you feel prone to offer a critical comment, resist the urge and try to replace it with a genuine word of support instead. While this may be challenging, the results will be ample reward.

All parts of the human body get tired eventually—except the tongue.
—KONRAD ADENAUER

TANDEM RUNNING

There are different kinds of spiritual gifts, but the same Spirit is the source of them all. There are different kinds of service, but we serve the same Lord. God works in different ways, but it is the same God who does the work in all of us. 1 CORINTHIANS 12:4-6

A RECENTLY PUBLISHED STUDY revealed that worker ants—those tiny little creatures that never seem to stop working—sacrifice time and efficiency in order to teach other ants how to find food.[9] When an ant goes out to find food, she will often choose another ant to accompany her. If the second ant doesn't know the way to the food source, the leader will teach her through a process called "tandem running." As the teacher runs along the path to food, the student follows behind and will often stop to locate landmarks. When the student is ready, she will run forward and tap her teacher on her back legs.

This process is extremely beneficial for the student. Ants participating in tandem running located a food source in an average of 201 seconds, while ants searching for food on their own took an average of 310 seconds (a 35 percent difference). However, the study found that the lead ants traveled up to four times faster when they were not accompanied by a student.

If the leader didn't want to be slowed down this much, researchers also observed that some would simply carry a follower on their backs and drop it off at the food source. This technique was three times faster than tandem running. But here's the catch: the carried ants were not able to remember how to get back to the food source again.

Learning to slow down goes hand in glove with cultivating patience with one another—and appreciating another's gifts. As you slow down enough to practice "tandem running" with your spouse, you'll cultivate patience in the process and enjoy a deeper connection with your unique mate. Since God works differently through different people, we are able to benefit from a variety of gifts, not just our own, and nowhere is this more satisfying than when we're running in tandem with our spouses.

There is no more lovely, friendly and charming relationship, communion or company than a good marriage. —MARTIN LUTHER

IF YOUR MARRIAGE
WERE A NORDSTROM

Among you it will be different. Whoever wants to be a leader among you must be your servant. MATTHEW 20:26

WE HAPPEN TO LIVE about four blocks from the Nordstrom headquarters and flagship department store in downtown Seattle. On more than one occasion we have had the privilege of speaking in the boardroom of this company to some of the executives and employees. As you walk through the various floors of office suites, you can't help but notice the same sign hanging in different places. It says, "The only difference between stores is the way they treat their customers."

Now, if you've done much shopping at Nordstrom, you know exactly what that sign means. You see, most stores advertise the quality of their merchandise or the wide selection of their goods. But not Nordstrom. The difference between Nordstrom and most other stores is that other stores are product oriented—Nordstrom is people oriented. Their employees are trained to respond quickly and kindly to customer questions and complaints. As a result, according to business consultant Nancy Austin, "Nordstrom doesn't have customers; it has fans."

You can probably think of a few other businesses like that, stores or businesses that treat people so well that their customers might more aptly be described as fans. They have tapped into genuine service, and they have earned the loyalty and even sometimes the love of their customers. The same can be said of marriages. The only difference between marriages is the way spouses treat their spouses. And for a husband and wife who are "spouse oriented," they don't just have a partner, they have a fan.

So what could you do in the next twenty-four hours to become a bit more "spouse oriented," more spouse friendly, for your partner? Can you identify one tangible act of service that would please your partner?

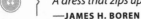

A dress that zips up the back will bring a husband and wife together.
—JAMES H. BOREN

YOUR SIDE OF THE BED OR MINE?

The peace of God, which transcends all understanding, will guard your hearts and your minds in Christ Jesus. PHILIPPIANS 4:7

OKAY, LADIES, THIS ONE'S FOR YOU.

Science has finally confirmed what you've long known: your own husband, who snores and tosses and turns at night, can significantly compromise your sleep. A study at the Mayo Clinic in Rochester, Minnesota, found that when men who have sleep apnea (a condition commonly associated with snoring in which breathing stops periodically during sleep) wore a device that helped them breathe at night, the continuity of their wives' sleep improved 13 percent—they got the equivalent of an extra sixty-two minutes of shut-eye a night.

But that's not all. When researchers at Loughborough University in England kept track of how forty-six couples moved their bodies as they slept, they found that women were disturbed by their partners' movements more frequently than men were.

We're not trying to start a fight here. But if you're like the typical couple and wanting to improve your quality of sleep, we want you to be aware of a couple of coping strategies for both of you during your pillow talk tonight. First off, experts say you can aim for better snooze control by encouraging your spouse to avoid alcohol, caffeine, heavy meals, and exercise within a few hours of bedtime. These preventive measures may help him sleep more soundly and move around less, which means you'll do the same. And if you are a snorer, sleep on your side, instead of your back, to reduce your snore potential.

Let's face it, men and women are different—even in how we sleep. Husbands and wives survive and thrive based on how well we flex, cope, and care for one another in the midst of our differences. At times that can be trying, but it's precisely what builds a better marriage, especially in the bedroom.

Laugh and the world laughs with you, snore and you sleep alone. —ANTHONY BURGESS

WHAT MOVIE TITLE DESCRIBES YOUR SEX LIFE?

Let the marriage bed be undefiled. HEBREWS 13:4, ESV

WE WERE SPEAKING AT a large marriage conference not long ago and after one of our sessions we slid into a workshop by Pam and Rich Batten, whose lecture title caught our eye: "How to Have Kids and a Sex Life, Too." They warmed up the group by asking couples which movie title best described their sex lives, with suggestions like *The Fast and the Furious, What's the Worst That Could Happen?,* or *The Mummy Returns.* There wasn't a show of hands, but *Dr. Doolittle* got the most chuckles.

In the discussion that followed, couples were quick to rattle off obstacles to a satisfactory love life: no energy, no privacy, no spontaneity, kids banging on doors, barging in, and so on. Each complaint engendered nods and groans of agreement. It seems nearly every couple, married long enough, understands the struggle to keep their sex life filled with passion. What most couples don't understand is how an intentional effort—once every thirty days—can keep the flames of passion burning on all the others.

Let's make this clear: sex is critically important for a quality marriage. We'll say it again: sex makes a significant impact on whether you will rate your marriage as satisfying or not.

In one survey on the importance of sex for marriage, the results were compelling: Couples who rated their sex lives positively also rated their marriages positively, and those who rated their sex lives negatively rated their marriages negatively as well. In other words, if couples report that sex is unimportant to them, it is very likely that they view their entire marriage as unhappy. Both the quantity and quality of sex in marriage are central to a good overall relationship.

You might be relieved to know that a number of factors other than frequency of sexual interaction have also been linked to satisfaction with marital sex. Mutuality in initiating sex can be an important contributor to sexual satisfaction of both wives and husbands. It also appears that women who take an active role during sexual sharing are more likely to be pleased with their sex lives than those who assume a more passive role.

No study states that a high quality sex life is an absolute requirement for a high quality marriage, nor that a good sex life guarantees a good marriage. Nonetheless, studies consistently suggest that quality of sex and quality of marriage do go together in most cases. That's why this topic is so important for married couples to discuss. So today we leave you with this question to discuss: How would you rate your current love life on a scale of one to ten and why?

> *The instinct of fidelity is perhaps the deepest instinct in the great complex we call sex. Where there is real sex there is the underlying passion for fidelity.* —D. H. LAWRENCE

IF YOU COULD TURN BACK TIME

Forgetting the past and looking forward to what lies ahead, I press on to reach the end of the race and receive the heavenly prize for which God, through Christ Jesus, is calling us. PHILIPPIANS 3:13-14

THRIFTY CAR RENTAL SPONSORS an annual Honeymoon Disasters Contest, and when they say they have received stories, they mean *all* kinds.

For example, one couple on their way to Nevada flipped their car. When they emerged, the husband, who had hit his head, could not remember the accident, recognize his bride, or recall the wedding.

Then there is the California couple who honeymooned in Cancun, Mexico, and had a terrific time swimming, feasting, and dancing. The fun ended when the husband playfully threw his bride onto the bed, fell on top of her, and broke two bones in her right leg. Three hours, one plate, and eight screws later, they were left with an $11,000 hospital bill that insurance wouldn't cover.

A couple from Virginia, finalists in the contest one year, sat through a comedian's shtick about *The Titanic* during one evening of their honeymoon cruise. Later, they awoke to the sound of crunching metal and the captain's order to abandon ship. The couple's lifeboat made it to shore, and the cruise line paid for accommodations—at a nudist colony.

If there were ever any couples who wish they could turn back time, it would have to be these poor souls. Don't we all have that wish sometimes? Don't you have a few conversations with each other you'd like to do over? Doors of opportunity you wish you had walked through? Decisions you would reverse? As Garrison Keillor says, "Show me a person without regret, and I'll show you a person with memory loss."

We've seen some couples poison their lives with regret—but we've also seen couples use their bad experiences to propel them to a better way of living. The former spend their days punishing themselves for something they should have done differently: "If only we had checked the weather report before we left," they say. "If only we had torn up our credit cards before we got into this kind of debt." "If only . . ." Whether it's over the road not taken or the one taken too long, if-onlys can hound a couple to death.

Other couples overcome everything from angry words to bankruptcy and somehow rise above it. They've wrestled their regrets to the ground and walked away victorious. They no longer allow their yesterdays to use up their todays. How? They make a choice.

You can't change your past. But you can take it to God and let him use your past as a springboard to a better tomorrow—or you can let it be the proverbial albatross that drags you down today. The choice is yours. What shouldas, couldas, and wouldas do you both need to surrender?

Don't let yesterday use up too much of today. —WILL ROGERS

THE MEANING OF YOUR RITUALS

I lay down and slept, yet I woke up in safety, for the LORD was watching over me.

PSALM 3:5

"IN THE GREAT GREEN ROOM there was a telephone and a red balloon and a picture of a cow jumping over the moon." So begins the first line of a children's book we read nearly nightly for many months to both of our boys when they were little. When they were each about three years old, they could barely put their heads on the pillows of their "big boy beds" without one of us reading this story narrated by a pajama-clad bunny. And we aren't the only parents who have this one memorized.

Margaret Wise Brown wrote the now-classic children's story *Goodnight Moon* in 1947. It sells better today than it did back then, and it has created a nightly ritual for legions of little ones who have to say goodnight to the red balloon and the moon before turning in.

Reading this story night after night got us to thinking about our own rituals. Why? Because couples who have rituals, research shows, have a stronger sense of identity as a couple and feel far more connected than couples who do not.

On any given evening at our house, about the time our local nightly news begins to air, you're likely to find both of us perusing the cereal boxes lined up in our kitchen pantry. Bran Flakes or Frosted? Shredded Wheat or Special K? It's a scene that has occurred countless times over the course of nearly two decades of marriage. We never planned this nightly ritual. It just happened. And now it's reflexive. A habit. Whoever gets there first typically sets out a bowl and spoon for the other. We do it by instinct, and this seemingly inconsequential and mundane act at the end of our day has become one of the many panels in the quilt of behaviors we've sewn together as a couple.

Each husband and wife, knowingly or not, has dozens of deeds similar to this that he or she does out of habit—some more meaningful to the relationship than others. So take a moment to inventory a few of yours. They may have to do with how you greet each other or say good-bye in the mornings. One ritual, in fact, may be the moments you share in reading through this devotional on a daily basis.

What meaningful rituals do you have as a couple? Keep in mind, these are repeated activities that have particular significance to you. They may seem insignificant on the surface, but they carry meaning and importance to you on a deeper level, nonetheless. Rituals ground you, fortify your relationship, and provide security and comfort. So give them a little attention to ensure they keep going or perhaps even to cultivate a new one.

Rituals are repeated and coordinated activities that have significance . . . . Otherwise, it is a routine but not a ritual. —**WILLIAM DOHERTY**

STANDING ON THE PROMISES

It is impossible to please God without faith. Anyone who wants to come to him must believe that God exists and that he rewards those who sincerely seek him.

HEBREWS 11:6

IT SHOULD COME AS NO SURPRISE, really. We stake everything most precious in our lives on promises that have been made. And promises we expect to be kept—by our parents, our spouses, our friends. So when it comes to hoping for God's commitment to us, it is the same as any other relationship. We know that pinning our hopes on promises always comes down in the end to one thing: trust in the person who makes them. The more we trust the promise-maker, the more hope we have in the promise being kept. That's why, for people of faith, knowing God is paramount (see Hebrews 11:6). Of course, knowing God does not eliminate our doubts of God's closeness. Even Jesus, in his desperation, echoed the cry of the psalmist David: "My God, my God, why have you forsaken me?" (Psalm 22:1, ESV).

The movie *A Beautiful Mind* tells the story of John Nash, played by Russell Crowe, who is a brilliant mathematician struggling with mental instability. His marriage is a testimony to true commitment through years of illness and trial. On the evening he proposes, the following conversation ensues.

Nash says, "Alicia, does our relationship warrant long-term commitment? I need some kind of proof, some kind of verifiable empirical data."

Alicia, amused by his awkwardness, says, "I'm sorry, just give me a moment to redefine my girlish notions of romance. A proof. Verifiable data. All right, how big is the universe?"

"Infinite."

"How do you know?"

"I know because all the data indicates it's infinite."

"But it hasn't been proven yet. You haven't seen it."

"No."

"Then how do you know for sure?"

"I don't. I just believe."

"It's the same with love, I guess."

It's the same for faith, too. You just believe. And as you believe, you come to know God. And the more you know God, the more you trust his promises—and a meaningful hope emerges. This becomes the foundation for our own ability to remain faithful and trustworthy as we live out our promises to our spouses.[1]

Unless . . . commitment is made, there are only promises and hopes, but no plan.
—PETER F. DRUCKER

DOES IT MATTER?

Pride leads to conflict; those who take advice are wise. PROVERBS 13:10

"LAST THURSDAY I was coming up Westlake Avenue and saw Jerry walking out of his office. I honked but I don't think. . . ."

"Honey," you speak up, "Jerry's office is on Denny, not Westlake."

"Well, whatever, I was downtown and saw him," your spouse continues. "He has this huge potted plant and I'm guessing . . ."

"Wait a second," you interrupt again. "You were still out of town last Thursday, so it had to be Friday."

Do you ever see a little bit of yourself in this scenario? Do you notice that you sometimes interrupt to be sure your spouse's facts are straight? You may not even be aware of doing this. But some spouses can't help but correct misinformation from their partners. Unfortunately, this comes across as inconsiderate and even rude, especially when it's in front of other people.

Of course, other little habits of ours are just as inconsiderate and rude, especially in front of others. Do you stretch the truth? Criticize your spouse? Hoard his or her attention? Prevent the two of you from leaving an engagement at the time you know your spouse would like to leave?

If there's a habit you think you might indulge a little too much and you'd like to curb this distressing tendency, there's a simple strategy. It has to do with increasing your level of awareness. Once you become aware of the fact that you're correcting irrelevant details, you can immediately stop doing so. A tip that's helpful to many, especially in public settings, is to simply devise a little signal that your spouse can use to let you know you're doing it again, whatever it is. Your spouse might simply give a gentle tug on his or her earlobe, for example.

Let your spouse know that you want to improve this behavior and decide on the signal together. Even expressing the desire to change this annoying habit will be a loving gesture your spouse will appreciate.

Ruth and I don't have a perfect marriage, but we have a great one. How can I say two things that seem so contradictory? In a perfect marriage, everything is always the finest and best imaginable; like a Greek statue, the proportions are exact and the finish is unblemished. Who knows any human beings like that? . . . To expect perfection in each other is unrealistic. —BILLY GRAHAM

FRIEND AND LOVER

His mouth is sweetness itself; he is desirable in every way. Such, O women of Jerusalem, is my lover, my friend. SONG OF SONGS 5:16

GOOD FRIENDS. Over the years, they have comforted you, irked you, and more than a few times, saved your skin. They are the friends you have known for years but still can't wait to see next week for lunch. Loyal and lasting, these friends have stood by you in good and bad, like a pair of boots that have worn well. They are the people you wouldn't trade for anything—and if you didn't have them, you'd trade almost everything to get them. Without good friends, the world is a wilderness.

The young Persian soldier must have felt this acutely when he was asked by his king, Cyrus the Great, whether he would trade the horse on which he had just won a race for an entire kingdom. "Certainly not, Sire," the young soldier replied, "but I would gladly part with him to gain a good friend, if I could find anyone worthy of such fellowship."

Good friends can be hard to find. Acquaintances, associates, partners, colleagues—these are found in abundance. Even a friend of the fair-weather variety is not uncommon. But the person worthy of being a good friend can be as scarce as lemonade in the desert. That's why couples in love are doubly blessed to be good friends as well as lovers.

When asked about the qualities of a good friend, Ralph Waldo Emerson said, "I find very little written directly to the heart of this matter in books." We agree. During the last couple of decades, we have seen an inexhaustible supply of studies on marriage and family relationships. Yet the relationship between two good friends has hardly been touched. A recent study at the University of Hartford looked at scores of articles in a sample of many popular magazines and found fourteen articles on marriage and family relationships for every one article on friendship. "Our culture is obsessed with romance," the researchers concluded. "Friendship is seen as secondary; no one thinks it has to be talked about."

But it should be. Friendship deserves far more attention than it gets, especially friendship in marriage. Allow yourself to be grateful for the ways your spouse is a dear friend and companion on life's journey, and ask yourself how you might cultivate more of a friendship with your spouse.

To the world you may be just one person, but to one person you may be the world.
—BRANDI SNYDER

IMPROVING YOUR HIGH-MAINTENANCE RELATIONSHIPS

The godly will flourish like palm trees and grow strong like the cedars of Lebanon.

PSALM 92:12

ABOUT 40 YEARS AGO, William Schutz was requested by the US Navy to construct an assessment that would help them assemble compatible submarine crews, groups of men who could live together, elbow to elbow, for extended periods of time with minimum conflict among themselves. Schutz found, not surprisingly, that compatible behavior was determined primarily by "natural fit." In other words, people who get along well with each other do so without much effort. Their relationship doesn't require much work; in fact, you could say it is low maintenance.

Hopefully, the two of you have a low-maintenance relationship. Sure, if you're like most couples, you have your trying times, but you are together because you enjoy a natural fit with your personalities. You may hit temporary turbulence together, but you know it's periodic, and your relationship stays on course.

If you are like most people, however, you also have some relationships that aren't so easy. These are the people who beef, bite, and bellyache. They give you the cold shoulder, spread rumors, seethe jealousy, play the victim, or trample your feelings. To sum it up, these people comprise your high-maintenance relationships. Well, you may wonder, are you simply left to wallow in the misery they create? Hardly.

After combing libraries, listening to clients, and surveying dozens of people, we have concluded that it is possible to make most high-maintenance relationships much better—especially when the two people help each other in the process.

Scripture not only says, "Do all that you can to live in peace with everyone" (Romans 12:18), but it also promises that when we work at turning from our self-centered ways to building up our relationships, we "flourish like palm trees." The effort you exert to improve a difficult relationship is almost always rewarded with new vitality and personal strength. Other dividends include fewer worries, a clearer mind, a more positive outlook, a stronger sense of efficacy, and better physical health. The bottom line is that improving your difficult relationships makes your life easier.

Take a quick inventory of any difficult relationships you are dealing with, and let your spouse know if there is any way he or she can offer encouragement or support.[2]

> *Irritation in the heart of a believer is always an invitation to the devil to stand by.*
> —ELEANOR DOAN

QUICK—ELIMINATE HURRY!

Be still in the presence of the LORD, and wait patiently for him to act. PSALM 37:7

WE READ NEARLY EVERYTHING John Ortberg writes. We went to graduate school with John and have long known him to be one of the most down-to-earth writers on heavenly issues you'll ever find. In his book *The Life You've Always Wanted*, he has a chapter called "An Unhurried Life" in which he tells the story of getting some spiritual direction from a wise friend shortly after moving to Chicago.

"I described [to my friend] the pace at which things tend to move in my current setting," John writes. He also told his friend about the fast clip of his family life and asked what he might need to do "to be spiritually healthy" in the midst of that flurry of activity.

After a quiet moment, his friend finally spoke: "You must ruthlessly eliminate hurry from your life." And that's all he said.

"Okay, I've written that one down," John told him. He was a little impatient. "That's a good one. Now, what else is there?" John writes that he had a lot to do just then and he was talking to his friend long distance, so as he puts it, "I was anxious to cram as many units of spiritual wisdom into the least amount of time possible."

His friend was quiet a long time before he spoke again.

"There is nothing else," his wise friend said. "You must ruthlessly eliminate hurry from your life."[3]

That's it. His spiritual mentor could have given him a laundry list of things to do that would have aligned his spirit with the Almighty. But that's all he suggested. There's nothing else but to eliminate hurry from your life.

Brilliantly simple, don't you think? Don't hurry past that. Take it to heart. Take time to be still before the Lord, and ask him to show you what the two of you could ruthlessly eliminate this very day that would eliminate hurry from your life together.

You're only here for a short visit. Don't hurry. Don't worry. And be sure to smell the flowers along the way. —**WALTER HAGEN**

LET IT BE

He did not retaliate when he was insulted, nor threaten revenge when he suffered. He left his case in the hands of God, who always judges fairly. 1 PETER 2:23

ON MAY 8, 1970, legendary rock band The Beatles released their twelfth and final studio album, *Let It Be*, recorded at Abbey Road in London. Apparently, the rehearsals and recording session for the album did not run smoothly. The acrimony between the band members was palpable. At one point, George Harrison walked out and quit the group after arguing with both Paul McCartney and John Lennon, only to be coaxed back some days later. The documentary recording the making of this last album became, in truth, a documentary about the breaking up of the band.

It's all a bit ironic, if you consider the title of the album. Apparently, "Let it be" is the phrase McCartney's mother, Mary, sometimes used to console Paul when there were tensions or problems. It's a good phrase—especially in marriage—even if it isn't uttered aloud. Consider this scenario:

"You really look tired," he says to her, as they climb into the car to run a quick errand.

"What do you mean by that?" she snaps.

"Just what I said," he counters. "I know you haven't gotten much sleep, and it shows."

"Well, I'm not tired," she declares, "and I find your comment very insulting."

Ever had one of these conversations? They're a little like trying to swat mosquitoes. The insults are not very big, but the more annoyed you get with them, the more irritating they become, and the more difficult they are to squelch. Such exchanges are not uncommon in marriage. After all, when a man and a woman live under the same roof and spend enough time together, insults—intentional or not—are bound to occur on both sides.

Happy couples, however, have learned the principle practiced in this passage: When one partner feels that a comment could have been meant as a zinger, he or she makes a decision to overlook it and move on. They don't retaliate when insulted. They don't seek revenge. They let it be. Think of the excruciating time this saves and the hassles it avoids, and decide to overlook a fault today, practicing "let it be" marital philosophy.

All the art of living lies in a fine mingling of letting go and holding in.
—HAVELOCK ELLIS

BATTLING THE BAD THINGS

Can anything ever separate us from Christ's love? Does it mean he no longer loves us if we have trouble or calamity, or are persecuted, or hungry, or destitute, or in danger, or threatened with death? . . . No, despite all these things, overwhelming victory is ours through Christ, who loved us. ROMANS 8:35, 37

EVERY GOOD MARRIAGE eventually bumps into something bad. It may be infertility, financial debt, emotional turmoil, or even something as earthshaking as infidelity. Problems are inevitable; no couple is immune. And in general, once a couple runs into some serious ones, they are not likely to recover quickly. Slow progress is the typical course—steadily building one marriage accomplishment upon another, like a game that is won one play at a time, or a building that is built brick by brick.

Smart couples don't expect the world to fall into their laps. It never has. But somewhere deep in the soul of every marriage, a husband and wife will find what Orison Marden calls their "slumbering powers." And these astonishing powers, when awakened, will rise up, look bad fortune in the face, and begin to revolutionize the relationship. It may be a gradual revolution, but it is a trust-building, heart-healing, love-renewing revolution, just the same.

We've been on a quest for some time to discover what strong couples do right in the midst of their calamities. Among other things, we found that these couples do at least two things:

First, good couples take responsibility for the good as well as the bad. They don't believe their problem rests with the other person. They don't waste their time pointing out each other's flaws and foibles. They own up to their parts of the marriage pie. They bring up their own mistakes so their partners don't have to.

Second, good couples believe that good wins over bad. They plant a seedling of hope in their relationship and allow its tiny roots, in time, to sprout optimism. And that optimism about their future together gives them a picture they can hang on to even in tough times.

This very short list is a tall order for mere married mortals, but with God's help, it is within reach. It is his love, from which we cannot be separated by any kind of bad times, that enables us to tap into these slumbering powers.

Deep within man dwell those slumbering powers; powers that would astonish him, that he never dreamed of possessing; forces that would revolutionize his life if aroused and put into action. —ORISON MARDEN

THE ULTIMATE HOPE

Blessed are those who trust in the LORD and have made the LORD their hope and confidence. JEREMIAH 17:7

ANY STUDENT OF BRITISH HISTORY knows what happened on this date in 1940. After the resignation of Neville Chamberlain, Winston Churchill became prime minister of the United Kingdom and eventually led Britain to victory during World War II. Few historical figures in the modern world have had more influence than Churchill.

On a trip to England a few years ago, we had the opportunity to tour his historic home in Chartwell, where he lived for more than forty years. In the exhibit room were incredible displays of uniforms and mementos as well as sound recordings of his speeches. We walked through his painting studio where he surely found a soothing escape from the oppressive weight of leadership in such trying times. We enjoyed Lady Churchill's rose garden and the lush landscape.

But one of the most memorable moments of our tour was a display of some of Churchill's sayings where we were drawn to an interaction he had with a foreign reporter who asked him about the greatest weapon his country possessed against the Nazi regime of Hitler. Without pausing for even a moment, Churchill said, "It was what England's greatest weapon has always been—hope."

Hope, one of the most powerful, energizing words in the English language, refers to a power that keeps us going in tough times, that energizes us with excitement and anticipation as we look to the future. It's been said that a person can live forty days without food, four days without water, four minutes without air, but only four seconds without hope.

David wrote music during turbulent times, which we know as psalms, and it seems that hope runs through them like a ribbon. Consider just a few of his verses:

> *The LORD watches over those who fear him, those who rely on his unfailing love. (33:18)*

> *Lord, where do I put my hope? My only hope is in you. (39:7)*

> *O Lord, you alone are my hope. I've trusted you, O LORD, from childhood. (71:5)*

> *I am worn out waiting for your rescue, but I have put my hope in your word. (119:81)*

Notice that David's hope is in the Lord and his love—in God's saving grace. Why? Because this is the source of ultimate hope, and it forever sustains us. That's why we can say, as Churchill would, "Never give up."

 } *Difficulties mastered are opportunities won.* —WINSTON CHURCHILL

LOVING ABOVE AVERAGE

Whatever you do, do well. ECCLESIASTES 9:10

WHILE SPEAKING AT THE National Press Club, President Eisenhower told his audience that he regretted that he didn't have a better political background and that he was not more of an orator. He said his lack of these qualities reminded him of his boyhood days in Kansas when an old farmer had a cow for sale. The buyer asked the farmer about the cow's pedigree, butterfat production, and monthly production of milk. The farmer said, "I don't know what a pedigree is, and I don't have an idea about butterfat production, but she's a good cow, and she'll give you all the milk she has."[4]

Everybody appreciates a person, or even a cow, who gives it his or her all. Yet how many times do we find ourselves just doing enough to get by—especially in our marriages? It's so easy to short the person we love, but it doesn't have to be that way. Not when it comes to love. Surely that's why Paul called love "the most excellent way" (see 1 Corinthians 13).

Historically, the word *excellence* has been used as a title of honor. It derives from the verb *excel*, which means "to go beyond average." And that is exactly what's required when you offer your very best. Debbi Fields, founder of Mrs. Fields cookies, understood this when she said, "Good enough never is." The difference between ordinary and extraordinary is that little extra.

What is that little extra, in concrete terms, when it comes to loving each other with all you've got today? Do you try to do well as a spouse, or are you just coasting along? You don't have to have everything figured out in order to give this relationship your all—so do it today.

If it falls your lot to be a street sweeper, go on out and sweep streets like Michelangelo painted pictures; sweep streets like Handel and Beethoven composed music; sweep streets like Shakespeare wrote poetry; sweep streets so well that all the host of heaven and earth will have to pause and say, "Here lived a great street sweeper who swept his job well."
—MARTIN LUTHER KING JR.

I'VE BEEN TALKING TO HER ALL WEEK

The Spirit of God has made me, and the breath of the Almighty gives me life. JOB 33:4

EVER WONDERED ABOUT that classic difference in "word count" that some spouses seem to have in a given day? A true story our friend Gary Thomas tells in his book *Sacred Marriage* illustrates the subject.[5]

A businessman on an airplane made room for a younger man who had just sat down next to him. As they fastened their seat belts, the businessman, starting up a friendly conversation, asked whether the young man was traveling on business or pleasure.

"Pleasure," said the young man. In fact, he was on his honeymoon. Seeing that the groom was alone, the businessman asked where the bride was.

"Oh, she's a few rows back. The plane was full, so we couldn't get seats together."

Offering to change seats with the young man's wife so that the couple could sit together, the businessman was surprised by the young man's reply: "That's okay. I've been talking to her all week."

Ouch! That's not a good sign for a brand-new marriage. On the other hand, some personality types actually do grow wearier of talking than others do—and it's not necessarily a matter of gender. Some people, men and women, are simply content to be more quiet. They get "talked out" on occasion. And, as it happens, these people often end up marrying someone who, relative to themselves, is a "talker." Of course, when the quiet partner begins to shut down—and doesn't have the excuse of getting some alone time by being assigned a different airline seat—the talker can start to feel hurt and even lonely.

This is just one example of the great importance for spouses of studying each other's personalities. If the two of you have never taken a personality assessment, it's worth considering. Once you compare your results, you just might find that what you've been taking personally has little or nothing to do with you or the state of your relationship, and instead has to do with your partner's personality. The Spirit of God made each of us, individually, and we are unique. That means there's a lot to know about your spouse. It's worth your while to get to know him or her!

So does this excuse the new husband on the airplane from not wanting to sit next to his bride? We'll leave that up to you to discuss.

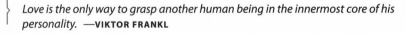

Love is the only way to grasp another human being in the innermost core of his personality. —VIKTOR FRANKL

EVERY COUPLE
NEEDS A SABBATH

God will do this, for he is faithful to do what he says, and he has invited you into
partnership with his Son, Jesus Christ our Lord. 1 CORINTHIANS 1:9

SOME TIME AGO, we spoke in a downtown church in Seattle that had a sense of humor. How do we know? This was on the sign in their parking lot: "Church parking only. We will not forgive those who trespass against us."

Every church has its own personality. And when you find a church that fits with yours, as a couple, you are blessed.

Research has shown that couples who attend church even once a month increase their chances of staying married. Studies have also shown that churchgoers feel better about their marriages than those who don't worship together. Attending church provides couples with a shared sense of values and purpose in life. It also provides couples with a caring community of support.

To cultivate spiritual intimacy in your marriage without incorporating the church is like trying to drive a car without a steering wheel. Billy Graham says, "Churchgoers are like coals in a fire. When they cling together, they keep the flame aglow; when they separate, they die out." Charles Colson goes as far as to say in his book *The Body* that "there is no such thing as Christianity apart from the Church." You see, the church is more than just a group of people who meet on a regular basis. If that were the sole criterion, your workplace might be a church. But a church is a group of people who are called together by the gospel—the Good News—of Christ's love and forgiveness. As the apostle Paul puts it, the church is called into partnership with God's own Son (1 Corinthians 1:9).

From the beginning of our marriage, observing the Sabbath has been a systematic time of rest and renewal for our relationship. Dedicating a day of the week to attend church and worship with the body of Christ stabilizes our marriage and liberates us from the tyranny of productivity that drives our other days. How can you and your spouse observe the Sabbath together—finding worship and fellowship, rest and renewal?

Church attendance is as vital to a disciple as a transfusion of rich, healthy blood to a
sick man. —DWIGHT L. MOODY

PAIN IS PART OF THE PACKAGE

Hatred stirs up quarrels, but love makes up for all offenses. PROVERBS 10:12

IT HADN'T BEEN A good morning. Just before breakfast they had blown up at each other.

"You are so self-centered and insensitive," she told him.

"Well, you overreact to everything," he retorted.

She wanted to take some time to talk about the situation. He couldn't get out of there fast enough. Before they hopped in separate cars to drive to work, each got in a few final jabs on the fly.

The truth is that the argument had been building up over several weeks, maybe even longer. Linda thought about all the times Ron was preoccupied with his job, his friends, his hobbies, his favorite team—anything other than her. She began to wonder, *Does he really love me anymore? If he really loved me, would he treat me this way?*

Ron was irritable when he got to work that morning. *What's gotten into Linda?* he wondered. *She's really turned into a nag—just like her mother!*

That morning both Ron and Linda felt terribly alone. They both wondered if they were going to make it as a couple. With their hurts running so deep, marriage loomed over them like an endurance contest.

Have you ever felt that way? If not, you have certainly felt the stinging pain, if only briefly, of something your spouse said or did. With marriage comes pain. It's part of the package. And whenever we are hurt, we usually see ourselves as innocent victims. Someone has done us an injustice, and now we're left to pick up the pieces. While it's true that we may be victims, we are not helpless victims: we can choose how we'll respond. We can choose to be angry, self-righteous, and resentful; or we can choose to rise above the negativity, forgive whoever hurt us, and move on.

That's what this proverb is all about: forgiveness. Unless we live in total denial, it's the only way to cover over all wrongs. And it begins when we free ourselves from any vindictiveness and desire to hurt back. "Never pay back evil with more evil. . . . Never take revenge," the Bible says (Romans 12:17, 19). When we realize that we have a choice about our response to pain, and we make the right choice, we will start to see love working on our behalf—and on behalf of our marriage as well.

Given the choice between the experience of pain and nothing, I would choose pain.
—WILLIAM FAULKNER

YOUR FINEST HOUR

Thank God! He has made us his captives and continues to lead us along in Christ's triumphal procession. 2 CORINTHIANS 2:14

IN APRIL 1970, the command module *Odyssey* for the Apollo 13 lunar mission was crippled by an in-flight explosion. A slight miscalculation could have sent the ship spiraling thousands of miles off course into outer space. Even if navigation back into earth's orbit succeeded, fears remained that the heat shield and parachutes were not functional. In addition, a tropical storm was brewing in the landing zone.

It's at this grim point in the movie *Apollo 13* that a press agent for NASA, recounting the many dangers facing the crew, asks an official for more information. Clearly stressed, the official snaps, "I know what the problems are. It will be the worst disaster NASA's ever experienced."

A NASA chief overhears this pessimistic assessment and responds sharply, "With all due respect, I believe this is going to be our finest hour."

A mixture of fear and hope etches the faces of the NASA team, friends, and family of the astronauts as they watch for any sign of a successful reentry. Three minutes after the reentry process begins, Walter Cronkite's voice informs the viewing audience that no space capsule has taken longer than three minutes to complete reentry. A NASA employee continues to attempt to contact the *Odyssey*, saying, "*Odyssey*, this is Houston. Do you read me?" The silence is agonizing. Suddenly, the receiver at NASA crackles. A capsule seems to materialize out of thin air on the screen, and the parachutes look like giant flowers that have burst into bloom.

A voice responds loud and clear, "Hello, Houston. This is *Odyssey*. It's good to see you again."

After that, few would dispute the opinion of the NASA official who said it was their finest hour. After all, the times that test one's mettle are the times the human spirit can shine the brightest. That's true not only of efforts like the space program; it's true of marriages, too. Your finest hour is not when everything is going well and you're on easy street. Truly, your finest hour is when times are tough and you stick it out, fight for your marriage, function under pressure, and make it to the other side—triumphantly.

If you are going through a difficult time, remember that there is no better cause than the person you have sworn to love, no more valiant goal than to fulfill the vows you made to your spouse. Though it may feel like your worst disaster, it is when you begin to fight for that cause and that goal that you will experience your finest hour.

A difficult crisis can be more readily endured if we retain the conviction that our existence holds a purpose—a cause to pursue, a person to love, a goal to achieve.
—JOHN MAXWELL

REVEALING THE REAL YOU

Make them holy by your truth; teach them your word, which is truth. JOHN 17:17

THINK ABOUT THE FIRST date the two of you ever had. Maybe you went to a nice dinner. We had ours at the Magic Pan in Kansas City on the famed plaza. Perhaps you went to a movie or a concert, played mini golf or attended a ballgame. You might recall what you were wearing, maybe what you had for dinner. You may even recollect what you talked about together. And you may be able to conjure up some of the feelings you had on that first date. Why? Because, if you are like most people, you put a lot of energy into that first date. You worked hard to create a positive impression of who you are for this person who eventually became your spouse. Even if you decided at the outset that you were just going to be yourself, you can't help but feel a bit of pressure to "perform" and be the best possible "you."

It's commonly believed that nearly everyone wears some sort of a mask on the first few dates. They may wear a mask for some time, wanting to continue a charade of the very best version of themselves as possible. Some would argue that mask wearing may even continue into the first bit of marriage. But sooner or later, the masks come off and the real people are revealed. We see what they do when they are hurt, angry, jealous, annoyed, and so on. It can't be helped. If you are with someone long enough in varying circumstances, you gradually discover the actual person. That's why some say love is blind, but marriage restores its sight.

So here you are—well after your first date. You've seen each other without the proverbial masks. What parts of your personality—the real you—do you think might be most challenging for your spouse to live with and why? Have you asked your spouse?

Think about today's verse. Do the traits you're thinking of line up with the Bible? If not, you can ask God to make you holy in those areas—to teach you his word, which is truth, about those aspects of your life.

> *An object in possession seldom retains the same charm that it had in pursuit.*
> —PLINY THE YOUNGER

LISTEN TO WHAT YOU'RE SAYING

I said, "It's all over! I am doomed, for I am a sinful man. I have filthy lips, and I live among a people with filthy lips." ISAIAH 6:5

"IF YOU BUGGED YOURSELF what would you hear?" It's a question I've been asking myself, on and off, since I (Les) was about ten years old, as a result of what started on this date in 1973. That's when the Senate Watergate Committee began its nationally televised hearings. I was too young to understand the national significance of what was taking place when it was revealed that the Oval Office of the White House in Washington, DC, was bugged with sophisticated equipment that went on at the sound of a person's voice. But I was old enough to know that secretly recording a conversation to play back later was intriguing.

The scandal became a national obsession. Every news broadcast and newspaper led with the story for days. Two people never came together on national talk shows or at the counters of coffee shops without discussing the tapes. All conversations, public and private, led to the West Wing of the White House.

Bugging became so pervasive that I had to give it a try in my own home. Halfway through a formal meal at the dining room table, a strange clicking came from the floral centerpiece. That's when I pulled a microphone from the arrangement my mother had made, triumphantly reporting that I had bugged the entire table conversation between my parents and my two older brothers. They thought I was joking until I rewound the tape and began playing back what each of us had said.

My dad, a pastor, used it as a sermon illustration some days later in a message he titled "If You Bugged Yourself What Would You Hear?" It's a good question even now, don't you think? What would you learn about yourself and your relationship with each other if your conversations for the past twenty-four hours had been recorded and played back to you? Would you find that your words were soft or harsh? Would your words ameliorate stress for your partner or compound it? Would what you hear be clean or filthy?

The real art of conversation is not only to say the right thing in the right place, but . . . to leave unsaid the wrong thing at the tempting moment. —DOROTHY NEVILL

SHE NEVER HEARS ME

We are each responsible for our own conduct. GALATIANS 6:5

A CONCERNED HUSBAND goes to see the family doctor: "I think my wife is deaf. She never hears me the first time I say something. In fact, I often have to repeat things over and over again."

"Well," the doctor replies, "go home tonight, stand about fifteen feet from her, and say something. If she doesn't reply, move about five feet closer and say it again. Keep doing this so we can get an idea of the severity of her deafness."

Sure enough, the husband goes home, and he does exactly as instructed. He stands about fifteen feet from his wife, who is standing in the kitchen, chopping some vegetables.

"Honey, what's for dinner?"

He gets no response, so he moves about five feet closer and asks again.

"Honey, what's for dinner?"

No reply.

He moves five feet closer, and still no reply.

He gets fed up and moves right behind her—about an inch away—and asks one final time, "Honey, what's for dinner?"

She replies, "For the fourth time, vegetable stew!"

Too often we project our own problems—our own character defects—onto our soul mates. After all, it's easier to assume he or she is the one with the problem, not us. It's all part of the blame game.

Some time ago in a counseling session, we saw a couple, one of whom was struggling with serious thoughts of infidelity. Instead of dealing with these undesirable thoughts consciously, it turns out, he began to project these feelings onto his wife. He began to think that she was having thoughts of infidelity and that she might be having an affair.

This situation illustrates the psyche's process of "acquittal by conscience." He projected his own impulses onto her so that he wouldn't have to grapple with them himself. Of course, this is a dramatic example of projection in relationships, but we do the same thing for less severe accusations. Have you ever said, "I'm not angry; you're the one who's angry!" when all the while you're shouting at the top of your lungs and you're red in the face? You get the idea.

So why not 'fess up and explore together, right now, the times or the topics where you think you are most inclined to project your problems onto your partner?

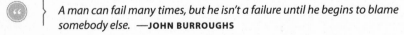

A man can fail many times, but he isn't a failure until he begins to blame somebody else. —JOHN BURROUGHS

MARRIAGE AND MONEY MATTER

Honor the LORD with your wealth, with the firstfruits of all your crops; then your barns will be filled to overflowing, and your vats will brim over with new wine.

PROVERBS 3:9-10, NIV

DID YOU KNOW YOU'RE getting paid to be married? That's what research from Ohio State University suggests. The study found that people who walk down the aisle and stay hitched accumulate nearly twice as much wealth as those who are single or divorced.

Economist Jay Zagorsky of OSU's Center for Human Resource Research tracked the financial and marital status of more than nine thousand people. Among that sample group he found that over a fifteen-year period, people who got married and stayed married acquired 93 percent more wealth than single or divorced people did in the same amount of time. That's amazing!

And what about the wealth of those who married and divorced? According to the study, it decreased by 77 percent, which is a greater loss than would occur by simply splitting a couple's assets in half. Why? Because after a divorce, a couple suddenly needs two of everything, which means two sets of payments—for rent or mortgage, car payments and auto insurance, households, furnishings, everything. Plus, there's the cost of the divorce itself, in lawyers and court fees, not to mention the time it requires, which may mean time off of work and loss of income.

On the other hand, marriage has financial rewards: "Married people boosted their wealth by about 4 percent each year—just as a result of being married—with all other factors held constant."[6] Now, you may not feel like your wealth is being boosted as a result of your marriage, but if you are like most couples, you need to count your blessings in this typically unnoticed reward.

Then, as today's verse reminds, you need to honor the Lord with this blessing of not only companionship but wealth as well. Talk with your spouse if you're not sure the two of you are giving your "firstfruits" to the Lord. It's important to manage your money as well as your relationship in a God-honoring way.

Money may buy you a fine dog, but only love can make it wag its tail.
—RICHARD "KINKY" FRIEDMAN

REVEALING YOUR DARK SIDE

Everyone has sinned; we all fall short of God's glorious standard. ROMANS 3:23

WE ALL HAVE SINNED. We all fall short. What does this mean?

It means every one of us, no matter how nice in general, has tendencies toward meanness, selfishness, envy, materialism, cruelty, dishonesty, lust, irresponsibility, and so on. But before you get too discouraged about our badness, think about it this way. Whatever miserable parts you have, if brought into the open, actually represent your potential for goodness. Why? Because good character is hammered out not in the absence of negative traits but in spite of them. It's your struggle to overcome greed, for example, that will make your generous spirit, once honed, far more prized, meaningful, and valuable than if it had come more easily or more naturally to you. There is no virtue in not acting on a desire that doesn't exist.

Yet so many people, especially well-intentioned people, work diligently to block out or bury their baser parts, to keep them from being quite that closely known by other people. They operate under the false assumption that if they ignore such bad tendencies, their dark side will disappear. Of course, that doesn't work. Stronger people come to terms with their rotten parts, eventually learning why they have them, and most importantly, how to transform them as best they can.

Transformation for the Christian, of course, begins with confession to God. He knows how short we fall from the glorious standard—it's his standard. But he also loves us with an everlasting love, and he is faithful to help us when we ask him for help.

Honest confession to someone else can help too. "I've got to tell you, I really struggle with celebrating somebody else's success," you might say. That's all. That's enough to test the waters with one another and see if you can risk going further. Your spouse should be a safe confidant for most issues, but consider a prayer partner as well.

The point is that we will never be known until we share the parts of our hearts that hurt or the parts of our hearts that hide—that is, the dark parts. Either way, it's a risk. But facing this risk is a prerequisite to being known, and it's a requirement for being loved. Try it with your spouse today.

As a very little dust will disorder a clock, and the least sand will obscure our sight, so the least grain of sin, which is upon the heart, will hinder its right motion toward God.
—JOHN WESLEY

EASY TO LIVE WITH

My people will live in peacful dwelling places, in secure homes, in undisturbed places of rest. ISAIAH 32:18, NIV

THE ODDSMAKERS SAY the chances are five in ten that a marriage will end in divorce. If one or both partners are still teenagers when they marry, they say the odds for divorce are even higher. If either partner witnessed an unhappy marriage at home, the odds increase again. If one or both partners come from broken homes, the odds rise yet higher. If either partner has been divorced before, the odds soar. If there has been regular sexual involvement before marriage, or if either or both partners abuse alcohol or drugs, the odds skyrocket.

Well, regardless of your marriage "odds," we have a soul-searching question for you that will help you beat them. Are you ready? Ask yourself: How would I like to be married to me?

That simple question can do more to help you ensure the success of your marriage and build a secure home than just about anything else. Think about it. How would you rate yourself as a marriage partner? Are you easy to live with? How do you enrich the relationship? What are the positive qualities you bring to your marriage?

Every marriage is unique, and though there is no definitive list of qualities that describes a good spouse, you can get a clue about what makes a good spouse by considering some of the traits that show up again and again in studies of lifelong love. For example, research has shown that the partner who is easy to live with feels good about himself or herself. He is not unduly concerned about the impression he makes on others. She can throw back her head, breathe deeply, and enjoy life. This kind of person is described in the Bible: "Then you will get the satisfaction of a job well done, and you won't need to compare yourself to anyone else" (Galatians 6:4).

The person who makes a good lifelong marriage partner and helps to build a "peaceful dwelling place" also has a way of passing over minor offenses and injustices. In other words, she is not easily offended. His general attitude is "not irritable, and it keeps no record of being wronged" (1 Corinthians 13:5). Some spouses punish their partner with time in the penalty box for ordinary bruises. But the person who is easy to live with doesn't even play the game.

What can you do to make sure your home is a place of safety and rest for both you and your spouse?

A smile is the beginning of peace. —**MOTHER TERESA**

THE EXTRA-MILE MARRIAGE

If a soldier demands that you carry his gear for a mile, carry it two miles.

MATTHEW 5:41

THIS ONE SHOCKING statement Jesus made holds enough power to revolutionize your marriage. He said if someone forces you to go one mile, go with that person two miles.

Have you learned to apply the extra-mile principle to your marriage? Every husband and every wife knows how to walk the first mile. After all, our relationships couldn't survive without it. The first mile is what we know we have to do. It is taking the trash out, preparing dinner, or balancing the checkbook because we said we would do it.

So what's the second mile? At the time Jesus made this statement, the Roman army had a pesky practice of forcing men and boys who were nearby to carry their soldiers' packs. Being civilized, the Romans limited the task to one mile, and every boy under Roman rule knew exactly how far that was. In fact, as a marker, most boys drove a stake into the ground precisely one mile from their house. This way, when a soldier required the task, the boy would walk exactly a mile down the road to the stake, set the pack on the other side, and be done with it. That was all he was required to do, and nobody expected more.

Jesus used this illustration to point out that we sometimes do the same thing in our relationships. We measure out exactly how much is expected and do just that, nothing more. Let's face it, with our hectic pace most of us do just enough to squeak by even in the relationship that matters most. So, yes, we take the trash out or we make the meal, but only because we have to, and our grumbling and whining make that clear. Jesus, however, says there is a better way—a way to do more than the minimum.

The extra mile turns the ordinary into the extraordinary, the expected into the unexpected. You walk the extra mile for your partner, for example, when you take the trash out with a smile or prepare a meal with a special touch, when you do your spouse a favor without expecting a reward. The extra mile turns responsibility into opportunity. When you are walking the extra mile in marriage, your attitude shifts from "have to" to "want to." Do you find that you "have to" do things for your marriage? If so, think about how you might turn that into "want to," and see what happens when you start going the extra mile.

 No one ever attains very eminent success by simply doing what is required of him; it is the amount and excellence of what is over and above the required that determines the greatness of ultimate distinction. —**CHARLES FRANCIS ADAMS**

WHERE YOUR TREASURE IS

Don't store up treasures here on earth, where moths eat them and rust destroys them, and where thieves break in and steal. Store your treasures in heaven, where moths and rust cannot destroy, and thieves do not break in and steal. MATTHEW 6:19-20

"WHEN MY HUSBAND AND I agreed that I should quit my job to stay home with our daughter," Jenny confided in us, "our income suffered an incredible hit. And at the beginning of each month, Dan and I nearly came to blows ourselves. As we faced a huge pile of unpaid bills, our arguments did nothing but escalate."

Interestingly, Jenny also told us that they had argued about money before she quit her job too. "It really doesn't matter how much we make or who makes it," she said. "Dan insists that I am irresponsible with money, and I maintain that he is a miserly doomsayer."

Sound familiar? Money is the number-one thing couples fight about. Since financial decisions have to be made almost daily, it's frequent fodder for fights. Many underlying emotional issues can cause money battles. Sometimes it's power and control. Sometimes the fights stem from the couple's different family backgrounds. What's surprising to many couples is that fights about money are not a function of how much money they have or don't have. Fights about money have more to do with the attitudes each person brings to money itself. The more important money is to you and the more you prize it—whether you are a hoarder or a spender—the more likely you are to have fights about it in your home.

Every marriage must protect itself against greed and self-centered consumerism. One of the best ways to do this is to give money away. God has given us all we have, and by giving a portion of what he has given us back to him, we free ourselves from its tyranny. The Bible calls us to break the idol of money by giving it away. And to do that, we must take Jesus' famous exhortation and apply it to our bank accounts: "Wherever your treasure is," he said, "there the desires of your heart will also be" (Matthew 6:21).

Talk with each other about your own desires or disappointments about giving, and set some new goals together for generosity in your marriage.

If you make money your god, it will plague you like the devil. —ANONYMOUS

GROWING MORE HOLY TOGETHER

I am the LORD your God. You must consecrate yourselves and be holy, because I am holy. LEVITICUS 11:44

WHEN RESEARCHERS ASK husbands and wives, "What is it you've gotten out of marriage?" couples often say something like, "My spouse has shown me parts of my personality I didn't know were there." In other words, "Marriage heightened my self-awareness and has helped me to grow."

Personal growth is one of the fringe benefits of a good marriage. Having a spouse, in a sense, is like having an intimate mirror that reflects who you really are and so provides more opportunities for personal change. That's why research shows that married people are healthier on nearly every spectrum than the rest of the population. That is also why Scripture says, "The man [or woman] who finds a wife [or husband] finds a treasure, and he [or she] receives favor from the LORD" (Proverbs 18:22). But that favor comes only when we consecrate ourselves—when we dedicate ourselves, solemnly, to the higher purposes of God.

The Bible calls our inward journey of change "holiness," being set apart, consecrated to a new relationship, a new purpose, a new identity. There is no greater personal growth than growth in the likeness of God! So as you consider today's verse from Leviticus—as you "consecrate yourselves"—consider how you and your partner might encourage each other to become more holy. What can you do to heighten each other's spiritual self-awareness today? What can you do today, and every day, to help each other become more holy?

Every single believer in the church of Jesus Christ is called to be holy, even as Christ is holy—to be pure and blameless in God's sight. So, if you have been born again, holiness must be the cry of your heart: "God, I want to be like Jesus. I want to walk holy before you, all the days of my life!" —DAVID WILKERSON

PARADISE FALLS

How do you know what your life will be like tomorrow? Your life is like the morning fog—it's here a little while, then it's gone. JAMES 4:14

WITH OUR TWO LITTLE BOYS we recently watched, once again, the Pixar animated movie *Up*, which follows the last adventure of a seventy-eight-year-old balloon salesman and widower named Carl Fredricksen.[7]

Carl's wife, Ellie, was more than the love of his life; she was the spark and spirit, as well. Their marriage is shown as a short vignette without dialogue—just a series of brief scenes perfectly complemented by a musical score—that nevertheless speaks volumes about the thrilling ups and terrible downs we all face in a lifetime of marriage.

The vignette begins with glimpses of Carl and Ellie's wedding day and their first home and first jobs—Carl as a balloon salesman at a zoo and Ellie as a zookeeper. The couple race up a grassy hill together, then look up at the sky and imagine pictures forming in the clouds. Suddenly the clouds are all shaped like babies, and Carl and Ellie are painting a nursery together. It's an idyllic look at young love and marriage.

But life isn't always idyllic. The scene shifts to Carl and Ellie in a hospital room with prenatal diagrams on the walls. Ellie is weeping into her hands. Next, Carl comforts his wife by reminding her of an old dream they shared when they were children—traveling to a place called Paradise Falls. Rejuvenated, Ellie creates a dream jar labeled "Paradise Falls," and into the jar goes all of the young couple's spare money.

Life steps in again; their car pops a tire, Carl is hospitalized, a tree falls and damages the roof of their home. For each inconvenience, the dream jar is depleted. Soon, Carl and Ellie have gray in their hair, and in a flash they are elderly.

Near the end of the vignette, Carl finally decides to fulfill their dream, and he purchases two tickets to Paradise Falls. But Ellie collapses on her way back up the grassy hill from their youth, where Carl plans to present the tickets. We see her in a hospital bed, with Carl holding her hand and kissing her forehead. Then we see Carl sitting alone at the front of a church. He holds a solitary balloon in his hand. The vignette closes as Carl carries the balloon into his house, which has turned cold and gray. The balloon is a lone spot of color against the gloom, and then everything fades to black.

Our lives are fun, deep, tragic, and tender. But they are also brief—here for a little while, then gone. What can you do today to be mindful of the blessings you share together in this present moment?

Every instant of time is a pinprick of eternity. All things are petty, easily changed, vanishing away. —MARCUS AURELIUS

THE RISK OF CHANGE

Jesus looked at them intently and said, "Humanly speaking, it is impossible. But with God everything is possible." MATTHEW 19:26

THE 1949 CLASS OF Harvard Business School graduates was stunningly successful. Fortune magazine dubbed them "The Class the Dollars Fell On."[8] But when these graduates were in their midfifties, a landmark study revealed that some ranked high on a scale of well-being and demonstrated passion for living while others came in at the bottom of the scale and showed little contentment, let alone passion.

Compared to any other group of Americans of their age, this entire class had done exceptionally well, but some were still soured on life. They suffered from boredom in their work and seemed to feel they could have excelled in their careers even more. Their ego wound in their business life spread discontentment to their marriages, their relationships with their children, and their health.

When researchers probed the data to understand the dynamics of the unhappy alumni, they came to realize much of their despondency was due to a single quality. In fact, it was the most salient quality separating them from their happier former classmates. That latter had a willingness to risk change while the unhappy group resisted it. Two-thirds of them, in fact, said they would love to change what they did—but they didn't. The researchers' conclusion: "Even among men for whom a superior education has opened many doors, well-being is not easily sustained without a continuing willingness to risk change."[9]

Don't misunderstand. The risk-taker's advantage is not about being impulsive or careless. It's about boldness, not bravado; action, not arrogance; risk, not recklessness. A calculated risk invigorates our souls and expands our lives. "Man cannot discover new oceans," said French author André Gide, "unless he has the courage to lose sight . . . of the shore."

We all have a shore that gives us security. It represents the comfortable and easy part of our lives that we know well. What might happen if you, as a couple, had the courage to lose sight of the shoreline that keeps calling you back from discovering new oceans? And what might those oceans be for the two of you?

One doesn't discover new lands without consenting to lose sight, for a very long time, of the shore. —ANDRÉ GIDE

PAY NOW, PLAY LATER

For everything there is a season, a time for every activity under heaven.

ECCLESIASTES 3:1

ANYONE WHO HAS EVER eaten the crusts of a peanut butter and jelly sandwich first, to enjoy the rest of the sandwich without the cumbersome crusts, knows the meaning of delayed gratification. It occurs anytime a person intentionally endures something less pleasant, no matter how big or how small, to benefit from something much more beneficial at a later time. In other words, delayed gratification happens when we pay now to play later.

When I (Les) was a child, I remember Mom and Dad giving me the opportunity to do my chores during the week so I could have my weekends to play. If I didn't do my chores during the weekdays, I would be stuck sweeping out the garage or cleaning out my hamster cage during a valuable Saturday, when I could have been at the beach with my buddies. It only took a couple of weeks for me to catch on, and the principle has stuck. Even in high school, my friends soon learned that I got my assignments done well before they were due. Why? Because early on I learned the value of delayed gratification.

Of course, this is a good quality that can be taken to a bad extreme. When Leslie and I were both students in graduate school, we had a sign over our computer we each used to write our dissertations. The sign said, "Some people spend their entire lives indefinitely preparing to live." It was a quote by Abraham Maslow, and it referred to the balance that is required when trying to delay one's gratification. It hung there for nearly five years and reminded us not to delay too much. There is a time to delay and a time to enjoy.

In what area would the two of you benefit from a little more delayed gratification? And where might you need to lighten up, ease off the preparation, and live a little bit more?

As we get past our superficial material wants and instant gratification we connect to a deeper part of ourselves, as well as to others. **—JUDITH WRIGHT**

THE FUEL OF AFFECTION

Don't just pretend to love others. Really love them. ROMANS 12:9

HERE'S A QUESTION: If your spouse were an automobile, what kind of fuel would keep him or her going?

Of course, the possible answers are endless. But if we had to choose one energizing fuel that would work for just about everyone, we'd say affection. Affection fuels loving feelings. And even if you're not used to it, affection is so easy to express. You have a million opportunities every day to express your fondness for your partner. You have countless ways to convey tender, warmhearted feelings for your spouse—because you are a unique couple, with your own set of shared experiences, conversations, memories, and inside jokes. It can be verbal or nonverbal. It could be a gentle caress, a loving wink, a turned-down blanket, or any other gesture of kindness and caring.

Jack never really understood the value of expressing affection to his spouse until he attended one of our seminars. A few weeks later, he sent us an e-mail: "I thought I'd give it a try. So I stopped by her office yesterday with her favorite coffee drink, and I asked the receptionist to bring it to her as a little surprise. I wrote 'Glad you're mine,' on the lid. That was it. Well, you would have thought I gave her a trip to Hawaii. She called me on the phone that afternoon and was gushing. And that evening, well, it was fantastic!"

Jack became a believer. You will too when you experiment with a few acts of warm affection for your spouse. Try it. Make a note to be genuinely, intentionally affectionate with your spouse in the next day, and see for yourself how far the fuel takes you.[10]

> *Affection is responsible for nine-tenths of whatever solid and durable happiness there is in our natural lives.* —C. S. LEWIS

A CRITICAL PLAN

They grumbled in their tents and refused to obey the LORD. PSALM 106:25

ONE OF THE TOUGHEST THINGS you might ever do to create a more loving marriage is to work on putting a clamp on criticism. When our deeper needs are not getting met, the tendency to criticize is so ingrained in some of us that it will require some serious discipline. The good news is, the tendency is likely to mellow the longer you are married. But it's worth the effort at any point to power down your critical comments toward your spouse.

Much of the time you may not even be aware of how often you utter critical comments. You may say things like, "You put these forks in here the wrong way. . . . Would you quit touching my pen? . . . Don't you know how to put a shirt on a hanger? . . . What did you do to make this so messy! . . . You're not in the left lane. . . . I can't believe you said that to him. . . . You bought the wrong kind of dressing. . . . Would you back off and give me some breathing room?"

If you find yourself being too critical, try these steps. First, apologize to your spouse. Say something like, "I know that I can be more critical than some people, and I want you to know that I realize this isn't always easy to live with. I'm really sorry."

Second, ask your spouse when he or she feels like you are most critical. You might be able to locate specific times (just before dinner when you are hungry, for example) or particular circumstances (when your monthly report at work is due).

Next, ask your spouse for suggestions on ways you could curb it. Don't make it the other person's responsibility, but invite input. You may discover that what you thought was critical isn't so much to your spouse and that what you haven't given much thought to really is. He or she can guide you a bit on how to lighten up.

Finally, invite your spouse to hold you accountable in one particular area where the critical comments hurt the most. Don't try to instantly diminish all criticism; that's too tough. Start by focusing on the area your spouse suggests.[11]

When we judge or criticize another person, it says nothing about that person; it merely says something about our own need to be critical. —**RICHARD CARLSON**

THE FREEDOM OF OWNING OUR MISTAKES

It is by believing in your heart that you are made right with God, and it is by confessing with your mouth that you are saved. ROMANS 10:10

NOT FAR FROM OUR HOME in Seattle is the corporate headquarters of Starbucks, and when Howard Schultz resigned from his position as the CEO of Starbucks in 2000, it was big news. The giant coffee chain was experiencing steady growth. But eight years later, when Starbucks was reeling from a bad economy and stiff competition, Schultz resumed his role as Starbucks's chief executive and faced a challenging mission: to lead a turnaround. In an interview with the *Harvard Business Review* about his return, Schultz commented that before they could move forward, they had to deal with the past by honestly admitting their mistakes.

> *When I returned in January 2008, things were actually worse than I'd thought. The decisions we made were very difficult, but first there had to be a time when we stood up in front of the entire company as leaders and made almost a confession—that the leadership had failed the 180,000 Starbucks people and their families. . . . We had to admit to ourselves and to the people of this company that we owned the mistakes that were made. Once we did, it was a powerful turning point. It's like when you have a secret and get it out: The burden is off your shoulders.*[12]

You know the feeling, don't you? To be released from the burden of trying to skirt responsibility is freeing.

Maybe you've seen the bumper sticker: "The man who can smile when things are going badly has just thought of someone to blame it on." Sadly, this is sometimes not too far from the truth. We tend to abhor vulnerability, and nothing makes us feel more vulnerable than admitting imperfection and confessing true need. We'd much rather find someone or something to blame.

Better yet, we'd like to guard against vulnerability in the first place by being blameless. If we could only manage to be perfect, we'd be blameless. So admitting any weakness or mistake, we think, makes us vulnerable to rejection.

And of course it does. When we take off our protective armor in the name of honest self-disclosure, someone may take advantage of us—even our spouses. But with God there is a twist, and it always works in our favor. Our vulnerability draws God to us. Our helplessness reveals his presence. Our weakness makes known his strength. And our confessions prompt his grace.

With God's help we can do the same thing for one another. We can make our relationship a safe place to become vulnerable and to own our mistakes. What is one practical way that each of you can offer the other person grace this very day?

Mistakes are always forgivable, if one has the courage to admit them.
—BRUCE LEE

LISTEN UP

Don't look out only for your own interests, but take an interest in others, too.

PHILIPPIANS 2:4

IN A *NEW YORK TIMES* ARTICLE titled "In One Ear and Out the Other," Natalie Angier examines the limited power of human memory. Among other things, she explores the common problem of being unable to remember a loved one's birthday . . . but being perfectly able to sing every word of an old TV theme song. We can all testify to the fact that if you add a little music to something, it's more likely to be remembered. That's because the brain is wired to work that way.

Unfortunately, most of us can't get our spouses to sing a conversation to us (or would desire that!). So when it comes to tuning in to each other, really engaging with one another, we've got to master the art of listening. And one of the most neglected fundamentals of listening is to eliminate all the potential barriers on the roadway to effective listening. That means we've got to become aware of what is keeping us from doing it. Here's a list to get you started:

Distractions: cell phones, TV, computers, iPods, magazines, and all the rest. If you want to truly listen to each other, you've got to remove these distractions.

Defensiveness: viewing complaints and criticism as a personal attack. Once you become defensive, once you begin to guard yourself, you are no longer truly listening.

Closed-mindedness: unwillingness to consider the opinions and ideas of others. If you've already made up your mind and closed the case, you'll never open your ears.

Projection: attributing your own thoughts and feelings to the other person. Once you lose objectivity, you'll never hear what's being said.

Assumption: drawing conclusions about the meaning or intention of what is said. Whenever you jump to conclusions, you convey that you aren't even interested in listening.

Pride: thinking you have little to learn from others. This is perhaps the most deadly of all distractions to listening. You'll never unplug your ears if your head is full of yourself.

The fundamental cause of almost all communication problems is that people do not listen to understand—they listen to reply.[13] Think about a time you've done that. It's not really a listening posture, is it?

If listening is not striking the right chord in your relationship, if either one of you is feeling misunderstood, this list may be worth pondering. But it's just a start. What would you say is most likely to get you listening with both ears?

Nature hath given men one tongue but two ears, that we may hear from others twice as much as we speak. —EPICTETUS

THE TIME MACHINE OF MARRIAGE

Cry out for insight, and ask for understanding. Search for them as you would for silver; seek them like hidden treasures. PROVERBS 2:3-4

ON THE FIRST MORNING IN her new home, a newlywed wife decided to make her husband breakfast. She fixed bacon, eggs, and toast, and poured him a big cup of coffee. After a few bites he said, "It's not like Mom used to make."

Trying not to let his comment hurt her feelings, she determined to get up the next morning and try again. The scene repeated itself three more days before the young wife got fed up. The next morning, she cooked two eggs until they were as hard as rubber, incinerated the bacon, and kept putting the bread back in the toaster until it turned black. She gave the coffee the same abuse.

When her husband came to the table, she put his food in front of him and waited. The man sniffed his coffee, took one look at his plate, and said, "Hey! It's just like Mom used to make!"

There's a profound truth in this silly story: the home we grew up in shaped forever our expectations. Not all, but many of our fundamental and sometimes quirky expectations stem from yesteryear.

Can you imagine if you had a time machine that enabled you to go back to your spouse's childhood and quietly observe him or her at home, at school, and with friends? Can you imagine the tremendous insight you would have? You'd be amazed to discover the answers to questions you've had about why he or she behaves in certain ways. And you'd be shocked to discover how much easier it is to empathize with your spouse, because you would understand more deeply what your spouse's life was like. You would have witnessed the times he was chided by his father or befriended by a classmate. You'd have seen her when she felt the most lonely or the most proud.

Of course, technology shows no signs of enabling such time travel, but that doesn't need to keep you from catching a glimpse of a few scenes from your spouse's childhood. Set aside some time in the coming days to devote an hour or so to visiting each other's childhoods. Each of you can pull together photos (maybe even home movies) and memorabilia about your life as a child. Start with your earliest memory and travel through your elementary-school years. Explore not only what happened along this formative time line but also how you felt and what you thought during your most vivid memories. Ask each other questions about important relationships.

Because you're married, you've already done this to some extent, but you've probably never done so with such intention. Of course, the choice is yours, but no matter how long you've known each other, we guarantee you that this little time-travel trip is sure to bring you closer together.

> *Out testing time machine, be back yesterday.* —DONALD DUCK

YOUR MOST IMPORTANT MARITAL ASSET

All of you should be of one mind. Sympathize with each other. Love each other as brothers and sisters. Be tenderhearted, and keep a humble attitude. 1 PETER 3:8

"ISN'T THAT THE TRUTH?" Leslie said as we sat quietly in our car waiting for the light to turn. She was referring to the bumper sticker on the car ahead of us. It read: "Misery is an option."

And it is. If you are miserable today, you can probably point to a set of circumstances that made you so. You may be justified in your miserable feelings. But, at the risk of sounding brash, you'd still be wrong. Your circumstances didn't cause you nearly as much misery as the attitude you chose in response to them.

W. C. Fields once said, "Attitude is more important than the past, than education, than money, than circumstances, than what people do or say. It is more important than appearance, giftedness, or skill."[1] And pastor Chuck Swindoll echoed those thoughts when he wrote, "The longer I live the more I realize the impact of attitude on life." He goes on to say, "The remarkable thing is we have a choice every day regarding the attitude we will embrace for that day. We cannot change our past . . . we cannot change the fact that people will act in a certain way. We cannot change the inevitable." He then makes this remarkable statement: "The only thing we can do is play on the one string we have, and that is our attitude."[2]

Happy couples don't have a certain set of circumstances; they have a certain set of attitudes. It's tempting, no doubt, to complain about our circumstances—or our partners—when they aren't what we want, but our complaining only makes matters worse. No one has ever heard a couple say, "We hit a real turning point in our relationship once we learned to complain and blame each other." It's absurd. Your destiny as a couple is determined not by your complaining but by your decision as two individuals to rise above whatever it is you are tempted to complain about, even if it is each other.

What is one situation or circumstance in your lives that might benefit from an attitude adjustment today? How can you give one another the gift of an uncomplaining disposition?

He who has so little knowledge of human nature as to seek happiness by changing anything but his own dispositions, will waste his life in fruitless efforts. —SAMUEL JOHNSON

ARE YOU SELF-AWARE?

There is more hope for fools than for people who think they are wise. PROVERBS 26:12

AS WITH EVERY OTHER marriage relationship on the planet, the well-being of yours depends on the well-being of each of you. In other words, your relationship can be only as emotionally and spiritually healthy as the two of you are. We make this foundational point just about every time we give a seminar for couples. And so much of our health has to do with maintaining balance—unless we are talking about self-awareness.

Think about it. Most attributes of mental health are found in the middle of a continuum that signifies a "balanced life." Self-worth, for example, is the midpoint between too much humility and too much pride. Delayed gratification is between compulsive restraint and freewheeling indulgence. The attribute of self-awareness, on the other hand, is unique. At one end of an imagined continuum of this trait we would find the people in denial, seeing themselves without any flaws, exaggerating their own abilities, and dodging feedback at all cost. These people are riddled with blind spots and reflect the common view of the narcissist. On the other end of this imagined continuum, however, well, we are at a loss. Is it possible to have too much self-awareness? Is it possible to be too open to feedback?

Remember that self-awareness is not the same thing as pride; in fact, you have to have the one to combat the other. Perhaps this healthy trait could be taken to an extreme, but we've never seen it. No matter how self-aware we are, we can always benefit from continued critique. We can always improve by being more conscious, more alert to our emotions, our motives, our thinking, and our behavior. Too much of a good thing? We don't think so.

Awareness does not guarantee psychological health, but psychological health is impossible without it. We'll say it again, self-awareness is one of the most significant keystones to emotional health—and thus to your relationship. So we ask: what are you doing today that will help you become aware of who you are in the context of your relationship?

 In other living creatures the ignorance of themselves is nature, but in men it is a vice.
—ANICIUS MANLIUS SEVERINUS BOETHIUS

CHICKEN SOUP FOR THE WHAT?

Let us not become weary in doing good, for at the proper time we will reap a harvest if we do not give up. GALATIANS 6:9, NIV

EVER HEARD OF CHICKEN SOUP FOR THE SOUL, the book series composed of inspirational, motivational, and uplifting stories? If you haven't, you're one of the very few. According to Harris Polls, 89 percent of the public not only recognizes the Chicken Soup brand but also knows what it is. With more than 112 million books sold to date, almost two hundred titles in print, and translations into more than forty languages, "Chicken Soup for the Soul" is one of the world's best-known phrases.

But long before the mega-success of that series, there was George Matthew Adams. You may not have heard of him, but if you were reading newspapers in the 1920s and 1930s, you would have surely seen his name. He wrote short essays of inspirational stories and was syndicated in about one hundred newspapers.

If there was a common theme in George's column, it would have to be encouragement and affirmation. "There are high spots in all of our lives," wrote George Matthew Adams, "and most of them have come about through encouragement from someone else. I don't care how great, how famous or successful a man or woman may be, each hungers for applause. Encouragement is oxygen to the soul. Good work can never be expected from a worker without encouragement. No one can ever have lived without it."[3]

It's so true. That's why we ask if the two of you are giving and receiving your daily required dose of encouragement and affirmation. To affirm, by the way, is to make firm. An affirmation is a statement of truth you make firm by repetition. It's what cultivates conviction. When you compliment your spouse's attitude, for example, you make that attitude more stable. More reliable. Because you noticed it, your partner's attitude is solidified and reinforced. He or she is more likely to demonstrate the same attitude again.

Like the repetition of a weight-lifting regimen, routine compliments build up a person's character qualities and strengthen his or her personality. So we ask you again: are you feeding each other a bit of chicken soup for the soul?

Correction does much, but encouragement does more.
—JOHANN WOLFGANG VON GOETHE

I'LL CHANGE HER

Let the Spirit renew your thoughts and attitudes. Put on your new nature, created to be like God—truly righteous and holy. EPHESIANS 4:23-24

A YOUNG BRIDE TO BE was very nervous on the day before her wedding, so she went to speak with her minister. "I'm afraid I might not make it through the ceremony properly," she confessed.

The minister assured her that everything would be fine: "When you enter the church tomorrow and the processional begins, you will be walking down the same aisle you've walked many times before. Concentrate on that aisle. When you get halfway down the aisle, you'll see the altar, where you and your family have worshiped for many years. Concentrate on that altar. Then, when you're almost to the altar, you will see your groom, the one you love. Concentrate on him."

The bride was relieved and left to prepare for her big moment. The next day, she walked down the aisle with her chin up and eyes bright—a beautiful, confident bride. But those along the center were a bit surprised to hear her muttering over and over: "Aisle, altar, him. Aisle, altar, him."

The "I'll alter him" mantra may not have been conscious for this new bride, but it's an outright expectation for some. On most Saturdays, you'll find us in a church somewhere in the country giving a day-long marriage seminar. And soon into the start of the day we often pose a task to the couples in the crowd: name one common myth of marriage. In other words, we want them to think of a familiar misconception that some couples hold. Inevitably, someone will say something along the lines of, "I'll change him after we marry." It's a common notion—but an obvious falsehood.

You can't change your spouse. A person has to want to change in order to make true and lasting behavior modifications. So what you can change is yourself. That's why we pose a different question for you today: what's one thing you'd like to change about yourself that would make you a better marriage partner?

> *I have learned that only two things are necessary to keep one's wife happy. First, let her think she's having her own way. And second, let her have it.*
> **—LYNDON B. JOHNSON**

YOU STILL HAVE VALUE

The very hairs on your head are all numbered. So don't be afraid; you are more valuable to God than a whole flock of sparrows. LUKE 12:7

WE WERE TWO OF THE SPEAKERS AT a marriage seminar in Branson, Missouri, when we saw another speaker, our friend and popular marriage author Gary Smalley, do something that captivated the crowd. Before an audience of thousands of people, Gary held out a crisp fifty-dollar bill and asked them, "Who would like this fifty-dollar bill?" Hands started going up everywhere. He said, "I am going to give this fifty dollars to one of you, but first let me do this." He proceeded to crumple up the bill. Then he asked, "Who still wants it?" The same hands went up in the air.

"Well," he replied, "what if I do this?" He dropped it on the ground and started to grind it into the floor with his shoe. He picked it up, all crumpled and dirty. "Now, who still wants it?" Again, hands went into the air. "You have all learned a valuable lesson," Gary said. "No matter what I do to the money, you still want it because it doesn't decrease in value. It is still worth fifty dollars."

Gary's simple illustration underscores a profound point. Many times in our lives we are dropped, crumpled, and ground into the dirt by the decisions we make or the circumstances that come our way. We may feel as if we are worthless, insignificant in our own eyes and in the eyes of others. But no matter what has happened or what will happen, we never lose our intrinsic value as God's children.

Have you internalized this message? If so, you know at the center of your being, deep down in your soul, that your value is established for all time. Your lovability is rooted deep in God's unending love for you. You don't have to work harder, look better, or win prizes of any kind. You know and live the most crucial message ever articulated: that you have inestimable worth because you are a creation of the Creator. Take this truth deep into your soul today, and allow it to serve as a springboard for the love and respect you offer to your spouse.

Though our feelings come and go, [God's] love for us does not. —C. S. LEWIS

GET REAL

People judge by outward appearance, but the LORD looks at the heart. 1 SAMUEL 16:7

A YOUNG PRIEST SAW a vision of God in a great cathedral. He ran to the bishop and, gasping to breathe, he said, "I have just seen a vision of God. He's behind that pillar over there. What should we do?" The bishop said, "Quick! Look busy!"

Do you ever feel like that with God? Sometimes we run around doing everything we can think of in an effort to impress God and everybody else—and sometimes it's just everybody else. That's because it's easy to be motivated by outward reward, or inward guilt or fear. People who rate high on spiritual and mental health, however, are motivated by a genuine hunger and thirst. For example, they love because love flows from their hearts—not because they want to prove how loving they are or to clear their consciences.

In the play *Murder in the Cathedral*, T. S. Eliot wrote these insightful lines: "The last temptation is the greatest treason / To do the right deed for the wrong reason." In the play the words are spoken by the character of Thomas Becket, who was to be martyred for his beliefs, and suddenly he saw that his final temptation would be to choose martyrdom for immortal fame—for the wrong reason, clearly. But how often in our own ordinary lives do we face the same temptation? No matter how small the situation, anytime we allow an outward appearance of a false motivation to cloak the true motivation in our hearts, we fall victim to this "greatest treason."

God does not want us doing "busywork" or suffering from the proverbial "disease to please." He does not want us to do what he says merely to have a clear conscience. He doesn't want us going through the meaningless motions. No, he wants us to follow him and his ways because we want to. In fact, we can't truly love any other way. God wants genuineness. We may look at the outward appearance, but according to today's verse, the Lord looks at the heart.

So how are you doing in this area? Are you being genuine with God—and with each other? Are you doing the right thing for the right reasons? If you're simply trying to "look busy," it's probably time to get real.

Genuine love is so contrary to human nature that its presence bears witness to an extraordinary power. —JOHN PIPER

GOD AND SEX

As the Scriptures say, "A man leaves his father and mother and is joined to his wife, and the two are united into one." This is a great mystery, but it is an illustration of the way Christ and the church are one. EPHESIANS 5:31-32

SEX IS ALL ABOUT RELATIONSHIP. That's the point. It's a personal encounter, not just a biological action. As Philip Yancey points out in his book *Rumors of Another World*, just thinking about how we humans have sex, as opposed to the mating of other mammals, should give us a clue. We are the only species that commonly copulates face-to-face, so that partners look at each other as they mate. Why? It's because human sex is designed to be more than physical. Sex certainly engages our bodies, but it also touches our souls. Perhaps that's why G. K. Chesterton made the memorable observation that "every man who knocks on the door of a brothel is looking for God."[4]

Yancey goes on to explore the connection of sex to the sacred—and how we as a culture have severed that connection. He says that when that happens, we neglect our spiritual longings because, as the French sociologist Jacques Ellul saw, our modern fixation with sex is really a symptom of an intimacy failure. Think of it this way: when a man and woman sever sex from relationship, they seem to gain much in the way of freedom, but they lose much in the way of spirituality. And we've worked with enough couples in counseling to see firsthand the desperate look of loneliness and despair when someone has compulsively relegated sex to simple self-gratification. But that's inevitable when we neglect the sacred aspect of the gift of sex.

The very word *sex* comes from a Latin verb that means to cut off or to sever. Yancey explains, "Sexual impulses drive us to unite, to restore somehow the union that has been severed." He points out that while Freud identified the deep pain within us as a longing for union with a parent, and Carl Jung linked the same as a longing for union with the opposite sex, the Christian sees a deeper longing—that is, a longing for union with the God who created us. After all, it was the Spirit of God who made the connection first, in the apostle Paul's letter to the Ephesian church, the source of today's verse.

Lean into your longings for connection and intimacy, and ask God to use them to bond the two of you together in deeper and more profound ways.

Sex is the most wonderful thing on this earth, as long as God is in it. When the Devil gets in it, it's the most terrible thing on this earth. —**BILLY GRAHAM**

WHAT DID YOU MARRY?

You will keep in perfect peace all who trust in you, all whose thoughts are fixed on you!

ISAIAH 26:3

WHEN PASTOR AND WRITER Skye Jethani and his wife, Amanda, were dating, she bought a car with the help of her dad. They found a car they liked at a local car dealership, and Amanda wanted Skye's opinion. His opinion of the car wasn't too good, but as he saw it, he was "just the boyfriend." Since Amanda's dad was the one helping to pay for the car, Skye didn't see that he had any ground to stand on when it came to swaying the decision. So he told Amanda to do whatever her dad thought was best. He figured it wasn't his car, so it wasn't his problem.

Two years later, however, Skye and Amanda were married. And that's when the car became his problem. A mere one thousand miles after the warranty expired, the transmission gave out. "Although I was tempted to do so," says Skye, "I didn't turn to Amanda and say, 'You bought this lousy car—this is your problem.' We were married. Her problems, regardless of where they came from, were my problems."[5]

And that's exactly right. When you marry a person, it doesn't mean you only marry the aspects of the person and the life that you want. You marry the whole person—goofy quirks, bad habits, and even the lousy car.

Of course, the same is true for your spouse: he or she married the whole *you*. To help you counter the natural inclination to dwell on how much you "have to put up with" because of your partner, we suggest you take a moment right now to note a handful of things your partner has to put up with because of you. This takes humility and grace, we know, but it's sure to realign your outlook.

> *When you find peace within yourself, you become the kind of person who can live at peace with others.* —**PEACE PILGRIM**

PLUGGING INTO POWER

Pride leads to disgrace, but with humility comes wisdom. PROVERBS 11:2

OVER TWO MILLION PEOPLE show up every day. In most cities, almost around the clock, there is a meeting starting in an hour fairly close to you. There are no dues, no budgets, no buildings. Attendance is free—as long as you admit your weakness.

On June 10, 1935, Bill Wilson, a stockbroker suffering from an uncontrollable drinking problem, started the first Alcoholics Anonymous group in Akron, Ohio, when he got in touch with surgeon Robert Holbrook Smith, a total stranger and also an alcoholic. Today AA groups number over 100,000 and meet in 150 countries. Millions upon millions have found healing and meaning as a result of these meetings. They have found strength to overcome what had rendered them helpless.

It all starts with a single step: admitting that you are powerless.

Why would admission of powerlessness be the starting place for breaking a habit? After all, the goal is to gain power and strength over an addiction that has knocked you off your feet. So why start with acknowledging your weakness in the face of that addiction?

It's a classic paradox: on the surface, it doesn't make sense. It's illogical. A contradiction. Yet this apparent oxymoron points out a great untapped reservoir of strength within the human heart. You see, contemporary studies have shown time and again that there is strength in owning up to our weaknesses—in admitting to ourselves that we need help, that we can't make it on our own, that we still have interior work to do. When weakness is concealed, when we attempt to keep it hidden even from ourselves, it is actually compounded. Bringing it out into the open, on the other hand, allows us to begin the process of change.

Are you ready for a daring and vulnerable question to explore with each other today? Here goes: what weaknesses are you harboring? Can you admit your powerlessness in one specific area to one another right now? What makes this challenging for you as a couple?

If we refuse to take the risk of being vulnerable we are already half dead.
—MADELEINE L'ENGLE

THE MOST VALUABLE GIFT

We will speak the truth in love, growing in every way more and more like Christ, who is the head of his body, the church. EPHESIANS 4:15

ON JUNE 11, 2002, one of the most popular shows on American television made its debut. *American Idol* set out to discover the best singers in the country though a series of nationwide auditions. The multiple-audition format features judges along the way who critique contestants' performances, culminating in a final panel of judges on the live program. At the show's inception, these three final judges' seats were filled by people whose personalities were easily identifiable. The passive Paula Abdul offered a gracious but not always truthful critique. Simon Cowell took the infamously aggressive approach that was truthful but rarely gracious. Randy Jackson was typically truthful and gracious at the same time.

We could all probably take a lesson from Randy. Why? Because most of us tend to lean either toward grace without truth or truth without grace. But when we combine the two, we "speak the truth in love."

Truth without grace is judgment. It says hurtful things in marriage like, "You're kidding me! I specifically asked you to leave the door unlocked, and because of you I've been waiting here, locked out, all this time. How dumb can you be?" Grace, on the other hand, says, "I know that I made an unusual request and that you locked the door out of habit. I could have done the same thing. Don't worry about it."

Grace comes from the Greek work *charis* that means "gift." It's not earned. It's not deserved. That's what makes grace so valuable in marriage. In fact, it just may be the most valuable gift you ever give your spouse. And of course, when we grow in grace, we become more like Christ.

Think about how you could be extending more grace to your spouse today, and then do it.

> *Grace isn't a little prayer you chant before receiving a meal. It's a way to live.*
> —JACQUELINE WINSPEAR

TOTAL COMMITMENT

For God has not given us a spirit of fear and timidity, but of power, love, and self-discipline. 2 TIMOTHY 1:7

WHEN THE LATE PATRICK SWAYZE wrote his memoir, he wasn't telling his story to others as much as to himself and his wife, Lisa. Actually, they wrote the book together, as a team. Though the book focuses on the dancer and actor's life, it also examines the couple's life and their nearly lifelong relationship.

Lisa and Patrick met when she was fifteen years old (he was eighteen) and a dance student of Patrick's mother. Four years later, on June 12, 1975, in Houston, Texas, they were married. Over the next thirty-four years, they worked together and dealt with success, disappointment (including two miscarriages and no children), addiction, and loss.

In 2008, Patrick was diagnosed with pancreatic cancer. His struggle to fight the disease captured headlines around the nation, and he died the following year at the age of 57. Since his book was begun after his diagnosis and came out after his death, its reflections had perhaps a more sober tone than many other memoirs of people so relatively young.

In *The Time of My Life*, his memoir with Lisa, Patrick wrote, "The one thing I realized as Lisa and I retraced the arc of our lives is that no matter what happened, we never, ever gave up—on each other, or on our dreams. I'm far from perfect, and I've made a lot of mistakes in my life. But that's one thing we both got right, and it's the one thing that's keeping me going today."[6]

As the saying goes, commitment in the face of adversity produces character—but another result is a rock-solid marriage. What can you do today to infuse your marriage with the kind of staying power that flows from forgiveness, trust, and unwavering commitment?

I suppose it's about keeping love alive, learning how to fall in love over and over again, not taking each other for granted, forgiveness, trust. Whatever it is, it works for us.
—PATRICK SWAYZE

SLOW DOWN, YOU AGE TOO FAST

I am about to do something new. See, I have already begun! Do you not see it?

ISAIAH 43:19

WHAT DID YOU HAVE for dinner last night? Where did you park your car last time you were at the grocery store? You probably can't quite remember, and according to a study done in 2004, that's because everyday routines are handled by our brains in autopilot, whereas new experiences require fuller attention. Because of this, routine experiences can be blamed for time seeming to pass more quickly as we age.

Dinah Avni-Babad, a psychologist at the Hebrew University of Jerusalem, explains that routine can be thought of as a straight line in one's memory, with new experiences represented as a jagged line. "The days feel much, much longer when you're a child," she says, with many experiences making jagged lines. On the other hand, we encounter fewer new experiences as adults, cruising through on a straighter line. So Avni-Babad suggests that you get out of your ruts if you want life to pass by more slowly.

Of course, that's not always as easy as it sounds. Some of us are stuck in a rut because we like it. We don't have to think about much when we are in our routine. But that's not always to our advantage.

Consider the current US standard railroad width: 4 feet, 8½ inches. How did we arrive at that very particular width? It's the one that English railroad-building expatriates brought with them to America. How did the English decide on that width? The first British rail lines were built by the same standard as the prerailroad tramways, which in turn were patterned after standard wagon-wheel spacing before the tramways. And before that, wagon-wheel spacing had been standardized by Imperial Rome—England's former ruler—whose war chariots used a standard spacing between their wheels.

Over time, the wheels would leave deep ruts along the extensive road network the Romans built. If the Romans didn't use a standard wheel spacing—and if the British wagon-wheel spacing didn't match Roman ruts—the wheels would break. The Roman standard was derived after trial-and-error efforts of early wagon and chariot builders. They determined the best width that would accommodate two horses was 4 feet, 8½ inches. Thus the United States standard railroad gauge is a hand-me-down standard based upon the original specification for an Imperial Roman war chariot.

Sometimes it seems easier to go with a prior "routine" rather than change something we might like better a different way. How often that same principle is at work in marriages!

Now that you know you can slow time in your relationship by doing something new, give it a try. What can the two of you do this week that will get you out of your routine?

 } *A person is always startled when he hears himself seriously called an old man for the first time.* —OLIVER WENDELL HOLMES

WHAT MEN NEED TO KNOW ABOUT WOMEN

Each of you will control his own body and live in holiness and honor.

1 THESSALONIANS 4:4

SO HERE WE ARE MIDWAY through 365 days of the year. . . . We think that's as good a reason as any to talk a bit about physical intimacy. In fact, we want to talk with the genders in mind. So, men, this one's for you (don't worry, women; tomorrow is your day).

Here's a little review from Females 101. Maybe you don't need it, but most men can benefit from this fundamental reminder. Women, unlike men, do not separate the physical from the relational and emotional aspects of the relationship. They want an ongoing sense of connection. They want an overarching atmosphere of intimacy and affection built on daily choices. As our friend Kevin Leman says it, "Sex begins in the kitchen." For this reason, it is critically important to communicate in loving ways throughout the day and give your wife special attention.

Your wife is also more vulnerable to distraction when it comes to physical intimacy. If she is fatigued, feeling hurt, or struggling with her body image, she may have difficulty focusing on intimacy. So do your best to minimize distractions by paying attention to what dampens her desires.

There you have it, some fundamental facts about female sexuality that husbands need to keep in mind. But we don't want to stop here. We have a suggestion—for your wife.

We suggest that you, the woman married to this man, help him see the relevance of these fundamental facts to your relationship. You can do this by recalling times when he got it right. No need to point out failures (every husband is keenly aware of those). Now, if you can't think of specifics right now, that's okay. Just keep in mind that what is central to *your* nature when it comes to physical intimacy is not the same for him. So helping him see the relevance of these truths within specific examples will go a long way toward helping your love life become everything you desire.

God intends . . . that the "one flesh" experience should be an expression and a highlighting of the partner's sense that, being given to each other, they now belong together, each meeting the other for completion and wholeness.
—J. I. PACKER

WHAT WOMEN NEED TO KNOW ABOUT MEN

The man and his wife were both naked, but they felt no shame. GENESIS 2:25

AS PROMISED, WOMEN, this one is for you. Just as we pointed out some fundamentals that men need to keep in mind about their wives, we have a similar set of truths for you.

First: men, unlike women, often view making love as a primary way of connecting with their wives. In other words, their patterns of intimacy can stem from an inability to connect in other ways, like conversations and nonsexual touching. For this reason (as well as others) your husband's physical drive may be more apparent than yours. If so, enjoy it as you allow yourselves to tap into your physical desires.

Men are geared more than women for immediate gratification. If he sees you getting ready for a party, he may not be satisfied with a long kiss and a few caresses. You may be thinking about being late or messing up your hair or lipstick, but he loves the excitement of the moment, even if it's brief.

You have undoubtedly noticed that your husband is prone to act on visual cues. So be ready for the unexpected and relish his attraction toward you.

So there you have it, three fundamental facts about men that you need to keep in mind. And just like yesterday, we have a suggestion, this time, for your husband.

As the man married to this woman, help her see the relevance of these three fundamental facts to your relationship. Talk to her about some recent times in your relationship where one of these facts has been apparent to both of you. This will help her underscore how important these are to you as a man. No need to point out failures or mistakes here. The goal is to help her see the relevance of these truths within specific examples of your life. As you do so, you'll both more fully enjoy God's great gift of physical intimacy.

> *[There is a] delusion that sex is an activity when it is primarily a relationship; if the relationship is faulty, the activity cannot long be self-sustaining or truly satisfactory.* —SIDNEY HARRIS

AN ABUNDANCE MENTALITY

If someone has enough money to live well and sees a brother or sister in need but shows no compassion—how can God's love be in that person? 1 JOHN 3:17

IN THE SUMMER OF 2009 at a Trader Joe's store in Menlo Park, California, a woman named Jenni Ware was standing at a checkout counter when she realized she had lost her wallet. Carolee Hazard saw that Ware wasn't going to be able to pay the bill, so she offered up the $207 that Ware needed to buy the items in her cart.

The next day, Hazard received a thank-you card and a check for $300 in the mail. In the card's note, Ware suggested that Hazard use the extra $93 to get a massage. But Hazard felt she needed to do something else with the money. Unable to come up with any good ideas, she turned to her Facebook friends, asking them what she should do with the extra cash. One of her friends suggested she give the money to the Second Harvest Food Bank of Silicon Valley. Hazard liked the idea, so she matched the $93 with her own money and sent in a check to the Second Harvest Bank for $186.

But the giving didn't stop there. After more and more people heard about Hazard's gift, the 93 Dollar Club was born on Facebook. With other donations of $93 (and other amounts as little as $0.93), this grassroots movement, which started out as a simple act to help a stranger, has led to others giving more than $100,000 to help combat hunger.

Here's what we know about generous people: They believe that if they give, they will not run out of resources. They work with what is called an "Abundance Mentality." It's what Stephen Covey was getting at when he used the analogy of Scarcity versus Abundance:

The Scarcity Paradigm	Abundance Paradigm
Defense	Offense
Escape Loss	Pursue the vision
Safety	Risk
Maintain	Create
Fear	Faith
Reactive	Proactive
Win-lose	Win-win
Tight	Generous

Magnanimous people have no vanity or jealousy. They aren't holding back their reserves. Of course, this applies to more than money. It has to do with how we give of ourselves. Talk together about how you can share the joy of generosity. What points of need are you each aware of and drawn to as a couple?

When we refrain from giving, with a scarcity mentality, the little we have will become less. When we give generously, with an abundance mentality, what we give away will multiply. —HENRI NOUWEN

WHO INVITED EGO?

Don't be selfish; don't try to impress others. Be humble, thinking of others as better than yourselves. PHILIPPIANS 2:3

IMAGINE THAT THE TWO OF you have just returned from an amazing vacation—to the Galapagos Islands, let's say—but after the obligatory "How was your trip?" from another couple you know, the conversation turns to them and stays there. They tell you about some new landscaping they're putting in, a conversation they had with their child, or a movie they just saw. They seem oblivious to you and your recent experience—and they are.

How does this happen? How can someone do this? In a word, egoism. Think of this couple as wearing mirrored sunglasses with the lenses flipped around. Everywhere they look they see a reflection of themselves and their own desires. They think they are looking at you, but they aren't. Their egoism pushes them to project feelings and thoughts on to you that have far more to do with their own emotions than yours.[7]

We've all experienced this with other people. And get ready to cringe—other people have probably experienced it with us. It happens. If we are not intentional about looking beyond our own egos, we end up looking at ourselves—and never knowing it. That's the embarrassing calling card of the ego. It doesn't alert us to the fact that it's paying a lengthy visit. If we're not careful, it just shows up unannounced, and we don't give it a second thought. And that's precisely the problem. Wondering how to solve it? We need to routinely keep our egos in check.

As a couple you can help each other, as iron sharpens iron (see Proverbs 27:17). In social settings you can help each other turn the conversation to others. When one of you begins to let ego drive the conversation a bit too long, the other can grab the wheel and put the focus elsewhere.

Can you think of a time when you have done this for each other? Or how about a time when you wish your partner would have done this for you? Talk about a gentle way you can do this for one another the next time you're out together, and see how well it works.

Perhaps middle age is, or should be, a period of shedding shells; the shell of ambition, the shell of material accumulations and possessions, the shell of the ego. —ANNE MORROW LINDBERGH

DOUBLE YOUR SERVE

Let us think of ways to motivate one another to acts of love and good works.

HEBREWS 10:24

GERMAN THEOLOGIAN Dietrich Bonhoeffer wrote a wonderful wedding sermon while he was in prison for his involvement with the anti-Hitler resistance, but he never had a chance to deliver it in person. Here is part of what he wrote:

> *Marriage is more than your love for each other. It has a higher dignity and power, for it is God's holy ordinance. . . . In your love you see only the heaven of your own happiness, but in marriage you are placed at a post of responsibility toward the world and mankind. Your love is your own private possession, but marriage is something more than personal—it is a status, an office. . . . It is marriage . . . that joins you together in the sight of God.*[8]

Have you thought about the "higher dignity and power" of your marriage? Have you thought recently about your marital "post of responsibility" to reach out to the world with your mate, doing good together as two married people transcending yourselves to become part of something larger?

One of the ways we have learned to reach out as a couple is by doing something anonymously, even something small. We call it a mission of service in secret. It is an act of kindness that is concealed from everyone but the two of us, and it helps us conform to the image of Christ.

Marriage is a great means to becoming more like Christ. It is a great means to "motivate one another to acts of love and good works" (Hebrews 10:24). Two people joined in marriage, as Bonhoeffer said, are ordained to serve others as a team. As a partnership, two people can serve other people better than they could as separate individuals. So don't neglect the practice of shared service. And know that when you join your efforts together, you are almost always doubly blessed.

Grief can take care of itself, but to get the full value of a joy, you must have somebody to divide it with. —**MARK TWAIN**

BETTER THAN YOU ARE

If you love only those who love you, what reward is there for that? Even corrupt tax collectors do that much. If you are kind only to your friends, how are you different from anyone else? Even pagans do that. But you are to be perfect, even as your Father in heaven is perfect. MATTHEW 5:46

AS AN AUTHOR, James Michener made his mark in the literary world by producing massive historical novels such as his Pulitzer Prize–winning *Tales of the South Pacific.* Ironically, Michener's style has drawn its strength and beauty from characters fleshed out with extensive genealogy and deep cultural roots, yet Michener himself is a man without a birth certificate. Abandoned as an infant, raised as a foster son in the Michener family headed by a widowed woman, James never knew his biological parents.

Despite his generous spirit and kind nature, Michener's accomplishments raised the ire of one of his adoptive family members who wrote hate-filled, hurtful notes to James whenever his name gained fame. Even after Michener's Pulitzer Prize, this poison-pen writer charged him with besmirching the good Michener name—which he said, "You have no right to use." But the phrase this anonymous hate monger thrust the most deeply under Michener's skin was, "Who do you think you are, trying to be better than you are?"

Michener says that the words of that note were "burned into my soul." But Michener turned the negative power of that question into a life challenge. Michener admitted to missing the nasty letters when his relative presumably died: "He was right in all his accusations." Michener confessed, "I have spent my life trying to be better than I was, and I am a brother to all who share the same aspiration."[9]

How about you? Are you trying to be better than you are? If so, it will be because you are aspiring to be the person God calls you to be. To be better than you are means choosing to love one another even when one of you becomes an uninvited critic. To be better than you are means choosing to become more Christlike. It means having more compassion, more grace, more forgiveness than you feel you are capable of.

Jesus asks a pointed question concerning this issue in the Sermon on the Mount, which is what today's verse is drawn from. We are to "be perfect" in love toward others— all others. How is this possible? Especially when not all others will be perfect in love toward us? Of course, we all struggle and stumble on our path to imitating the Father, but in the process we become better than we are.

To become like Christ is the only thing in the whole world worth caring for, the thing before which every ambition of man is folly, and all lower achievement vain.
—HENRY DRUMMOND

CARPE WHAT?

The thief's purpose is to steal and kill and destroy. My purpose is to give them a rich and satisfying life. JOHN 10:10

TO FIGURE OUT WHAT people do in a typical day, interviewers talked to four thousand Americans. Study participants were asked to split up the prior day into fifteen-minute periods and relive what they did, with whom, and how they felt. These four thousand people were selected to represent every part of the United States, matching census data on age, gender, ethnicity, and so on.

The findings? In a typical day we spend just over 1.7 percent of our time in activities that we personally find to be enjoyable and meaningful. That's just twenty-five minutes per day doing whatever we love: playing with children, listening to music, being in nature, and so on. And the vast majority of us spend nearly 20 percent of every day in unsatisfying activities such as commuting to work or fixing a broken appliance. That leaves 63 percent of our day—and that, according to the study, is spent in between the extremes, passively accepting whatever the day holds.[10] Clearly, the vast majority of us are not waking up and hollering "*carpe diem!*" in the morning. We're not seizing the day; we're all too often letting it seize us. We're not living with passion.

Why is this? Some would say it's that we're stuck in a rut, just trying to make it. We need whatever jobs we're in, and they're consuming our lives. Of course we need to provide for ourselves and our families. But as the years slide by, far too many of us don't so much live as merely exist. We play it safe, rarely venturing outside our emotional comfort zones. We trade passion for security.

So what about the two of you? As you enter this summer season, is your relationship characterized by passivity or boldness? If you were looking in as an outsider on your relationship, where would you say this couple needs to seize the day, and why? Is there something you've been wanting to do together that you could try out this summer?

The tragedy of life is what dies inside a man while he lives. —ALBERT SCHWEITZER

YOU SNOOZE, YOU LOSE?

In peace I will lie down and sleep, for you alone, O LORD, will keep me safe. PSALM 4:8

WE WERE HAVING DINNER with another couple, a very busy couple in the middle of launching their own business, when the subject of sleep came up. They were burning the proverbial candle at both ends. "We just don't have time to sleep," the husband said.

Wow! That's quite a claim, don't you think? After all, we all need our sleep—we can't function without it. But his statement got us thinking. As a busy couple ourselves, we've had plenty of late nights followed by early mornings. It seems every couple has a season or two when sleep suffers, and we're all in search of a secret for getting more done while remaining rested. In fact, the search for that elusive balance has been going on for centuries.

Leonardo da Vinci would bite his tongue to fend off fatigue, and he would sleep fifteen minutes every four hours for a grand total of an hour and a half a day. The painter Salvador Dalí napped sitting with a spoon in his hand and a tin plate at his feet so that the moment he was overtaken by deep slumber, the spoon would fall, clatter, and awaken him refreshed. Dustin Hoffman used to jump rope for twenty minutes whenever his eyelids sagged. Charles Lindbergh said he spoke with ghosts over the Atlantic in order to make his historic thirty-three-hour solo flight between New York and Paris.

Did these accomplished men find the secret to wringing more life out of life? Cornell psychology professor James Maas is among a growing number of sleep experts who worry that most of us spend our days desperately in need of a good night's sleep. In his book *Power Sleep*, Maas claims sleep deprivation has become a crisis. Here's how he says you can tell if you're sleep deprived: If you need an alarm clock to wake up, if you fall asleep during the day, and if you fall asleep soon after your head hits the pillow (it should take you at least fifteen minutes).

But here's the good news. It turns out that married couples can help one another have a better night's rest. How? By incorporating two simple rituals into their pillow talk: a tender touch and a kind word. It seems these two behaviors will set your minds for emotional safety and sweet slumber. And while the researchers didn't explore it, we have a pretty good hunch that a little prayer between husband and wife wouldn't hurt either.

You may want to pose a simple question to one another right now: how rested do you feel most mornings on a scale of one to ten? Then talk about what you can do for each other to create more restful nights in the future.

 I love that you are the last person I want to talk to before I go to sleep at night.
—WHEN HARRY MET SALLY

LESSONS OF AN INTRUDER

A third time he asked him, "Simon son of John, do you love me?" Peter was hurt that Jesus asked the question a third time. He said, "Lord, you know everything. You know that I love you." Jesus said, "Then feed my sheep." JOHN 21:17

DICK PETERSON called it "the intruder." And it was a fitting name for the multiple sclerosis that was invading his wife's body, as well as their marriage. He knew that his marriage to Elizabeth was about to be stretched to the max. What he didn't know was how many life-changing lessons he would learn along the way—lessons about practicing Christ's love.

> *"Her disease became my disease," he writes. "As she moved from cane to walker to electric scooter and finally to a powered wheelchair, then lost use of her right hand, I had to adjust my life to fit her needs. . . . We do have the choice to let it tear us apart or use it to strengthen our marriage bond as we face the adversity together. . . . It reaches to feelings, emotions, and attitudes about what we do, what's done to us, and who we are to ourselves and each other."[11]*

Do they pray for healing? Of course. They agonize before God for Elizabeth's health to return. Their hearts long for the days when she could offer a tender touch with her fingers instead of a permanently clenched fist. "But if we only grieve the loss," he says, "we miss the gain—that what this disease does to us may also be done for us. Even as the MS steals abilities from Elizabeth's life, a healing grows almost undetected inside. When we talk about this, Elizabeth wonders aloud, 'Did it really take this to teach me that my soul is more important to God than my body?'"

At the same time, Dick is asking,

> *Is this what Jesus meant when he taught his disciples to serve? When he washed their feet, did he look 2,000 years into the future and see me washing my wife's clothes and helping her onto her shower seat to bathe? Did it really take this to teach me compassion? God's healing can be sneaky. We pray that Elizabeth will resume her old life; he wants her to assume a new life. We long for change on the outside; he desires change on the inside. We pray for what we want; he answers with what he knows we need. [God] has made me question whom it is I love. When I pray for healing, is it for Elizabeth? Or is it because her healing would make life so much easier for me? I challenge, "Aren't you the God who heals? I love her and I want her well." But in the back of my mind I know I also want her healed for me.*

In response to this challenge, Jesus asks Dick as he asked Peter, "Do you love me more than these?" Dick's response: "I think He wants me to love him more than my wife. So I reply with Peter's words, 'Yes, Lord. You know that I love you.'"

Lord, grant that I might not so much seek . . . to be loved as to love.
—ST. FRANCIS OF ASSISI

THE GREAT COMPROMISE

Pride leads to disgrace, but with humility comes wisdom. PROVERBS 11:2

IT'S A POPULAR IDIOM to communicate the idea that if people don't do what you want, they need to change: "It's my way or the highway." Ever felt like that? Of course you have. If we are honest, we have all had times when we wanted something done our way while our spouses wanted it done another.

Make way for compromise. Not one of my favorite words. I (Leslie) view compromise in much the same way I view such things as sit-ups and checkbook balancing: necessary but evil.

Some people start out marriage with the belief that they shouldn't have to compromise because they should agree on everything. That's because during courtship they *seem* to agree on everything, and that seems to be the goal. But over time, different needs and issues are brought to bear on the committed relationship, and some disagreement about how to meet those needs and deal with those issues is inevitable. And if a husband and wife don't learn to eat a little humble pie and make some compromises now and then, they might as well give up. Marriage cannot survive without compromise.

Arriving at a mutually pleasing compromise doesn't just solve the immediate, specific problem of the conflict itself; it also ushers in a spirit of humility to the marriage. You see, selfish pride is the primary barrier to compromise in marriage. So by default, when we compromise, humility is infused into the relationship. No wonder the book of Proverbs states that when pride enters the picture it's a disgrace, but humility cultivates wisdom.

In the next few hours think about one way you could infuse your relationship with a spirit of humility and a willingness to compromise. How can you honor a specific desire of your spouse's that you do not share?[12]

> *For everything you have missed, you have gained something else; and for everything you gain, you lose something.* —RALPH WALDO EMERSON

WHAT A MEAL CAN MEAN TO MARRIAGE

Let your conversation be always full of grace, seasoned with salt. COLOSSIANS 4:6, NIV

"PASS THE CORN."

"Where's the salt?"

"Move over."

"Do you have to chew your ice so loud?"

These are just a few of the common utterances around most family dinner tables. Pleasant, huh? And too bad. Mealtime offers one of the best opportunities for human connection and companionship—especially for couples. Culinary writer M. F. K. Fisher is known for saying, "Sharing food with another human being is an intimate act that should not be indulged in lightly."

The writer of Proverbs would certainly share Ms. Fisher's sentiment. You can have a dinner table with every delectable delicacy and the bounty of each season, but if the emotional tone around the table hangs heavy with unpleasantness, you might as well be eating leftover pizza from somebody else's party: "Better a dry crust with peace and quiet than a house full of feasting, with strife" (Proverbs 17:1, NIV).

Think about it. The usual scenario is that two people reunite at dinnertime and grouse to each other about the events of their day: "Traffic was terrible on the way home tonight." "Did you pick up my dry cleaning?" "Your mother called again." "I need the car tonight." Or, even worse, they flip on the television and eat without saying a word.

If you want to reclaim table time with your spouse, make it pleasant—make it a time both of you look forward to. You don't have to cook like Julia Child or set a table like Martha Stewart to make mealtimes pleasurable. What matters most is the focus of your conversation. So tonight, whatever is on the menu, remember to let your conversation at the table be well seasoned with grace.[13]

A smiling face is half the meal. —**LATVIAN PROVERB**

BECOMING EACH OTHER'S SCULPTOR

This means that anyone who belongs to Christ has become a new person. The old life is gone; a new life has begun! 2 CORINTHIANS 5:17

AT A RENOWNED MUSEUM IN Florence, Italy, you will find four partially finished sculptures. Michelangelo originally intended each of them to be used on the tomb of Pope Julius, but midway through the project he decided not to use them and ceased his work. There is a hand protruding here, a torso of a man there, a leg, part of a head. None is finished.

Stand in this great hall, looking at these fragmentary figures, and you will sense the turmoil, the struggle embodied in these stones. It's as though the figures are crying to break free from the prison of the marble to become what they were intended to be.

Michelangelo called them *The Captives.* Study them for a time, and they are certain to stir up within you a deep longing to be completed, yourself. They are bound to bring more consciously into your awareness the ache in your soul to be free from that which imprisons or inhibits your wholeness.

This is a universal longing we humans share—to grow, to mature, to become complete, and to fulfill our destinies. But sometimes, like Michelangelo's captive statues, we are frozen in our efforts to realize who we were really meant to be.

But here's the good news. In a loving relationship in which two people are doing their best to serve God, we become, to some degree, each other's sculptors. It is God who does the work, but he allows us to hold the tools: not chisels, but words and actions. And as we prayerfully consider what God is helping our spouses to become, we can help them to break free of the captivity of their old selves to become new creations. As Michelangelo said of one of his efforts: "I saw the angel in the marble and carved until I set him free."

How can you support your spouse on a journey toward becoming free to be his or her best self?

The greater danger for most of us lies not in setting our aim too high and falling short; but in setting our aim too low, and achieving our mark. . . . Lord, grant that I may always desire more than I can accomplish. —MICHELANGELO

TWO ARE BETTER THAN ONE

Two people are better off than one, for they can help each other succeed.

ECCLESIASTES 4:9

BECAUSE OF THE WORK WE do with engaged couples, we get a lot of wedding invitations. And we attend a lot of weddings. Sometimes we feel like we have seen or heard of everything you could possibly do to make a wedding ceremony memorable and special. But not long ago we discovered something we had never seen before, and it impressed us.

You have probably seen the use of a unity candle where a couple joins two individual candle flames together to light a larger candle symbolizing their union. Well, in this case, the symbolism went much deeper. Our friends Jim and Jeannette wanted something that would express their trust and dependence on God in their marriage, so they came up with what they called the "unity cord."

In front of the congregation, they braided three cords together symbolizing the powerful strength of their marriage when they lean not on their own understanding but on the wisdom of God. The three separate cords represented the three participants in this lifelong union—Jim, Jeannette, and God's Son, Jesus Christ. By the braiding of these three cords, Jim and Jeannette visually illustrated their new oneness, intricately interwoven and strengthened by their love of God. The minister explained that the new, braided cord was far stronger than either of the individual cords representing Jim and Jeannette. He then read Ecclesiastes 4:9-12:

> *Two people are better off than one, for they can help each other succeed. If one person falls, the other can reach out and help. But someone who falls alone is in real trouble. Likewise, two people lying close together can keep each other warm. But how can one be warm alone? A person standing alone can be attacked and defeated, but two can stand back-to-back and conquer. Three are even better, for a triple-braided cord is not easily broken.*

When we acknowledge God's presence in our marriages, we are braiding our marriage with the strength of God's power. Think about your marriage in view of that image. Is it tightly woven, or has it come loose? Either way, pray today that God would tighten and strengthen the cord.

What is a friend? A single soul dwelling in two bodies. —ARISTOTLE

SHAKE IT UP

What sorrow awaits you who lounge in luxury in Jerusalem, and you who feel secure in Samaria! AMOS 6:1

WE WERE ATTENDING A conference on spiritual formation when the workshop leader asked this question: If you were doomed to live the same life over and over again for eternity, would you choose the life you are living now?

Wow! That will get you to ponder your life, don't you think? And it's sure to get you questioning the lethal attitude of complacency—that smug satisfaction that settles into low expectations and inaction.

Complacency seeps into the crevices of a marriage without anyone knowing. After so many years of the same old routine, a once-vibrant marriage slowly evolves into a stale relationship of the ho-hum. In its most toxic form, complacency becomes listless indifference, and it can kill a marriage. Referring to its depreciating effect on Christianity, Archbishop Richard Whately said that indifference "is a more insidious and less curable evil than infidelity itself." And it has that effect on the institution of marriage as well as the institution of the church.

It is because complacency is such a great enemy of the human spirit that the writers of the book of Proverbs have a lot to say about it. For example, Proverbs 27:23 says that the wise person is always on the lookout for early signs that entropy is setting in: "Know the state of your flocks, and put your heart into caring for your herds."

So how does a couple protect themselves against the cancer of complacency? With vision. Take a look around. Do you know of any couple who works at crafting a vision for their future that has fallen prey to complacency? Of course not. It's an impossibility. Once you take time to explore your future as a couple, you inoculate yourselves against indifference. You are taking action to create a life together that complacency cannot penetrate. So take a moment and ask yourselves what you want to have accomplished as a couple three months from now. One year from now. In a decade. Consider how you would like to improve such areas as communication, intimacy, financial management, outside relationships, traditions for holidays, spirituality, and so on. Then take your plans to the Lord and ask for his guidance as you consider how to spend the time he has given you together.

I hate to see complacency prevail in our lives when it's so directly contrary to the teaching of Christ. —JIMMY CARTER

HOW MUCH MONEY DO YOU NEED?

You have planted much but harvest little. You eat but are not satisfied. You drink but are still thirsty. You put on clothes but cannot keep warm. Your wages disappear as though you were putting them in pockets filled with holes! HAGGAI 1:6

DO YOU HAVE ENOUGH MONEY? Think about your answer. If not, would another 20 percent more income do the trick for you two? Would you then be satisfied?

No matter how much a couple has, they almost always believe a little bit more would be just enough. In fact, studies have shown that most couples believe they would be happier if their income were 20 percent higher. Of course, 20 percent more will never satisfy, at least not for long. As our increases are absorbed into the living standard, expectations rise and the cycle needs repeating.

Above a certain subsistence level, which varies with the life stage of each couple, happiness in marriage depends not on the quantity of money but on the quality of the relationship. And this is true at all stages of life: for richer, for poorer. That's why this passage from the Old Testament book of Haggai urges us to consider whether we will ever have enough. The writer of Ecclesiastes agrees: "Better to have one handful with quietness than two handfuls with hard work and chasing the wind" (Ecclesiastes 4:6; see also Proverbs 15:17; 17:1).

So whether you are living in a one-bedroom apartment and praying that your monthly income will outlast the month, or like Rockefeller you'll consider your wealth sufficient when you have "just one dollar more," remember these wise words: "Don't wear yourself out trying to get rich. Be wise enough to know when to quit. In the blink of an eye wealth disappears, for it will sprout wings and fly away like an eagle" (Proverbs 23:4-5). It is far more rewarding to put your hope in God, "who richly gives us all we need for our enjoyment" (1 Timothy 6:17).

Money never made a man happy yet, nor will it. . . . The more a man has, the more he wants. Instead of filling a vacuum, it makes one. —DAVID ALFRED DOUDNEY

LETTING GO

Since we are surrounded by such a huge crowd of witnesses to the life of faith, let us strip off every weight that slows us down, especially the sin that so easily trips us up. And let us run with endurance the race God has set before us. HEBREWS 12:1

MAYBE YOU'VE HEARD OF the strategy. It's clever. And it always works. In parts of India and Africa that are overrun with monkeys, officials control the monkey population by employing the help of professional monkey catchers. But the best part is that the catchers actually allow the monkeys to catch themselves.

Here's how it's done. The catcher hollows out a gourd no bigger than a basketball and cuts an opening in the gourd about the size of a silver dollar. He then carries the gourd to an area frequented by monkeys. He holds up the gourd above his head for all the monkeys to see before placing it on the ground in an open area near a tree. He then tethers the gourd, tying it so that its movement is restricted and so it can't be carried off.

The monkey catcher then walks over to a banana tree and selects a banana in plain view of the monkeys. He holds it high above his head for all the monkeys to see. He walks back and places it inside the gourd. Next, he walks back several paces out of view from the monkeys.

What happens next is rather startling. One of the curious monkeys will come over to the gourd, examine it, give it a push, and check out the banana within. Now, there are bananas all around, all easily obtainable. But this curious monkey wants *that* banana. He easily puts his hand into the small opening of the gourd, and he can easily take it back out—as long as he is not grasping the banana. But as long as the monkey holds onto the banana, he's stuck. His tight fist around the banana keeps him trapped.

You would think the monkey would simply let go so he could be free, but he doesn't. He holds onto what he wants. He makes noises, jumps around, and shakes the gourd, but he won't release his grip, making it easy for the catcher to catch him. The monkey could have had all the bananas he could eat hanging on trees, but he gets it in his head that he's got to have that solitary banana in the gourd. And he won't let go of it, literally.

We can all act like a monkey in this regard, can't we? So we ask a simple question today: What are each of you holding too tightly? What has a grip on you as much as you have a grip on it? And more importantly, what can you do to loosen your clinched fist and release it to God?

 The greatness of a man's power is the measure of his surrender. —WILLIAM BOOTH

SLOW FOOD

A bowl of vegetables with someone you love is better than steak with someone you hate. PROVERBS 15:17

WE GOT MARRIED IN CHICAGO ON JUNE 30, 1984. Since then we've done our best to celebrate this important anniversary in a variety of ways, sometimes with others but mostly on our own. But no matter where we are or what we're doing, the celebration seems to eventually center around food—especially on our twentieth anniversary.

We marked the milestone, as many couples do on their anniversaries, with a fancy meal—just the two of us. But this was like no meal we had ever experienced before. We arrived at the five-star Herbfarm in the foothills of the Cascade Mountains at six, and the meal did not end until well after eleven. No entertainment, no interludes, just five leisurely hours of a nine-course meal. Occasionally we'd take a walk around the gardens in between courses, but most of our time was spent talking about anything and everything that came to mind. Talk about having time to let your souls catch up! With our two boys safe at home with a babysitter, we relished the slow pace of the evening. We basked in the time we had with no agenda other than to be together.

Granted, this is not the kind of meal we'd want all the time. It was highly unusual, to say the least. But it underscored for us the value "slow food" brings to our relationship. Truth is, a slow approach to food strengthens any relationship. There is something in the nature of eating together that forms a bond between people. As Carl Honoré points out in his book *In Praise of Slowness*, "It is no accident that the word 'companion' is derived from the Latin words meaning 'with bread.'"[14]

Meals become meaningful when we share them with our partners in a "slow" way, in a way that allows our spirits to relax and makes us more loving. It's what caused famed playwright Oscar Wilde to say, "After a good dinner one can forgive anybody, even one's own relations." If that's not enough encouragement to eat well together, what is?

It's not really about what you eat, of course—or even eating, period. Find a way to create a relaxed moment to unite your spirits today, whether it's a slow meal or a lazy moment of conversation.

Nothing would be more tiresome than eating or drinking if God had not made them a pleasure as well as a necessity. —VOLTAIRE

THE NEW LUXURY OF SLEEP

Two people lying close together can keep each other warm. ECCLESIASTES 4:11

NOT SO MANY YEARS AGO, women's magazines encouraged readers to set the alarm half an hour earlier in order to find quiet time alone or to get more done. Dark raccoon circles under your eyes from too many short nights? Not to worry. The solution became, not more sleep, but artfully applied makeup known as "concealer." Now the same publications are running headlines touting the value of sleep.

It seems sleep is in. It's the new luxury—for those who have the time.

Capitalizing on the changing attitudes toward sleep, the Sealy Company is spending an estimated $20 million on print and television ads to emphasize the value of a good night's sleep. It also wants to change its image from being a mattress company to that of a "sleep wellness provider."

In many hotels, sleep has become the new status symbol. Westin advertises a "Heavenly Bed," offering "layers of comfort and relaxation." And certain Hilton Hotels feature "Sleep-Tight" rooms, complete with soundproofing, special drapes, and other sleep aids. A special promotion allowed guests in those rooms to even take their pillows home with them. And the corporate world also is beginning to catch on. A handful of companies now provide nap rooms, recognizing that a midday snooze can improve a worker's alertness.

Truth be told, however, in marriage the perfect bed is not simply about sheets and pillows. It's about the relationship of the husband and wife who sleep on them. It's about the tone they set in the late night hours as they are dozing off to sleep, side by side. More important than the quality of the linens is the quality of the relationship. And the time we spend as a couple in bed talking about the residue of the day and our plans for tomorrow, our pillow talk, becomes some of the most important and precious moments in marriage.

The time you have for pillow talk—when you are by nature slowing down, breathing more deeply, and relaxing your muscles—should never be taken for granted. It's too good an opportunity to be let go unnoticed. Did you know your pillow talk can dramatically determine your dreams? It can also influence how well you sleep and how you feel when you wake up in the morning. So don't waste this time. Before you hit the hay tonight, take a moment to savor the change in your pace. Notice your body's desire to lean into this antidote to stress and hurry. In a relaxed way, talk to each other about your busy day. What was your high and low? And check in with each other on how you can pray for the upcoming day.

Savor the time before you fall asleep. It's the perfect time to rejoin your spirits.

 } *Sleep is the golden chain that ties health and our bodies together.* —**THOMAS DEKKER**

CREATING A MARRIAGE

[Jesus] said, "This explains why a man leaves his father and mother and is joined to his wife, and the two are united into one." MATTHEW 19:5

TWO DAYS AFTER OUR WEDDING, Les and I were nestled into a cottage, surrounded by towering timbers along the picturesque Oregon Coast. A few miles to the south were the famous coastal sand dunes where we planned to ride horses later that week. And up the coast was a quaint harbor village where we thought we might spend another day leisurely looking at shops and eating our dinner by candlelight in a rustic inn some friends recommended. Other than that, we had nothing on our itinerary for the next five days except enjoying the beach and each other, rain or shine.

We couldn't have dreamed up a better scenario for our honeymoon—not that everything was perfect. We accidentally locked ourselves out of our rental car on day two, and Les offered to walk to the nearest filling station while I waited at the cabin. I wanted to go along.

"Are you sure?" he asked. "It might rain."

"It'll be fun. Let's go."

We walked and talked the two or three miles to find a pay phone, where we made arrangements for a locksmith to take us back to our car. Sitting on a curb, we waited, saying nothing, while a couple of seagulls chatted it up overhead. Les was fiddling with a stick he'd picked up on our walk, when I realized several minutes had passed without our having said a word. It was an easy stillness, a kind of eloquent voicelessness, in which we were content not to talk.

I think it was there and then, quietly sitting on a curb next to a phone booth under a cloudy sky, that the thought hit me: I had captured true love. The thing I'd been seeking ever since I was old enough to know it could be sought was now in my possession. I had married a man who loved me deeply, just as I loved him. We had committed ourselves to love together, forever. Love's ethereal mysteries were now unfolding before my very eyes, its elusive qualities fading. While I stood by doing nothing, love was enveloping my being.

I'm not talking about the dizzying, starry-eyed early stage of a relationship; Les and I had dated for nearly seven years before we found ourselves married and honeymooning on the Oregon Coast. The love I experienced that day was clear eyed and grounded. There was no sunset on the horizon, no piped-in background music. This was reality and I was simply taking it in, relishing the silence and stillness of having no other purpose than that of being together. Husband and wife.

Think about the marriage you have created, and relish the good.

A successful marriage requires falling in love many times, always with the same person.
—MIGNON MCLAUGHLIN

PERFECT PEACE?

You will keep in perfect peace all who trust in you, all whose thoughts are fixed on you! Trust in the LORD always, for the LORD GOD is the eternal Rock. ISAIAH 26:3-4

PERHAPS YOU'VE HEARD about a king who was building a new palace and wanted his main entrance hall to be decorated with a large painting. Because he saw his kingdom as a peaceful land, the king decided that the painting best representing peace would win the honored place.

Naturally, hundreds of paintings were submitted for consideration, and the king spent the next few months eliminating all but the best two. Before announcing the winner, he hung both paintings in the palace for public viewing.

The first painting was of an undoubtedly peaceful scene. It featured a majestic mountain lake so perfectly still that the landscape behind it was mirrored in its reflection. The sky, too, was idyllic: brilliant blue, with fluffy clouds floating above. Around the lake were beautiful wildflowers and a calmly grazing family of deer in the distance.

The second painting also portrayed a mountain scene, but of a dramatically different character. It featured a cliff, rugged and strong. A few small trees grew out of the cracks in the face of the cliff, with gnarled roots clinging for life. A waterfall crashed violently down the cliff and into the misty abyss. The clouds looming over this landscape were dark and ominous, and in the distance lightning flashed. Halfway up the cliff grew a small bush. In its branches, a bird sat in a nest, warming her eggs.

After several weeks, the king declared the second painting the winner. Surprised, the people asked the king to explain his decision. He said, "Peace is not the absence of conflict. Peace is a state of mind. Those who experience peace have clarity and calm even when turmoil surrounds them."

So how about the two of you? Which painting would you have chosen? What is your vision of a peaceful life? You've probably heard of the political doctrine of achieving "peace through strength." But for God followers, it's the other way around: strength through peace. When you are feeling your weakest, when you are broken and frail, God promises to keep you in "perfect peace" when your mind is focused on him. Why? Because as the prophet Isaiah said, God is the Rock eternal. God is your strength.

In what specific ways do you need God to be your strength this week? What about your spouse? Pray for each other to "trust in the LORD always."

 Peace is not something you wish for; it's something you make, something you do, something you are, and something you give away! —ROBERT FULGHUM

SWEET LAND OF LIBERTY

Don't copy the behavior and customs of this world, but let God transform you into a new person by changing the way you think. ROMANS 12:2

AFTER THE BATTLES OF LEXINGTON and Concord, the second Continental Congress realized that the possibility of reconciliation with Great Britain was fading fast. They debated the issues and then appointed Thomas Jefferson and a committee to write a document that declared their independence. After two weeks of writing, and with minor changes by Benjamin Franklin and John Adams, they signed it, all fifty-six members.

Several defiant expressions of freedom were expressed in the process, including John Hancock's signature, which was large enough for King George III to read without his spectacles. But perhaps the most dramatic symbol of freedom came in the ringing of a bell: the Liberty Bell. The famously cracked bell is no longer rung, but it is still revered as a powerful, if silent, voice of freedom. And it is enshrined for all to see with this silent message from the Bible engraved across its face: "Proclaim liberty throughout all the land unto all the inhabitants thereof" (Leviticus 25:10, KJV).

On this birthday of the United States, as we celebrate our political liberty as a nation, it is also good to think of our spiritual liberty as couples. That reminder comes when the bell of spiritual freedom rings in the collective soul of a couple. How? Perhaps the apostle Paul had something like this in mind when he said in today's verse, "Don't copy the behavior and customs of this world, but let God transform you into a new person by changing the way you think."

The mind is the place of residence for our attitudes. It is also the central power station for making decisions. And it needs renewing every day. Our minds set us free by our faith or hold us captive by our doubts. And the best way to ring the bell of liberty that resides in the mind is to choose to let God transform your mind daily.

Is there something in your relationship with your spouse that needs renewal? Something that keeps you from being free? As you focus on spiritual renewal, think about how transforming the way you think today can give you greater freedom in your marriage.

Liberty is always dangerous, but it is the safest thing we have.
—HARRY EMERSON FOSDICK

HELPING EACH OTHER HEAL

Each heart knows its own bitterness, and no one else can fully share its joy.

PROVERBS 14:10

ON MY (LESLIE'S) PARENTS' thirty-fifth wedding anniversary, our family suffered a meltdown.

Dad was a well-liked pastor, low key and hardworking. Under his leadership, congregations grew and deepened their faith. His ministry was marked by serenity, a rich investment in relationships, and a nonflashy style of teaching and preaching. But after what must have been a strained and eerie anniversary dinner, Dad told Mom a secret he had been keeping for months, disclosing a decision no one would have predicted. After thirty-five years of marriage and ministry, he was calling it quits. Dad was having an affair, and he didn't want it to end. The next day he turned in his ministerial credentials, moved in with his secretary, and walked away from his former life.

Devastated, Mom was left alone to pick up the pieces. Though in fragile health with severe diabetes, she had always been faithful, invested in her marriage, and obedient to God. She had been a committed partner in ministry and never imagined that adultery would shatter her world.

Neither did I. Disbelief and shock are the only words to describe the reaction Les and I had to the news. Our shock turned into anger, followed quickly by concern for my mother's survival. She had lost her marriage, the parsonage, her income—everything.

The crisis consumed me. I could think of nothing else. We went on with our lives, teaching, writing, grocery shopping, watching television, crawling into bed at night, but what had happened would not leave my mind. *How could Dad leave?* I asked again and again. *This goes against everything he ever taught me! Doesn't he see the incongruity of his decision?* Questions like these pummeled my mind. One day I cried for eight hours without stopping. That was several years ago, and even today the healing is not complete; on occasion the same questions pierce my stillness, and the tears flow freely.

Les never had to ask me what I was thinking; he knew. He patiently listened to expressions of my breaking heart. He absorbed every painful and ugly feeling he could. Even months later, when there were days as dark and tearful as the first one, or when I just couldn't decorate our home for Christmas because of painful memories, he never panicked or demanded that I pull myself together. He held me gently, listened, and gave me comfort.

No matter how caring Les was, I still felt alone. He can never fully know the pain of my heart. "Each heart knows its own bitterness." But given time, marriage cuts our personal pain in half. And even when it seemed impractical and indulgent, Les gave me time to heal. This gift brought a balm of understanding to my spirit.

In times of pain, remember that you can be a gift of healing to one another.

 Healing rain is a real touch from God. —MICHAEL W. SMITH

FISHING FOR A COMPLIMENT?

Kind words are like honey—sweet to the soul and healthy for the body. PROVERBS 16:24

A PRAIRIE HOME COMPANION WITH Garrison Keillor debuted as an old-style variety show before a live audience on July 6, 1974. The show is known for its traditional folk music and its tongue-in-cheek radio dramas. But many people seem to enjoy best Keillor's storytelling segment, "News from Lake Wobegon." There's a good example printed in Keillor's book *We Are Still Married*:

> The town ball club was the Lake Wobegon Schroeders, so named because the starting nine were brothers, sons of E. J. Schroeder. E. J. was ticked if a boy hit a bad pitch. He'd spit and curse and rail at him. And if a son hit a homerun, E. J. would say, "Blind man coulda hit that one. Your gramma coulda put the wood on that one. If a guy couldn't hit that one, there'd be something wrong with him, I'd say. Wind practically took that one out of here, didn't even need to hit it much"—and lean over and spit. . . .
>
> So his sons could never please him, and if they did, he forgot about it. Once, against Freeport, his oldest boy, Edwin Jim, Jr., turned and ran to the centerfield fence for a long long long fly ball and threw his glove forty feet in the air to snag the ball and caught the ball and glove and turned toward the dugout to see if his dad had seen it, and E. J. was on his feet clapping, but when he saw the boy look to him, he immediately pretended he was swatting mosquitoes. The batter was called out, the third out. Jim ran back to the bench and stood by his dad. E. J. sat chewing in silence and finally said, "I saw a man in Superior, Wisconsin, do that a long time ago but he did it at night and the ball was hit a lot harder."[1]

Some people, like poor E.J., pull back their compliments because they harbor an irrational fear of making someone feel better than he or she should. It's a fear, of course, that eventually makes them very lonely. And, sadly, it's a fear that even appears among couples. As Kin Hubbard says, "Some folks pay a compliment like they went down in their pocket for it." Don't let that happen in your relationship. Be as generous as you can with compliments—as long as they're coming from a genuine heart.

There is no effect more disproportionate to its cause than the happiness bestowed by a small compliment. —ROBERT BRAULT

FIFTY YEARS AND COUNTING?

A house is built by wisdom and becomes strong through good sense. Through knowledge its rooms are filled with all sorts of precious riches and valuables. PROVERBS 24:3-4

OUR FAMILY GATHERED AROUND a large circular table in an elegant restaurant that has unofficially become the backdrop for many of our most meaningful family celebrations. For literally decades, my (Les's) family has gathered here from around the country to mark holidays, birthdays, graduations, promotions, and farewells. But this time was different. The dinner was a celebration of Mom and Dad's wedding anniversary on July 7—their fiftieth.

They didn't want a big party. This celebration was strictly a family affair. The food, as always, was exquisite. The anniversary cake was lovely. The presents were nice, but what gift could be worthy of such a noble occasion? What impressed me most about the entire event wasn't tangible; it was something my father said. We had just offered grace and thanked God for the family and the many years Mom and Dad had lived together. Then, before picking up his fork, he looked around the table and said: "I can't believe it has been fifty years! The time is so short!"

The rest of the meal was devoted to reminiscing. Mom talked about the times when each of her three sons was born. She could describe in detail the various homes we had lived in. Dad talked about the churches and colleges he and mom had served. There was the first pastorate they took during the Korean War, and the transition to being a college president during the Middle East oil crisis. They both reminisced about their first trip to London and many other journeys around the globe. They must certainly have had some hard times, like all married couples do, but all they seemed to remember were things they enjoyed together. What a contrast it was to the last anniversary Leslie's parents celebrated.

It made us think a lot about our own marriage, short in comparison to Mom and Dad's fifty years. What will we reminisce about after that long? Have you ever asked yourself the same question? After fifty years, what memorable treasures will your house of love include?

 } *To love is to receive a glimpse of heaven.* —KAREN SUNDE

SHAPING ETERNITY

Those who are wise will shine as bright as the sky, and those who lead many to righteousness will shine like the stars forever. DANIEL 12:3

WE HAVE BEEN TEACHING relationship courses at the university level for nearly two decades, and if there's one thing that this experience has taught us, it is this: If you want to learn something, teach it. It's an age-old adage that we're reminded of nearly every time we finish a lecture.

Have you discovered this insight? If you're a teacher, you surely have! Once you try to effectively convey principles or skills to someone else, you realize you have to become expert in those principles and skills yourself. If you want to help another couple manage conflict more effectively, for example, you can't help but improve this aspect of your own relationship. Perhaps this is why today's verse from Daniel notes that those who lead others to righteousness shine like the stars.

Have you considered teaching together as a couple? You don't have to have a teaching position or be widely read or even published in order to "teach." If you have a solid marriage and the willingness to share your own struggles and successes as a couple, you have what it takes to make a difference in another couple's lives. And that difference doesn't necessarily have to be made in the traditional classroom. It may come in the form of marriage mentoring, where you meet couple to couple. If you do, you're sure to experience a boomerang effect that blesses you every bit as much as you're blessing another couple.

Is there anyone whom the two of you could mentor together? Your willingness to walk alongside another couple is likely to shape eternity. As Henry Adams said: "A teacher affects eternity; he can never tell where his influence stops." Or maybe you're at a stage at which you could really benefit from another couple's mentoring you. Is there anyone you could ask? Your own "eternity" might be shaped by the influence of someone you know. Give it some thought.

Teaching is leaving a vestige of oneself in the development of another. And surely the student is a bank where you can deposit your most precious treasures.
—EUGENE P. BERTIN

A KIND WORD

An anxious heart weighs a man down, but a kind word cheers him up.

PROVERBS 12:25, NIV

PEOPLE ROUTINELY UNDERESTIMATE the importance of their relationship's "small talk," those little, unmemorable things we say to one another in the course of a day. It's easy to miss the opportunities we have in those casual moments to speak kindly to one another. And though they could stand to benefit the most from speaking kindly to one another, spouses are no exception.

We're not talking about elaborate praise or a heartfelt poem, as wonderful as those things are. We're talking about simple, everyday kindness in conversation. Kind expressions, such as, "Thanks," "You're great," or "I missed you today." So often we take it for granted that our spouses know we appreciate them, but those little words of encouragement make a big impact.

"The small day-to-day things you say are more important than any of the overarching communication issues," says Clifford Notarius, author of *We Can Work It Out*. Most marriage experts agree. Thomas Holman, a professor of family sciences at Brigham Young University who studies ways to increase marital quality, has found that making time for small talk is at least as important to couples' happiness as agreement on values and role expectations, demographic similarities, emotional health, or parents' marriage success.

When a couple is just sitting around talking, one of the things they are saying is, "You are important enough to me just to sit here with you." It's what Dr. Holman calls a "Maxwell House moment" because it is the kind of casual exchange that usually takes place over a cup of coffee. The subject isn't relevant; it's the kindness of the words expressed that matters.

Do you and your spouse just sit together talking like that from time to time? You might try it today. And the next time your spouse has a heavy heart, remember the wise words of today's verse. You don't have to throw a party, buy presents, or hire a clown. All you need is a kind word.

Those who loved you, and were helped by you, will remember you when forget-me-nots are withered. Carve your name on hearts, and not on marble.
—**CHARLES H. SPURGEON**

WHAT'S YOUR METAMOOD?

Even if we feel guilty, God is greater than our feelings, and he knows everything.

1 JOHN 3:20

SCIENTISTS CALL IT "METAMOOD": an awareness of one's own mood, or the ability to pull back and recognize what one is feeling as anger, sorrow, shame, or whatever emotion is foremost. It's a difficult skill because our emotions so often appear in disguise. A person in mourning may know she is sad, but she may not recognize that she is also angry at the person for dying—because this seems somehow inappropriate. A parent who yells at the child who ran into the street is expressing anger at disobedience, but the degree of anger may owe more to the fear the parent feels at what could have happened. The boss who feels attacked by an employee's question about a new policy may be completely unaware that the innocent question seems aggressive to him only because his father used to ask the same kinds of things to point out his shortcomings.

Not recognizing how we really feel is one of the most troubling blind spots we have as human beings and one of the most common causes of interpersonal conflict. When we don't see how we really feel, our emotions start to manage us rather than the other way around. We begin to mask our emotions, and that simply puts off solving one problem and usually creates another one. For example, you may be ticked off at your spouse, who is late to meet you at an appointed time, and that's one problem. But if anger is too threatening for some reason, you simply smile and ignore your churning stomach. Later that evening, you find yourself snapping at your spouse for no good reason at all. *Where did that come from?* you both wonder. And that may develop into a new problem.

When we don't acknowledge our true emotions, we give up our ability to control them. They bleed into other areas of our lives where they have no right to be. The next time you experience an unusually strong emotion, take a moment to reflect and try to recognize any emotional undercurrents that may be contributing to it. Allow this deeper awareness to bring insight, and ask God for help sorting through your emotions, especially where your spouse is concerned. After all, as today's verse says, he knows exactly what they are, and he is greater than them.

You cannot make yourself feel something you do not feel, but you can make yourself do right in spite of your feelings. —PEARL S. BUCK

JULY 11

THE FIRST OF HIS MIRACULOUS SIGNS

When the master of ceremonies tasted the water that was now wine, not knowing where it had come from (though, of course, the servants knew), he called the bridegroom over. "A host always serves the best wine first," he said. ". . . But you have kept the best until now!" This miraculous sign at Cana in Galilee was the first time Jesus revealed his glory. And his disciples believed in him. JOHN 2:9-11

MINISTER AND STORYTELLER Frederick Buechner was born on this day, July 11, 1926. He is the author of more than thirty critically acclaimed books, including *A Long Day's Dying, Godric, Listening to Your Life,* and *The Sacred Journey.* The *New York Times* has called him the finest Christian writer in America. But it's his book *Whistling in the Dark,* originally published in 1988, that we've come to appreciate for the way he describes marriage:

> *They say they will love, comfort, honor each other to the end of their days. They say they will cherish each other and be faithful to each other always. They say they will do these things not just when they feel like it but even—for better for worse, for richer for poorer, in sickness and in health—when they don't feel like it at all. In other words, the vows they make at a marriage could hardly be more extravagant. They give away their freedom. They take on themselves each other's burdens. They bind their lives together in ways that are even more painful to unbind emotionally, humanly, than they are to unbind legally. The question is: what do they get in return?*

And here's his answer:

> *They get each other in return. . . . They both still have their lives apart as well as a life together. They both still have their separate ways to find. But a marriage made in Heaven is one where a man and a woman become more richly themselves together than the chances are either of them could ever have managed to become alone. When Jesus changed the water into wine at the wedding in Cana, perhaps it was a way of celebrating this miracle of commitment and the transformation it fosters.*[2]

He's saying that the married couple never has to face the world alone. You have each other with whom to get through the night and wake to the day. And as married individuals you have the opportunity to become better versions of yourselves than on your own.

> We hear of the conversion of water into wine at the marriage in Cana as of a miracle. But this conversion is, through the goodness of God, made every day before our eyes. Behold the rain which descends from heaven upon our vineyards; there it enters the roots of the vines, to be changed into wine; a constant proof that God loves us, and loves to see us happy. —BENJAMIN FRANKLIN

WHAT'S THE SECRET?

If we confess our sins to him, he is faithful and just to forgive us our sins and to cleanse us from all wickedness. 1 JOHN 1:9

TWO EXPERIENCED FISHERMEN went ice fishing. They chopped holes in the ice, put worms on their hooks, dropped their lines into the water, and three hours later, they had caught nothing. Then, a boy came along with his fishing gear. He cut a hole in the ice midway between the two fishermen, put a worm on his hook, dropped his line into the water, and immediately, he caught a fish. He repeated the process, over and over again, until he soon had a catch of a dozen fish. The two fishermen watched and were flabbergasted.

Finally, one of the men approached the lad and said, "Young man, we've been here for more than three hours and haven't caught a single fish. You've caught at least a dozen in just a few minutes. What's your secret?" The boy mumbled an answer, but the man didn't catch a word of it. Then he noticed a large bulge in the boy's left cheek. "Take the bubble gum out of your mouth so I can understand what you're saying," the man said. Whereupon the boy cupped his hands and spat it out. "It's not bubble gum," he said, "it's my secret. You've got to keep the worms warm."

Everybody likes to be in on a secret. Why? For the simple reason that secrets are often helpful. Who doesn't want to know the secret to baking a great chocolate cake? Or avoiding a traffic jam? Or raising good kids? We like to be "in the know."

But there are secrets we keep to ourselves that are definitely not helpful. These are the things about ourselves—our character flaws—that keep us from being authentic. They are little secrets (sometimes big ones) about our selfish sides that we don't want anyone to discover.

So are you feeling brave enough to let the secret out and confess? Some little selfish side that comes out at certain times? Confession to God, who knows it all anyway, is the path to being cleansed from unrighteousness. And confession to one another keeps the marriage relationship open and honest. And here's a little known and helpful secret: you'll be amazed at how a little revelation can bring you closer together.

The naked truth is always better than the best-dressed lie. —ANN LANDERS

MORE THAN CONQUERORS

Dear brothers and sisters, when troubles come your way, consider it an opportunity for great joy. For you know that when your faith is tested, your endurance has a chance to grow. So let it grow, for when your endurance is fully developed, you will be perfect and complete, needing nothing. JAMES 1:2-4

WE HAVE SOME FRIENDS WHO have been married more than thirty years. In their mid-fifties now, they seem to enjoy all the blessings possible for a healthy married couple—a beautiful home, good friends, bright children, and fulfilling careers. But their marriage hasn't been a walk on easy street. Their second child, a boy, was just four years old when he wandered into a neighbor's yard and drowned in their swimming pool.

The mother found her son face down in the water and worked frantically to revive him, as did the emergency crew, but his life was lost. Faced with this tragedy and the unbearable grief that followed, this couple could have given up. After all, it is not uncommon for a marriage to dissolve in the face of overwhelming suffering. Strangely, sorrowful partners sometimes retreat to separate and bitter corners of misery. And because misery doesn't always love company, their circumstances tear them apart instead of bring them together. But not this couple. They chose to call upon the power of love to help them weather their tragedy as partners.

Are you and your spouse cultivating the power of love? We hope you will never be forced to test its strength, but we pray you will always rest in the courage that comes from a healthy Christian marriage. "Can anything ever separate us from Christ's love? Does it mean he no longer loves us if we have trouble or calamity, or are persecuted, or hungry, or destitute, or in danger, or threatened with death? . . . No, despite all these things, overwhelming victory is ours through Christ, who loved us." (Romans 8:35, 37).

What a marvelous resource husband and wife can be to one another. For as we cultivate love, we are strengthening our ability to cope with all that life might bring. And when the times of trouble come, we can help one another remember that we are never separated from the love of Christ.

 Our strength grows out of our weakness. —**RALPH WALDO EMERSON**

ENJOYING YOUR DIFFERENCES

Is there any encouragement from belonging to Christ? Any comfort from his love? Any fellowship together in the Spirit? Are your hearts tender and compassionate? Then make me truly happy by agreeing wholeheartedly with each other, loving one another, and working together with one mind and purpose. PHILIPPIANS 2:1-2

IT HAS BEEN SUGGESTED that two strangers could be married to each other off the street and make a pretty good marriage together if only they were mature enough to work their way through the inevitable differences.

How do you and your partner handle differences? If you are like most couples, you have probably tried one of two things: sweeping your differences under the rug by ignoring them altogether, or trying to make one another become like yourselves. Unfortunately, as you may have found out, both strategies are doomed to frustration. As for the first, it's only a matter of time before repressed differences reemerge; and as for the second, we miss out on a tremendous gift of marriage when we do not enjoy our partners' uniqueness. That's right, enjoy the differences!

Every person is unique (see Psalm 139:14). God never intended couples to approach life as if they were twins separated at birth. He made us with unique strengths and weaknesses. He gave each of us special gifts. The difference in temperament that allows your partner to deal with situations that would drive you crazy is something to be thankful for. Sure, some of his or her traits make living together tough at times, but those very differences can account for some of the best aspects of your marriage too. Appreciating the positive side of your differences will make your marriage more balanced and complete.

What is one way your spouse's uniqueness enriches your life today? Once you identify it, why don't you share that with your spouse?

We continue to shape our personality all our life. —ALBERT CAMUS

THE FRUIT OF THE SPIRIT

The whole law can be summed up in this one command: "Love your neighbor as yourself."
But if you are always biting and devouring one another, watch out! Beware of destroying
one another. GALATIANS 5:14-15

IN THE CENTER OF YOUR HEAD is a structure of the brain whose purpose is survival. It is the intensive care unit of the nervous system, the part of the supersystem that helps you stay well. Medical students are taught to remember the functions of this part of the brain, called the limbic system, by knowing that it is consumed with either fighting, fleeing, or feeding. Body temperature, heartbeat, breathing, sweating, and the general response of the body to the world begin here.

The limbic system reacts to any change in our internal or external world, a type of biological Geiger counter. But it does not read, consider, evaluate, or assess anything in regard to the welfare of the rest of the world. It is only concerned with its own survival. Unless told otherwise, there is no "us" in the lower levels of the brain, only "self." This is borne out by some of the verses we can read about our basic selfishness (see 2 Timothy 3:2). But according to Galatians 5:22-23, there are qualities that transcend a selfish focus on "me." These qualities are the fruit of inviting the Holy Spirit to transform our self-centered tendencies: "The Holy Spirit produces this kind of fruit in our lives: love, joy, peace, patience, kindness, goodness, faithfulness, gentleness, and self-control. There is no law against these things!"

What person would not like to make a home with someone who demonstrates these qualities? These are the marks of the individual who, through the power of God, has transcended selfishness and seen "me" turned into "we." Every marriage runs the "limbic system" risk of becoming two self-centered persons consumed with individual survival. But when the Holy Spirit is allowed to transform each one's self-gratifying nature, the real miracle of marriage occurs: the more we give of ourselves, the more fruit we enjoy.

All the fruits of the Spirit, which we are to lay weight upon as evidential of grace, are
summed up in charity, or Christian love; because this is the sum of all grace.
—JONATHAN EDWARDS

THROUGH THE DARKNESS

He pours disgrace upon princes and disarms the strong. JOB 12:21

NANCY KNEW HER BABY HAD problems almost immediately, but she and her husband named the baby girl Hope. Born with clubfeet and extreme lethargy, among other problems, Hope was officially diagnosed with Zellweger Syndrome. There is no treatment or cure for this rare metabolic disorder. Most babies with the disease live less than six months.

As Nancy looked at Hope, she thought, *Here's my chance to respond to the worst thing I can imagine in a way that is pleasing to God.* It wasn't easy. Nancy had to make that decision over and over again during the next few months. The grieving didn't get easier. Hope wasn't healed. On her 199th day of life, Hope took her last breath. But that was not the end of hope. Each day, Nancy trusted God to do something meaningful despite her loneliness and grief.

Both parents must be carriers of the recessive gene in order for Zellweger Syndrome to occur, so the Guthries decided David would have a vasectomy to prevent another pregnancy. Only one in two thousand vasectomies fail, so the couple felt secure. But one year after Hope died, Nancy was pregnant again. Prenatal testing revealed this child would also have Zellweger Syndrome. Named after the angel, Gabriel was born on July 16, 2001. They knew what to expect. Their son's first day would be his best. Gabriel died 183 days later.

Nancy says that answering how or why begins with another question: what? What do we believe about God? "Do I trust God enough to believe he's in control and whatever he allows in my life will be for my ultimate good—not that whatever he allows in my life is good?"[3]

It's been said that faith isn't faith until it's all you're holding on to. Nancy's hope had left her clinging to nothing more than a conviction that God would carry her though her dark and deep abyss of grief. Her expectant faith was not about to let her waste her pain on perpetual anger and forever asking "Why?" Her faith resuscitated her hope when it seemed that all was hopeless. Her faith and trust in God's heavenly perspective pulled her through the darkness. It was her expectant faith that gave her strength she didn't know she had.

In your marriage, you may know very well a situation requiring the kind of faith Nancy displayed. Or you may not yet. The Guthries have survived their personal tragedy by holding on to this faith in God together and watching him bring them through. What about you? How can you allow hope to permeate any corners of your marriage darkened by grief and doubt today?

The person who is plunged into doubt is not the unbeliever, but the person who has no other hope but hope. —JACQUES ELLUL

THE MIRACLE OF MARRIAGE?

Look beneath the surface so you can judge correctly. JOHN 7:24

COMEDIAN BILL COSBY SAID, "For two people in a marriage to live together day after day is unquestionably the one miracle the Vatican has overlooked." He's got a point. Once the masks are put aside and a couple settles into married life with their differing personalities, year after year, it can indeed seem miraculous that the relationship endures.

What may even be more phenomenal is that a marriage need not only survive but it can actually thrive in the face of two differing and strong personalities that face off day after day. There is no one-size-fits-all solution to making different personalities work together over time. But one of the ways this can be possible is by simply observing one another's personalities and respecting them. Of course, we can't x-ray a personality, but we can observe it. How? By looking at the way we act.

There is much about personality that we can pick up simply by watching. We can deduce something, for example, about personality when we notice that a person does very careful research before buying a camera, just as we can deduce something about personality when we see someone else purchase a high-priced gadget on impulse. And as Yogi Berra so famously said, "You can observe a lot just by watching." Especially when that "watching" is done around the clock in a marriage.

Think about it. You know your spouse's particular habits pretty well by now, don't you? We naturally become witnesses to one another's traits simply because we're there living with them day in and day out. It's almost as if we are on surveillance without ever intending it. The mere time that marriage consumes cannot help but to make us keen observers of each other's traits as they become visible in our reactions, our expressions, and our behaviors.

So what traits do you think are most consistently seen by your spouse in you? Right now, come up with two personality traits that you think your spouse would note about you, and then test your accuracy by asking each other if you're right. Do those traits make your spouse's tolerance of them seem miraculous? Give him or her whatever apologies or thanks your discovery warrants.

In a time when nothing is more certain than change, the commitment of two people to one another has become difficult and rare. Yet, by its scarcity, the beauty and value of this exchange have only been enhanced. —ROBERT SEXTON

EVEN AN OGRE CAN CHANGE

This means that anyone who belongs to Christ has become a new person. The old life is gone; a new life has begun! 2 CORINTHIANS 5:17

THINK OF A BIG GREEN OGRE and who comes to mind? If you've seen the popular animated movie series you're bound to say Shrek.[4]

In the sequel to the first film Shrek falls in love with the princess Fiona. They eventually get married and then travel to the castle of Fiona's parents in order for Shrek to receive her father's blessing. The visit does not go well, and Shrek and Fiona start to fight.

After disagreeing with Fiona's father, Shrek barges into Fiona's chambers and starts throwing their things together. As the newlyweds' first crisis unfolds, their voices get louder and louder until they're shouting at each other.

Shrek says, "I told you coming here was a bad idea."

"You could have at least tried to get along with my father," Fiona replies.

"You know, somehow I don't think I was going to get Daddy's blessing even if I did want it."

"Well, do you think it might be nice if somebody asked me what I wanted?"

In a sarcastic tone, Shrek responds, "Sure. Do you want me to pack for you?"

"You're unbelievable," says Fiona. "You're behaving like a . . . a . . ."

"Go ahead and say it!" Shrek challenges her.

"Like an ogre!" Fiona shouts.

Shrek yells, "Well, here's a newsflash for you. Whether your parents like it or not, I am an ogre. And guess what, princess—that's not about to change."

Fiona pauses for a moment and takes a deep breath. Then she composes herself and walks slowly to the door and opens it. In a gentle tone that invites reconciliation she simply says, "I've made changes for you, Shrek. Think about that." Then she quietly shuts the door behind her, leans up against it, and begins to cry. Shrek, cut to the heart, walks to the door and hears her crying, then leans up against his side of it and sighs.

Like all of us, Shrek knows it's true. Every spouse has to make changes for the other person. Why? Because marriage entails some necessary losses. It requires sacrifice and adaptability on both sides. None of us can claim that our negative natures are unchangeable, that we simply are who we are. The truth is that we are all, through Christ, in the process of becoming what God wants us to be.

Is there an area in your marriage in which a little more adaptability on your part would go a long way? Think about that.

When you are through changing, you are through. —BRUCE BARTON

PLAYING FAVORITES?

My dear brothers and sisters, how can you claim to have faith in our glorious Lord Jesus Christ if you favor some people over others? JAMES 2:1

A GROUP OF CHILDREN were once asked, "What does 'love' mean?" You may have heard some of their answers:

Rebekah, age 8: "When my grandmother got arthritis, she couldn't bend over and paint her toenails anymore. So my grandfather does it for her all the time—even when his hands got arthritis, too. That's love."

Nikka, age 6: "If you want to learn to love better, you should start with someone you hate."

Tommy, age 6: "Love is like a little old woman and a little old man who are still friends even after they know each other so well."

Cindy, age 8: "During my piano recital, I was on a stage, and I was scared. I looked at all the people watching me, and I saw my daddy waving and smiling. He was the only one doing that. And I wasn't scared anymore."

Jessica, age 8: "You really shouldn't say 'I love you' unless you mean it. But if you mean it, you should say it a lot."

Out of the mouths of babes, right?

When James writes of not showing favoritism in verse one, he is speaking of having an inclusive and loving attitude with others—the kind some of these kids are talking about. He is talking about letting outsiders in. Do you do that in your marriage?

Most of us become pretty comfortable in our tightly knit social circle and don't even think about stepping outside it to see who might be in need of inclusion. The most glaring example, as James 2:2-7 points out, concerns socioeconomic status. But playing favorites can be seen even at a church picnic. How many new people have attempted to plug into the body of Christ only to feel sidelined and forgotten? It's difficult to know. But when we become less discriminating and give a "good seat" to an outsider, something wonderful happens in a marriage. It's called shared service—reaching out to another person as a caring couple. And ironically, few things bring a couple closer together than reaching out to others together.

So the next chance you get an opportunity—at a party or simply socializing in the church foyer as a couple—try a little experiment and don't play favorites. You might be surprised what it does for your marriage to reach out and include a new friend.

The giving of love is an education in itself. —**ELEANOR ROOSEVELT**

ACTIVE LISTENING

Understand this, my dear brothers and sisters: You must all be quick to listen, slow to speak, and slow to get angry. JAMES 1:19

WHAT IF YOU COULD PRESS a magic button in your marriage that would instantly create positive and warm emotions about your relationship? What if it would automatically increase your sense of satisfaction, intimacy, and fun? Well, in a sense, you can. Here's how: when your partner shares good news, you simply need to actively respond. That's it!

"It isn't enough just to listen passively," says Dr. Shelly Gable, who authored a UCLA research report on the subject. When you hear good news from your spouse, you need to be active, give eye contact, and offer a tender touch. Because when you do this, your spouse immediately has tender feelings toward you. They can't help it. This kind of warm response automatically engenders warmth in return. It's a practical way of simply saying *listen.* After all, we all want to be heard and understood.[5]

Consider the facts: most people talk at the rate of 120 words per minute. But most spoken material can be comprehended equally well at rates up to 250 words per minute. What does this mean? It means we all have plenty of extra time to be distracted or pre-occupied during a typical conversation. That's what causes us to do just the opposite of what this verse in the first chapter of James urges. Most of us, most of the time, are quick to talk and slow to listen.

Jesus certainly understood the value of taking time to listen. When he encountered the emotionally disturbed demonic men who lived among the tombs in Gadara, the men were shouting at Jesus: "Who are you? Have you also come here to torment us?" Jesus could have turned and walked away. He certainly didn't deserve to be talked to like that. Jesus would have been justified in leaving the poor men to their own devices. But instead, Jesus listened. He not only heard the words that the men shouted, but he listened for the message of the emotions behind the words. Jesus understood that the men's outburst was really a cry for help, and he helped (see Matthew 8:28-32). This was listening to more than words; it was listening for the feelings behind them.

Try to convey love today by actively listening to the emotional messages beneath your spouse's words and reflecting those feelings back so he or she can feel the depth of your connection.

There is hardly ever a complete silence in our souls. God is whispering to us wellnigh incessantly. Whenever the sounds of the world die out in the soul, or sink low, then we hear these whisperings of God. . . . He is always whispering to us, only . . . we do not always hear, because of the hurry, noise, and distraction which life causes as it rushes on. —FREDERICK W. FABER

LOVE CONQUERS ALL

Most important of all, continue to show deep love for each other, for love covers a multitude of sins. 1 PETER 4:8

WE PACKED A PICNIC LUNCH with tuna fish sandwiches and Diet Pepsi and drove from Pasadena up the coast to Santa Barbara, three or so hours away. It was Les's idea—we'd been married just a year. *Okay,* I thought, *this could be fun. We'll have time to talk as we drive, and we can eat our lunch on the beach.* But Les, now in graduate school, had a different idea. He was one week into a stressful summer school course, taking Greek! So he brought along a taped lecture to listen to on our drive and a pack of flash cards to study for his next exam. So much for romance, at least on that day.

I don't want to paint an incorrect picture; Les can be very romantic. On my birthday this year, for example, he took me to the swankiest restaurant in town and had prearranged with the maître d' to have a gift delivered to our table with my favorite dessert.

Still, in our home, romance can be a hit-or-miss endeavor. Of course, I own my part of the misses. Like the time I planned a weekend getaway as a surprise for Les. That's when I learned he doesn't think surprises are very romantic! Or the time I thought he would enjoy going to a theater production instead of skiing with his friends. He didn't.

Well, if you can't already tell, we haven't discovered the secret to romance in marriage. Maybe that makes us romantically impaired. But we have discovered that a big part of cultivating romance is learning to love each other in spite of expectations for romance that aren't met—even when our partners seem blatantly unromantic. That's a lesson couples can learn from Peter when he writes, "Continue to show deep love for each other, for love covers a multitude of sins."

Whether it's different romance instincts or something else altogether, you and your spouse will have certain areas of mismatch, and that's when true love, covering over those areas in grace, can triumph. Think about one such area for your marriage. How can you "show deep love for each other" today?

> *You will find as you look back upon your life that the moments . . . when you have truly lived, are the moments when you have done things in a spirit of love.*
> —HENRY DRUMMOND

IT'S OKAY TO CRY

You keep track of all my sorrows. You have collected all my tears in your bottle. You have recorded each one in your book. PSALM 56:8

"DON'T CRY!"

"It's okay to cry," Leslie whimpered.

We were having lunch at a favorite restaurant, talking about I don't know what when out of nowhere, or so it seemed, Leslie's eyes flooded with tears. Only moments before they were sparkling with quite a different emotion.

"I know it's okay to cry," I confessed, "but can't you wait until we get in the car?"

Of course, what seemed like a simple request to me only exacerbated the emotion I was insensitively trying to stifle. Leslie dabbed her eyes with a napkin, trying to retain her mascara, but the floodgates soon opened, and the tears flowed like a stream.

I can't tell you how many times we have lived through similar scenes. And although neither of us could tell you what the underlying issues were, we can assure you that to one degree or another, tears are a part of every marriage relationship. But there's good news about those tears: did you know that God keeps a record of your tears? The psalmist says they are listed on a scroll—in other words, in a book (see Psalm 56:8). God values our tears. And as this passage makes clear, God pays attention when we cry. Following his example, we should respect the tears of our spouses.

Part of cultivating intimacy is learning that there is no shame in tears. Sure, crying in the middle of a restaurant is nobody's idea of a good time, but if an onlooker doesn't understand the tenderness of tears between a married couple, that's his or her problem!

When you allow for the full expression of your spouse's emotions, you create a safe place for your spouse to be fully authentic. How can you make your marriage a safer place for emotional authenticity today?

The same tears that break our hearts may also nourish us in ways that matter most to God. —**PHILIP YANCEY**

TELLING LITTLE WHITE LIES

This is what you must do: Tell the truth to each other. Render verdicts in your courts that are just and that lead to peace. ZECHARIAH 8:16

EVERY COUPLE TELLS little white lies to one another in an attempt to be more "loving." If we don't like something our partners do for us, like cooking a meal or fixing something in the house, for example, we might say, "Oh, it's wonderful!" It's a little lie that couldn't hurt a flea, right? Not necessarily.

Consider Ron and Cindy, who had been married only a few weeks when he cooked his "world famous BBQ hot ribs" on their brand-new grill. As they were eating, Ron asked Cindy if she liked the ribs. Cindy knew Ron had worked hard to make them and was afraid that she would offend him if she was honest. "Oh yes," she told Ron, "they're great!"

Believing that Cindy really liked his famous dish, Ron began barbecuing quite regularly as a kind of family tradition, and there were always leftovers, which had to be eaten. After a while, Cindy could bear it no longer, and in a moment of anger about something else she confessed that she hated Ron's ribs, that they made her gag, that she never wanted to see ribs on her table again! Ron was shocked and hurt. She had lied to him. "How can I ever believe you again?" he asked.

Should Cindy have told Ron right from the beginning that the ribs made her gag? Not if she cared about her marriage. Marriage requires honesty, but honesty does not require brutality. Truth is brutal only when it is meant to cause pain or when it is a partial truth. If Cindy said she hated the ribs, that would only be part of the truth. To be honest she could say something like, "Not really, I've never liked barbecue on the grill—but it doesn't make a bit of difference to me. I like the side dishes and love seeing you cook."

The tragedy of most seemingly insignificant experiences of deception is that they take on a life of their own and become bigger than we expected. That's why we must do as Zechariah's book says, and tell the truth to one another in a way that is just and promotes peace.

Those that think it permissible to tell white lies soon grow color-blind.
—AUSTIN O'MALLEY

FAITHFUL AND TRUE

Understand, therefore, that the LORD your God is indeed God. He is the faithful God who keeps his covenant for a thousand generations and lavishes his unfailing love on those who love him and obey his commands. DEUTERONOMY 7:9

"IT IS EASIER IN THESE UNITED STATES to walk away from a marriage than from a commitment to purchase a used car," said an attorney at a conference we attended. "Most contracts cannot be unilaterally terminated; a marriage commitment, however, can be broken by practically anyone at any time, and without cause."

He is right. A friend of ours went to traffic court, where he heard two divorce decrees from the judge before his turn came to be heard. He dropped by our office later to tell us about his experience. He said, "I told my wife when I got home that we could have had a divorce any number of times if those reasons I heard in court were good enough for a legal separation."

The "till death do us part" of marriage is not merely an ideal. It is a reality that is insured by an unswerving commitment—a willful agreement to keep love alive. "Do two walk together unless they have agreed to do so?" asked the prophet Amos (3:3, NIV). Commitment is the cerebral part of love. It is the part that comes more from our minds than our hearts.

Why do so many marriage commitments fall flat these days? We believe it is because too many promises are made without the promises of God. We can "hold tightly without wavering to the hope we affirm, for God can be trusted to keep his promise" (Hebrews 10:23). Our commitment to each other in marriage is sustained by God's model of faithfulness to us. When a man and woman covenant with one another, God promises faithfulness to them (see 1 Corinthians 1:9). There is no way to overemphasize the centrality of commitment in God's character. It is woven into every part of the Bible—from Genesis, in which God initiates his promise of faithfulness, through Revelation, in which John's vision depicts a white horse, whose "rider was named Faithful and True" (19:11). Allow God's faithfulness to infuse your marriage covenant with staying power.

A covenant made with God is not restrictive, but protective. —**RUSSELL M. NELSON**

SETTING ASIDE SELFISH DESIRES

There will always be some in the land who are poor. That is why I am commanding you to share freely with the poor. DEUTERONOMY 15:11

SOMETIMES A LITTLE STORY, apocryphal or true, can make a point that stays with us. So here's one about a little boy that carries an underlying message for every couple.

Many years ago, a ten-year-old boy walked up to the counter of a soda shop and climbed onto a stool. He caught the eye of the waitress and asked, "How much is an ice cream sundae?"

"Fifty cents," the waitress replied.

The boy reached into his pockets, pulled out a handful of change, and began counting. The waitress frowned impatiently. After all, she had other customers to wait on.

The boy squinted up at the waitress. "How much is a dish of plain ice cream?" he asked.

The waitress sighed and rolled her eyes. "Thirty-five cents," she said with a note of irritation.

Again, the boy counted his coins. At last, he said, "I'll have the plain ice cream please." He put a quarter and two nickels on the counter. The waitress took the coins, brought the ice cream, and walked away. About ten minutes later, she returned and found the ice cream dish empty. The boy was gone. She picked up the empty dish—then swallowed hard.

There on the counter, next to the wet spot where the dish had been, were two nickels and five pennies. The boy had had enough for a sundae, but he had ordered plain ice cream so he could leave a tip.

What does this heartwarming story have to do with marriage? Like the little boy, no matter how small our resources may seem—in money, time, or energy—we have the opportunity to give to one another. We can carefully set aside our selfish desires, budgeting our time and energy to make sure we have enough for our spouses. And also like the boy, if we simply commit to doing it, regardless of the size of our resources or the treatment we are getting at the moment, we will make an impression.

> *Selfishness is that detestable vice which no one will forgive in others, and no one is without in himself.* —HENRY WARD BEECHER

ARE YOU CRITICIZING OR COMPLAINING?

Make allowance for each other's faults, and forgive anyone who offends you. Remember,
the Lord forgave you, so you must forgive others. COLOSSIANS 3:13

THE REVEREND BOWEN WAS struck with an inspired idea while taking a shower. He
was tired of hearing the parishioners at his Kansas City church complain about everything from the choice of hymns at the Sunday service to the informal dress code at the
church's Saturday night worship. So he asked his flock to take a pledge: vowing not to
complain, criticize, gossip, or use sarcasm for twenty-one consecutive days. People who
joined his cause were issued little purple bracelets as a reminder of their pledge to quit
complaining. If they caught themselves complaining, they were supposed to take off the
bracelet, switch it to the opposite wrist, and start counting the days from scratch.[6]

Pretty good idea, huh? After all, who wouldn't like to eliminate complaining—
especially from your own marriage? Well, a little-known secret among marriage specialists is the fact that complaining is actually good for your marriage. You read that right!
It's *good* for your marriage. Research at the University of Washington has shown that
complaining, at a moderate level, helps couples air their grievances and keep improving.
What isn't helpful to a marriage is criticism.

So what's the difference between criticism and complaining? Criticism almost always
begins with you ("You always make us late!"), whereas complaining almost always begins
with I ("I feel so frustrated when we are late to something that matters to me"). This may
seem like a small matter of semantics, but it makes a big difference in our marriages.
Today's verse tells us we must forgive others for their faults—after all, think of all the Lord
has forgiven us. But expressing our frustrations in a loving way is sometimes necessary
in order for healthy change to occur.

How can you work to eliminate criticism from your marriage? Would a twenty-one
day challenge work for you? Or is there another way you could challenge yourself to start
forgiving your spouse for his or her faults and expressing complaints in a loving way?

It is only imperfection that complains of what is imperfect. The more perfect we are, the
more gentle and quiet we become toward the defects of others. —FRANÇOIS FÉNELON

IF I SHOULD WAKE BEFORE I DIE?

Faith is the confidence that what we hope for will actually happen; it gives us assurance about things we cannot see. HEBREWS 11:1

DO YOU REMEMBER YOUR first nighttime prayers? If you were like countless other children, you prayed, "Now I lay me down to sleep . . ." Remember that? There's a line from that prayer that's worth reconsidering. In fact, it was our friend Tony Campolo who brought it to our attention.

Tony was taking a course in Chinese philosophy during his graduate education. The Buddhist monk who taught the course told him, "As a Christian, you teach your children to pray all wrong. You teach them to pray, 'If I should die before I wake.' It would be better if you taught them to pray 'If I should wake before I die.'"[7]

The monk went on to point out that most of the people he knew were half awake when they ought to be asleep. But even worse, when they were asleep, they were half awake. No one seemed to be totally alive. Nobody seemed to be turned on to what was going on around them. He's got a point, doesn't he?

Too often we meander through our days without purpose, without energy, and without life. "We examine each day before us," says Tom Hennen, "with barely a glance and say, 'no, this isn't one I've been looking for,' and wait in a bored sort of way for the next, when we are convinced, our lives will start for real."[8] It's his way of saying we are like sleepwalkers who hope to wake before we die.

So maybe today, whatever time you happen to be reading this, you can pray that God would wake you before you die, and consider how you can live tomorrow for all it's worth. How can you make your day count? What can you do to find meaning in your moments?

Here's a place to start: identifying what you really want in your life and in your marriage. Maybe it's more time with your children. Maybe it's financial freedom. Maybe it's to complete a project you've been postponing. The key is to identify what you want most from tomorrow. This is what will give you purpose and direction. We have a friend who puts it this way: Know what you ardently desire, sincerely believe in it, vividly imagine it, enthusiastically act on it, and you will live each day for all it's worth. We couldn't agree more.

Because of the routines we follow, we often forget that life is an ongoing adventure. —MAYA ANGELOU

KNOWING WHAT TO EXPECT

You can make many plans, but the LORD's purpose will prevail. PROVERBS 19:21

DID YOU KNOW THAT KNOWING what to expect gives you power? It's true. Psychologists call it "cognitive control." With even a small bit of information about a situation we feel more in control and have better outcomes than those who don't have it.

Consider a simple experiment conducted on women entering a supermarket. Each group of women was given a long shopping list on which they were to select the most economical purchase in the store for each item. One group was told, "While you are carrying out the task, the store may become crowded. So if you feel a little anxious while you're shopping, that may be why." That was it. That's all the added information they received. The other group of shoppers didn't get this information. But that little piece of knowledge seemed to make a big difference. The informed group got more shopping items correct, was more satisfied with the store, and felt the experience was comfortable. The uninformed group felt stressed, missed items on their list, and didn't like the experience. Having information about a situation, as this study and many others have shown, frees people from "searching for explanations" and empowers them to give their attention and energy to the task.

This scenario pales in comparison to the knowledge God wants us to have—the information he provides to give us the upper hand in life. He says it plainly: "Here on earth you will have many trials" (John 16:33). You can expect them. Problems rain on all of us. Nobody gets through this life without troubles. "I have told you all this," he says, "so that you may have peace in me." In other words, by knowing what to expect, we have "cognitive control" that brings about direction, focus, strength, and contentment. When we take God at his word and understand that trials will simply be part of our lives, we can also take him at his word to bring us peace in the midst of the trials.

[Hope] means a confident, alert expectation that God will do what he said he will do. It is imagination put in the harness of faith. It is a willingness to let God do it in his way and in his time. —EUGENE PETERSON

WATCH WHAT YOU SAY ABOUT EACH OTHER

What you say flows from what is in your heart. LUKE 6:45

DID YOU KNOW THAT how you talk about each other to your friends and family and even strangers can predict your success as a couple? That's what researchers at the University of Washington in Seattle report. A ten-year study followed ninety-five couples beginning six months into their marriages. The initial hour-long interview together probed their relationships, their parents' unions, and their philosophies of marriage.

More than what was actually said, researchers noted whether they expressed fondness and admiration for their partners, if they talked about themselves as a unit, if they finished each other's sentences, referenced each other when they told a story, and whether what came to mind was pleasant. Turns out that couples characterized by these ways of talking about one another and their relationship are far more likely to enjoy lifelong love.

In fact, with this information alone, researchers can predict with 87 percent accuracy whether a couple will end up divorcing. Think about that. How you talk to others about your spouse and your relationship is a huge indicator of the state of your union. Even within just the first six months of marriage, the signs become pretty clear. The authors of the study found that couples who endure talk to others about their spouses as if they are wearing "rose-colored glasses." Those who will divorce talk to others about their spouses with cynicism.

How can this be? It comes down to how your attitude shapes the way you view your spouse. If you give public praise to others about your spouse, you will inevitably look more favorably upon him or her yourself. You will discover a deeper appreciation for your partner than you had before. In fact, the more opportunities you find to talk positively about your partner when he or she isn't present, the more likely you are to increase your loving attitudes and behaviors toward him or her. In other words, what you say about your spouse, for good or ill, shapes the way you think, feel, and act in your marriage.

How do you speak about your spouse? Do you point out the good or the bad? Could your relationship benefit from an increased loving attitude about him or her?

Forgive me my nonsense, as I also forgive the nonsense of those who think they talk sense. —ROBERT FROST

WHY ARE WE HERE?

You have been called to live in freedom, my brothers and sisters. But don't use your freedom to satisfy your sinful nature. Instead, use your freedom to serve one another in love. GALATIANS 5:13

WHILE SITTING AT A STOPLIGHT, Lorraine noticed a woman on the corner, slumped over a crate. There was a bundle in her lap; Lorraine could see a tiny child's arm sticking out. The woman was dozing off, and the baby was about to hit the ground. When the light changed, Lorraine drove past them, but then, about three blocks away, she decided to go back.

Gently touching the woman's shoulder, Lorraine handed her a piece of paper and told her if she needed help with her baby, she could take it to the address she had written on it. The address was her mother's apartment.

The next day the woman on the crate left her baby at Clara Hale's house. And as she did, Hale House was born. Since 1969, hundreds of children have found sanctuary in Mother Hale's brownstone in Harlem. In 1985, Ronald Reagan said this about Clara in his Presidential State of the Union address: "Go to her house some night and you may see her silhouette against the window as she walks the floor talking softly, soothing a child in her arms—Mother Hale of Harlem is an American hero."

Clara Hale died in 1992, but her legacy has gone on—providing a warm, loving, nurturing home for infants and young children in need.

In addition to providing a temporary holding facility for children until their mothers can get help and resume care on their own, the organization went on to provide transitional housing and relapse prevention for formerly drug-addicted mothers.

When asked why she worked so diligently to meet the difficult needs of abandoned and often drug-addicted infants, Clara Hale would say, "You've got to help other people in this world; otherwise why are you here?"

That's a great question for all of us to ask ourselves. In your marriage specifically, why are you here—for yourself? Why are you two here, together as a couple—for yourselves? Asking ourselves these direct questions is sure to cause any of us to consider the difference we are making, as a couple or on our own, and what we can be doing to make more of one.

He profits most who serves best. —A. F. SHELTON

THE STRANGULATION OF TRIANGULATION

[When Jacob told Rachel and Leah about his plans to return to his homeland,] Rachel and Leah responded, "That's fine with us! We won't inherit any of our father's wealth anyway. He has reduced our rights to those of foreign women. . . . So go ahead and do whatever God has told you." GENESIS 31:14-16

HELEN AND A GIRLFRIEND from church were going to Italy for ten weeks to work temporarily at a design studio where her friend had connections. Helen, a single woman in her thirties, had always dreamed of traveling abroad. For the first time in her life she had the opportunity, and she was very excited to go.

Helen was an adult, but she still lived in the same small town as her parents and attended the same church. In fact, the three often enjoyed Sunday lunch together. And it was at one Sunday lunch that Helen told her parents the exciting news about her trip. As it turned out, however, her parents, who had never even thought about traveling overseas, weren't so excited. Her father asked why she would need to take such a trip. Then her mother stepped in, aggressively suggesting that Helen seemed depressed and despondent. Helen couldn't believe her ears.

The next thing she knew, her mother had scheduled an appointment for Helen to see a psychiatrist, and her relatively uninvolved father suddenly encouraged her to go. Helen endured a couple of interviews with a puzzled psychiatrist and fought her parents' escalating efforts to cancel her trip. Eventually, though, she gave in and passed up the opportunity to go abroad.

Why is it that, just as Helen was doing something she felt excited about, her parents moved in to resist it? Or consider Laban and his daughters, Rachel and Leah: because of Laban's underhanded dealings, they were left unsupported by the person who should have been most helpful in the establishment of their marriages. How can otherwise loving family members be capable of directly moving to thwart our opportunities?

The answer is found in a family triangle. In some families, a person becomes so entrenched in a triangulated role that his or her identity cannot be separated from it. That was Helen's problem. Over the years, she had served as mediator between her mother and father, and her plan to leave for ten weeks was so threatening to the family's delicate relational balance that a crisis ensued.

Eventually, Helen transcended the "strangulation of triangulation." She realized that her role in the triangle sabotaged her attempts to develop a separate identity and invest in other relationships. Though she had missed her opportunity to travel abroad, like Rachel and Leah, Helen eventually took other steps that set healthier boundaries between herself and her parents.

Do you see emotional triangles in the family you came from? How do they affect your life and your marriage today?

I have found the best way to give advice to your children is to find out what they want and then advise them to do it. —HARRY TRUMAN

WHAT ARE YOU WAITING FOR?

If we hope for what we do not yet have, we wait for it patiently. ROMANS 8:25, NIV

A MAN AND A WOMAN NOTICED each other on the morning New York-to-Washington air shuttle. Sparks flew, but no words were exchanged, even as they stood together in the taxi line at Washington National. She got in a cab, looked back, and saw him running after her. She begged the cabbie to stop, but he kept going. She scrawled her phone number on a piece of paper and pressed it against the back window, but she knew the man was too far away to read it.

So she went to her meeting. But she couldn't stop thinking about him. Realizing the man had had no luggage, so he would surely be returning to New York that day as well, she feigned illness and returned to the airport to wait for him to catch the shuttle back to New York. She waited all day and got on the 9 p.m. flight alone. "Stepping into the gate area, she looked ahead. And there he was. 'What took you so long?' he asked. 'I've been waiting all day.'"[1]

The story has been published in a book called *The 50 Most Romantic Things Ever Done.* But whether it's an urban myth or a true story, it reveals the sage advice of the old proverb: Good things come to those that wait. And they do.[2]

Of course, few of us enjoy waiting. It seems like a waste of time yet often reaps a reward. One famous example is that of perfume and cosmetics mogul Estée Lauder. After starting her business, Lauder realized she had to persuade a cosmetics buyer to place her products in stores. One day at 9 a.m., Lauder was waiting to see Marie Weston, the cosmetics buyer. Since Lauder had no appointment, she was advised to come back another day. But Lauder decided to wait, even though the buyer was booked solid all day. Finally, after 5 p.m., Marie Weston came out of her office. She looked at Estée Lauder in disbelief, then admiration, and said, "Well, do come in. Such patience must be rewarded."

What are the two of you waiting for? Chances are you know the answer to this question immediately. Maybe it's a job promotion or a raise in salary. Maybe you're waiting for the slow grief of a lost loved one to dissipate. Perhaps it's an upcoming vacation or a new life phase, like enjoying an empty nest. Or maybe it's the arrival of a new baby. Most of us, most of the time, are waiting for something. And that's why a prayer for patience is always in order. Have you asked God to give you this gift in your marriage lately?

Waiting is a period of learning. —HENRI NOUWEN

GETTING REAL

Dear friends, do not believe everyone who claims to speak by the Spirit. You must test them to see if the spirit they have comes from God. For there are many false prophets in the world. 1 JOHN 4:1

I (LES) DEMONSTRATE IT EVERY autumn in one of my entry-level psychology courses at the university. I administer a simple survey to my two hundred students that has them ranking their interpersonal abilities relative to other students on campus. In other words, they are ranking how well they get along with others as compared with their peers. I collect the information, tabulate the results, and display them on the screen. The results are predictable. All of them, every single one, see themselves as "above average." They can't help but laugh out loud as they see the results. "Isn't it amazing," I say, tongue-in-cheek, "that in this class of two hundred students we lucked out by having everyone be above average?" They laugh some more.

Then I reveal on the screen another tidbit from the survey: An astounding 25 percent see themselves in the top one percent in terms of their ability to get along with others. This time, the students don't laugh—they gasp.

How is it that fifty students out of two hundred see themselves in the upper echelons of interpersonal savvy compared to their peers? Simply because it's more satisfying to believe good things about oneself than to face the truth.

Of course, self-deception doesn't always work. Sometimes we are flat-out forced to see that we failed. We can't deny failing an exam or the fact that we drove the car into a mailbox. That's when we try rationalizing our behavior: "I didn't have time to study" or "My spouse messed with the rearview mirror."

We may frequently avoid telling ourselves the truth, but that's not always bad. "Truths and roses have thorns about them," said Thoreau. The truth can hurt, and it can take time to see it clearly. That's the point: the abilities that contribute to self-deception are not necessarily wrong in themselves. We go wrong with them when we use our deceiving abilities to routinely convince ourselves that we are better than we actually are. That's when we buy the lie that says, "If I'm not so bad, I don't have to change."

So here's the question: When it comes to your relationship, how are you deceiving yourself about the kind of spouse you are? In other words, in what area are you trying to convince yourself that you're a better partner than you really are? If you're feeling brave enough, ask your partner to shed some light for you.[3]

 The easiest person to deceive is one's own self. —EDWARD BULWER-LYTTON

TWENTY-FOUR-KARAT FRIENDSHIP

A man of many companions may come to ruin, but there is a friend who sticks closer than a brother. PROVERBS 18:24, NIV

ON THIS DAY IN 1936, American track-and-field star Jesse Owens was on a course to win the long jump at the Olympic games in Berlin, Germany. After all, he had set three world records in one day in 1935. He had a running broad jump record of 26 feet 8¼ inches that would stand for twenty-five years. But at one crucial moment in his career he needed the encouragement of a friend, and just about the unlikeliest person stepped up to be that friend.

As he walked to the long jump pit to make his jump for qualification, Owens saw a German competitor taking practice jumps—in the twenty-six-foot range. Owens, fully aware of the racial tension caused by his presence, was nervous. He knew about the Nazis' desire to prove Aryan superiority, and here was a German who looked quite capable of doing just that.

Fumbling under the pressure, Owens made his first jump from well beyond the takeoff board—a foul. Then he fouled the second attempt. One more, and he would be disqualified from the event.

It was at that point that the tall German approached Owens. He introduced himself as Luz Long and proceeded to talk to Owens for a few minutes. Lest you miss the significance, remember that this was the black son of a sharecropper and the white German, in Nazi Germany, chatting in view of the entire stadium. What were they saying?

Long had recognized Owens's skill and, apparently, his nerves. He pointed out that Owens could easily jump the qualifying distance, so he suggested starting several inches before the takeoff board, to avoid a fatal third foul.

Taking Long's advice, Owens qualified easily, going on to set an Olympic record and earn the second of four gold medals during the 1936 Olympics. And the first person to congratulate Owens was Luz Long—in full view of Adolf Hitler.

At the beginning of World War II, a paragon of Germany's strength offered technical assistance and words of encouragement to someone who, according to the rules of the game, was technically a foe both on and off the field. Owens never saw Long again, because Long was killed in the ensuing war. But he never forgot him. "You could melt down all the medals and cups I have," Owens later wrote, "and they wouldn't be plating on the twenty-four-carat friendship I felt for Luz Long."[4]

This unlikely friendship demonstrates an invaluable lesson in close connections: When someone goes out of the way—regardless of what others may think or say—to put our interests above his or her own, that person is sure to earn our affection and loyalty. How much more so for marriage!

A friend is one who walks in when others walk out. —WALTER WINCHELL

WALKING IN EACH OTHER'S SHOES

Because of the privilege and authority God has given me, I give each of you this warning: Don't think you are better than you really are. Be honest in your evaluation of yourselves, measuring yourselves by the faith God has given us. ROMANS 12:3

"OUR VIEWERS WANT TO KNOW the most important thing they can do for their relationships," the producer told us. We were sitting in plush leather chairs, sipping bottled water out of straws in the green room of the famous Harpo Studios in Chicago. "Oprah is likely to ask you," the producer continued, "if you could give only one suggestion for improving relationships, what would it be?"

We didn't have to think twice. It wasn't the first time we'd been asked; we hear this question a lot. In fact, for nearly every interview we do, the question is inevitable.

When it comes to that crucial component in a successful relationship—whether it be at work, with family, or on the church board—there's no need to guess. We stand on a mountain of research when we tell you the answer. In a word, it's empathy. It's putting yourself in another's shoes.

Let's not kid anyone. Empathy is not always easy. But empathy can be easier than you think. In fact, it can become downright habit forming. The catch? Empathy can never do its invaluable work unless it's predicated on emotional self-awareness. Let's look into that a little bit.

In 1990 Yale psychologist Peter Salovey coined the phrase *emotional intelligence* to describe qualities that bring human interactions to their peak of performance. Harvard psychologist Daniel Goleman brought the phrase into the national conversation with his groundbreaking book on the subject. He calls empathy our "social radar" and believes that, at the very least, empathy enables us to read another's emotions. And at the highest levels, empathy understands the concerns that lie behind the person's emotions. But all this emotional processing is predicated on being aware of what *we* are feeling at a given moment.

In other words, the key to identifying and understanding another person's emotional terrain, experts agree, is an intimate familiarity with our own. Trading places demands that we put aside our own emotional agendas for the time being in order to clearly receive the other person's signals. The point is that if we don't know what we are feeling, we can't set our own emotions aside—temporarily—to enter the emotional world of another.

Does all this research come as a surprise to God? Of course not. He's the one who wired us to work this way. "Be honest in your evaluation of yourselves," his Scriptures say, according to the standard of "the faith God has given us." When you harness the power of empathy based on a standard of faith, you will enjoy a connection with your spouse like you never have before.

Empathy builds on self-awareness. —DANIEL GOLEMAN

HOW TO SAY "I LOVE YOU" WITHOUT UTTERING A WORD

Dear children, let's not merely say that we love each other; let us show the truth by our actions. 1 JOHN 3:18

OF ALL THE LITTLE EXPRESSIONS of love—a box of chocolates, a handwritten poem, or a bouquet of handpicked wild flowers—I think my favorite is a good old-fashioned kiss. Whether it be the gratuitous kind that comes with greeting my husband after a day at work or the surprising ambush kiss while standing together in line at the grocery, I always feel especially loved when Les gives me a simple kiss.

Did you know the word *kiss* comes from a prehistoric syllable that is believed to be the sound of kissing? However it originated and whoever named it really don't matter to me. I just know I like it. And why shouldn't I? Kisses, according to a Danish saying, are the messengers of love.

But when it comes to public expression of love, married couples have more than kisses in their nonverbal vocabulary. Holding hands is another favorite of mine. It communicates affection, safety, and comfort. Science has even shown that simple hand-holding blunts the brain's response to threats of physical pain (as any couple can attest to who is walking through a hospital ordeal together). Perhaps the loudest statement hand-holding makes is to others. It communicates more clearly than nearly anything else that you are a couple. Whether it is the simple grasp or the more intimate interlocking of fingers, holding hands is a great expression of love that keeps couples bonded.

Even more intimacy than holding hands is found in a hug. A warm embrace can be practiced publicly or privately without stigma. A hug is not only an expression of support and comfort but of romance and intimacy. Studies even indicate numerous biological benefits, like lowered blood pressure, to husbands and wives who frequently hug. But the greatest benefit of a hug is the love and affection it engenders for both the initiating and reciprocating spouse.

So if it's been a little too long since these three common expressions of love—kissing, hand-holding, and hugging—have found their way into your daily marital routine, you may want to turn up the heat and be a bit more intentional about renewing your public and private displays of affection. These expressions may be the most important words you don't speak all day.

The most important things are the hardest to say . . . because words diminish them.
—STEPHEN KING

YOU'RE SO PREDICTABLE— THANK GOD!

Encourage each other with these words. 1 THESSALONIANS 4:18

LESLIE AND I WERE DRIVING around town doing some errands when the conversation turned to a familiar subject. You know the one: "What do you want to do for dinner tonight?" In our home we're a bit on the spontaneous side with this activity. While some couples plan out their meals by the week, we often seem to decide on what we'll eat about the time we're starting to feel hungry.

That's why, after naming a few options for our meal, I suggested the old standby: spaghetti.

"I knew you were going to say that."

And I'm sure she did. I bet we have spaghetti at my suggestion almost every week. We almost always have what's needed to make it in the pantry, and it always tastes good. I guess you'd call it a routine. And chances are you have certain routines too. How many times have you and your spouse uttered the words *I knew you were going to say that* to one another? If you're like most married couples, even if you've been married for just a short while, you've come to expect certain reactions and behaviors from your spouse. Why is that? It's because personalities are fundamentally predictable. Thank God!

Can you imagine trying to be married if you never knew what to expect from your spouse? A marriage couldn't survive if behavior was not basically predictable. Imagine if one day your spouse was extremely laid back and easygoing and then the next day was extremely intense and regimented! You'd be living in chaos. Without relative consistency from your spouse, marriage would be an unbearable roller coaster ride.

Of course, we've all had married moments when we say something like this: "I would never have predicted you would want to do that!" That's because even with a relatively consistent set of traits, our personalities make room for a smidge of the unpredictable. And that's not bad, either. Changing things up, on occasion, can get us out of boring ruts. But for the most part, you can take comfort in knowing that your spouse's personality (as well as your own) will remain pretty predictable.

Take a moment right now to note a character quality in your spouse's personality that gives you comfort, a trait that you are especially thankful for today, and why.

There is no substitute for the comfort supplied by the utterly taken-for-granted relationship. —IRIS MURDOCH

THE VALUE OF SHARED ACTIVITY

For everything there is a season, a time for every activity under heaven.

ECCLESIASTES 3:1

IT WAS THE ANCIENT GREEK philosopher Aristotle who said, "The quality of life is determined by its activities," and he was right. But have you noticed that his statement is especially true when the activity is shared? It is. And for that reason we are devoting this meditation to one simple suggestion: If your spouse has been longing to share an activity with you and you've been resisting, give it some serious consideration. Maybe your spouse wants to share a bike ride or a walk around the neighborhood. Maybe it's a game of tennis or antique shopping. It could be anything, big or small. Don't make your spouse beg for it. Surprise him or her with a ready willingness to go.

Paula, who prized reading and a good nap during her free time, knew her husband wanted to rent a kayak at a nearby lake. He'd been talking about it all summer. But Paula dragged her feet on the idea because it just wasn't something she wanted to do. So her husband eventually went off kayaking on his own. When he returned home, he went on and on about how great it was. "It's so relaxing and freeing to be out there on the water," he told Paula. But she interpreted that as pressure to join him. So she resisted even more. "That all sounds good for you, but it's not my kind of thing," she'd say. The topic was dead. He didn't mention it anymore. The next Saturday, however, when her husband was going out again to kayak by himself, she volunteered to try it with him. "You would have thought I'd given him a gold bar or something," Paula confessed. "I literally had no idea that this would mean so much to him. I hadn't made him that happy for a very long time."

You can do the same thing. It doesn't take much. If you've been resisting a shared activity that your spouse wants you to join in on, consider an about-face and do it. You'll double the fun for your partner, and it will surely bring you closer together.

Shared joy is a joy doubled. —**SWEDISH PROVERB**

THE PRICE OF PASSIVITY

You must have the same attitude that Christ Jesus had. PHILIPPIANS 2:5

WHETHER IT BE IN A HOSPITAL, a nursing home, a college classroom, a concentration camp, or even a marriage, helpless, oppressed people often perceive control to be beyond them, and this perception deepens their resignation.

This is precisely what researcher Martin Seligman and others found in experiments with both animals and people.[5] When dogs were strapped in a harness and given repeated shocks, with no opportunity to avoid them, they felt helpless—obviously. But later, when placed in another situation where they could escape the punishment by merely leaping a hurdle, these same dogs cowered without hope. Faced with traumatic events over which they have no control, people, too, come to feel helpless and hopeless. This was discovered near the end of World War II when death camp prisoners were being released, only to discover they could have easily escaped on their own through holes in fences and unlocked gates. It's what researchers call "learned helplessness." And it's the price we pay for giving up control.

Whether we are in control or not does not seem to be the ultimate issue. It's whether we believe we have control that really counts. Think about it: since we can reduce the intensity of our stress by simply thinking about our problems in a more positive light (without "catastrophizing" them), we must have within us the ability to control the effect that adversity has on us.

Jill Kinmont, who was once the country's top female skier, is a great example of the choice we have over not our circumstances but their effects on our spirits. She became quadriplegic when she fell and severed her spine in a race just before her twentieth birthday and a year before the 1956 Olympic games, for which she had been a top prospect. Jill went on to graduate from UCLA, pursue a lifelong teaching career, become an exhibited painter, and marry. Interviewed when she was forty-one, she was asked what accounted for her bright and positive outlook on life. Was it, the questioner suggested, because she had nineteen great years in the beginning? "I beg your pardon," she replied. "I've had forty-one great years."

Can you imagine the price Jill would have paid if she had given up her ability to choose her attitude along with her ability to walk? Can you imagine the price any one of us pays when we surrender our life—or our marriage—to fate? John Milton was right when he said, "We can make a heav'n of hell, or a hell of heav'n." The choice is ours.

Could you choose to make more of a "heav'n" out of a situation in your marriage?

 } *The mind . . . can make a heav'n of hell, a hell of heav'n.* —JOHN MILTON

A PRESIDENTIAL PASSAGE

Trust in the LORD with all your heart; do not depend on your own understanding. Seek his will in all you do, and he will show you which path to take. PROVERBS 3:5-6

FOR THREE DAYS IN AUGUST OF 1974, Richard Nixon considered whether or not to leave the presidency willingly, or to go through impeachment. Meanwhile, Gerald Ford, serving as a nonelected vice president for the nine months since Spiro Agnew resigned, realized he would not be moving into the vice president's house as vice president after all, but into the White House, as president—the first and still the only president not elected to either office.

Ford and his wife, Betty, never expected to be in that position under any circumstances, but certainly not in the ones that faced them at the time. Not only would Ford be assuming that awesome responsibility on August 9; he would be doing so at a time when the country was in chaos. Economic instability, the Vietnam War, and now impeachment seriously strained the goodwill between the nation and the White House.

"There had never been a time in our lives when we so much needed a source of strength beyond ourselves," Betty says in Marlo Thomas's book *The Right Words at the Right Time.* "Jerry reminded me of the fifth and sixth verses of chapter three of the Book of Proverbs, a prayer he learned as a boy, which reads: 'Trust in the Lord with all thine heart; and lean not unto thine own understanding. In all thy ways acknowledge Him and He shall direct thy paths.' This became our prayer."[6]

Betty Ford says that depending on God helped her through many challenges the Fords faced during their White House years. Besides those associated with her husband's position, there were the challenges of her breast cancer and later her recovery from addiction to alcohol and prescription drugs. She says that those verses were "a great source of strength for me." Betty Ford, an Episcopalian, had always looked to God, but as she endured one difficult challenge after another, her dependence on God grew.

People usually learn to lean on God the best when times are tough. As marriage counselors we've talked with so many couples who confess that a crisis is what brought them back to a radical dependence on God—and we know just what they mean. In a recent medical emergency with one of our sons, we did nothing if not trust in the Lord with our whole hearts.

Maybe it's because God seems more present in our desperate pain and grief. Or maybe it has more to do with the times we feel most out of control. But don't wait for that kind of situation to strike you: seek to "acknowledge him" in all your ways today.

You never know what you can do until you have to do it. —BETTY FORD

YOUR ROMANCE QUOTIENT

May the Lord make your love for one another and for all people grow and overflow.

1 THESSALONIANS 3:12

WHEN THEY MARRIED EIGHTEEN MONTHS AGO, Kim never would have dreamed she'd find herself complaining that her husband, Steve, didn't show her enough affection. "He was so attentive that he would notice if I changed a part in my hair or bought a new blouse," Kim says. But the loving words and compliments come a little less often now, and frankly, Kim misses the special attention. "He thinks I'm the one who's cooling off," she says, "but I just can't get interested in sex when I feel I'm being ignored."

Kim and Steve aren't alone. The frequent expressions of affection and approval that couples give each other during the courtship and honeymoon stage can dwindle during the first years of marriage. You may love each other as much, but you tend to talk about it less. There's a peak of emotional intimacy during the early phase of a relationship, and then the "I love yous" dwindle and the romance fades. And if we are not careful, they can remain at low ebb for years to come.

Let's make this perfectly clear. Contrary to the fairy tales we were weaned on, romance runs the risk of fading. No, let us rephrase that—romance always fades. As human beings, we aren't built to maintain the high levels of feverish passion and romance experienced during the early days of engagement and the honeymoon. Even the more mature stories of doomed love reinforce this notion. Remember the tragic twosome Romeo and Juliet? How about Lancelot and Guinevere? Rhett and Scarlett? In each case, love was snuffed out while the heat of passion was still turned up full blast. Why? Because it couldn't last. The heat of passion was never meant to.

However, that doesn't mean we are doomed to never enjoy the romance of a honeymoon again. Not by a long shot. In fact, researchers have found that the deepest and most satisfying moments in a couple's marriage are enjoyed during their second half. It often takes effort to get there, though. So the question is, what are you doing to ensure your romance quotient doesn't fade? Sure, the engagement and honeymoon are over, and maybe all your "early married" years, too. But the married years you're in now can be full of romance too. What can you do now to make your love overflow?[7]

And what's romance? Usually, a nice little tale where you have everything As You Like It, where rain never wets your jacket and gnats never bite your nose and it's always daisy-time. —D. H. LAWRENCE

GIVING SOME TIME AT BAT

We who are strong ought to bear with the failings of the weak and not to please ourselves.

ROMANS 15:1, NIV

ON AUGUST 11, 2002, the Chicago Cubs were at Coors Field playing the Colorado Rockies. Although the Cubbies had no chance of making the play-offs, their most celebrated player was committed to doing whatever he could to help his team win as many games as possible. Sammy Sosa was also intent on adding to his impressive home run total.

Each of his first three times at the plate, Sosa hit home runs with two runners on base. That meant that by only the fifth inning, Sosa had hit a trio of three-run homers and tied a franchise record with nine RBIs. Even the Colorado Rockies fans were thrilled with the possibility that Sosa could hit a fourth homer in the game, which would tie the major-league record. They knew (as did Sosa) that in the thin, mile-high air, home runs were more frequent than in other ballparks. The odds were in Sosa's favor.

To everyone's amazement, the Cubs' right fielder decided enough was enough. Sosa voluntarily exited the game before his next at bat. According to Cubs manager Bruce Kimm, Sosa wanted to be rested up for the next day's game. But that wasn't all. According to the Chicago skipper, "Sammy was thinking about the other players a little bit, too. It was a good time to get them some at bats. It was a very unselfish move."[8]

Every couple has the same opportunity. We may not be playing ball, but the game of marriage is ripe with opportunities for an unselfish move. Whether it be with the TV remote, the restaurant you choose, the temperature of the room, or anything else, you might consider what it will do for your "team" to give your spouse some at bats.

I have been a selfish being all my life, in practice, though not in principle.
—JANE AUSTEN

MEMORY LANE

Look, the winter is past, and the rains are over and gone. SONG OF SONGS 2:11

CURRENT RESEARCH SAYS that memory is reconstructed as much as it is reproduced. In other words, we may be just as likely to re-create events as we are to remember them exactly. In many experiments, involving more than twenty thousand people in all, professor of psychology and law Elizabeth Loftus and her colleagues have shown that eyewitnesses actually reconstruct their memories. For example, in one experiment a filmed traffic accident was shown to subjects who were then asked different questions about what they had seen. While one group was asked, "How fast were the cars going when they smashed into each other?" the other was asked, "How fast were the cars going when they hit each other?" Those who heard the word *smashed* gave higher speed estimates than those who heard the word *hit* and, a week later, recalled seeing more than twice as much broken glass at the scene as the other group did. In fact, there had been no glass broken in the accident, but the question was enough to suggest that there was, and that was enough to re-create a memory.

What Loftus's experiment demonstrated is known as the misinformation effect, which describes the phenomenon of people misremembering reality even when supplied with only subtle misinformation. Apparently the misinformation effect is so subconscious that later on it is nearly impossible for witnesses to tell the difference between actual memories and those that were only suggested to them.[9] That's because when we fill in our memories' gaps by guesses or assumptions, those guesses now truly become part of our memories. As novelist Anaïs Nin put it, "Memory is a great betrayer."

How does this subtle memory creation affect marriage? Well, let's say you notice a pattern of lashing out in anger at your spouse. You may start to recall how your father did that very same thing to you. *Ah, no wonder I have issues with anger—it all makes sense now.* Or does it? Obviously it is possible to remember what actually happened to you, but the point is that sometimes your memory may say it was so whether it was or not.

Is there some unfortunate behavior in your marriage that you are a little too willing to blame on your past? Why not focus on the present? Are you willing to let your spouse speak into your life on that issue? What can you do today to put your memories behind you and revise your present?

We cannot change our past. We cannot change the fact that people act in a certain way. We cannot change the inevitable. The only thing we can do is play on the one string we have, and that is our attitude. —CHARLES R. SWINDOLL

A LIFETIME LOVE AFFAIR

My lover is mine, and I am his. SONG OF SONGS 2:16

HE HAS PREACHED IN PERSON to more people around the world than any other preacher in history. More than 2.5 million people have stepped forward at his crusades to accept Jesus Christ as their personal Savior. Of course, you already know we're talking about Billy Graham.

Have you ever heard of the Billy Graham Rule? As a guard against even the appearance of wrongdoing, the great evangelist had a policy that he would never be alone with a woman, other than his wife Ruth. Perhaps it's one of the reasons their marriage thrived for more than sixty years.

Billy met Ruth at Wheaton College. "I saw her walking down the road towards me and I couldn't help but stare at her as she walked. She looked at me and our eyes met and I felt that she was definitely the woman I wanted to marry." Ruth thought that he "wanted to please God more than any man I'd ever met."[10]

Billy and Ruth married on August 13, 1943. To close observers, Graham was like a schoolkid with his beloved wife right to the end of her life. "Though she's been gone three years," says Graham biographer Jerry Jenkins, "he still speaks dreamily of her."

Jenkins recalls a luncheon several years ago that he and his wife, Dianna, were scheduled to have with the Grahams. It was close to Billy and Ruth's sixtieth wedding anniversary, but because of failing health, Ruth was unable to join her husband and friends for the meal. Billy, who held his wife's hand in public and talked lovingly about her often, didn't allow Ruth's absence to pass unremarked. The great evangelist, himself on a cane, told his companions, "We've learned at this stage of our lives, we can maintain our lifetime love affair with our eyes."

For six decades, together or apart, in sickness and in health, the Grahams enjoyed a lifetime love affair. Can you think of a couple that you know whose marriage you admire? Let them know what a blessing their relationship is to you and consider inviting them to share from their rich experiences as marriage mentors for the two of you. And while you're at it, don't underestimate the encouraging power you two have as a couple to be an inspiration in the lives of another married couple who might benefit from your own marriage wisdom.

A good marriage is made up of two good forgivers. —GIGI GRAHAM TCHIVIDJIAN

HEALING THROUGH HUMOR

Sing for joy, O heavens! Rejoice, O earth! Burst into song, O mountains! For the LORD *has comforted his people and will have compassion on them in their suffering.* ISAIAH 49:13

LAUGHTER HAS IMPORTANT physiological effects on the body. Laughter is good medicine. Modern research indicates that people with a sense of humor have fewer symptoms of physical illness than those who are less humorous. This idea, however, is nothing new. Since King Solomon's time, people have known about and applied the healing benefits of humor. Proverbs 17:22 tells us, "A merry heart does good, like medicine" (NKJV). And as the French philosopher Voltaire wrote, "The art of medicine consists of amusing the patient while nature cures the disease."

In spite of its historical legacy, the healing power of laughter was not taken seriously by the scientific world until Norman Cousins, former editor of *Saturday Review* and subsequent professor at UCLA's School of Medicine, wrote about his life-changing experience with humor. As he reported in his book *Anatomy of an Illness*, laughter helped turn the tide of a serious collagen disease. "I made the joyous discovery," Cousins reported, "that ten minutes of genuine belly laughter had an anesthetic effect and would give me at least two hours of pain-free sleep." He surrounded himself with Marx Brothers films and *Candid Camera* videos. He also checked out of the hospital and moved into a hotel where, as he says, he could "laugh twice as hard at half the price."

Cousins called laughter "inner jogging" because every system in our body gets a workout when we have a hearty laugh. Laboratory studies support Cousins's hunches. Our cardiovascular and respiratory systems, for example, benefit more from twenty seconds of robust laughter than from three minutes of exercise on a rowing machine. Through laughter, muscles release tension, and neurochemicals are released into the blood stream, creating the same feelings that long-distance joggers experience as "runner's high."[11]

What amuses you as a couple? Is there some equivalent of Cousins's comedy videos that you could surround yourselves with on some kind of a regular basis? Brainstorm your options together today. Make it a point to maintain a sense of playfulness and humor together. You might even think of it as a workout for your soul![12]

 Laughter is like a shock absorber that eases the blows of life. —BARBARA JOHNSON

TIME IS WHAT YOU MAKE IT

Teach us to realize the brevity of life, so that we may grow in wisdom. PSALM 90:12

CHUCK COLSON TELLS the story of visiting Mississippi's Parchman Prison, where he found most of the death-row inmates killing time by watching TV.

> But in one cell a man was sitting on his bunk, reading. As I approached, he looked up and showed me his book—an instruction manual on Episcopal liturgy.
>
> His name was John Irving. On death row for more than 15 years, he was studying for the priesthood. John told me he was allowed out of his cell one hour each day. The rest of the time, he studied—preparing to meet Christ or serve him here.
>
> Seeing that John had nothing in his cell but a few books, I thought, God's blessed me so much, the least I can do is provide something for this brother. "Would you like a TV if I could arrange it?" I asked.
>
> John smiled gratefully. "Thanks," he said, "but no thanks. You can waste an awful lot of time with those things." For the 15 years since a judge placed a number on his days, John has determined not to waste the one commodity he had to give to the Lord—his time.[13]

Kind of gives you pause, doesn't it? A prisoner on death row who doesn't have time for television! Wherever you spend it, time is truly what you make it. Sally Cunneen, writing in *The Christian Century*, tells a story of how reflecting on the principles of E. F. Schumacher, statistician and economist during World War II, spurred her own thinking about counting her resources rather than simply living with them.

> Evaluating my everyday use of time and resources, I noticed how often I tended to count and measure—abstracting from a situation rather than living it. Take the routine of soft-boiling an egg. After the water came to a boil—a goal for which I would wait impatiently—I would slowly count to 100 while the egg cooked to the desired firmness. In this numerical mode, I would keep an eye on the clock and sometimes snap at my husband, absorbed in the newspaper.

Thinking about it, Sally came up with a new way of timing her egg cooking: she began to say three Hail Marys after the water began to boil. "Then," she says, "I use the boiling time to place myself in touch with earlier generations of cooks who measured their recipes with litanies, using time to get beyond it."[14]

So what about the two of you? Are you simply passing time when you could be making it better? After all, time is what you make it. Don't allow your next twenty-four hours to pass without making them what you want. Consider how each of you can help one another do just that.

Where, except in the present, can the Eternal be met? —C. S. LEWIS

NO-FAULT MARRIAGE

Don't pick a fight without reason, when no one has done you harm. PROVERBS 3:30

VIRTUALLY EVERY COUPLE *we see in therapy is interested in what, or who, caused their problems; they're looking for a place to lay blame. What they do not understand about problems in marriage, technically speaking, is that causes are not simple matters. Finding fault—in the truest sense—is not easy. Why? Because the influences on a problem are reciprocal. They cannot be pegged on one thing or one person.*

It's one of the most profound secrets of human relationships we know: causality is circular. In a marital problem, choosing the point at which the causal chain begins is pointless and arbitrary. There is no one single cause for anything in marriage.

Does that make you feel uneasy?

Most of us are far more comfortable with a linear cause-effect approach where an unhappy childhood or bad nerves can explain undesirable behavior. The truth is that human relationships are not that simple. A better approach is to focus not only on what goes on inside a person, but what takes place between two persons.[15]

The point is that no one is really to blame in a marriage relationship. Both of you have established your routines. And by heightening your self-awareness of the patterns in your relationship, you will learn what moves you can make to positively affect your marriage—without playing the blame game about which of you is the problem. This will free you to be a part of the solution, instead. And you will see that taking ownership for making change will have a synergistically positive effect between you.

Teach me to feel another's woe, to right the fault I see; that mercy I to others show, that mercy show to me. —**ALEXANDER POPE**

THE MARK OF A REAL FAIRY TALE

Dear brothers and sisters, one final thing. Fix your thoughts on what is true, and honorable, and right, and pure, and lovely, and admirable. Think about things that are excellent and worthy of praise. PHILIPPIANS 4:8

ONCE UPON A TIME THERE was a prince who wanted to marry a princess, but she would have to be a real princess, and there were many counterfeits. You remember the story. The king traveled all over the world to find one, but nowhere could he get what he wanted. Finally one evening the old king heard a knock at the city gate, and it was a woman claiming to be a princess. But to find out for sure, the queen devised a plan. She took off all the bedding from the guest's bed and laid a pea on the bottom; then she took twenty mattresses and laid them on the pea. In the morning the princess was asked how she had slept. Because she mentioned having felt an uncomfortable lump in the bed, her fate was decided. The prince now knew he had a real princess.

Hans Christian Andersen wrote that story in 1835, and published it on May 8 for the entertainment of children. But all these years later, we think there is a little lesson in it for every married couple. What is it? That a true "prince" or "princess" notices the little things. Especially those little things that can make a big and positive difference.

For example, a "real" husband or wife recognizes when his or her spouse needs an extra hand with bringing in the groceries, or is feeling overwhelmed by something at work and could use a tender back rub. In other words, a sensitive and responsive spouse is on the lookout for ways to be helpful.

Aside from looking out for little needs, "real" husbands and wives also recognize the positive little things that go unnoticed by most. When their spouses take out the trash, they say thanks. Like the princess and the pea, they notice a change in the bed—like when the bed has been freshly made with clean sheets—or when their partners have picked up the coat they left hanging over the back of a chair, or filled the car with gas, or when they took care to make the yard look nice.

Bottom line is we strengthen our marriages whenever we take time to lend a hand and whenever we notice and appreciate the little things our partners do to help us out. Little acts of kindness go unacknowledged, and eventually undone, in most marriages. Don't let yours be one of them. In fact, you may want to say thanks right now for something little you've noticed today that your spouse said or did.

Every man's life is a fairy tale written by God's fingers. —HANS CHRISTIAN ANDERSEN

THE *S* WORD

Submit to one another out of reverence for Christ. EPHESIANS 5:21

SEVERAL YEARS AGO, a young and recently married man named Tim invited me (Les) to lunch one day and asked, "How can I get my wife to submit to me?" His question threw me. I have counseled many newlyweds, but I had never heard the question phrased so bluntly.

Tim was a devout Christian trying to build his new marriage on biblical principles, and he wanted to be the "head" of the home. He read about headship in the verse that says "The husband is the head of the wife as Christ is the head of the church, his body, of which he is the Savior" (Ephesians 5:23, NIV). Tim interpreted this statement to mean literally that it was his job to be the boss of his wife. And it was her job to be submissive to his demands. Tim's wife, however, didn't see things that way because she lived in the twentieth century, not the first. She saw herself, understandably, as an equal partner in the marriage.

Tim, sincere as he was, didn't fully understand what it meant to be "the head of the wife as Christ is the head of the church." It never seemed to occur to Tim that in the Bible the husband is never called to make his wife submit. The Bible doesn't call husbands to rule over their wives. It calls them to renounce the desire to be master and be the first to honor and respect their wives. It is all out of reverence for Christ.

What then is headship? Let me tell you what I told Tim. Headship is not being the first in line. It is not being the boss or ruler. It is being the first to honor, the first to nurture, the first to meet your partner's needs.

A healthy marriage is built on a mutual desire to submit one's needs to the other. As Ephesians 5:21 says: "Submit to one another out of reverence for Christ." That's the basic principle. Emptying ourselves of our self-centered desires is the bridge to becoming soul mates. Without mutual submission, every marriage, no matter how romantic, will eventually falter.

The key is understanding that submission is a two-way street in marriage. Scripture not only calls husbands and wives to "submit to one another," but we are to also submit to God (see Job 22:21; Hebrews 12:9; James 4:7).

The only right a Christian has is the right to give up his rights. —OSWALD CHAMBERS

BETA SPOUSE

Each time he said, "My grace is all you need. My power works best in weakness." So now I am glad to boast about my weaknesses, so that the power of Christ can work through me.

2 CORINTHIANS 12:9

IT'S COMMON PRACTICE FOR A new website or software to go public in what is referred to as a "beta" version. When Microsoft, for example, launches a new system upgrade, it will come out in beta before the "official" or final version is released. For years Google called their e-mail feature, Gmail, a beta site. What does that mean? The idea behind the term is that the system or program is still in test mode. In other words, it is available for the public to use, but with the understanding that you may find bugs in it. The site is not making any claims to have everything worked out to perfection. Understanding what that means, you don't get angry with a beta site if some aspect of its functionality is not doing what you think it should. You give a beta version plenty of grace, and the site is counting on you to do it.

The same principle holds true in marriage. Think how much conflict, frustration, and friction we could avoid in our relationships if we treated each other as "beta spouses." If we could remember that we are all a work in progress—ourselves as well as our partners—life would be exponentially easier.

So why don't we do that? For many, the reason rests on an unrealistic level of perfectionism. And perfection was never meant for marriage.

Of course, this does not mean we should not aim for high standards in our relationships or within ourselves. But there is a huge difference between excellence and perfectionism. Excellence is not attaining an impossibly out-of-reach goal. It has to do with living up to our potential. Everyone, no matter how lowly, has the potential to attain excellence in his or her life—no one, no matter how lofty, has the potential to attain perfection.

When you wake up each morning, give both yourself and your spouse permission to live in beta mode, surrounded with lots of grace. And if you insist on perfection, let it have to do with God's power being made perfect in your weakness.

Perfectionism is the voice of the oppressor. —ANNE LAMOTT

GROWING TOGETHER OR GROWING APART?

The thief's purpose is to steal and kill and destroy. My purpose is to give them a rich and satisfying life. JOHN 10:10

ONCE IN A WHILE COUPLES come to our counseling offices with a decision for divorce already determined. They are headed to divorce court and are just stopping by our place along the way, or so it seems. Their motivation for therapy is usually focused on how to break the news to their children, and they usually explain their situation to us something like this: "We aren't ending our marriage with a lot of hard feelings; we simply discovered that we no longer had anything in common. I guess we grew apart."

We wince each time we hear it. It has got to be the lamest excuse possible for ending a marriage. Why? Because the way it is described, it sounds as if a divorce were inevitable—as if something in their personalities destined them to gradually separate. The truth is we all grow in the directions we choose, and if our mates' trajectories are different from ours, it need not be the end of the relationship. It simply calls for some intentional adaptation. "Drifting apart" is an excuse for not wanting to realign our attitudes and actions with those of our partners.

An enduring marriage requires possibility thinking, elasticity, and resilience. It needs continual attention and adaptation to grow together. It requires a shift in interests as our partners' interests shift. In other words, to remain good and strong, marriage entails a lifelong project of adjusting and readjusting our attitudes. For this is the only path to finding positive options to our most perplexing circumstances.

Take a hard look at your own level of adjustment today. Is it set too high, with an impossible standard your spouse must meet before you'll bend toward him or her? Talk to the Lord today about the state of your heart toward your spouse, and ask him to bring about a rich and satisfying life in your marriage.

> *A loyal friend laughs at your jokes when they're not so good, and sympathizes with your problems when they're not so bad.* —**ARNOLD H. GLASGOW**

IT'S NO FAIRY TALE

Now there is no condemnation for those who belong to Christ Jesus. And because you belong to him, the power of the life-giving Spirit has freed you from the power of sin that leads to death. The law of Moses was unable to save us because of the weakness of our sinful nature. So God did what the law could not do. He sent his own Son in a body like the bodies we sinners have. And in that body God declared an end to sin's control over us by giving his Son as a sacrifice for our sins. ROMANS 8:1-3

IT WAS FIRST PUBLISHED IN 1812 by the Brothers Grimm in their *Children's and Household Tales*, though it has even older origins than that. Today it's better known as "Rapunzel," and it has been told and retold again and again, recently by Disney in the animated film *Tangled*, which claimed to be "taking adventure to new lengths."

The fairy tale "Rapunzel" is the story of a beautiful young girl, imprisoned in a tower by an old witch who insistently tells her she is ugly. One day when Rapunzel gazes from the window in her tower, she sees a handsome prince standing below. He is enchanted by her beauty and tells her to let her long golden tresses down from the window. The prince then braids her hair into a ladder and climbs up to rescue her.

The implicit message of this fairy tale is simple but profound. Rapunzel's prison is really not the tower but her fear that she is ugly and unlovable. The mirroring eyes of her prince, however, tell her that she is loved, and thus she is set free from the tyranny of her own imagined worthlessness.

We are all, in a sense, like Rapunzel, enslaved by the fear of rejection, yearning to be valued by someone special. But in our counseling office we have seen enough couples to know that some spouses are especially troubled by the fear of being unlovable. They are afraid they are not loved because they feel unlovable, and this fear directly affects their marriages.

The grace of being loved and accepted unconditionally is incomprehensible, and we all fall short of deserving this kind of perfect love. But we must still accept the gracious gift of God's eternal love. There is "no condemnation" for those of us in Christ Jesus. And when we accept this love, we are freed to love one another as we should.

Think about this crucial dynamic today. Do you accept God's unconditional love for you?

He led her to his kingdom where he was joyfully received, and they lived for a long time afterwards, happy and contented. —JACOB AND WILHELM GRIMM

PESSIMISM KILLS ENCOURAGEMENT

Judas and Silas, both being prophets, spoke at length to the believers, encouraging and strengthening their faith. ACTS 15:32

FEW THINGS ARE MORE deadly to marriage than negativism—especially in its most alluring form of pessimism. In fact, we suspect that if couples could be given a vaccine against pessimistic thinking we would see the divorce rate all but drop off. The good news is that in a sense, you can protect your marriage against a pessimistic virus. How? All it takes is a little encouragement.

Some marriage partners see every problem in their lives as interminable. They believe one problem will ruin everything. So they quit trying. They give up, resigned to passivity. They raise the white flag and surrender to the problems of life they could otherwise beat.

A different group of spouses see their outside problems as mere obstacles, as challenges to overcome. They face a difficult situation at work or with a friend and work hard to get through. They don't give up.

Do you know the difference between these two groups of married couples? Marriage experts do. Research has shown time and again that all it takes for many people to persevere in the midst of a difficulty is an encouraging word from their spouses: "I believe in you," "You have what it takes," "You are doing great." Seemingly small and insignificant, these simple statements almost go unnoticed. But not by the person on the receiving end. Encouragement brings strength and can make the difference between a spouse who gives up and a partner who perseveres.

No wonder it was remarkable that Judas and Silas did what they could to encourage and strengthen the early believers! In the same way, don't neglect the powerful role you can play in each other's lives just by offering the simple gift of encouragement.

 The optimist sees the rose and not its thorns; the pessimist stares at the thorns, oblivious of the rose. —**KAHLIL GIBRAN**

MARRIAGE MOCCASINS

Keep on loving each other as brothers and sisters. Don't forget to show hospitality to strangers, for some who have done this have entertained angels without realizing it! Remember those in prison, as if you were there yourself. Remember also those being mistreated, as if you felt their pain in your own bodies. HEBREWS 13:1-3

WE CAN ALL LEARN SOMETHING from this well-known Sioux Indian prayer: "Oh Great Spirit, grant me the wisdom to walk in another's moccasins before I criticize or pass judgment." Learning to walk in your mate's moccasins is at the heart of a healthy marriage relationship. It is the rare capacity to put yourself into the shoes of your partner and accurately see life from his or her perspective. Psychologists call it empathy.

Empathy combines two important capacities, to analyze and to sympathize—to use our heads and to use our hearts. Our analytical capacities involve collecting facts and observing conditions. We look at a problem, break it down into its causes, and propose solutions. That's analyzing. Sympathizing is feeling for another person. It is feeling the pain of someone who's suffering or feeling the anger of a person in rage. Together, sympathizing and analyzing are the twin engines of empathy. One without the other is fine, but their true power is found in combination. We need to love with both head and heart in order to empathize.

The apostle Paul encouraged empathy in Hebrews when he said: "Remember those in prison, as if you were there yourself. Remember also those being mistreated, as if you felt their pain in your own bodies" (13:3).

When we empathize with our partners, we put aside our expectation that they should be like us. We accept the fact that they have brought their unique personality into our marriage, and we ask ourselves questions like "What is *he* feeling? What pressures does *she* have to cope with? What does *he* fear? What does *she* need? How, if at all, should I help my spouse?"[16]

Remember there's no such thing as a small act of kindness. Every act creates a ripple with no logical end. —SCOTT ADAMS

A HAPPY ACT OF KINDNESS

Whoever wants to be a leader among you must be your servant, and whoever wants to be first among you must be the slave of everyone else. For even the Son of Man came not to be served but to serve others and to give his life as a ransom for many. MARK 10:43-45

BOSTON IS ONE OF OUR favorite cities. Les grew up there. And each time we get back to "Beantown" for a speaking engagement we try to do something different with our down time. Last year we visited the Holocaust Memorial at Quincy Market, where five of six pillars are inscribed with stories that speak of the cruelty and suffering in the camps. The sixth features a story that Gerda Weissmann Klein tells about her friend Ilse Kleinzahler. She tells that story, among others, in an interview with the *Chicago Tribune*:

> *My friend Ilse Kleinzahler, who died a week before we were liberated, once found a raspberry in the gutter on the way to the factory. It was in Grunberg, one of the most miserable camps, and she saved it all day long. She carried it in her pocket— the temptation must have been incredible—and she gave it to me that night on a leaf. She had plucked a leaf through the barbed wire, washed it, and presented me with one slightly bruised raspberry. Most people think of (the Holocaust) as unrelieved horror. I like to remember some of the things in camp, how people helped each other . . . that there was friendship and love and caring.*[17]

As difficult as it may be for us to fathom the world those girls were living in at the time, it's easy to be inspired by such a gracious and happy act of kindness: a simple berry, treasured and presented to a friend. It's a breathtaking example of the generosity one person can offer another—and nowhere is that truer than in marriage.

Imagine a marriage in which you offer your prized possession to your mate, whatever it might be. Maybe it's your time, when you have a pile of work; or your listening ear, when you'd planned on watching TV; or your presence, when a friend has invited you to do something else. Your simple yet spectacular gift may be known to you only. But you will enjoy all the rewards a happy act of kindness offers.

How can you use Ilse's kind act, in the midst of all her suffering, as an inspiration to show extraordinary kindness to your spouse?

To be rich in admiration and free from envy, to rejoice greatly in the good of others, to love with such generosity of heart that your love is still a dear possession in absence or unkindness—these are the gifts of fortune which money cannot buy.
—ROBERT LOUIS STEVENSON

LIFE IS NOT A DRESS REHEARSAL

Brothers and sisters, we urge you to warn those who are lazy. Encourage those who are timid. 1 THESSALONIANS 5:14

AFTER A LIFELONG SEARCH for meaning in life, one of the conclusions King Solomon of Israel drew was this: "Whatever you do, do well. For when you go to the grave, there will be no work or planning or knowledge or wisdom" (Ecclesiastes 9:10). This is not in contrast to what he says just a few verses prior: "Eat your food with joy, and drink . . . with a happy heart, for God approves of this!" (9:7). In fact, the idea is to live every day to its fullest, which includes both working and playing hard.

Nadine Stair got the message, if only too late. You may not know her name, but you may have heard about something the late Mrs. Stair, of Louisville, Kentucky, said when she was asked several years ago, at age eighty-five, what she would do if she could live her life all over again. She had a memorable answer:

> *If I had my life to live over, I'd try to make more mistakes next time. I would relax. . . . You see, I was one of those people who lived prophylactically and sensibly and sanely, hour after hour and day after day. Oh, I've had my moments. And if I had it to do over again, I would take more chances. I would scale more mountains, I would swim more rivers, and I would watch more sunsets. . . . I would have more actual troubles and fewer imaginary ones. . . . I would travel lighter, much lighter, than I have. If I had my life to live over, I would start barefoot earlier in the spring, and I'd stay that way later in the fall. And I would ride more merry-go-rounds, and greet more people, and pick more flowers, and dance more often.*[18]

Ever feel like the days of your life have become too sensible, too sane—too safe? To put it another way, if you were to rate how well you as an individual are living life to the fullest on a scale of one to ten, how would you answer and why? Does your answer change for you as a couple? What's one area of your life together in which you would like to be living with more passion and boldness?

He who is overcautious will accomplish but very little. —FRIEDRICH VON SCHILLER

SEEKING WISE COUNSEL

When the Father sends the Advocate as my representative—that is, the Holy Spirit—he will teach you everything and will remind you of everything I have told you. JOHN 14:26

"ARE YOU SAYING I need counseling?" Caleb says with a sneer.

"Well, I think everybody needs counseling," Michael replies.

"Look, man," Caleb says, "I am not about to go talk to somebody I don't even know about something that's none of their business!"

"Look—Karen needs to respect you," Michael says. "But just remember: a woman is like a rose—if you treat her right, she'll bloom; if you don't, she'll wilt."

"Where did you get that?" Caleb asks.

Michael smiles and says, "Counseling."

This little dialogue from the film *Fireproof* underscores what we can testify is common resistance among couples to seeking wise counsel. However, as we have pointed out in our book *Meditations on Proverbs for Couples*, marriage therapy and even just plain good counsel from a wise friend or mentor isn't only for embattled marriages like the character Caleb's was.

> *What used to be a last resort, in fact, is now an increasingly popular option for any state of a marriage. Counselors who used to focus exclusively on the make-or-break variety of interventions are now equipping themselves for doing basic marriage tune-ups on successful relationships. And with good reason. There is so much good research and information on marriage that is just sitting around waiting for real life couples to put it to good use.*
>
> *But while the stigma of going to counseling is lessening, far too many couples allow pride to stand in the way of receiving a bit of advice. It seems many couples would rather have their fingernails pulled out than visit their local marriage counselor. I suppose this shouldn't be too surprising when you consider that therapy demands emotional vulnerability, not to mention admitting that you can't solve every problem by yourself. That's especially difficult for men. After all, men are socialized to repress feelings of hurt, shame, or caring. Push a young boy into the playground dirt, and he knows it's his job to come back with a fistful of gravel rather than a face full of tears.*[19]

Whatever the aversion to counseling may appear to be, pride is almost always a factor. And that holds true when it comes to seeking help from the ultimate counselor—the Holy Spirit.

 } *Preaching is personal counseling on a group basis.* —**HARRY EMERSON FOSDICK**

THE WEDDING AT CANA

There was a wedding celebration in the village of Cana in Galilee. Jesus' mother was there, and Jesus and his disciples were also invited to the celebration. The wine supply ran out during the festivities, so Jesus' mother told him, "They have no more wine." . . . Jesus told the servants, "Fill the jars with water." When the jars had been filled, he said, "Now dip some out, and take it to the master of ceremonies." So the servants followed his instructions. . . . This miraculous sign at Cana in Galilee was the first time Jesus revealed his glory. JOHN 2:1-3, 7-8, 11

> **PREPARING FOR THE WEDDING** *has been compared to readying for a trip into the wild unknown. The wedding dress and bride's trousseau, according to some, need to be as carefully set as a compass pointed toward new territory. As Dr. Mary Roberts wrote in her 1912 book* Why Women Are So, *"A trousseau was as essential to the prospective bride as an outfit to the explorer of arctic or tropical wilds. . . . Who knows what might be needed and yet unattainable in the great adventure upon which she was about to embark!"*
>
> *To prepare the trousseau, a prospective bride spent the final days of her engagement stitching linens and clothing. She sewed and shopped, packed and cleaned, sewed and packed some more. There was no time to spare. The process became her transition into wifehood, and she certainly wanted to come out of it looking her absolute best.*
>
> *A century later, some of us may think that modern women have moved beyond that. Clearly, we've become more cultured through careers and education. But the wedding dress and ceremony are still a big deal. The millions of dollars spent annually on mere magazines about weddings can attest to that fact.[20]*

In the above passage from John 2, Jesus is at a wedding in Cana for a family whom he and his mother probably knew. His disciples were included in the invitation. What is interesting to note, many commentators say, is that the miracle he performed at this wedding was actually for his disciples. Few besides them saw it. The miracle signaled the unveiling of his glory, and his disciples put their faith in him (see verse 11). As you look back at your own wedding, is there a sign of Jesus' presence and glory that you recall?

If you're like most other couples married in this country, your wedding represents many hours, days, and even months of intense preparation of things roughly equivalent to the old trousseau. In the midst of preparing for that special ceremony put on for others to see, were you able to see the miracle that God was performing in your own life? Does your marriage now give testimony to God?

*There is something about a wedding gown prettier than in any other gown in –
the world.* —DOUGLAS JERROLD

PRAYING FOR EACH OTHER

They all met together and were constantly united in prayer. ACTS 1:14

PRAYING WITH EACH OTHER is not easy for us. Oh, we pray together before meals, and we pray together when there is a special need or crisis, but we aren't the kind of couple who kneels beside our bed each night. We might be better persons if we did, but we don't. I suppose we could blame our busy and fickle schedules, but the truth is we just haven't made the effort to build a consistent shared prayer time into our lives. We pray as a family every night when tucking our boys into bed, but we don't set aside a routine and specific time to pray as a couple.

We admire couples who do, and we covet the rewards they surely reap. For as Jesus has said, "If two of you on earth agree about anything you ask for, it will be done for you by my Father in heaven. For where two or three come together in my name, there am I with them" (Matthew 18:19-20, NIV).

Still, one thing we do every day is pray *for* each other. Whether together or in separate cities, we remember each other in our daily prayers. We made that commitment on our wedding day, and Leslie had the reference of Philippians 1:3-5 engraved inside my wedding band. It's a prayer that says, "I thank my God every time I remember you. . . . I always pray with joy because of your partnership in the gospel from the first day until now." (NIV).

Sometimes one of us will say to the other, "I'll be praying for you today," but most of the time there is just a quiet assurance that the one partner is lifting up the other with prayers.

Set aside even five minutes today to pray specifically for your spouse, and if possible, with your spouse. Invite God to reveal to you how you can share his love with your spouse today.

> *If you are a stranger to prayer you are stranger to the greatest source of power known to human beings.* —BILLY SUNDAY

YOUR SPIRITUAL STYLE

If the whole body were an eye, how would you hear? Or if your whole body were an ear, how would you smell anything? 1 CORINTHIANS 12:17

FOR MOST OF OUR MARRIAGE, we have been out of sync with each other in how we relate to God. Early on we realized we were on relatively divergent paths. Not that we didn't share the same values or maintain our individual walks with God. It was more that we didn't understand each other's way of relating to God individually, which made it seem impossible to relate to God together as a couple. But, as we eventually learned, it all comes down to knowing and affirming each other's spiritual style.

I (Leslie) am contemplative, through and through. I like nothing more than to spend a few hours each day alone with God. Having little boys has put a crimp in my style, but this remains my primary pathway to God. I have had the same prayer book for years and the same well-worn Bible, too. They keep me company as I seek to love God with the purest and deepest love I can. I like to rise early to enjoy the quiet morning hours as I spend time with God. This isn't out of duty; it isn't a discipline I work at. It comes naturally. Nothing about this style, however, seemed natural to Les. He saw it as too time consuming and unproductive.

My spiritual pathway is more intellectual. I (Les) don't know if it's in my blood—I share this style with some family members—or if it's from my academic training (including seminary), but I feel closest to God when I am studying a truth or insight new to me. If I can conceptualize some aspect of my spiritual life in a fresh way, if I can wrap my mind around a truth, I come alive in my relationship with God. The time I most often spend with God is while I'm reading a new book or in my study, lined with reference tools that help me in my spiritual pursuit. Not so for Leslie. She viewed my approach as too academic and emotionally removed.

So how do the two of us relate to God together? We each still walk the paths that bring us closer to God—but now we also value each other's paths. In the past, we selfishly expected the other to conform to our individual leanings. After all, that felt like the best way to relate to God. And it is for us individually—but not as a couple. This simple revelation was a breakthrough for our marriage.

How would you describe what brings you closest to God? Do you and your spouse respect each other's spiritual style?[21]

While we have the gift of life, it seems to me the only tragedy is to allow part of us to die—whether it is our spirit, our creativity, or our glorious uniqueness. —GILDA RADNER

BUILDING A HOUSE OF LOVE

Whatever you say or whatever you do, remember that you will be judged by the law that sets you free. JAMES 2:12

YOU'VE HEARD OF Habitat for Humanity, the international nonprofit organization devoted to building "simple, decent, and affordable" housing. The organization creates housing for low-income families using volunteer labor and donated money, materials, and, sometimes, land. And you probably know the volunteers represent a broad range of professions, including stay-at-home moms, teachers, lawyers, and doctors.

What you may not know is that it all started with one woman's frustration with her workaholic husband. Linda and Millard Fuller married on August 30, 1959. But neither one of them would have ever predicted the course their life would take some years later. Millard became a millionaire. And he worked hard for his money. But Linda was sick and tired of Millard's money-grabbing lifestyle. While some envied her big house, fancy cars, vacation homes, and all the rest, Linda couldn't have cared less. She wanted Millard, not money. That's why she announced one day that she was going to New York to think about the future of their marriage.

"I was in agony," Millard said. "Never before had I suffered as I did during those days. Everything else—business, sales, profits, prestige, everything that seemed so important—paled into total meaninglessness." Linda's actions were not part of Millard's plan. It stopped him dead in his tracks. And in a tearful meeting in New York City, Millard and Linda were eventually reunited. They decided to sell their successful business, give the money to charities, and go on a missions trip to Africa, touring schools, hospitals, and refugee programs. Not long after they returned home to Georgia, they gave birth to Habitat for Humanity, a nonprofit, ecumenical Christian housing ministry—now the largest nonprofit housing organization in the United States.

Actions speak louder than words, as we all know. But in case you're doubting that, you can talk to any one of the hundreds of thousands who have been helped into a new home by Habitat, and they'll make you a believer.

If you're like us, you can sometimes talk a good talk when it comes to faith issues. But the story of this "house-building" couple challenged us to make sure we were also walking our talk.[22]

 I see life as both a gift and a responsibility. My responsibility is to use what God has given me to help his people in need. —MILLARD FULLER

TALK ABOUT A LOVE DARE!

You desire honesty from the womb, teaching me wisdom even there. PSALM 51:6

BECAUSE WE SEEM TO speak at the same conferences from time to time, Gary Thomas, author of such bestselling books as *Sacred Pathways*, has become a good friend. We sometimes share our thoughts about writing and speaking over dinner. And we occasionally read portions of each other's manuscripts (offering a bit of peer critique) before they are published. And because we travel so often, we also share stories of the road.

A while back, Gary told us about a hotel manager who had grown weary of being yelled at on occasion by dissatisfied customers who expected five-star service at Motel 6 prices. One day, enduring yet another tirade, the manager couldn't believe how rude and crazy a customer had become, and he imagined that if she saw herself in a mirror, she wouldn't believe it either.

That thought sparked a daring idea. He put up a giant mirror behind the hotel's front desk—and the tirades from dissatisfied customers all but ceased. When people saw how crazy they looked while yelling and screaming, they stopped.

That's why we're asking you to do something daring today. We're asking you to swallow your pride and ask your partner to help you see one part of yourself that you may not be seeing on your own. We know. You're already cringing. But this is one of the great benefits of being in a loving relationship. It's a bit like having a mirror that can reflect something about you that you'd never see otherwise. So are you game? Can you muster the courage to ask your partner a tough question? Here it is: What's one thing you see in me that I may have a tough time seeing myself?

Now, here's the catch. You've got to receive this information without defense. It's the only rule in this little exercise. Just receive the information by saying, "Thank you." That's all. Take the information in, and ponder it without coming back with explanation or defensiveness. After all, everyone has blind spots. And as Thomas Carlyle said, "The greatest of faults, I should say, is to be conscious of none."

Oh, that God the gift would give us to see ourselves as others see us! —**ROBERT BURNS**

NOW IS ALL WE HAVE

This is the day the LORD has made. We will rejoice and be glad in it. PSALM 118:24

WHAT'S THE FIRST THING you want to know when you wake up each morning? Think about it. Every one of us wakes up with the same question on our minds: What time is it? That's why we check the clock the moment our eyes open.

Knowing the time not only helps you stay on schedule, but the question can really give you pause if you ask it from a more contemplative place, as in what time is it in my life? In other words, the question becomes, What time is it right now for me (regardless of what the clock says)? Is it time to recharge my batteries? time to take care of an errand that is long overdue? time to phone a friend I've neglected? In other words, what time is it, really?

Asking that question keeps us fully present—right now. Too often we get dragged down by the past, wallowing in regret, or pulled forward by the future, dreaming of what might be tomorrow. Either habit sways us from living fully in the here and now. When someone says, "I'm just killing time," that person might as well say, "I'm throwing away my life." As Alice Bloch said, "We say we waste time, but that is impossible. We waste ourselves."

In his book *Today Matters*, our friend John Maxwell says, "It may sound trite, but today is the only time you have. It's too late for yesterday. And you can't depend on tomorrow. That's why today matters."[1] We've seen John live out this principle with Margaret, his wife. John is one of the most conscientious timekeepers we know. He milks every moment, wanting to bring Margaret into his life at every turn. Sure, he plans for the future and he ponders the past, but make no mistake that John doesn't live for the moment.

You can choose to live in the moment too. Being fully present results from being mindful of what this hour holds. It's being aware that yesterday ended last night and tomorrow hasn't arrived. All you can be certain of is *now*, so decide to use it.

The fact that you are reading these words, focusing on how to use your time together, tells us you are light years ahead of other couples in practicing this principle. But everyone can benefit from a reminder to be fully present in the moment. So, what can you do in your relationship this week to do just that? How can you help each other live fully in your moments together?

Here's a tip that's helped us: Return to the simple question, What time is it, really? That's probably all it will take to snap back into the moment and remember that now is all you have. And that's enough.

 He who neglects the present moment throws away all he has.
—**FRIEDRICH VON SCHILLER**

UNFORGETTABLE

Let all that I am praise the LORD; may I never forget the good things he does for me. PSALM 103:2

YOU MAY FIND THIS STORY hard to believe, but a British newspaper began an article with the following sentence: "Heartfelt commiseration to Dorothy Naylor of Plymouth, whose recent daytrip to Bridgewater was spoiled when her husband, Oliver, left her on the forecourt of a garage . . . and drove seventeen miles before noticing his wife was not in the car."

"I couldn't believe he'd gone without me," Mrs. Naylor told the *Western Morning News*. "I usually sit in the back because I can move around more, but normally we talk to one another."

The couple, both in their seventies, had pulled into a filling station to change a tire. After replacing the tire, Mr. Naylor drove off and didn't notice his wife's absence until he had arrived in another town. After stopping in town, he asked his wife a question. When she didn't answer, he turned around and discovered that he had left her behind. The paper added that the couple had been married for forty years. They both chalked it up to faulty memory.[2]

That raises the question, How's your memory? We don't mean in general. We mean how is your memory when it comes to remembering each other? Now, we don't expect that you're at risk for driving off from an event and not noticing that your spouse isn't with you. But all of us from time to time could benefit from letting our partners know we think about them often. That's what Nat King Cole was singing about in his award-winning song "Unforgettable."

So here's our challenge for you today. Sometime in the next twenty-four hours, do something out of the ordinary that lets your spouse know you are thinking of him or her. It may be as simple as a little e-mail or a voice-mail message. Then again, it may be singing to your spouse your own rendition of the Nat King Cole classic (but only if you have a singing voice). What you do is up to you. Just make sure your spouse knows that he or she is in your thoughts today.

And while you're at it, why don't you ask God to help you to never forget the good things he does for you? In fact, why not say a prayer together right now, thanking God for a couple of good things he's doing for you this week?

Memory . . . is the diary that we all carry about with us. —OSCAR WILDE

BEING YOUR PARTNER'S PUBLICIST

Let someone else praise you, not your own mouth—a stranger, not your own lips.

PROVERBS 27:2

ENGLISH AUTHOR Samuel Butler once said, tongue in cheek: "The advantage of doing one's praising for oneself is that one can lay it on so thick and exactly in the right places." I know what he means.

Maybe it's because I had two older brothers to compete against, but I grew up with a compulsion to blurt out my own self-praise: "Did I tell you about my promotion?"; "Did you know I met with the governor?" Leslie, on the other hand, is quite the opposite, rarely bringing extra attention to herself.

As you might imagine, our polar differences in this area have caused some inner reflection and a bit of soul searching. And after more than twenty-five years of marriage, each of us is beginning to find a better balance. I have a ways to go, but I'm not as self-promoting as I used to be. And inch by inch, Leslie is getting a little more comfortable discussing her accomplishments when appropriate. But above all, we are learning to practice the proverbial secret of affirmation: Let someone else praise you and not your own mouth. This truth may not have been written with couples in mind, but the wise husband and wife will quickly see its applicability to marriage.

In social situations it's often easy to distinguish loving couples from warring ones. Most everyone has been at a party where one half of a couple has taken a public jab at the other. Perhaps it was along the lines of "I keep wishing that John would get out of his recliner, turn off the television, and help me out in the garden like he keeps saying he will!" It's a bad idea to use the cover of an audience to say something you wouldn't say in private. Couples who can't contain their criticisms in public are in serious trouble.

Loving couples, on the other hand, enjoy boosting each other in front of others and casting each other in the best light—much as they did in their courting days, when they wanted their friends and family to like their new love. They say things like "Sarah just got a promotion, but she won't tell you that" or "Rick may not mention it, but he secured a huge grant for his company this week." Loving couples praise one another in private and public. They tell each other's stories; they cover for each other and work as a team.

When you have an opportunity to praise yourself, take a rain check. Remember Proverbs 27:2. But when an opportunity arises to tactfully compliment your spouse, don't let the opportunity slip by.

> *If I have seen further it is only by standing on the shoulders of giants.*
> —ISAAC NEWTON

GIVING YOUR PARTNER "GOOD PRESS"

There are many virtuous and capable women in the world, but you surpass them all!
PROVERBS 31:29

IF YOU WERE TO HOLD high something you appreciate about your spouse right now, what would it be? Chances are it would take you some time to think about that. For some reason, we humans don't always lean into noticing and remembering the things we value in our spouse. That's why some find a gratitude journal dedicated to their marriage to be especially helpful.

You've probably heard about keeping a gratitude journal in which you record the things you are grateful for in a notebook at the end of each day. This is a powerful way to cultivate gratitude, and many will testify to its effectiveness. But we have something a little different in mind. We're talking about a gratitude journal specifically for each other.

Here's how it works. Use a little notebook or even a simple note card, and take turns passing it back and forth. You may exchange it once a month, once a week, or once a day. That's up to you. You may even be sporadic. The goal is to simply use this journal as a way to tell your spouse one thing about him or her that you're especially grateful for that day. You might write something like, "I've noticed today just how amazing you are with our daughter when she gets frustrated, and I'm so grateful that she has you as a parent." Then set the journal on your spouse's desk or pillow or wherever you know it will be found and read. Then your spouse will make a gratitude entry about you and eventually pass it back so you can read it.

Of course, you have to be intentional about doing this. And one more thing: you've got to be genuine. The late comedian George Burns told a group of acting students in Hollywood, "Once you can fake genuineness, you've got a career." Of course, you can't fake it. Everyone has a built-in radar detector for phoniness. So if you're going to give good gratitude to your spouse, don't do it merely as a task to check off your to-do list. Make sure it's coming from the heart.

Praise the bridge that carried you over. —GEORGE COLMAN

SEPTEMBER 5

WHAT'S DRIVING YOU?

A house is built by wisdom and becomes strong through good sense. Through knowledge its rooms are filled with all sorts of precious riches and valuables. PROVERBS 24:3-4

BACK IN THE 1950S, with prosperity on the rise and automated machines entering the workplace, experts warned of an excess of free time. They thought Americans, with computers and other gadgets of convenience, were headed into a time of less work and more leisure. Sociologists even founded an institute to prepare for the dangerous glut of leisure time they envisioned.

Well, society's fortune-tellers couldn't have been more wrong. Today's workforce puts in long, hard hours. Since 1973, the typical adult's leisure time has shrunk by 40 percent—from twenty-six to sixteen hours a week in 2008.[3] Work is consuming. We complain about them, but only a minority of us say we could do without our jobs. Not just because we need the money, but because we like them.

Our desire to work fills weekends, the traditional time for leisure and recuperation, with more work: catching up on chores and errands.

Ask anyone what most robs their marriage of time together and you will likely hear a one-word answer: work. Why do we allow work to steal our time together? Experts point out that we often mistake what we do with who we are. We hang our worth and significance on our work.

When I (Les) was training as a medical psychologist, a highly respected scientific thinker gave a lecture for the hospital interns. I don't remember much of the lecture, but I will never forget what he said near the end:

> I was asked to speak to you on my most recent findings and I have done that. Now let me tell you young doctors what I wish someone would have told me when I sat where you are. You can save yourself unnecessary frustration in the course of your careers if you ask yourself why you are doing what you are doing. For more than thirty years I have struggled and strained to make an impact in my field, and some would say I have.

The room was still as he continued. "But only recently have I learned that I cannot measure my self-worth by the number of articles I publish or the number of people who applaud my findings." That was it. He gathered his lecture notes and sat down. As his mini message sank in, he obviously had touched a nerve with us hard-driving students.

In his book *Ordering Your Private World*, pastor Gordon MacDonald writes, "A driven person is usually too busy for the pursuit of ordinary relationships in marriage or family, not to speak of one with God."[4] So what's driving you? Why are you working so hard? Maybe it's time to cash in on all your hard work and spend a little extra time together.

Men tire themselves in pursuit of rest. —LAURENCE STERNE

SAYING THE RIGHT THING AT THE RIGHT TIME

The words of the godly are a life-giving fountain. PROVERBS 10:11

IN 1982, JAIME ESCALANTE left a well-paying job as a computer engineer to become a math teacher at Garfield High School in East Los Angeles. You may remember his creative teaching techniques, discipline, compassion, and encouragement depicted in the movie *Stand and Deliver*. By saying the right words at the right time, he awakens the potential of a group of inner-city Latinos.

During his first year, eighteen students willingly give up their Saturdays and vacations to prepare for the Advanced Placement Calculus Exam. When they finally take the test, Escalante's students unexpectedly pass with flying colors. These unprecedented high marks from this particular Hispanic demographic prompt suspicious testing officials to disqualify the scores, alleging the students cheated. The only way the students can prove they didn't cheat is to retake the test. They reluctantly agree to take it again.

Crowded in a classroom in sweltering summer heat, the kids huddle around their teacher. Mr. Escalante breaks the news to them that they have only one day to prepare. The students are understandably disheartened.

Mr. Escalante begins to pace the classroom and offer encouragement. "Just go step by step and play defense," he advises like a coach in a locker room at halftime. "Don't bring anything. No pencils. No erasers. Nothing. Don't wear clothes with too many pockets. Don't let your eyes wander. No spacing out. Don't give them opportunity to call you cheaters."

He pauses, takes a breath, and then speaks proudly: "You are the true dreamers, and dreams accomplish wonderful things. You're the best!" Escalante cheers. "Tomorrow you'll prove that you're the champs. Now let's start with chapter one."[5]

If there's one thing Jaime Escalante understood, it was the value of saying the right words at the right time—and making sure those words engendered optimism. How about you? Is there something your spouse needs to hear from you that you may not be saying?

Remember not only to say the right thing in the right place, but far more difficult still, to leave unsaid the wrong thing at the tempting moment. —BENJAMIN FRANKLIN

THE BEST THERAPY

Give to those who ask, and don't turn away from those who want to borrow.

MATTHEW 5:42

SINCE 1925, PEOPLE suffering from severe mental illness have turned to The Menninger Clinic in Topeka, Kansas. It was the first psychiatric treatment alternative to the nearly inhuman conditions of the asylums of the day. Today it is often ranked as the number one psychiatric hospital in the nation. And it's all due to Dr. Karl Menninger.

Dr. Menninger specialized in neurology and psychiatry and is well known for his writing. His first of fourteen books, *The Human Mind*, attempted to educate the public in psychiatry. Writing the book was not an easy task for a busy doctor. Yet despite his hard work, the thirty-seven-year-old psychiatrist didn't have much faith in the success of his project. He told a friend that it would not get noticed. He was very wrong.

The Human Mind was published in 1930 and immediately became a Literary Guild selection and sold two hundred thousand copies. It was one of the first books in which a psychiatrist explained the everyday workings that went on in his office, and showed the world as it is seen through the eyes of a psychiatrist.[6]

In his later years, Dr. Karl Menninger gave a lecture on mental health and was answering questions from the audience. "What would you advise a person to do," asked one man, "if that person felt a nervous breakdown coming on?"

Instead of giving the expected reply, "Consult a psychiatrist," he shocked everyone by saying, "Lock up your house, go across the railway tracks, find someone in need, and do something to help that person."

His point? Serving others cultivates health and brings about peace and contentment. It's what the colloquial proverb says:

If you want happiness for an hour—take a nap.
If you want happiness for a day—go fishing.
If you want happiness for a month—get married.
If you want happiness for a year—inherit a fortune.
If you want happiness for a lifetime—help others.

So if you want to experience the ultimate psychotherapy, there's no need to pay a psychiatrist. Simply recognize the needs around you and meet them—starting in your own home by serving your spouse. Soon you'll see that the best form of therapy is helping others.

Love cures people, the ones who receive love and the ones who can give it, too.
—KARL A. MENNINGER

A TRUE LOVE DARE

The purpose of my instruction is that all believers would be filled with love that comes from a pure heart, a clear conscience, and genuine faith. 1 TIMOTHY 1:5

WHILE COACHING FOOTBALL at the University of Colorado, Bill McCartney dared his 1991 team to play beyond their normal abilities. He had heard that most people spend 86 percent of their time thinking about themselves and only 14 percent of their time thinking about others. The coach was convinced that if his team could stop thinking about themselves and begin to think of others, a whole new source of energy would be available to them.

McCartney challenged each player to call someone they loved and tell that person that they were dedicating the upcoming game to him or her. The team members were to encourage those persons to carefully watch every play they made, because the game was dedicated to them. McCartney arranged to distribute sixty footballs, one for each player to send to the person he had chosen, with the final score written on the football.

Colorado was playing its archrival, the Nebraska Cornhuskers, on Nebraska's home turf. Colorado had not won a game there in twenty-three years, but Coach McCartney had challenged his players to go beyond themselves—to play for love. The Colorado Buffaloes won the game, and the score written on sixty footballs was "27 to 12."

Could it be that thinking of others provides a new source of energy? Scripture sure seems to back up this theory. The theme of putting others first resonates throughout the Bible in verses such as Acts 20:35 (NIV): "It is more blessed to give than to receive." You've likely heard that so often that it nearly bounces off your ears. But don't overlook it today. Realize just how powerful it is to "play for love."

He lives the poetry that he cannot write. The others write the poetry that they dare not realize. —OSCAR WILDE

THE RULE OF RELATIONSHIPS

Do to others as you would like them to do to you. LUKE 6:31

IN 1963, MARY KAY ASH was passed over for a promotion in favor of a man whom she had trained. You can imagine her frustration. After all, she'd worked at Stanley Home Products in Houston for quite some time. She'd paid her dues, and she deserved the promotion.

So Mary Kay quit her job and decided to write a book to help women in business—women like herself. The book, as it turned out, became a business plan for her ideal company, and in September 1963, she began Mary Kay Cosmetics. She had just a five-thousand-dollar investment to get it started, but that's all it took. The company became highly successful, and she became highly respected. The company now has more than five hundred thousand independent beauty consultants in twenty-nine markets worldwide. And Mary Kay Inc. is ranked as one of the 100 Best Companies to Work for in America, according to *Fortune* magazine.

A guiding light for her company was the Golden Rule. She considered it the founding principle for her business interactions. In fact, her marketing plan was designed to allow women to advance by helping others succeed. Think of that! And her slogan "God first, family second, career third" expressed her insistence that the women in her company keep their lives in balance.

"Everyone has an invisible sign hanging from his neck," according to Mary Kay Ash. It says, "Make Me Feel Important!" Mary Kay drilled this principle into her sales team. She told them again and again, "Never forget this message when working with people." She knew compliments and affirmation were critical to enjoying success with others.

You may never sell cosmetics or anything else in the business world, but this principle is essential to the success of your relationships—especially with each other. So how are you doing when it comes to practicing the Golden Rule with one another?

Think through the next twenty-four hours of your life. What's about to happen? What can you predict—especially as it relates to your spouse? Do you know when your spouse might be in need of some affirmation? Do you know when he or she might need a compliment or a little favor? Why not plan right now on putting the Golden Rule into practice in that moment and do unto your spouse as you'd like him or her to do unto you?

You never know, this guiding principle just might become the business plan for your ideal marriage.

> *We have committed the Golden Rule to memory; let us now commit it to life.*
> —EDWIN MARKHAM

LOVING UNTIL IT HURTS

There is no greater love than to lay down one's life for one's friends. JOHN 15:13

ON THIS DAY IN 1946, a little-known nun experienced what she later described as "the call within the call." She was thirty-six, and she heard God telling her to leave the convent and help the poor while living among them. Two years later she replaced her traditional nun's habit with a simple white and blue cotton sari, adopted Indian citizenship, and ventured into the slums of Calcutta to work with India's poor, sick, orphaned, and dying. Forty years later, Mother Teresa was an internationally renowned humanitarian and advocate for the poor. She became nothing less than an iconic symbol of compassion and love.

Shane Claiborne, author of *The Irresistible Revolution*, spent a summer in the slums of Calcutta with Mother Teresa and wrote the following about one of his experiences there:

> *People often ask me what Mother Teresa was like. Sometimes it's like they wonder if she glowed in the dark or had a halo. She was short, wrinkled, and precious, maybe even a little ornery—like a beautiful, wise old granny. But there is one thing I will never forget—her feet. Her feet were deformed. Each morning in Mass, I would stare at them. I wondered if she had contracted leprosy. But I wasn't going to ask, of course. "Hey Mother, what's wrong with your feet?"*
>
> *One day a sister said to us, "Have you noticed her feet?" We nodded, curious. She said: "Her feet are deformed because we get just enough donated shoes for everyone, and Mother does not want anyone to get stuck with the worst pair, so she digs through and finds them. And years of doing that have deformed her feet." Years of loving her neighbor as herself deformed her feet.[7]*

Think of it! She loved so much that her feet became deformed from placing others above herself. Love almost always has a way of changing us—if not physically, emotionally. How has your love for each other changed you as individuals?

Intense love does not measure—it just gives. —MOTHER TERESA

WHAT MATTERS MOST IN YOUR MARRIAGE?

I well remember them, and my soul is downcast within me. Yet this I call to mind and therefore I have hope: Because of the LORD's great love we are not consumed, for his compassions never fail. They are new every morning; great is your faithfulness.

LAMENTATIONS 3:20-23, NIV

IN THE AFTERMATH OF the horrific Twin Towers tragedy that struck our nation on September 11, 2001, we were amazed by some of the notes and letters we received from couples around the country. They wrote to tell us how this act of terrorism impacted their marriages. More specifically, they told us how hearing some of the conversations between couples—when they knew they would never speak again—moved them.

"When I heard the cell phone calls made by loved ones soon before their deaths," wrote one man. "I thought about what I would say to my wife if I were to call her in the seconds before I die. I recognized that I could not possibly tell her all the beauty that she had brought to my life, and what an incredible person she is to me—not in those few moments, not on short notice." He went on to tell us that he took the time to tell his wife what mattered most to him, on his own schedule, "not on death's timetable."

Sharing our true feelings is an opportunity we all have. As you consider the anniversary of this horrific tragedy, we urge you to tell your spouse all he or she means to you, too. Take some time to inventory what really matters most to both of you in your relationship. What are the things you prize about what you have built together? Maybe it's the way you lift one another up in tough times. Maybe it's your shared sense of humor. Perhaps one of the things you value most in your marriage is how you bring one another closer to God. And what do you prize about your partner? Maybe you love the way your spouse hones your personal vision and gives you confidence. Whatever it is, make a list of what matters most.

In fact, if you want to get practical, take a moment right now to let each other know what you would say on a cell phone recording to each other if you feared the worst. And then celebrate the fact that you can verbalize to each other what you cherish in your marriage—on your own schedule.

Time is passing. Yet, for the United States of America, there will be no forgetting September the 11th. We will remember every rescuer who died in honor. We will remember every family that lives in grief. We will remember the fire and ash, the last phone calls, the funerals of the children. —GEORGE W. BUSH

GRIEF IS A GIFT

Son of man, groan before the people! Groan before them with bitter anguish and a broken heart. EZEKIEL 21:6

WITHIN JUST A FEW DAYS OF the September 11 tragedy in New York City, I (Les) found myself in Manhattan, working with a team of psychologists who were flown in to assist in the aftermath. Soon I was speaking with a man who showed me a crinkled photo of his sister who worked in the World Trade Center. She didn't survive. I walked with a firefighter to the emergency morgue as he delivered a body part in a red plastic bag. I prayed a solemn prayer, and then he and I walked back into the hole of Ground Zero. I spoke with a mom who held out hope beyond hope that her son who drove a delivery truck would be found and identified in the twisted steel.

I spoke with so many whose countenances showed palpable loss. And now, years later, I have spoken to many of these same people and have joyfully discovered that, in spite of this horrific trauma, they are learning to trust life once more. Along with millions of others, they are learning some important truths about grief.

Grief is a gift. It is as natural and normal as sleeping when you are tired. Although it might sound backward, grief actually works to restore your soul. Very succinctly, grief is the process of separation of one's emotions from the jolt of any loss. Of course, grief is preoccupying and depleting. Some well-intentioned friends may think it is their job to "talk you out of it," but it's your right to grieve—individually and as a couple—if you have suffered loss of any kind. Bereaved people move through various stages of grief that allow them to reorganize life in positive ways. In other words, grief is a healing agent.

So if you happen to find yourselves grieving during this season for any reason, give yourselves permission to mourn your loss. Don't try to act "recovered" when you aren't. Doing so would only short-circuit the healthy progression of grief. Instead, cry when you want to. Talk about your pain when you can. And give yourself freedom to mourn your loss.

Give sorrow words; the grief that does not speak whispers the o'er-fraught heart and bids it break. —WILLIAM SHAKESPEARE

DO I UNDERSTAND YOU CORRECTLY?

Such stupidity and ignorance! Their eyes are closed, and they cannot see. Their minds are shut, and they cannot think. ISAIAH 44:18

ON A DOWNTOWN BUS, just as it is pulling into its next stop, a woman stands up, slaps the face of the man next to her, and hurries to the exit. Each of the passengers who saw what happened reacts in their own way. A middle-aged man feels sad for the man who was slapped. A younger woman is frightened. A teenage boy is angry. Another woman feels excited. How could the same event trigger such an array of varying emotions? The answer is found in self-talk.

The middle-aged man who reacted with sadness thought to himself, *He's lost her and he'll never get her back.*

The fearful woman thought, *She is going to really pay a price for that tonight when he sees her at home.*

The angry teenager says to himself, *She humiliated him; like most women, she must be a real jerk.*

The woman who felt excited said to herself, *Serves him right. What a strong woman; I wish I was more like that.*

In each case, the event was almost instantly interpreted, judged, and labeled. And each individual's unique self-explanation resulted in a distinctive emotional experience—sadness, fear, anger, or excitement. Truth is, the emotional consequences of an event like this vary as much as the people observing it.

This variation is exactly why, even in relationships with the people we love the most, we must clarify our perceptions before we jump to faulty conclusions. How often have you made an assumption that led you down an unnecessarily bumpy conversation with your spouse? We've all done it. And often, that mistake can be remedied or avoided altogether with a simple question: Do I understand you correctly?

> *When the mind is thinking, it is simply talking to itself.* —PLATO

THE SINGLE SENTENCE

I pray that from his glorious, unlimited resources he will empower you with inner strength through his Spirit. EPHESIANS 3:16

IN THE AUTUMN OF 1992, we did something unusual. We offered a course at Seattle Pacific University that promised to answer questions openly and honestly about family, friends, dating, and sex. In short, its purpose was to teach the basics of good relationships.

Colleges around the world offer instruction on nearly every conceivable topic, but try to find a course on how to have good relationships, and you'll look for a long time. We wanted to change that. As a psychologist (Les) and a marriage and family therapist (Leslie) teaching on a university campus, we had our hands on stacks of relationship research showing that, with a little help, most of us can make our bad relationships better and our good relationships great. And that's exactly what we wanted to teach students to do.

Since that first autumn, we have lectured to thousands of students on campuses and in churches across the country, teaching the basics of good relationships. And we always begin with the same sentence: If you try to find intimacy with another person before achieving a sense of wholeness on your own, all your relationships become an attempt to complete yourself.

This single sentence holds the key to finding genuine fulfillment for every relationship—including your marriage. If you do not grasp its message, the best you can hope for is a false and fleeting sense of emotional closeness, the kind that comes from a series of temporary attachments. Once you understand and internalize the truth of this sentence, however, you'll discover the abiding comfort of belonging—to each other and ultimately to God.

Pay mind to your own life, your own health and wholeness. . . . A bleeding heart is of no help to anybody if it bleeds to death. **—FREDERICK BUECHNER**

THE HEART OF THE MATTER

I will give them singleness of heart and put a new spirit within them. I will take away their stony, stubborn heart and give them a tender, responsive heart. EZEKIEL 11:19

WHAT A MARVEL! The human heart beats seventy-five times a minute, forty million times a year, or two and a half billion times in a life of seventy years. At each beat, the average adult heart discharges about four ounces of blood. This amounts to three thousand gallons a day or 650,000 gallons a year—enough to fill more than eighty-one tank cars of eight thousand gallons each. The heart does enough work in one hour to lift a 150-pound man to the top of a three-story building, enough power in seventy years to lift the largest battleship afloat completely out of the water.[8]

In spite of the miraculous power of this vital human organ and what it represents in the human spirit, our hearts—as this verse points out—can become divided and even turn to stone. The cause? It's not cholesterol or high blood pressure. It's what Ezekiel calls "vile images and detestable idols" (Ezekiel 11:18) that cause our hearts to harden. So we ask you, what images and idols is your heart given to? Is there something that has hardened your heart? Perhaps it is the idol of resentment or the vile image of retribution. It could be any number of things that cause a stony, stubborn heart. The question is, What will it take to have a tender, responsive heart? As you probably know, the answer is not an easy one. More often than not, our hard hearts need a bit of breaking to soften them up.

Anglo-Irish author and playwright Oscar Wilde asked a poignant question of anyone who has "heart problems": How else but through a broken heart may the Lord Christ enter in?

> *I would rather have eyes that cannot see; ears that cannot hear, lips that cannot speak, than a heart that cannot love.* —**ROBERT TIZON**

FINDING
RELATIONSHIP RENEWAL

Have you never heard? Have you never understood? The LORD is the everlasting God, the Creator of all the earth. He never grows weak or weary. No one can measure the depths of his understanding. He gives power to the weak and strength to the powerless. Even youths will become weak and tired, and young men will fall in exhaustion. ISAIAH 40:28-30

WE HAVE ATTENDED MORE marriage retreats than we can count. Some in hard-to-find, out-of-the-way, rustic settings. Others in posh hotels or resort getaways. No matter where they are or how they are structured, they always serve the same purpose—renewal. They are dedicated to improving, refreshing, and strengthening marriages. On some occasions, the organizers of the retreat will even offer an opportunity for couples to renew their wedding vows.

Whether vows are renewed or not, every couple, no matter how strong and secure, needs occasional renewal in their relationship. We all need time to recharge our emotional and relational batteries. We need inspiration. And don't think that newlyweds still enjoying the "honeymoon phase" don't need the same thing. "Even youths will become weak and tired" (v. 30). All of us need to renew our strength—no matter our age or stage.

So take a moment to consider how you and your partner do just that. Study together Isaiah 40:31, and take to heart what boosts your marriage vitality; it's a truth that is introduced by the little word *but*: "But those who trust in the LORD will find new strength. They will soar high on wings like eagles. They will run and not grow weary. They will walk and not faint."

What can you do this week that will help you soar on wings like eagles? On a personal and specific level, what helps you run and not grow weary? Are you familiar with what helps your spouse find new strength?

A rent garment is catched by every nail, and the rent made wider. Renew therefore thy repentance speedily, whereby this breach may be made up, and worse prevented.
—WILLIAM GURNALL

THE ONE-MINUTE MARRIAGE?

There is more hope for a fool than for someone who speaks without thinking.

PROVERBS 29:20

THE SCENE? Our counseling office. The clients? Rick and Amy, a married couple of less than a year.

"I hear the words coming out of your mouth, but I just don't understand what you mean!" Rick's frustration was unmistakable. "It's like you're speaking a foreign language."

"Well, you're the only person I've ever known who didn't understand me when I talked," she replied angrily.

"What you say sometimes just isn't logical," he countered.

"I'm not like you, Rick, analyzing everything, picking apart every word." Amy was close to tears.

"I know. I just wish you weren't so emotional when you talk. I don't get what you're saying. We just can't communicate."

That's it, the number-one complaint in marriage: we just can't communicate. The truth is every couple communicates whether they want to or not. Saying nothing is communicating. What most couples mean by this complaint is that they don't understand one another.

Like Rick and Amy, many of us have difficulty talking to each other from time to time. He answers a question simply and succinctly; she says he's not "listening" to her. She tells him she knows exactly how he feels; he thinks she's trying to put him in a box.

In order to understand better and communicate more effectively with our partner, we have to slow down and think. Good communication takes time. When the bestselling business book *The One Minute Manager* was popular, there were a hundred spin-offs, including "The One Minute Marriage." Give me a break. Maybe managers can accomplish their goals through quick contacts, but a husband and wife? Not likely.

When we slow down the conversation with our partner, we are less likely to give hasty orders, snappy solutions, and thoughtless comments. When we slow down, we are more likely to listen to the emotions that underlie our partner's words and pay more attention to the nonverbal messages. Taking care in these ways helps us avoid foolish conversations and brings about true understanding.

Talking can happen on the run, but understanding requires less hasty intervals. Listen again to the wise message of Proverbs: "There is more hope for a fool than for someone who speaks without thinking."

> *The single biggest problem in communication is the illusion that it has taken place.*
> —GEORGE BERNARD SHAW

EVEN ITS NAME HISSES

A gossip goes around telling secrets, so don't hang around with chatterers.

PROVERBS 20:19

"THE SNAKE THAT POISONS everybody. It topples governments, wrecks marriages, ruins careers, busts reputations, causes heartaches, nightmares, indigestion, spawns suspicion, generates grief, dispatches innocent people to cry in their pillows. Even its name hisses. It's called gossip. Before you repeat a story, ask yourself: Is it true? Is it fair? Is it necessary? If not, shut up."

United Technologies, the conglomerate, placed this mini lecture in newspapers across the country for no other reason than to make people take a second look at gossip. And with good reason. Gossips have plagued the earth since people began to talk. The apostle Paul warns about the destructive power of gossip and the condemnation that comes to "gossips and busybodies" who say "things which they ought not" (1 Timothy 5:13, NKJV).

Most people have certain stereotypical ideas about gossip and gossipers. Think about gossip and you might envision housewives gabbing over the clothesline about a neighbor's drinking problem. Or you may think of teenage girls exchanging malicious remarks about their classmates over the telephone. These perceptions, however, are not only sexist, but they are wrong. Women are no more likely to gossip than men. So, no matter what your gender, don't be afraid of a little self-reflection when it comes to gossip—even within your marriage.

Be honest. In the supermarket line, when no one you know is around, you speed-read and hope the cashier is even slower than usual. You would never, of course, actually buy the tabloid paper, but something within you enjoys a tidbit of gossip now and then. What harm is there in knowing the Hollywood rumors about who is dating and divorcing and which celebrities are having plastic surgery? Maybe none, but what about your desire to get the scoop on people in your church? Does a part of you want to hear the dish, dirt, and scandal about the people in your life? The temptation is powerful.

Gossip can harm any relationship, and particularly a marriage. Husbands and wives are supposed to be each other's cheerleaders, guarding each other's reputations. So, if you are wondering whether what you want to say about your spouse is gossip or not, ask yourself a few questions: *Would I say this to his or her face? Would I want my spouse saying this about me?* If the answers are no, then you probably should keep it quiet.

Gossip needn't be false to be evil—there's a lot of truth that shouldn't be passed around.
—FRANK A. CLARK

ARE YOU A CONTROL FREAK?

People with understanding control their anger. PROVERBS 14:29

ISN'T A LITTLE CONTROLLING behavior healthy? Sure. Recent research indicates that feeling in control is vital to mental and physical health, as well as happiness at home and satisfaction at work. In fact, feeling to some degree that you are master of your own fate is one of the key traits of happy people, according to David Myers, author of *The Pursuit of Happiness*. What's more, psychologist Judith Rodin has demonstrated in experiments at Yale University how merely feeling in control can alter the functioning of a person's immune system.

Being in control, however, can be too much of a good thing. It certainly was in my case. I'm the first to admit that I can be controlling. In fact, the people who know me best will admit it for me. When I first told Leslie I was going to write a book called *The Control Freak,* she joked about it being my autobiography.

Some of the best advice I ever received on my road to recovery from being a control freak was from my father. As a retired college president with many years of knowing what it's like to be in charge as well as to have fun, my dad sat me down as an adult child and asked me a question: "Why are you driving so hard, son?"

My knee-jerk response was a joke: "To keep up with you, Dad."

He thought I was serious. We talked about the psychological pressure that is trans-mitted, intentionally or not, from one generation to the next. We talked about the drive to produce and our mutual compulsions for control. Then my dad told me his secret for keeping life under control without being a control freak. "Count your blessings," he said. "Don't let a day slip away without taking time to appreciate God's gifts."

How about you? Do you have some controlling tendencies? If so, how have those tendencies affected your marriage? What blessings are you counting today?

 } *It seems easier to be God than to love God, easier to control people than to love people.* —HENRI NOUWEN

FROM YOU TO WE

First get rid of the log in your own eye; then you will see well enough to deal with the speck in your friend's eye. MATTHEW 7:5

THERE'S AN OLD JOKE ABOUT a couple, married for decades, living in a small town. Two elderly men are sitting on a bench, and the one asks the other how this local couple is doing. "You know how it is," comes the laconic reply. "They've only ever had one argument in their married life—and they're still having it."

Let's face it. Conflict is inevitable, even in the parsonage and even if it's the same fight over and over. But most of us don't limit our conflict to one area. After all, it takes very little for the fur to fly in most marriages. We end up arguing about silly little things: "Who took my pen?" or "You just passed a parking space right there!" Such seemingly innocuous questions and statements, when laced with a particular attitude, can ignite a major blowout. It's almost unavoidable. We can't eliminate conflict completely—not if we are being authentic with our feelings. But if we do our best to see the issue from our partner's perspective, we can reduce conflict's life span and minimize its negative impact.

How does simply broadening our perspective limit conflict's damaging effects for us? By trading in the blame game for positive solutions. By exchanging "you" statements for "we" statements. The results of one study showed that the "best" arguers are those who don't point their fingers. According to the study, the person who says "we" the most during an argument suggests the best solutions.

So the next time conflict erupts—and it will—try trading in your "you" statements for "we" statements. You'll be amazed how such a simple vocabulary swap can change everything.

The course of true love never did run smooth. —WILLIAM SHAKESPEARE

CATCHING THE CATCHER

Sing to him; yes, sing his praises. Tell everyone about his wonderful deeds.

1 CHRONICLES 16:9

THE GREAT SPIRITUAL WRITER Henri Nouwen's final book before he died on September 21, 1996, was a diary of his last year. Throughout his journal he talks about trapeze artists known as the Flying Rodleighs. He was touched by their skill and grace on the trapeze. Much of his attraction to their circus performance had to do with the special relationship between the flyer and the catcher. Swinging high above the crowd, the daredevil flyer lets go of the trapeze simply to stretch out his arms and wait to feel the strong hands of the catcher pluck him out of the air. "The flyer must never catch the catcher," one member of the troupe had told him. "He must wait in absolute trust."

What a powerful message for those of us who are driven by control. Can you imagine the strong-minded discipline it takes to surrender your own efforts to the hands of another? Could the two of you do this together? Could you fly helpless through the air and yet resist your internal compulsion for control, relying solely on someone else to save you?

Thankfully, we can leave the trapeze act to the professionals. This kind of trust seems beyond comprehension to most of us, yet it is the very quality that saves us from ourselves and brings us to a place of genuine worship. Why? Because the major obstacle we have in entering true worship is ourselves. Worship, by its very nature, helps us transcend our self-reliance and trust more wholly in God. Worship releases us from our self-focus and puts our eyes on Christ.

Only when we surrender our own efforts to the hands of our Creator do we truly worship. In worship we set aside our compulsion for control to hear what God might say to us. Through music, through words, through fellowship, God speaks because we have surrendered ourselves to him.

Imagine how your marriage might be improved if you exchanged your desire to control your spouse for a wholehearted trust in God.

Worship changes us into the likeness of the one we worship. —JACK HAYFORD

TAKING RESPONSIBILITY

Pay careful attention to your own work, for then you will get the satisfaction of a job well done, and you won't need to compare yourself to anyone else. For we are each responsible for our own conduct. GALATIANS 6:4-5

A CEO HAS TAKEN ON a new job, and the outgoing CEO says to him, "Sometimes you'll make wrong choices. You will. You'll mess up. When that happens, I have prepared three envelopes for you. I left them in the top drawer of the desk. The first time it happens, open #1. The second time you mess up, open #2. The third time, open #3."

For the first few months, everything goes fine. Then the CEO makes his first mistake, goes to the drawer, opens up envelope #1, and the message reads, "Blame me." So he does: "This is the old CEO's fault. He made these mistakes. I inherited these problems." Everybody says, "Okay." It works out pretty well.

Things go fine for a while, and then he makes his second mistake. So, he goes to the drawer and opens up envelope #2. This time he reads, "Blame the board." And he does: "It's the board's fault. The board has been a mess. I inherited them. They're the problem." Everybody says, "Okay, that makes sense."

Things go fine for a while, and then he makes his third mistake. So, he goes to the drawer and opens up envelope #3. The message reads: "Prepare three envelopes."[9]

The inclination to point fingers is not exclusive to CEOs. The same victim mentality and finding someone to blame can permeate a marriage, too. Once a husband or wife gets wrapped up in blaming others, a vicious cycle permeates the relationship. Soon each partner is looking for ways to avoid responsibility and shift the blame. Ever since Adam blamed Eve and Eve blamed the serpent, we have learned the trick of finding excuses. Accused of wrongdoing, we respond, "I didn't do it," "Well, you asked for it," or "I didn't mean to."

But let's be honest. We are responsible. Nobody makes our choices for us. While we are not necessarily the cause of all that happens in our lives, we are responsible for what we make of what happens. As Scripture says, "You have been called to live in freedom. . . . But don't use your freedom to satisfy your sinful nature. Instead, use your freedom to serve one another in love" (Galatians 5:13).

Don't let your marriage become a blame game. Don't lay the blame on your parents, schooling, income, siblings, friends, government, each other, or anything else. Take responsibility for your feelings and your actions, and watch your marriage mature.

Let everyone sweep in front of his own door, and the whole city will be clean.
—JOHANN WOLFGANG VON GOETHE

A WEE LITTLE MAN'S LESSON

Zacchaeus stood before the Lord and said, "I will give half my wealth to the poor, Lord, and if I have cheated people on their taxes, I will give them back four times as much!" LUKE 19:8

"ZACCHAEUS WAS A WEE LITTLE MAN. . . ." If you grew up in the church as we did, you probably know this little song whether you want to or not. Even as small children, many of us learned through song the story of this tax collector who took advantage of everyone else.

But the profound message of Zacchaeus's conversation with Jesus and what brought it about may take a bit of maturity to fully comprehend. Think about the scenario. Jesus knew all about Zacchaeus and his reputation as a dishonest tax collector. When he saw him up there in that sycamore-fig tree, he could have pointed a finger of condemnation and ridiculed him in front of the crowd. But he didn't. He called him down from his perch and went to his home. The townspeople scoffed at Jesus, but it didn't matter.

What mattered was that Jesus took the heavy blanket of condemnation off of Zacchaeus's back and gave him an opportunity to change. No blame. No ridicule. No harsh words. In effect, Jesus was saying to this greedy little man, "I don't condemn you, but how would you like your life to be different?" And different it became! Zacchaeus made restitution and then some for his misdeeds.

There is a lesson for every married couple in this story. It has to do with how we respond to our spouse when we could rightfully point to his or her faults. We somehow think that "help" will be the catalyst for change. But it's not. True change comes only when the heavy blanket of condemnation is removed and the guilty person has the opportunity to choose a different way—not out of fear or pressure, but because he or she wants to be a better person.

 As much as we thirst for approval we dread condemnation. —HANS SELYE

BLURRING THE LINE

An offended friend is harder to win back than a fortified city. Arguments separate friends like a gate locked with bars. PROVERBS 18:19

WE WERE FLYING HOME to Seattle after a speaking engagement in Atlanta when we sat down on the plane next to a professor at the University of Washington, Pepper Schwartz, whom we'd met a time or two. She'd recently written a book called *Peer Marriage* and was returning home on this flight after a long media tour.

We were all a little tired but not enough to keep us from talking. Pepper still had enough energy to tell us about her recent research findings, and her enthusiasm was contagious. "Loving couples negotiate," she said. In her study of couples who enjoy their marriages, Dr. Schwartz found that there's less of the rank pulling and power playing seen in unhappy unions. Schwartz reports that these egalitarian twosomes have conversations filled with supportive questions and what she calls tag questions, such as "Do you agree?" and "What do you think?"

Think about that for a moment. Do the two of you use these little questions as you're negotiating what to do or where to go? It turns out that these little questions are vital. They open the conversation to the other person's views, just as two business people who respect each other might. They allow a couple to hash out a fair agreement on anything important, from day care for the kids to what kind of vacation they will take. "Our solemn oath is: Never give up, never walk out—until we are both satisfied," one woman in a peer marriage told Schwartz.

British statesman Winston Churchill once said, "The English never draw a line without blurring it." We love that statement. Why? Because that should be true of the couple who learns to compromise. When a husband and wife come to believe that equality means splitting things down the middle, keeping score, then marriage becomes a contest of who can get a better deal. And that wipes out the true spirit of compromise. Marriage is not about score keeping. It's not about equitable distributions. It's about compromise. It's about bending rather than breaking. Agreeing to find an agreeable solution to one's disagreements means that on some occasions one partner gets a bigger piece of the pie, and on other occasions the pie is cut differently.

So when was the last time you learned from the British sentiment that both sides win when the lines are blurred and no one is keeping score in your relationship?[10]

Better bend than break. —SCOTTISH PROVERB

FAITHFUL AND TRUE

The man who commits adultery is an utter fool, for he destroys himself. PROVERBS 6:32

THE LONG LIST OF PUBLIC OFFICIALS, celebrities, sports icons, and other noteworthy individuals engaging in extremely tawdry behavior, if not infidelity, has made cheating a common headline. We all know that infidelity is older than David and Bathsheba; however, the media saturation, public interest, and hyperspeed revelations of mistresses makes it feel more commonplace than it is.[11] Still, we've all heard the stories about men or women who have affairs or abruptly walk out of long-term marriages. In fact, it's difficult these days to find a person who does not personally know of a situation exactly like this.

We live in a culture that values tolerance and the individual's pursuit of happiness. However, the flip side can be the sense that any kind of behavior is permissible as long as one is "following his or her heart." Many of us feel vulnerable when we hear stories of a person who walks out on a relationship, and we can't help wondering whether our spouse would ever do such a thing.

It raises a question: Can you tell whether your spouse will betray you? Not really. No research has been able to identify reliable predictive factors. But one sign is fairly consistent. A marriage partner who commits a major betrayal—not only an affair or a sudden decision to walk away from the marriage, but also a risky business deal that jeopardizes the family's future—has probably given off warning signals all along, signals that his or her spouse often chose not to see. Throughout the marriage, this spouse consistently shows by his or her behavior that protecting the relationship is not a priority.

Consistent failure to protect the relationship in other areas is as close to a predictor of unfaithfulness as you are ever going to find. But it's an important one. One that has a message for all of us. We need to do everything we can to protect our marriages. The consequences are too dreadful not to. As this Proverb says, anyone who does not do so "destroys himself."

> Be faithful in little things, for in them our strength lies. —MOTHER TERESA

LIVING LIFE TOGETHER

If we are living in the light, as God is in the light, then we have fellowship with each other.

1 JOHN 1:7

"LISTEN TO THIS," LES SAID. He was reading an article in *Wired* magazine. "'Despite all we've learned over the past few decades about psychology, neurology, and human behavior, contemporary medicine has yet to devise anything that works markedly better.'"[12]

"What's it talking about?" I asked.

Les went on to tell me that according to the article, Alcoholics Anonymous has helped millions of people recover from alcohol addiction, but nobody really knows why. The one factor that seemed to offer a compelling reason for AA's success is "the power of like-minded friends who provide support, honesty, and accountability." The article described how sharing problems with a small group of supportive friends has been shown to help people overcome what they're struggling with.

Now, we're not experts on AA and its success rates, but we do know a thing or two about the power of a small group. We joined our first small group as a couple less than a month into our new marriage. And we've been in small groups of one kind or another ever since. There is something almost inexplicable about the collective power of community. When people "do life together," they seem to do life better.

You don't have to be in AA to benefit from this supportive power. You don't even have to be struggling with a problem. Starting a small group with other couples can have no other purpose than fellowship or friendship. A weekly or monthly meeting where you simply share what's been on your mind—and listen to what others are sharing from their lives—can help you gain clarity, a new perspective, and fresh insight into everything from finances to in-laws.

The question we have for you today is about starting a small group with other couples. If you're already a part of one, you may have experienced the benefits of this time-tested endeavor. But if you're not, we urge you to give it serious consideration. It's easier than you think. Just make a list of a few couples you'd enjoy gathering with on a regular basis. Ask them what they think of the idea, and you'll be on your way—living life together—sooner than you think.

The community stagnates without the impulse of the individual. The impulse dies away without the sympathy of the community. —**WILLIAM JAMES**

A QUICK CURE—FOR REAL!

[Jesus] understands our weaknesses, for he faced all of the same testings we do.

HEBREWS 4:15

SOME PEOPLE ARGUE THAT empathy—the practice of putting yourself in your partner's shoes—takes too much time and effort. We couldn't disagree more. Empathy is the fastest way to make progress in a relationship. It saves untold time in moving past difficulties.

Think of any convoluted conversation you've ever had. Perhaps it involved misread motivations concerning a joke in front of friends. Or maybe it was a lack of appreciation that caused you to clam up. Whatever the problem, wouldn't you like a way to make it immediately disappear? Wouldn't you like a magic button that would suddenly make things better? Sure. Who wouldn't? Well, that's what empathy can do.

It's quick.

Empathy does not require a long, drawn-out conversation to get things back on track. It can literally happen in an instant. For example, we recently had a conversation that became increasingly heated. It involved what to serve for a dinner party we were hosting in our home.

"You can just do enchiladas," Les asserted. "People love those."

"I'm not serving enchiladas," I protested. "These people are expecting a nice dinner."

"Well, then I don't know what to say." Les shrugged and left the room.

"Where are you going?" I shouted.

"I've got ice cream out on the counter in the kitchen," he hollered back.

I followed him into the kitchen, and he could feel me gearing up for a hardheaded discourse on why enchiladas were not appropriate for the party and how he needed to be invested in this event as much as I was.[13]

Before we made it to the softening ice cream, Les turned to me, put his hands on my shoulders, and said, "Help me see this from your side."

That's all it took. In less than a minute I told him how I had a limited amount of time to choose a menu, make the food, get the house ready, arrange for child care, prep our second-grader for a spelling test, take my mom to a doctor's appointment, and so on.

"No wonder you're feeling frazzled," Les confessed. "I didn't realize you had all that on your plate."

That was it. In a moment's time, Les suddenly saw my world from my perspective, and the tension melted long before his ice cream. He offered to take a few of my tasks, and we moved forward. The point is that if he hadn't put himself in my place, our enchilada exchange would have evolved into an emotional and time-consuming upheaval that neither of us wanted.

You get the point. Nothing works faster than empathy.

 The solutions all are simple—after you have arrived at them. But they're simple only when you know already what they are. —ROBERT M. PIRSIG

ROOTED IN THE WORD

The word of God is alive and powerful. It is sharper than the sharpest two-edged sword, cutting between soul and spirit, between joint and marrow. It exposes our innermost thoughts and desires. HEBREWS 4:12

THE ROOT SYSTEM OF MOST trees is as wide and deep as the leaf line is wide and high. That is not true, however, of the redwood, which has a shallow root system that spreads out in all directions. It is just not very deep. That fact of life creates a problem for a redwood standing alone. It can easily be blown over because the lack of deep roots gives it little stability. However when two redwoods grow together, their root structures intertwine with each other and give one another strength. Though weak as separate trees, they become strong together. The same is true for soul mates. "Two are better than one," said King Solomon (Ecclesiastes 4:9, NIV).

Whether you live in one place for many years or relocate around the country according to job requirements, the most important roots you'll ever establish are in God and his Word. For this spiritual root system will bear much fruit. Jesus said, "I am the vine; you are the branches. Those who remain in me, and I in them, will produce much fruit. For apart from me you can do nothing. . . . But if you remain in me and my words remain in you, you may ask for anything you want, and it will be granted! When you produce much fruit, you are my true disciples. This brings great glory to my Father" (John 15:5, 7-8).

As a couple grows together in their understanding of God and his Word, they become all the more "rooted and established in love" (Ephesians 3:17, NIV). So if your circumstances take you from coast to coast or anywhere around the world, never forget that the two of you, like the redwoods, become stronger together.

A seed hidden in the heart of an apple is an orchard invisible. —**WELSH PROVERB**

HOW'S YOUR LOVE LIFE?

Since they are no longer two but one, let no one split apart what God has joined together.

MATTHEW 19:6

THAT'S A FAIR QUESTION, isn't it? After all, sexuality is not a given, something that somehow miraculously takes care of itself once we enter marriage. It needs nurture, tenderness, education, and—are you ready for this?—religion.

It's a fact. Religion, according to some studies, is good for your sex life. As strange as it may sound, there is a strong link in marriage between spirituality and sexuality. Married couples who cultivate spiritual intimacy are far more likely to report higher satisfaction with their love lives than other couples.

This fact makes sense if you think about it. The mysteries, wonders, and pleasures of sex in marriage are a divine gift to celebrate. Those who try to limit sex to procreation are simply ignoring the Bible. Scripture—right from the beginning—enthusiastically affirms sex within the bonds of marriage.

Start with the first chapter of the Bible. It contains a magnificent comment on the meaning of sexuality in marriage. As God is bringing the universe into existence, we are told that the human creation is set apart from all others, for it is the Imago Dei, the image of God: "God created human beings in his own image. In the image of God he created them; male and female he created them" (Genesis 1:27). Our maleness and femaleness is not just an accidental arrangement of the human species. Our male and female sexuality is related to our creation in the image of God. This point is echoed throughout Scripture. And Jesus certainly underscores a high view of sex in marriage when he refers to the Genesis passage and then adds, "Since they are no longer two but one, let no one split apart what God has joined together" (Matthew 19:6).

In the Old Testament and in the New Testament, in the Gospels and in the Epistles, we find the call to celebrate sexuality in marriage. There is no denying that your spiritual growth helps to enhance your sexual intimacy in marriage. So, we'll ask it again. How's your love life?

What a happy and holy fashion it is that those who love one another should rest on the same pillow. —NATHANIEL HAWTHORNE

A PORTABLE HEART MONITOR?

As pressure and stress bear down on me, I find joy in your commands. PSALM 119:143

A COLLEGE PROFESSOR WAS given a portable heart-rate monitor to wear because of his heart problems. Doctors feared that little oxygen was reaching the professor's heart muscle, but they needed to accurately assess how his heart was beating throughout a typical day. On this day the professor attended one of his regular and far too frequent departmental meetings—something he considered a waste of time.

But this typical day revealed something the professor was surprised to find, something he was completely unaware of. He learned from the monitor that, while he thought he was cynically detached from the discussions, his heart was pounding away at dangerous levels during his meetings. He had not realized until then how distressed he was by the daily scuffle of departmental politics—even when he felt uninvolved.[14]

In a very real sense, marriage can be a bit like wearing a portable heart monitor. The relationship comes with a built-in feedback system. And that's a good thing. Why? Because marriage heightens our self-awareness. Our partner helps us see things about ourselves, especially our emotions, that we may not see otherwise. And, believe it or not, that unique insight about ourselves can actually be soothing.

How so? For starters, self-awareness diminishes the time you spend stewing over stressful emotions. For example, when you accurately identify how you feel, you recover from distress more quickly. An experiment focused on people who were laid off from their jobs. Many were understandably angry. Half were told to keep a journal for five days, spending twenty minutes writing out their deepest feelings (a common exercise in raising self-awareness). Those who kept journals found new jobs faster than those who didn't.[15] Their heightened self-awareness lowered stress and more quickly enabled productivity.

While keeping a journal is a great method for heightening self-awareness, nothing we know of beats the loving dialogue between a husband and wife for helping us monitor our emotions and bringing us to a God-honoring place with our feelings.

No one can get inner peace by pouncing on it. —**HARRY EMERSON FOSDICK**

THE LIFEBLOOD
OF YOUR RELATIONSHIP

The believers devoted themselves to . . . fellowship. ACTS 2:42

ONE OF THE MOST FAMOUS timepieces on television has appeared every Sunday night for decades. The hard-hitting *60 Minutes* newsmagazine's stopwatch has been ticking away since the day it first aired on September 24, 1968. Well, almost. The actual timepiece is in the Smithsonian. Regardless of the watch itself, the notable sound of its "tick . . . tick . . . tick . . ." is synonymous with some of the most scintillating news stories on television.

For years we've watched the program, the most successful broadcast in television history, and it almost always generates a healthy discussion in our home. We can talk for long periods about the shady diploma mill Mike Wallace uncovered. Or the inexplicable streak of genius displayed by a savant in a story from Morley Safer. And whether he makes us smile or makes us mad, Andy Rooney is hard to ignore. As we said, the program almost always gets us talking.

And that's the point. Talking. Did you know that communication is the very lifeblood of your relationship? And yet it is the number-one complaint most couples have about their relationships. "We just don't communicate" is a common refrain in many counselors' offices. Or "We never have time just to talk" is one we hear a lot. But the one that makes us cringe the most is "When we finally find the time to talk, we don't have anything to say."

Whether a relationship sinks or swims depends on how well a husband and wife send and receive messages, how well they use their conversations to understand and be understood. Think about it. If you are feeling especially close to your partner, it is because you are communicating well. Your spirits are up. Your love life is full. You are in tune. And when communication falls flat, when you feel stuck and you're talking in circles, relational satisfaction drops. As we said in our book *Love Talk*, communication—more than any other aspect of your relationship—can either buoy relational intimacy or be the deadweight of its demise.

That's why this aspect of your relationship can always benefit from an infusion of time. Time and talk are always a winning combination. A good conversation simply doesn't happen while traveling at breakneck speed. Experts agree that most couples need a good sixty minutes each day to converse. Lingering over the evening meal can often serve this purpose. For some couples it means taking advantage of a quiet house when the kids are in bed. For others, maybe it means turning off the radio when driving together or turning off the TV to prioritize talking time.

> When I think of talking, it is of course with a woman. For talking at its best being an inspiration, it wants a corresponding divine quality of receptiveness; and where will you find this but in woman? —OLIVER WENDELL HOLMES

POOR CHARLIE BROWN

*May the L*ORD*, the God of Israel, under whose wings you have come to take refuge, reward you fully for what you have done.* RUTH 2:12

A LITTLE BOY IN MINNESOTA, nicknamed "Sparky," drew a picture of his family dog, Spike, who ate unusual things such as pins and tacks. He sent it to Ripley's Believe It or Not! and the little comic got published with this caption: "A hunting dog that eats pins, tacks, and razor blades is owned by C. F. Schulz, St. Paul, Minnesota, drawn by Sparky."

That little boy was Charles Schulz, and on October 2, 1950, his syndicated cartoon strip called "Peanuts" made its first appearance, featuring a dog named Snoopy. It also featured a lovable loser named Charlie Brown, a character named after one of Schulz's coworkers at an art school. The "Peanuts" series ran for nearly fifty years, and at its peak it appeared in more than 2,600 newspapers in seventy-five countries.

Despite his relentless determination, Charlie Brown is a child who is continually discouraged by his own insecurities and is often taken advantage of by his peers, especially Lucy. Here's an example: Lucy asks Charlie Brown to help with her homework. "I'll be eternally grateful," she promises. "Fair enough. I've never had anyone be eternally grateful before," replied Charlie. "Just subtract 4 from 10 to get how many apples the farmer had left."

Lucy says, "That's it! That's it! I have to be eternally grateful for that? I was robbed! I can't be eternally grateful for this, it was too easy!"

With his blank stare, Charlie replies, "Well, whatever you think is fair."

"How about if I just say 'thanks, Bro?'" replied Lucy.

As Charlie leaves to go outside, he meets Linus, "Where've you been, Charlie Brown?"

"Helping Lucy with her homework."

Linus asks, "Did she appreciate it?"

Charlie answers, "At greatly reduced prices."[1]

Ever felt like Charlie? You're not alone. We all need to know we are needed and that we offer something of value. But too often most of us feel like the appreciation we receive is offered at reduced prices. As we're edging toward the Thanksgiving season in the weeks to come, don't let your appreciation of each other and those around you go on sale.

It always gets darkest just before it gets totally black. —CHARLIE BROWN

BRIDGING THE SEX GAP

The wife gives authority over her body to her husband, and the husband gives authority over his body to his wife. 1 CORINTHIANS 7:4

ALTHOUGH THE TYPICAL red-blooded American male would never dream of publicly admitting his hunger to be held or his craving to be caressed or his yearning to be massaged, those desires are often as real for men as for women. It's true. In his private and vulnerable moments, even an unaffectionate man will confess that he wants his wife to touch him more often.

Okay, you might say as a wife, but isn't the type of touching at issue here—those gentle caresses to arouse and seduce—exactly the time-consuming foreplay that sometimes exasperates men (at least according to conventional wisdom)? Don't men prefer to move straight toward the "main event"?

Not exactly. It's just that, relative to women, men lack the language and the courage to express specific physical needs—to ask for what they really want. So what ends up happening simply perpetuates the myth. Instead of working to improve the process, the goal-oriented male focuses on the prize at the end of the rainbow.

In a recent counseling session, after taking a brief inventory about their sex life, a husband told me (Les) that he loves touching his wife. "She has the softest skin, and it feels so good to caress her," he confessed. "But I wish she would do the same for me." It's not the first time I've heard that.

So tonight as you slip between the sheets, set aside your expectations and use your pillow talk to explore one of the most important things that happens in your bed: lovemaking and all that leads to it. Use today's meditation as an opportunity to bridge the communication gap about your sex life. Do your best to uncover what your partner likes and dislikes about being touched in the preamble to your lovemaking.

Recount an occasion when you felt in sync sexually. And if that's a distant memory (as it is for many couples), think of what that would mean for you and discuss it. What makes you feel like your partner is in tune with your physical desires? On a scale of one to ten, how open do you feel you can be with each other on this topic and why?

Anybody who believes that the way to a man's heart is through his stomach flunked geography. —ROBERT BYRNE

BEAUTY SLEEP FOR THE SOUL

Those who live in the shelter of the Most High will find rest in the shadow of the Almighty.

PSALM 91:1

IT'S 7:30 A.M. when a knock on the door rousts Miss Universe from a deep slumber. The twenty-year-old native of Botswana groggily rises, looking more like Miss Bad Hair. "Phone for you," says the manager of the apartment, apologetically. At 7:45 in the next bedroom, the alarm buzzes—the cue for twenty-two-year-old Miss USA to shuffle down the hall and plug in her curlers before flopping back into bed.

It could be reveille in any college dorm—except these roommates really do need their beauty sleep.[2] And truth is, we all do. It's tough to look good without that regulation eight hours. A decent night's sleep is important because while you're sleeping your cells' renewal process is working at its hardest. Nighttime is when damaged skin cells repair themselves and recoup their energy to protect the skin again the following day. That's why many women apply night creams jam-packed with goodies for optimum nourishment of the nocturnal skin. To get the maximum benefit from those hardworking cells, and look your best, you have to first be assured of a good night's sleep.

Tonight, however, we want you both to consider a different kind of "beauty sleep." This kind requires no expensive creams or lotions. We're talking about beauty sleep that focuses on your character—how beautiful you are on the inside.

Here's your assignment. Focus your pillow talk tonight on what kind of magical "cream" you'd like to apply to your character if you could. After a night's sleep, maybe this lotion would help you become more patient with others, for example. Or maybe the beauty cream you would apply would make you more disciplined or goal oriented. Perhaps it would help you delay your gratification or increase your level of kindness or generosity. Maybe your magical cream would give you more empathy and understanding to soothe conflicts.

As you are turning in tonight, be sure to get your beauty sleep—for your face, sure— but for your soul as well.

A thing of beauty is a joy for ever: Its loveliness increases; it will never pass into nothingness; but still will keep a bower quiet for us, and a sleep full of sweet dreams and health. —JOHN KEATS

SHIPSHAPE RELATIONSHIP

Those who refresh others will themselves be refreshed. PROVERBS 11:25

A BATTLESHIP IS AN UNLIKELY place to learn a tender lesson in love, but that's exactly where one can be found when Mike Abrashoff is in command. You may know his story of taking the worst-performing ship in the US Navy fleet and turning it into number one.

As commander of a one-billion-dollar warship and a crew of 310, Mike Abrashoff used grassroots leadership to increase retention rates from 28 percent to 100 percent, reduce operating expenditures, and improve readiness. How did he do it? Among other things, he placed supreme importance on public compliments.

"The commanding officer of a ship is authorized to hand out 15 medals a year," he writes. "I wanted to err on the side of excess, so I passed out 115." Nearly every time a sailor left his ship for another assignment, Captain Abrashoff gave him or her a medal. "Even if they hadn't been star players, they got medals in a public ceremony as long as they had done their best every day. I delivered a short speech describing how much we cherished the recipient's friendship, camaraderie, and hard work." Sometimes the departing sailor's shipmates told funny stories, recalling his or her foibles, trials, and triumphs. But the bottom line was to make the person feel good by complimenting him or her in front of others.

"There is absolutely no downside to this symbolic gesture," said Abrashoff, "provided it is done sincerely without hype." Captain D. Michael Abrashoff knew how to make his sailors feel like a million bucks. [3]

And you can do the same thing for your partner. In fact, when was the last time you gave him or her some public praise? You don't have to create a ceremony like Captain Abrashoff. You can do so whenever you're with friends or family—whether your spouse is there or not. Whenever you have the opportunity to publicly praise another person, don't let it slip by.

So think about a time that is coming up when you will be with other people. Maybe it's out to dinner with friends. Maybe it's a small group study. Whatever the situation, think in advance about how you might put this suggestion into practice. In specific terms, how might you compliment your spouse in front of others?

And while we're at it, take this moment together, right now, to imagine that you had a medal to award your spouse for the past few days. You may not have a public ceremony in which to make a little speech. That doesn't matter. Just tell each other about the reasons you'd award each other a medal right now.

Praise in public; criticize in private. —VINCE LOMBARDI

A SIMPLE SOLUTION
TO TOSSING AND TURNING

Cling to your faith in Christ, and keep your conscience clear. 1 TIMOTHY 1:19

FEW PEOPLE WOULD ARGUE that an overly busy lifestyle and stress-filled days and weeks can affect our ability to sleep well. If we're not worried about work or finances, we have concerns about children, aging parents, health, fragmented families—and the list goes on and on. Articles abound on how to get a good night's sleep, and more than one author has written an entire book on the subject. One such book lists sixteen tips for eliminating sleep problems. Among them are get up and go to bed the same time every day, don't take daytime naps, avoid drinking alcohol and smoking, and follow a bedtime routine to help you unwind. But the author also includes an item that some other writers don't: keep a clear conscience.[4] Imagine that! Unfinished business with our spouses—unkind or thoughtless remarks, encouraging words left unsaid, unwillingness to put our spouse's needs ahead of our own—any or all of these and more can keep us from maintaining a clear conscience and cause us to toss and turn when we could be sleeping peacefully.

So what's the practical solution? It's not always easy, but it is simple. As soon as you make a thoughtless remark or behave in a way that is hurtful toward your spouse, be prepared to offer a sincere apology and ask forgiveness. In fact, to prepare for the time when you may need to apologize—and all of us do—consider these questions to generate a discussion: Can you recall a time when you didn't apologize for doing or saying something you felt bad about? What did it do to your insides? What did it do when it was time to go to bed for the night? Conversely, can you recall a time when coming clean on something gave you a fresh start and a peaceful night's sleep?

Poet Thomas Hood wrote, "O bed! O bed! Delicious bed! That heaven upon earth to the weary head." And that is so true—but only if you and your spouse work at keeping your consciences clear with each other.

A quiet conscience sleeps in thunder. —THOMAS FULLER

KNOWING YOUR LIMITS

Common sense and success belong to me. Insight and strength are mine. PROVERBS 8:14

A STUDY IN CORPORATE America has something to teach couples. It compared executives who floundered and those who succeeded. Both groups had weaknesses, of course, but the critical difference was that those who did not succeed failed to learn from their mistakes and accurately assess and accept their shortcomings.[5] The unsuccessful executives ignored their faults, often rebuffing those who tried to point them out.

In a similar study of several hundred managers from twelve different organizations, Daniel Goleman, author of *Emotional Intelligence*, found that "accuracy in self-assessment was a hallmark of superior performance." It's not that top performers have no limits, he says, but "they are aware of their limits."[6]

So what's the lesson for couples? It's this: When a couple lacks an accurate assessment of their problems, they never figure out how to progress beyond them. You can see this phenomenon on almost any day in the offices of most marriage counselors. Sure, couples know they are struggling, but many don't see the real problem.

Every couple has deficits. But these struggling couples don't know what theirs are. "We just don't know how to communicate," they might say. In a sense this may be true, but their real deficit is that they don't know how to make time for meaningful communication, or they may keep their feelings boxed up, or any number of things. Communication breakdowns are only a symptom of their real problem. And if they could identify their real trouble, they could do something about it.

Successful couples, on the other hand, learn from their mistakes by accurately assessing their shortcomings. They don't ignore their challenges, and they don't deny their limits. They face challenges head-on, looking for practical solutions to build the most God-honoring relationship possible. And when they run into personal limitations, they get help.

Accuracy is twin brother to honesty. —CHARLES SIMMONS

SPIRITUAL OPTIMISM

He is the one who mediates a new covenant between God and people, so that all who are called can receive the eternal inheritance God has promised them. For Christ died to set them free from the penalty of the sins they had committed under that first covenant. HEBREWS 9:15

SHORTLY AFTER GRADUATE SCHOOL, and early into taking on our teaching assignments at the university, we found a helpful mentor in H. Norman Wright. In fact, you'll see him in a framed photo that rests on a prominent shelf in our study. Norm was one of the early pioneers when it comes to giving married couples practical help from a biblical perspective. He's written dozens of helpful books for couples. And if you spend time with him, you'll learn very quickly that he's an optimist. He likes to learn from the past, but he's drawn to the present and the future. He's a "glass half-full" kind of guy.

Someone defined a pessimist as one who feels bad when he feels good for fear he'll feel worse when he feels better. Pessimists have simply made negative thinking a habit, a way of life. Optimists, on the other hand, are undaunted by defeat. When they are confronted with the inevitable hard knocks of life, they immediately look for solutions. They see defeat as temporary. Most of all, they look to a bright future.

It is difficult to read about the new covenant of Christ and not become an optimist. Through his death and resurrection, Jesus is promising an eternal inheritance. He is setting us free from sin. Of course, the Bible has a different word for optimism: hope. In the New Testament "hope" appears more than eighty times, and it usually includes references to Christ, who is the hope of this world (see Titus 2:13; 1 Peter 1:3, NASB). Colossians 1:4-5 tells us that love springs from hope. That's a good message for married couples. We can't really love one another without hope.

Hope is the "strong and trustworthy anchor for our souls" (Hebrews 6:19), and "will not lead to disappointment" (Romans 5:5). Paul also alluded to hope as being an attitude of optimism when he urged the Thessalonians to put on the helmet of hope (I Thessalonians 5:8, NIV). Hope protects our head. It is an attitude that safeguards optimism—and protects a marriage. And that's a lesson we learned early on from our optimistic friend Norm Wright.

An optimist is the human personification of spring. —SUSAN J. BISSONETTE

OUR INNER EYJAFJALLAJÖKULL

Dear friends, never take revenge. Leave that to the righteous anger of God.

ROMANS 12:19

ABOUT THIS TIME OF YEAR IN 2010, much of the world breathed a collective sigh. Earlier that year the volcano Eyjafjallajökull in Iceland had belched ash and dirty ice into the atmosphere at a rate of 750 tons per second and shut down air traffic over Europe for months. But it was officially over. Thousands of canceled flights could take to the air again.

Author and speaker Gordon MacDonald likened Eyjafjallajökull to the volcanoes of anger that mark the landscape of the human soul. "These interior Eyjafjallajökulls of varying sizes can erupt when one least expects it: in traffic, in a routine conversation when disagreement rises, in a moment when someone denies us something we believe we deserve."

He makes a great point. Our subterranean emotions can explode without warning. MacDonald writes, "I grew up thinking I was a pretty calm person and that it was others—not me—who had anger issues. My wife, Gail, once pointed out to me that while I often said nothing in such moments, the glare on my face told a more accurate story of my inner disposition.

"Then one day I discovered Eyjafjallajökull within myself. I became embroiled in a disagreement that caused feelings to ignite in ways I'd never experienced before. . . . When the volcano inside of me blew, it brought my life, for all practical purposes, to a halt, much as the real Eyjafjallajökull has paralyzed northern Europe. I was surprised, amazed at myself: all of this meanness that suddenly came from who-knows-where. . . . I have not fully mastered this area of life, but I have learned to spot the uprisings of feelings that can eventually morph into needless anger."[7]

Perhaps no other emotion has caused married couples more difficulty than anger. We have seen how people explain away their anger. Some deny it by calling it fatigue, nervousness, or being uptight. Others suppress their anger, making every effort to keep it from showing (this usually leads to a phony emotional saccharine sweetness). Still others try to spiritualize it by talking about righteous and unrighteous anger. Some people flaunt anger over their partners. "This is the way God made me, so you might as well get used to it. It's in my genes."

Well, anger is not inherited. It is learned and can be unlearned. And anger by any other name is still anger. Whether suppressed, spiritualized, or flaunted, anger will do its destructive deeds to even the best of marriages. What matters is not whether you feel angry, but what you do with your anger once it kicks in. That's why Paul encourages us to "do things in such a way that everyone can see you are honorable. . . . Live in peace" (Romans 12:17-18).

 A man is about as big as the things that make him angry. —**WINSTON CHURCHILL**

DON'T QUIT

He will give eternal life to those who keep on doing good, seeking after the glory and honor and immortality that God offers. ROMANS 2:7

JUST TWO DAYS BEFORE Columbus sighted land, his men were on the verge of mutiny. They had sailed the longest voyage ever out of the sight of land and wanted to turn back.

The October 10, 1492, entry in Columbus's journal stated, "Here the people could stand it no longer and complained of the long voyage. . . . The Admiral cheered them as best he could, holding out good hope of the advantages they would have. And he added that it was useless to complain. He had come to the Indies, and so had to continue until he found them, with the help of Our Lord."[8] Two days later they discovered America.

A folk proverb says, "Perseverance is everything." The apostle Paul would likely agree. As he makes clear in today's verse, God gives eternal life to those who persevere and don't give up on their faith when the going gets rough.

Ignacy Paderewski, the great Polish pianist, composer, and statesman was waiting to begin one of his recitals when an eight-year-old boy from the audience slid out of his seat and headed for the stage before his parents could stop him. The young man seated himself at the piano and began playing "Chopsticks." The audience scowled at this brash lad with his jarring sounds. From the side of the stage, however, Paderewski entered and quietly slid up behind the boy, reaching his long arms out to the right and left of the two small hands. Paderewski began to improvise on the "Chopsticks" theme. Suddenly the simple melody, played imperfectly, took on a sound of beauty, blessed with the master's approval and touch. The audience burst into applause. Everybody noticed that Paderewski kept whispering into the boy's ear. It was later revealed that he just kept saying, "Don't quit, don't quit."

We have a similar opportunity in marriage to keep one another keeping on. At those times when one partner is weak, the other can be strong. And when both husband and wife are losing strength, the Master always comes alongside to make our imperfections beautiful. God's voice saying "Don't quit, don't quit" can keep us persevering.

Our greatest weakness lies in giving up. The most certain way to succeed is always to try just one more time. —**THOMAS EDISON**

YOUR SPIRITUAL PATHWAY TO GOD

Be strong and courageous! Do not be afraid and do not panic before them. For the LORD your God will personally go ahead of you. He will neither fail you nor abandon you.

DEUTERONOMY 31:6

A KINDERGARTEN TEACHER was observing her classroom of children while they drew. She would occasionally walk around to see each child's artwork. As she got to one little girl who was working diligently, she asked what the drawing was. The girl replied, "I'm drawing God." The teacher paused and said, "But no one knows what God looks like." Without missing a beat or looking up from her drawing the girl replied, "They will in a minute."[9]

We sometimes think everyone sees God and how to relate to him exactly as we do. In fact, our focus can become so narrow that we expect everyone else—especially our spouses—to see him the very same way. And that's a terrible mistake for most married couples. Why? Because each person has unique experiences of learning God's character. Some people have gone through life experiencing a great sense of his justice or his joy. Others may have spent years marveling at the grace and protection that he has personally shown them. Is God limited to being more about justice or joy or grace or protection? Not at all—he embodies all those qualities.

Some time ago we were speaking at Willow Creek Community Church in Barrington, Illinois. Bill Hybels, the pastor of this great church, told us about a book that has since helped us greatly in our desire to deepen our own level of spiritual intimacy as a couple. So much so that we feel compelled to share with you the gist of its message. The book is called *Sacred Pathways*, and Gary Thomas is the author. Though the book is not written with couples in mind, we immediately saw the application of Gary's message to easing the soul-searching ache for spiritual connectedness that so many couples experience. In fact, we recently talked with Gary about our observation, and he was quick to confess that his own marriage was the catalyst for his thinking. "I knew my wife loved God," he said, "but I didn't understand why she didn't relate to him the way I did."

So how about the two of you? How do your spiritual pathways to God differ?

The soul can split the sky in two and let the face of God shine through.
—EDNA ST. VINCENT MILLAY

HOW OFTEN IS ENOUGH?

My lover said to me, "Rise up, my darling! Come away with me, my fair one!

SONG OF SONGS 2:10

STUDIES SHOW THAT married couples make love an average of 98 times per year.[10] So what do you think? Is that good or bad? It's a relative question, we know. How you answer depends on your perspective and your expectations. If you want to have sex once a day versus once a month, you'll look at this news differently.

Consider the following comments made by a pretty typical wife and husband after just three or four years of marriage.

Wife: "He keeps saying he wants to make love, but it doesn't feel like love to me. Sometimes I feel bad that I feel that way, but I just can't help it."

Husband: "I don't understand. She says it doesn't feel like love. What does that mean, anyway? What does she think love is? I want to have sex with her because I love her!"

We've done enough marriage counseling to tell you that this kind of talk is not unusual. In this marriage, as in many others, the husband sees himself as showing his love to his wife by engaging her in sexual activity. It's genuine. He feels connected to her, and lovemaking is an expression of that. He doesn't need much "warm up" to get started. In fact, little to no conversation is required.

The wife, on the other hand, sees sexual activity as something that should evolve out of verbal expressions of affection and love. She doesn't understand the mere act of lovemaking as being loving at all unless it's contextualized in a conversation that brings it about. Like a scene from a Woody Allen movie that cuts too close to home, this couple bickers continually about how frequently they have sex.

"I'd be happy if we had sex just once a week," the husband will say.

"He wants to have sex all the time—at least once a week," the wife will tell us.

Of course, the question about how much lovemaking is enough is not a matter of counting the number of times per week or per month. There is no prescription, no magic number. For partners who are dedicated to each other, the question of frequency will be answered in terms of concern for the needs and desires of the other person.

The only stable happiness for mankind is that it shall live married in blessed union to woman-kind. —D. H. LAWRENCE

FEELING THE PAIN?

He will wipe every tear from their eyes, and there will be no more death or sorrow or crying or pain. All these things are gone forever. REVELATION 21:4

AN ARTICLE IN *NEW SCIENTIST* magazine states that during the years before he died, English poet John Keats wrote hundreds of letters and sonnets to Fanny Brawne, the woman he would have married but for his lack of financial security.[11] In one letter to her, Keats wrote, "My love has made me selfish. I cannot exist without you; I am forgetful of everything but seeing you again; my Life seems to stop there; I see no further."[12]

Tuberculosis took hold of Keats about the time he penned these words, and he died just a year later at age twenty-five. Of course, his poetic work lives on. If fact, his love poems and letters are considered among the most popular in English literature. No doubt about it, Keats's love for Fanny inspired great poetry, but new research suggests it may have also provided some relief from the discomfort of Keats's tuberculosis.

A recent Stanford University study explored the analgesic effect of love and found that it directly impacts our overall experience of pain. The study recruited fifteen undergraduates, each of whom described themselves as "intensely in love." The students were asked to bring along photos of their loved ones and of a good-looking acquaintance. The researchers first asked the participants to hold a block whose temperature could be controlled and report how much pain they felt at different temperatures.

The brain of each person was then scanned while they performed one of three tasks. They did this while holding the temperature-controlled block. For the first two tasks, participants were shown either a picture of their attractive acquaintance or their loved one, and told to think about the person in the picture. The final task was a word-puzzle designed to distract them and known to reduce levels of pain they report.

The temperature block was set at three different levels: no pain, moderate pain, or high pain. After completing each task, each person rated the level of pain. The study showed that both love and distraction reduced pain, and by the same amount—about 40 percent! The photo of the attractive acquaintance provided much less relief.[13]

Fascinating, don't you think? God designed us in such a way that a loving relationship would ease our pain. Good thing, too. Pain has been with us since the beginning (see Genesis 3:16). And it will be with us to the end (see Revelation 21:4). That's why the comfort of loving each other is doubly rewarding.

 } *The pain passes, but the beauty remains.* —PIERRE-AUGUSTE RENOIR

THE SO-SO SAMARITAN?

Love your neighbor as yourself. LUKE 10:27

PRINCETON UNIVERSITY psychologists John Darley and Daniel Batson conducted a landmark study years ago that is now recounted in nearly every university course on social psychology. Here's what happened:

> *Darley and Batson met with a group of seminarians, individually, and asked each to prepare a short, extemporaneous talk on a biblical theme, then walk over to a nearby building to present it. Along the way to the presentation, each student ran into a man slumped in an alley, head down, eyes closed, coughing and groaning. The question was, who would stop and help? Darley and Batson introduced three variables into the experiment, to make its results more meaningful. First, before the experiment even started, they gave the students a questionnaire about why they had chosen to study theology. . . . Then they varied the theme the students were asked to talk about. Some were asked to speak on the relevance of the professional clergy to the religious vocation. Others were given the parable of the Good Samaritan [see Luke 10:25-37]. Finally, the instructions given by the experimenters to each student varied as well. In some of the cases . . . the experimenter would look at his watch and say, "Oh, you're late. They were expecting you a few minutes ago. We'd better get moving." In other cases, he would say, "It will be a few minutes before they're ready for you, but you might as well head over now."[14]*

Now, which of these seminary students do you think was most likely to stop to help the man in need? Most of us would expect that those who had just read about the Good Samaritan would have been the most likely to stop and help. But we would be wrong.

> *It is hard to think about a context in which norms concerning helping those in distress are more salient than for a person thinking about the Good Samaritan. . . . Indeed, on several occasions a seminary student going to give his talk on the parable of the Good Samaritan literally stepped over the victim as he hurried on his way. The only thing that really mattered was whether the student was in a rush.[15]*

We all struggle to set aside self-interest and let go of our personal agendas. Pride, not to mention our schedule, seems to continually interfere with our loving efforts. If we're honest, on occasion we can even step right over a need that our partner has as we hurry on our way. We have needs, drives, rights, and goals that do not easily harmonize with selfless love. The question is, how can we be a "Good Samaritan" in the relationships that matter most? Can you identify one way you can embody this kind of love today? Keep in mind, self-giving love does not demand a huge sacrifice. Small things done with great love most often characterize the actions of a person who loves like the Good Samaritan.

Don't look for big things, just do small things with great love. —**MOTHER TERESA**

LIFE IN THE FAST LANE

Jesus said, "Come to me, all of you who are weary and carry heavy burdens, and I will give you rest. Take my yoke upon you. Let me teach you, because I am humble and gentle at heart, and you will find rest for your souls." MATTHEW 11:28-29

A SCHOOL CROSSING GUARD in Florida was frustrated that cars refused to slow down as they went through the zone where he was in charge. Dale Rooks had tried everything, but nothing seemed to work. Nothing, that is, until he took matters into his own hands by wrapping a blow dryer in electrical tape to make it look like a radar gun.

The next day, when speeding drivers noticed Dale pointing his "radar gun" at cars, they instantly slammed on their brakes. "It's almost comical," Dale said. "It's amazing how well it works."[16]

Dale's clever idea got us thinking about what it would take to get people to slow down in general—not just in their cars. Can you imagine if your spouse could hold up a radar gun when you were falling victim to hurry sickness? On a particularly rushed day, he or she could clock your speed and pull you over for a respite. Wouldn't that be convenient when our day gets too busy to connect or even pause for a meal? Maybe after three tickets in an allotted period of time we would have to go on vacation together. It's all wishful thinking, we know. But it does give one pause to consider how we might help each other slow down.

Jonathan Tunrbough tells the story of his mother who was driving his sisters and him to school when a policeman stopped her for speeding. When his mom drove off again, she was being very careful to stay under the speed limit. After a few minutes had passed, they all started hearing a strange noise coming from their vehicle. "What's that noise?" his mother asked. Laughing, he replied, "That's the sound of slow. We've never heard it before!"[17]

What does slow sound like in your marriage? What does it look like? Chances are at least one of you wants to ease up the pace. How will you know when you've slowed down?

For us, a sure sign of slowing down means we're both home with our boys for an evening with nothing scheduled past five o'clock except time together. It also means not holding phone conferences while driving in the car with the family. It means taking our little ones to the park without a time limit. And the sound of slowness means hearing casual conversation around the dinner table and hearing the waves on the beach while we're watching the sunset together.

So we'll ask you again. What are the sounds and sights of slow in your relationship? Answering this question just might help you find more of them.

 } *Running on empty, running blind. Running into the sun, but I'm running behind.*
—JACKSON BROWNE

EATING HUMBLE PIE

He said, "I tell you the truth, unless you turn from your sins and become like little children, you will never get into the Kingdom of Heaven. So anyone who becomes as humble as this little child is the greatest in the Kingdom of Heaven." MATTHEW 18:3-4

HANNAH, A COUNTRY CHURCH organist for many years, had taken to falling asleep during the sermon. As she was loved by all, this fault was easily overlooked. Besides, the position of the organ at the east end of the platform kept her pretty much away from the congregation's normal line of vision.

One Sunday as the sermon was building to a climax, the minister swung his arm forcefully and cried: "Look to the East!" The congregation, following his gesture, gasped and then chuckled softly. There sat Hannah, head back and mouth open, sleeping the sleep of the innocent. The minister regained his composure and concluded his message with equal poise. Hannah awoke at her usual time and played the closing hymn, temporarily unaware of what had happened.[18]

The circumstances may have been different, but we've all been in Hannah's shoes. We've all suffered a humiliating experience that brought us down a notch or two. And that's not a bad thing.

Just as a self-inflating mattress becomes puffed up with nothing but air, we can puff ourselves up with hollow pride. You know the syndrome. You've seen it in others, and if you're honest you've seen it in yourself. We can become so impressed with who we think we are that we lose all sight of our humility. And humility is a key ingredient to any healthy relationship, especially marriage. William Gurnall said, "Humility is the necessary veil to all other graces." Without humility, it's nearly impossible to engender kindness and warmth with our spouse.

So when was the last time you monitored your unhealthy pride quotient? If it's been a while, consider what the famous preacher Charles Spurgeon said: "Humility is to make a right assessment of oneself." That's all. It's not complex. And as a married couple, you have a built-in way for doing just that. Though it takes some courage, you can invite feedback to help you honestly assess how you're doing with pride. But by all means, be gentle with each other. And pray the prayer of Thomas Merton: "Give me humility, in which alone is rest, and deliver me from pride, which is the heaviest of burdens."

If you want to get practical, ask your spouse to help you identify one area in your life where it wouldn't hurt to have a bit more humility. Listen to his or her feedback without being defensive. The goal here is to help, not hurt, one another.

What makes humility so desirable is the marvelous thing it does to us; it creates in us a capacity for the closest possible intimacy with God.
—MONICA BALDWIN

HAPPILY EVER AFTER?

Talk is cheap, like daydreams and other useless activities. Fear God instead.

ECCLESIASTES 5:7

OSCAR WILDE, the nineteenth-century writer, once wrote, "In this world there are only two tragedies. One is not getting what one wants, and the other is getting it." Deep down, our greatest hope is not for fame, comfort, wealth, or power. Those rewards create almost as many problems as they solve. If you reach your goal, if your dreams come true, you're bound to eventually wake up someday and ask, "Is this it?"

We will never be happy or fulfilled until we stop measuring our real-life achievements against the dream of whatever we imagined would make us happy. It's what psychologist Daniel Levinson called the "tyranny of the Dream." Each of us developed this dream when we were young. Maybe it was planted by parents or teachers, or maybe our own imaginings. The Dream was to someday be truly special. We dreamed that our work would be recognized, that our marriages would be perfect, and that our children would be exemplary. We may have dared to dream we'd be famous or affluent.

If we've been hit by a major jolt—diagnosed with cancer, for example—our Dream has been deferred while we hope for a cure. But whatever we are dreaming of, we keep holding out hope that it will be realized and the fairy tale complete. But, as Anaïs Nin reminds us, "We've been poisoned by fairy tales." They don't come true. The Dream can never make us happy. Even if you reach your goals to become the success you imagined, you're likely to feel empty. Why? Because our greatest hope is not for fame, comfort, wealth, or power. These are shallow hopes. Our greatest is far deeper. Our greatest hope is for meaning.

What does this have to do with your relationship? Everything. You've no doubt hung hopes—perhaps very high hopes—on your relationship. You've got your own version of the fairy tale you want to write together, and it's all about living happily ever after, right? But truth be told, it will be the meaning that you create together that matters most. Sure, the rewards and pleasures you experience as part of your Dream are great blessings, but don't take your eyes off the meaning of your relationship in the eyes of God. That's where the ultimate dream becomes real.

 } *Live out thy life in its full meaning for behold, it is God's life.* —JOSIAH ROYCE

FOR THE TO-DO LIST SPOUSE

When the Father sends the Advocate as my representative—that is, the Holy Spirit—he will teach you everything and will remind you of everything I have told you. JOHN 14:26

SOME YEARS AGO I (LES) THOUGHT I could check a bunch of "loving behaviors" off my to-do list with Leslie by using a nifty feature on our voice-mail system. It's called "future delivery." It allows you to record a message now and then determine the day you want it to be delivered in the future. I recorded a dozen or so loving messages to Leslie and then programmed them to be sent on various days in the coming month. Boom! I could check that issue off my list for a while.

At first, Leslie was pleased to receive them. "Hey, thanks for that nice message today," she'd say.

"What message?" I'd ask, before remembering what I had done days earlier. But a few messages into this, Leslie began to catch on to what I had done. Suddenly the messages weren't so meaningful. And truth be told, they weren't coming from the heart. I was trying to take a shortcut, and it left both of us unsatisfied.

Are you like me, a to-do list spouse?

In reality, I simply needed some reminders to focus my attention on my spouse. I needed a prompt from the Holy Spirit to be sure I was sincerely tuned in to my marriage—rather than being consumed by an upcoming book deadline, a university project, or a speaking engagement. So I began to send myself a few "future delivery" reminders, this time via my own electronic calendar. At times that I designate, I plug in reminders for various things I want to convey or do with my wife: Ask Leslie how I can help her this week; wash her car and fill it with gas; take her to dinner; take the kids out and give her a quiet evening at home. You get the idea. I simply place reminders on my calendar that increase the odds of me investing in my marriage.[19]

To love for the sake of being loved is human, but to love for the sake of loving is angelic.
—ALPHONSE DE LAMARTINE

A DIFFICULT GIFT TO GRASP

I am convinced that nothing can ever separate us from God's love. Neither death nor life, neither angels nor demons, neither our fears for today nor our worries about tomorrow— not even the powers of hell can separate us from God's love. ROMANS 8:38

JOHN OF KRONSTADT WAS a nineteenth-century Russian Orthodox priest, born on October 19, 1829—a time when alcohol abuse was rampant. None of the priests ventured out of their churches to help the people. They waited for the people to come to them. John, compelled by love, went out into the streets. People said he would lift the hungover, foul-smelling people from the gutter, cradle them in his arms, and say to them, "This is beneath your dignity. You were meant to house the fullness of God."[20]

What a powerful message! And truth be told, you don't have to be on skid row to hear it. We are all in need of a continual reminder of God's love for us. And if we struggle more than most with feelings of inadequacy, we need it all the more.

Susan, married just under a year, came to us with her husband, Don, because she repeatedly questioned her worth, her dignity. "Sometimes I just don't know how Don can love me," she would say. "I feel so guilty; like I don't deserve to have such a good husband."

Jonah would have understood Susan's feelings of inadequacy. When God called Jonah to preach to the city of Nineveh, Jonah ran away. And when a storm threatened to capsize the boat he was on, Jonah knew immediately whose fault the storm was. "Throw me into the sea," he said, "and it will become calm" (Jonah 1:12). Only when he was trapped in the belly of the great fish did Jonah stop running and face up to God. Yet when he went to Nineveh and they repented, he again withdrew.

Sometimes love is a difficult gift to grasp. Like Susan, some of us fear we are not lovable—to our spouse or even to God. And some of us, like Jonah, cannot fathom why God would choose us to love. That is why Paul reminds us in this passage of Romans that nothing can separate us from the love of God.[21]

It is not the most lovable individuals who stand more in need of love, but the most unlovable. —**ASHLEY MONTAGU**

GUILT AND GRACE

Now I am glad I sent it, not because it hurt you, but because the pain caused you to repent and change your ways. It was the kind of sorrow God wants his people to have, so you were not harmed by us in any way. For the kind of sorrow God wants us to experience leads us away from sin and results in salvation. There's no regret for that kind of sorrow. But worldly sorrow, which lacks repentance, results in spiritual death.

2 CORINTHIANS 7:9-10

EARLY CATHOLIC GUIDES for priests taking confessions warned about a type of person called "the scrupulous," people who held on to guilt no matter what. They were "unrelieved confessors" who, in spite of all assurances, could not accept grace.

If you are "scrupulous," if you are holding on to your guilt like a security blanket, you can be assured that it is doing damage to your marriage. Guilt is like a toxin to relationships. There is a better way. The secret is found in this passage of 2 Corinthians, and it is called "godly sorrow"—as opposed to "worldly sorrow" or guilt.

While guilt and sorrow are sometimes seen as the same emotional experience, they could not be further apart. Sorrow, unlike guilt, does not wallow in self-punishment and self-abasement. Instead, it is grounded in a deep concern for relationships and constructive change.

German reformer Martin Luther struggled with unbounded feelings of guilt. He expended great energy meeting the requirements of his religious order, confessing his sins repeatedly, and on one occasion, for six hours. He was so obsessed with confessing even the minutest sins that once his superior chided him by saying, "If you expect God to forgive you, come in to confession with something to forgive."

When we relate to God out of a guilty conscience, rather than godly sorrow, we try to earn our worth by being severely critical of ourselves. Rather than rely on God's mercy, we struggle to show God—and sometimes our spouse—how good we are.

Of course, that's no way to live. And it's certainly not the life God called us to. So what can you do today if you're living under the weight of guilt and condemnation? Maybe you can list anything and everything you are feeling guilty about. Then ask each other what things you listed might fall into the category of "false guilt." Gaining some objective perspective from each other may be all you need today to get a fresh glimpse of God's grace in your life.

Grace is not simply leniency when we have sinned. Grace is the enabling gift of God not to sin. Grace is power, not just pardon. —JOHN PIPER

YOUR HOUSE OF LOVE

Many waters cannot quench love, nor can rivers drown it. If a man tried to buy love with all his wealth, his offer would be utterly scorned. SONG OF SONGS 8:7

ABOUT THIRTY MILES FROM Belfast, Northern Ireland, close to the shore of Strangford Lough, is a stately home called Castle Ward that tourists can visit. The house was built in the 1760s, and its original owners were Bernard Ward, the first Viscount Bangor, and his wife, Lady Anne.

The most striking feature of the house is its display of two different styles of architecture. The rear of the house is Gothic, while the front is neoclassical. Why the different styles? Because Bernard enjoyed one while Lady Anne another. Today, the house still stands—as a monument to stubbornness, some would say—but to others, it is a celebration of diversity.

Do you ever feel as if your proverbial house of love is being built with the same mentality? As if your marriage is becoming too focused on who gets what? We've known some couples who are so consumed with their individual concerns that they miss one of the great joys that can be found in learning to compromise.

Can you recall the last issue where either one of you, or both of you, demonstrated a marked ability to compromise? What was that issue, and why did you choose to compromise on it? Can you recall how you felt as a result? More likely than not, you eventually felt a great sense of satisfaction. You felt as if you'd accomplished something and grown as a person. Mature and emotionally healthy people learn to become professionals in the fine art of compromise.

The truth is that most marriages are going to have opposing features, some quite striking, because of the distinct personalities of the spouses. But remember this: the healthiest marriages allow for the full expression of both personalities. As iron sharpens iron, they help one another become who God intended them to be. And as this verse reminds us, you can't buy this kind of love.

Love is the only way to grasp another human being in the innermost core of his personality. —**VIKTOR E. FRANKL**

THE PURPOSE-DRIVEN MARRIAGE

As the Scriptures say, "A man leaves his father and mother and is joined to his wife, and the two are united into one." This is a great mystery, but it is an illustration of the way Christ and the church are one. EPHESIANS 5:31-32

WE KNOW A COUPLE WHO celebrated their first anniversary with a romantic candlelit dinner at home. Near the end of the main course, the wife slipped away only to emerge from the kitchen with the perfect dessert for the finishing touch: the top of their wedding cake. With the first cut into the cake, both knew something was wrong. The cake squeaked. With a little more cutting, they discovered the problem. For an entire year, they had saved a round chunk of frosting-covered Styrofoam in their freezer.

Looks can be deceiving. As this silly but true story illustrates, we can focus so much on the externals of a relationship that we neglect to see what we are actually preserving in our marriages. Which brings up a serious subject: Deep down, what do you believe is the core purpose of your marriage? To be happy? We trust you've learned by now that marriage was never designed to act as insurance against sadness. Good marriages, and even great ones, are by no means protected from bad things. So we ask again. What is the central purpose of your marriage?

We have thought long and hard about this question, and here is our answer: The purpose of our marriage is to draw us closer to God. We used to think that God would help us draw closer to each other, that he would help us build a better marriage. And he does. But our emphasis in recent years has focused more on how our marriage helps us build a better relationship with God. This turnabout in thinking has revolutionized our relationship. Instead of asking God to help our marriage, we are more apt to ask each other how we can help the other walk closer to God. Marriage, in other words, is becoming an important means to our Creator. The challenges we face, the joys we celebrate—more than most anything—are bringing us into an intimate relationship with God.

The bonds of matrimony are like any other bonds—they mature slowly.
—PETER DE VRIES

FINDING INSPIRATION

The LORD is my strength and my shield. I trust him with all my heart. He helps me, and my heart is filled with joy. I burst out in songs of thanksgiving. PSALM 28:7

SOME TIME AGO WE read the memoirs of Christopher Reeve, the *Superman* actor, who fell from a horse in a riding accident that severed his spinal cord and paralyzed him from the shoulders down. In the days that followed the accident, both he and his mother considered pulling the plug on his life-support system. We got to the point in his book, *Still Me*, where he mouthed his first lucid words to Dana, his wife: "Maybe we should let me go." But his wife, through tears, persuaded him to fight back, saying, "I want you to know that I will be with you for the long haul, no matter what. You're still you, and I love you."

Stories like this can't help but inspire husbands and wives—bringing us closer together. Why? It's almost inexplicable. Moments of inspiration, when shared by a couple, create a bond. We've shared inspirational moments watching a news report. We'll never forget the tragic scene of mistreated orphans in Romania and the story of one couple's quest to rescue and adopt a deformed little boy. We've shared inspirational moments in worship. We'll never forget standing in a church and listening to Wayne Watson sing "For Such a Time As This." Our hearts have rarely been more full. Or the time we heard Lloyd Ogilvie preach at Hollywood Presbyterian Church on "Finishing the Race." We felt our spirits soaring together.

What about you? When was the last time the two of you were inspired together? In case you don't know, there are countless inspirational moments waiting to be discovered by the two of you. All that's required is that you are willing to find them. And when you do, your lives become richer, your connection deeper, and your spirits lighter.

Every character has an inward spring, let Christ be it. Every action has a key-note, let Christ set it. —HENRY DRUMMOND

TAKING YOUR TIME

Seek the Kingdom of God above all else, and he will give you everything you need.

LUKE 12:31

MICHIGAN GOVERNOR Granholm issued an official proclamation recently in her state: "On behalf of the citizens of Michigan, Governor Jennifer M. Granholm hereby proclaims October 24 as 'Take Back Your Time' Day. Whereas too many are suffering from overwork, over-scheduling and time poverty . . . and whereas, many Americans are working extremely long hours, taking shorter vacations and suffering from stress and burnout, . . . and whereas, time pressure has a negative impact on family life, . . . therefore be it resolved, that I, Jennifer M. Granholm, Governor of the State of Michigan, do hereby proclaim this day as 'Take Back Your Time' Day."

We'd never heard of such a proclamation. It almost made us want to pull up our roots in Seattle and move to the Great Lakes State. Who wouldn't want to live in a place where even the governor wants you to not be so busy? If only it were that easy. Unfortunately, it takes more than a proclamation to actually win the war on busyness. So here is a simple suggestion for doing just that.

Are you ready? Here it is: Slow down.

No duh! Right? Of course, the cure for hurry sickness is to slow down. Lily Tomlin's quote is one of our favorites: "For fast-acting relief, try slowing down." If you prefer a more contemplative thinker, here's what Gandhi said: "There is more to life than increasing its speed."

Okay. So we all know we should slow down more often, but how? Well, at the end of reading this sentence, close your eyes, take a deep breath, and put your hand over your heart and feel the beat for about fifteen seconds. Did you do it? If so, you know how something as simple as this can slow you down.

But if you didn't, if you kept on reading, let us ask you a question. You seriously don't have time to pause for fifteen seconds before completing this paragraph? If so, we have a more challenging assignment. Try not wearing your watch tomorrow. If you're really brave, take the clock off the wall. Just for a day. You'll be amazed to discover how tuned into time you are and how your watch speeds you up more than you think. It's a little exercise that can't help but get you to ease your foot off the gas pedal of your day and slow down.[22]

For fast-acting relief, try slowing down. —**LILY TOMLIN**

STOP STEWING
AND START DOING

Can all your worries add a single moment to your life? And if worry can't accomplish a little thing like that, what's the use of worrying over bigger things? LUKE 12:25-26

A UNIVERSITY OF MICHIGAN study determined that 60 percent of human worries are totally unwarranted. Of the remaining portion of our worries, 20 percent are about already past activities and completely beyond our control. And another 10 percent are so petty that they don't make much difference at all. Of the remaining 10 percent of our worries, only 4 to 5 percent are really justifiable. And even half of this residue of viable worries is beyond our capacity to change! The final half, or 2 percent of our worries which are real, can be solved easily, according to these researchers, "if we stop stewing and start doing!"[23]

Whether these statistics are reliable or not doesn't really matter. The indisputable point is that most of our worries are not worth the stress they generate. How many times have the two of you let worry cloud your dinner conversation? How often do you lie awake at night consumed with an obsessive worry?

You don't have to let the poison of worry contaminate your marriage. Jesus Christ came to give us eternal life, but also abundant life (see John 10:10, NASB). He came to give us life to the fullest and to set us free from the harmful effects of worry. By the way, Jesus practiced what he preached. When faced with the hostility of Herod and the pressure of the public clamor for healing, for example, he had plenty to worry about. Instead, Scripture tells us, he and the disciples rested. Jesus said to his disciples: "Let's go off by ourselves to a quiet place and rest awhile" (Mark 6:31).

So don't allow worry to get a foothold in your marriage. Life is too short. The possibilities are too great. Instead, you can help each other to "give all your worries and cares to God, for he cares about you" (1 Peter 5:7).

> *When I had a sleepless night, I learned to turn my insomnia over to God. I'd just say, "Lord, you know I've got to get my rest. You worry about these problems. You're going to be up all night anyway."* —MARY C. CROWLEY

RULES OR RELATIONSHIPS?

No one can ever be made right with God by doing what the law commands. The law simply shows us how sinful we are. ROMANS 3:20

FOR SEVERAL YEARS, an anti-lawsuit group from Michigan has held "The Wacky Warning Label Contest" to show the effects of lawsuits on warning labels. A warning sticker on a small tractor that reads, "Danger: Avoid Death" took home the top prize recently. Another was found on a label of an iron-on T-shirt transfer that warns, "Do not iron while wearing shirt." A baby stroller that featured a small storage pouch was also submitted. It warns, "Do not put child in bag."[24]

Absurd, right? It's legalism taken to crazy town. But companies who post such warnings obviously feel they need to protect themselves under the law by doing so. Why? Because some people seem dead set on finding legal holes in the system of laws and using them to their advantage.

The early church struggled with legalism. Because Judaism emphasized keeping God's law, the first Christians had to decide what place laws and rules would play in their new lives in Christ. In the book of Galatians, Paul goes to great lengths to convince new Christians that circumcision is not necessary for their salvation. Following the rules by keeping the old Jewish laws will not save you. Only a relationship with Christ will bring you redemption.

Truth be known, many contemporary Christians have never really felt comfortable balancing rules and relationships. But if there was ever an earthly testing ground for this important task, it is in marriage. We've all known of couples who become so uptight and rigid about the way things should be done in marriage that the relationship never stands a chance. It is too weighed down with rules. On the opposite end of the continuum is the so-called "open marriage" where anything goes and there is barely a rule to be found.

Let's make this clear: Laws and rules have their place. We need them in our society, and we need them in marriage. But here's what rule-bound couples often forget: rules turn sour when they become more important than relationships. Legalism kills joy in marriage. It breeds oppressiveness and judgment. Legalism sucks grace from relationships and drains grace from the home.

If Jesus had thought the Kingdom could be built through law, legalism and fundamentalism, He would have worked with the Pharisees rather than call disciples. —DAVID CURRIE

ONE SIMPLE QUESTION

Don't worry; we wouldn't dare say that we are as wonderful as these other men who tell you how important they are! But they are only comparing themselves with each other, using themselves as the standard of measurement. How ignorant! 2 CORINTHIANS 10:12

EVERY AUTUMN AROUND this time of year we begin teaching a course at our university called Relationships 101. It's not required. It's a general elective. But students fill the auditorium on Monday evenings to hear us lecture on relationships. We love teaching this class. Why? For starters, it's exciting to have students in a college classroom who don't have to be there. But mostly, we love teaching this course because we know it makes a difference.

After more than a decade of teaching this course, we now routinely receive e-mails and notes from former students who express appreciation for something we said or something we demonstrated in class that seemed to stick with them and help them out.

And one of the notes we sometimes receive has to do with a simple question we pose to these students. We're about to ask you the same thing. Before we do, however, we want you to know that how you answer it will reveal a bit about your interpersonal approach. So we want both of you to take a contemplative moment to consider it. And be honest. Here's the question: What thought races through your head when you walk into a room of people?

While there are countless responses to this question, all of them are likely to fall into one of two basic camps. These two fundamental responses, in our experience, come in the form of two quiet questions: "How am I doing?" or "How are they doing?"

A social setting fundamentally elicits one of these two positions. You walk into a room of other people, and you are either concerned with yourself and the impression you are about to make or you are focused on them and what is taking place. Whenever your approach falls into the category of "How are they doing?" you are priming the social pump for empathy, sensitivity, and a listening ear. Alternatively, when your basic social approach is to ask "How am I doing?" you are more likely to feel insecure, uneasy, and self-focused.

Of course, nobody is always operating from the how-are-they-doing platform. We all tend to fluctuate between the two. And when it comes to our marriages, we tend to do the same thing. But with the help of the Holy Spirit, we can lean more and more frequently toward the empathy side of the scale. And when two people are doing that for each other, they are creating the safest and most loving place on earth.

If you compare yourself with others, you may become bitter or vain, for always there will be greater and lesser persons than yourself. —MAX EHRMANN

IN THE BEGINNING GOD CREATED FAMILY

My child, listen when your father corrects you. Don't neglect your mother's instruction.

PROVERBS 1:8

FOR MORE THAN FIVE DECADES a thousand people wrote to her every day—before the age of e-mail. She had eight secretaries and two clerks who would winnow the letters down to about two hundred and then sort those into categories. Each letter told a story and then asked a question of a woman who had spent her life dispensing advice to the lovelorn, the afflicted, the battered, the diseased, the lonely, and the confused. Her name was Ann Landers.

"The changes I have seen," she once wrote, "would twirl your turban." Over the years her advice shifted from bad breath to AIDS, from spoiled brats to gun-toting ten-year-olds. Despite the changes, Ann Landers stated that the number-one issue people have questions about is families. "It's always been that way," she says, "and I suspect it's always going to be that way."[25]

How could it be otherwise? It is within the family that our personhood, our very identity, first takes shape. Our family provides us with a blueprint for ways of being and behaving. We pick up on rules, regulations, and expectations about our own and other people's behavior from our family. It is in the family that we learn about what kinds of feelings are acceptable, appropriate, and tolerable. Every conceivable subject is taught in the family, from politics to religion, from psychology to philosophy. And, of course, Christianity. John Wesley once said, "I learned more about Christianity from my mother than from all the theologians of England." Lessons are learned at home more quickly than any university professor could ever hope for in a classroom. It is within family that life's lessons are internalized and become the substrate from which our thinking, our motives, our very personalities are formed.

It's no wonder that God designed human beings to live in families. Throughout human history, the family has fulfilled God's intent to provide a context for creation and care. Charles Colson wrote, "The family, ordained of God as the basic unit of human organization, is necessary not only for propagating the race but as the first school of human instruction."[26] Colson couldn't be more right. We learn almost everything from our families. That's the way God made it. So what life lessons did your family teach you? What life lessons are you as a couple passing on?

Call it a clan, call it a network, call it a tribe, call it a family. Whatever you call it, whoever you are, you need one. —JANE HOWARD

HIDING BEHIND A MASK?

Confess your sins to each other and pray for each other so that you may be healed. The earnest prayer of a righteous person has great power and produces wonderful results.

JAMES 5:16

"YOU'RE THE FIRST PERSON I have ever been completely honest with." Every psychologist hears these words from time to time, but it was Sidney Jourard who made sense of them in his in-depth book, *The Transparent Self*. He was puzzled over the frequency with which patients were more honest and authentic with a clinician than they were with family or friends. After much study, he concluded that each of us has a natural, built-in desire to be known, but we often stifle our vulnerability out of fear. We're afraid of being seen as too emotional or not emotional enough, as too assertive or not assertive enough, too whatever, or not whatever enough. We're afraid of rejection.

The result? We wear masks. We put up our guard. We become what Abraham Maslow called "jellyfish in armor" by pretending to be, think, or feel something we aren't. Consider the words of a letter whose author is unknown, but it could have easily been written by each of us:

> *Don't be fooled by me. Don't be fooled by the face I wear. I wear a mask. I wear a thousand masks—masks that I am afraid to take off; and none of them are me.*
>
> *Pretending is an art that is second nature to me, but don't be fooled. For my sake, don't be fooled. I give the impression that I am secure, that all is sunny and unruffled within me as well as without; that confidence is my name and coolness my game, that the water is calm and I am in command; and that I need no one. But don't believe me, please. My surface may seem smooth, but my surface is my mask, my ever varying and ever concealing mask.*[27]

We often vacillate between the impulse to reveal ourselves and the impulse to protect ourselves. We want to be known, of course, but not if the risk of rejection is too high. Wearing masks is a common practice, even among loving couples.

So are you both feeling safe enough to talk about a mask you sometimes wear in your own relationship? How about revealing one of your masks right now? What would it be, and when are you most likely to wear it? Why?

Everything is usually so masked or perfumed or disguised in the world, and it's so touching when you get to see something real and human. I think that's why most of us stay close to our families, because no matter how neurotic the members [of the group], how deeply annoying or dull—because when people have seen you at your worst, you don't have to put on the mask as much. And that gives us license to try on that radical hat of liberation, the hat of self-acceptance. **—ANNE LAMOTT**

COUPLES THAT PRAY TOGETHER

Pray in the Spirit at all times and on every occasion. Stay alert and be persistent in your prayers for all believers everywhere. EPHESIANS 6:18

"I FEEL CLOSER TO YOU when we pray together," Leslie recently told me. "It's probably the most intimate thing we do." And she's right. It's part of God's desiring that we walk together with him—not in a formal or legalistic way, but in a way that is genuine and natural. God longs to be part of each and every marriage, and prayer is one of the best ways we know of for inviting him into yours.

But let's get real. Spiritual intimacy, while vital to a healthy marriage, so often seems elusive. We are the first to admit that we don't pray together as often as we'd like. We're not the types to kneel beside the bed each night or morning and hold hands while we call on God together. We'd probably be better for it, but more often than not our prayers together (other than at meal times) are spontaneous and often unexpected. But with the nightly ritual of tucking our little boys in bed, we've discovered how meaningful it is to say a prayer together before falling asleep.

Maybe you already do this. If so, you know the harmony it brings to your marriage. As Swiss physician Paul Tournier pointed out, praying together enriches a couple's home.[28] Heartfelt prayer together lowers our defenses and heightens our teamwork. It joins our sprits together—even when our differing temperaments, ideas, and tastes threaten to divide us. And by the way, for all those skeptics who think that prayer is for uptight people who can barely mention the word sex, researchers have found something surprising: Couples that pray together have better sex lives. Why? Well, when two people's bodies, souls, and spirits are in harmony with one another and with their Creator, physical intimacy becomes reminiscent of Paradise, and love returns to Eden.

So say your prayers tonight, and every night you can. It just may be the most important thing you do all day.

To be a Christian without prayer is no more possible than to be alive without breathing.
—MARTIN LUTHER KING JR.

A MARITAL REFORMATION?

Sensible people control their temper; they earn respect by overlooking wrongs.

PROVERBS 19:11

IT WAS ON THIS DAY, October 31 in 1518, that Martin Luther, the German priest and scholar, posted the Ninety-Five Theses to the door of the Wittenberg Castle Church (which served as a kind of bulletin board). His intent was to spur debate. Little did he know that his questioning of certain church practices would lead to the Protestant Reformation that would change the state of the church forever.

Luther could have just as easily begun a movement in modern-day marriages with this buried quote: "It is impossible to keep peace between man and woman in family life if they do not condone and overlook each other's faults but watch everything to the smallest point. For who does not at times offend?"

It's difficult to improve on that. Luther could not have spoken a truer word. Can you imagine what would happen in your home if both of you suddenly began overlooking petty problems? if you each decided to bypass each opportunity to criticize? What would happen if suddenly tomorrow this grace occurred in every home? It would be nothing short of a revolution—perhaps the greatest social revolution ever!

Love must be blind—at least to petty offenses—if it is to grow. We all supply plenty of opportunities for our spouse to find fault. That goes with the territory of being human. The trick is learning how to shut our eyes when we encounter each other's minor faults. How do you actually put this biblical principle into practice? Here are a couple of suggestions.

First, take inventory on what you especially appreciate about your spouse. Why? Because doing so recalibrates your mind-set. In one of the classes we teach, we sometimes have our students take ten seconds to notice everything in the room that's green. Suddenly, they see green everywhere. Why? They invoked a green mind-set. They couldn't help but see it because that's all they were looking for. The same is true in marriage. When we invoke a positive mind-set for our partner, we begin to see so many more things they do well. A positive mind-set can't help but engender appreciation and positivity.

Second, own up to your own faults. Is there some log in your eye that you have missed in the fixation on the speck in your spouse's eye (Matthew 7:3-5)? Consider what it would be like to be married to you. What about you makes you challenging to live with? The more you recognize the difficulties you bring to the table, the more acceptance you will have of your partner's foibles.

Try these two steps today, and start your own marital reformation.

 It is the glory of a man to overlook an offense; it is a foolish and prideful man who feels every little offense is worthy of confrontation. **—TIM CHALLIES**

WHERE DO YOU NEED GRACE?

Be kind to each other, tenderhearted, forgiving one another, just as God through Christ has forgiven you. EPHESIANS 4:32

THE 2003 FILM *OPEN RANGE*, directed by Kevin Costner (who also stars in the movie), is not only an old-fashioned Western. It is also a story about second chances. Kevin Costner's character comes to town seeking revenge for the killings of his friends:

> *His plans for bloodshed, however, reawaken memories of the Civil War. As an assassin, he had killed hundreds, and as the war grew long, he stopped discriminating between soldiers and civilians, between men, women, and children. He had killed them all.*
>
> *But when Charley meets Sue Barlow, played by Annette Bening, Charley sees the possibility of a different life for himself—a life filled with love, home, and family. Until he met Sue, Charley considered such a life out of reach for a man with his murderous past. Yet, Sue's love calls him to that different life.*
>
> *Charley's violent side re-emerges in a shootout in which he is wounded. He resolves to leave Sue and his dreams of a changed life. As Charley prepares to leave, Sue tells of her patient love for him, despite his past.*
>
> *In a dusty, shot-up saloon, Sue tells him, "I don't have the answers, Charley, but I know that people get confused in this life about what they want, and what they've done, and what they think they should have done because of it. Everything they think they are or did takes hold so hard that it won't let them see what they can be."*
>
> *She continues, "I've got a big idea about us, Charley . . . and I'm not going to wait forever, but I am going to wait. And when you're far away, I want you to think about that . . . and come back to me."*[1]

And he does.

Love, infused with patience, will always pass the test of time. Few acts are more grace-full than waiting on and loving a husband or wife who is still in process. And aren't we all? Each and every one of us is in need of patient grace from our spouse.

And so instead of asking where are you giving grace to your spouse, the more poignant question is where do you need grace from your partner today? Once you can begin to answer this question, you are more likely to receive grace. Humility engenders grace and cultivates patient love. Can you talk about this concept with each other?

Here's a tip that has helped us when pride keeps us from offering patient and merciful love to each other. Simply take that behavior, that trait, that bad habit, that thing that irritates you or angers you and say, "There but for the grace of God go I."

Grace is given not because we have done good works but in order that we may have power to do them. —ST. AUGUSTINE

STOP AND SMELL THE SPICES

Your wife will be like a fruitful grapevine, flourishing within your home. Your children will be like vigorous young olive trees as they sit around your table. PSALM 128:3

IT'S DIFFICULT TO EXAGGERATE the value of sharing a slow-paced family meal together. Study after study finds that kids who eat dinner with their families regularly are better students, healthier people, and less likely to smoke, drink, or use drugs than those who don't. Such benefits are enough to make you get up and set the table.

> Three nights a week, Kristi and Roger Strode turn the lights low, put on soft music and sit down to eat by candlelight. This isn't a romantic dinner. It's supper with the kids. The Strodes have three children, two jobs and very little time. . . . But dinner in their Shorewood, Wisconsin, household has been transformed with the introduction of the candles, music, and one simple, cooked meal for everyone. "There's real conversation now and less bickering," Ms. Strode told Hilary Stout of the Wall Street Journal. "It brings the whole energy level down to a good place."[2]

But be assured, lingering over a meal benefits everyone, not only the kids. A husband and wife are guaranteed to draw their spirits together when they make table time for meals a common practice. Sure, it takes preparation time, and you're bound to run into logistical challenges involving schedules, but the bonding that results from eating together at the end of a workday is worth the effort—really. If the kids squabble more than share around the table, Dr. Bill Doherty, professor of family social science at the University of Minnesota, offers the following suggestions:

> Ask yourself: "What am I doing that makes it worse?" The answer in many cases is unnecessary reprimanding. The classic no-dessert-unless-you-behave-and-eat turns dinner into a control struggle which defeats the purpose. If they don't eat their vegetables, he suggests, let it go.
>
> Also, don't turn the conversation into an interrogation session about school or activities. A more off-the-wall conversation starter might get everyone engaged. One of his suggestions: If you could meet someone from history, who would it be?
>
> A little more creativity may be in order to keep smaller kids seated. Try a one-color meal—everything green might even help in the eat-your-vegetables department. Or an alphabet dinner, with every dish beginning with the same letter (pasta with plums and pears). Get them excited by picnicking in the living room one night or even eating under the table. . . .
>
> And if dinner is simply too much to handle, try breakfast. Or start with just one night a week. Most important, Mr. Doherty says: "Make it special. Light candles, put a tablecloth out." In other words, make a distinction between a routine meal and a meaningful family ritual.[3]

A mealtime ritual is a keystone for finding time together. —BILL DOHERTY

STAYING IN TOUCH—LITERALLY

Moved with compassion, Jesus reached out and touched him. . . . Instantly the leprosy disappeared, and the man was healed. MARK 1:41-42

TIMMY WAS VERY AFRAID of lightning and thunder. His mom and dad would say, "Now, Timmy, don't be afraid. God is right here in the room with you." He would agree, but then as Mommy and Daddy went into their room, the lightning clapped, and the thunder rolled, and Timmy screamed bloody murder. Timmy's daddy and mommy went back into his room: "Honey, we thought we told you, you don't need to be afraid. God is right here in the room with you."

"I know God is right here in the room with me," Timmy responded, "but I need someone with skin on."[4]

It's easy to identify with this kid. We all want someone with skin on, and that's one of the great blessings of going to bed as a married couple. The holding, cuddling, and spooning we enjoy as husband and wife is wonderful. You know the feeling of holding each other tight under the covers during a rainstorm and the comfort of warming each other's bodies as you climb into bed on a crisp autumn evening. You know the feeling of a gentle caress after a tough day or holding hands across the bed as you fall asleep on a summer's eve. Sometimes just the touch of a toe (even if it's cold) is all it takes to be assured of your partner's presence. Gentle, warm, magnificent touch is glorious.

It can happen at any point throughout the night. At 3:00 a.m., when the world is silent and you're awake contemplating how you parent your child. Or you're pondering the fate of your investments in the stock market. Or you're thinking about your career. Or the future of the country. Or your relationship with God. A few thoughts along these lines can sometimes be enough to banish sleep for hours. But just when your fretting reaches a crescendo, you reach over to your spouse and place your hand on his arm or around her tummy. That's when the world stops spinning out of control. Your heart slows. You drift off to sleep.

Touch. Glorious touch. Scientists have found that touch between a husband and wife can reduce tension, elevate mood, enhance self-esteem, and even strengthen the immune system. Granted, not all touch in marriage is welcome. At certain moments, and for certain people, it can be seen as a demand or even a rebuff. But much of the time, touching between couples can actually be more emotionally potent than the sex act itself.

To us family means putting your arms around each other and being there.
—BARBARA BUSH

THE SEASON OF HARVEST?

Let us not become weary in doing good, for at the proper time we will reap a harvest if we do not give up. GALATIANS 6:9, NIV

OUR FRIEND MARSHALL SHELLEY is vice president of Christianity Today International. We first got to know Marshall through his practical writings on marriage. He inherited his no-nonsense writing style from his father, Bruce, who wrote about church history in a way that any layperson could understand. In fact, when Les was taking an advanced graduate course in church history as part of his seminary education, he'd often read Bruce Shelley's explanation so that he could better understand the scholarly text assigned in the class.

Marshall has a keen knack for finding practical applications within the context of everyday experiences. An experience he had with his wife's father, a Kansas farmer, is a great example. All his life he raised corn, wheat, milo, and beef cattle. Along the way he also raised sheep and chickens. One morning Marshall was tagging along with his father-in-law around the farm when they talked about the differences between city dwellers and those who live on farms.

Most city people, he explained to Marshall, expect each year to be better than the last one. "They think it's normal to get an annual raise, to earn more this year than you did last year," he said. But a farmer has good years and bad years, depending on the weather. A single storm can wipe out a year's crops, just as a series of well-timed rains can improve them. Some years farmers have more, some years less.

Marshall said that moment with his father-in-law became an indelible memory. It gave him clarity about his own life. Growing in spiritual maturity requires gratefully accepting the "seasons of more" and the "seasons of less" that God weaves into the specific areas of our lives, areas like marriage. After all, every couple experiences changing seasons, and some years a particular season can be especially tough. Other times, a season can be especially fulfilling.

Whether this autumn season is rich with harvest for your marriage or not nearly what you expected or hoped, God's Word urges you to keep your hands on the plow and not become "weary in doing good." It encourages us not to give up.

Are you experiencing a "season of less" right now and feeling tempted to give up doing good in some area? If so, what specific thing can you do today to keep your hand on the plow?

If, on the other hand, you are in a "season of more," take a lesson from a wise Kansas farmer, and thank God for this season's blessings.

Always do your best. What you plant now, you will harvest later. —OG MANDINO

THINKING TOO MUCH?

Be clear minded and self-controlled. 1 PETER 4:7, NIV

"LIFE IS DEEP AND SIMPLE, and what our society gives us is shallow and complicated." Fred Rogers, the Mister Rogers of children's television, said this in a thoughtful interview shortly before he passed away. What a wise and compassionate man. And what an amazing and insightful sentence. Life is deep and simple. And yet we so often make it more complicated than it needs to be—because we think too much.

Just about anything can trigger overthinking: Your boss makes a sarcastic comment, your spouse doesn't call when you expect, a colleague seems short with you in an e-mail, a friend makes a flippant comment about your weight, you're nervous about a doctor's appointment. The list is endless. You find yourself ruminating on these situations, postulating on possible explanations for other people's actions, nitpicking scenarios, replaying the events in your head, and coming up with alternate endings—basically making a thought fog out of your brain.

You may think you're gaining valuable insight by ruminating and analyzing every detail, but you're not. Overthinking is not your friend. It makes your mind tense, keeps you stuck in your head, and immobilizes your motivations. So the question remains: are you thinking too much?

Almost all of us do this on occasion. The good news for couples is that we have a built-in sounding board because of our relationship. Experts find that couples are less likely to think too much the moment they begin talking about what's weighing them down. Why? Because as we talk about what we've been overthinking, the complexity of the issue often becomes more simple, and the load begins to lighten.

And of course, praying together about it is at least as important as talking about it. Releasing our burdens to the Lord is a luxury every Christian can afford. So what's weighing on your mind today? Why not release that tyranny? It may sound clichéd, but right now you can talk it over and pray it through.

Of all the tyrannies on humankind, the worst is that which persecutes the mind.
—JOHN DRYDEN

WEAVING OUR SPIRITUALITY WITH OUR SEXUALITY

Let there be no sexual immorality, impurity, or greed among you. Such sins have no place among God's people. EPHESIANS 5:3

WHAT HAPPENS WHEN WE connect our spiritual self with our sexual self? We like what Philip Yancey says in *Rumors of Another World*: "When I experience desire, I need not flinch in guilt, as if something unnatural has happened. Rather, I should follow the desire to its source, to learn God's original intent." He's saying that a sexual impulse can and should take us to God's original purpose in creating us as sexual beings. He created us for relationship. And a relationship does not get more personal or more sacred than when it is consummated in making love.

We want to say it straight. Sex is more than physical. It's more than treating another human being like a sexual plaything. It is spiritual. And that's why it is designed to make us holy. You read that right! Sex is designed to make us holy.

Now, we can already hear your questions: "Are you saying that the more sex I have the more spiritual I am? Are you saying that I'm supposed to be thinking religious thoughts while making love?" Of course not. Don't misread us here. We all know that sex is complex. It's influenced by mood, levels of stress, constraints of time, sleep, and so on. Remembering that sex is spiritual as well as biological—that it's about a deep and profound connection of two souls—does not guarantee that we will realize anything more than physical gratification in our sex lives.

Sex doesn't promise a spiritual epiphany. After all, marriage is composed of two people who have bad moods, stressful schedules, and imperfect hygiene. As a spouse, you live with a person who needs patience, respect, understanding, kindness, nurturing, acceptance, devotion, forgiveness, and so many other honorable qualities. And you need the same from your spouse. Admit it. For when you do, you've recalibrated your sex life to honor the whole of your relationship, not merely the physical aspect. And within those deeper bounds is where the holiness of sex resides.[5]

Sex may be redeemed in our secular age not by denying it and not by indulging it but integrating it into our quest for depth, loyalty, and permanence in interpersonal relationships. —EDWARD THORNTON

ARE YOU A CONTROL FREAK?

Can all your worries add a single moment to your life? LUKE 12:25

"I AM SURE THAT WHEN *we spoke our marriage vows," said Janet, "Bob added 'to have and to hold as long as I'm the boss.'" She was sitting in my office after four years of trying to stand on equal ground with her husband. According to her, Bob never lets go of the reins. Literally. "He would have to be in a complete body cast before he would let me drive the car," she complains. On a few rare occasions where Janet does get behind the wheel with Bob in the car, he tells her everything to do: "Stop here." "Speed up." "Pass this guy."*

"Then there is the remote," Janet said. . . . "Need I say more," she gracefully dismissed this easy target. But before the end of our counseling session, Janet summed up her husband this way: "He believes he knows how to do everything, and, by natural right, he is boss of anybody found standing in his vicinity."[6]

Sadly, Bob is known as a control freak. And truth be told, overcontrolling tendencies are always linked to anxiety. They're the result of over-amped worry. That's why almost all of us are overcontrolling on occasion—whether we admit it or not.

Isn't a little controlling behavior healthy? you might be asking. Sure. Research indicates that feeling in control is vital to mental and physical health, as well as happiness at home and satisfaction at work. In fact, feeling to some degree that you are master of your own fate is one of the key traits of happy people, according to Christian psychologist David Myers, author of *The Pursuit of Happiness*. And even Scripture urges us to be in control of our tongues (see James 3:2).

Being in control, however, can be too much of a good thing. That's why it's beneficial for all of us who value our relationships to take a personal inventory of our controlling ways. If you become aware of how you can be overcontrolling, this proven strategy can help: know where you can and can't exert explicit influence on each other.

We know of a pastor who nearly lost his marriage because he was treating his wife like a staff member. He would order her around the home, never asking for her advice or input. If you want to keep your controlling tendencies from getting out of control, you have to decide where you can exert your influence and where you can't. And that usually comes down to handing over your anxieties to God. As Luke asks, "Can all your worries add a single moment to your life?" Of course not!

"Kindly let me help you or you will drown," said the monkey, putting the fish safely up in a tree. —ALAN WATTS

KEEPING YOUR DREAM

Where there is no vision, the people perish. PROVERBS 29:18, KJV

OUR FRIEND JOHN MAXWELL once told us a story he read about a man who caught a vision for his life—in spite of what others said. His name was Monty Roberts.

Monty owns a ranch in San Ysidro, California, and is the son of an itinerant horse trainer who traveled to farms and ranches training horses. As a result, Monty's high-school career was continually interrupted. When he was a senior, he was asked to write a paper about what he wanted to be and do when he graduated.

That night Monty wrote a seven-page paper describing his goal of someday owning a horse ranch. He even drew a diagram of a two-hundred-acre ranch, showing the location of all the buildings, the stables, and the track. Then he drew a detailed floor plan for a four-thousand-square-foot house that would sit on the two-hundred-acre dream ranch. The next day he handed it in to his teacher. Two days later he got it back and on the front page was a large red F with a note that read, "See me after class."

When he went to see the teacher he asked, "Why did I receive an F?" The teacher said, "This is an unrealistic dream for a young boy like you! You have no money, you come from an itinerant family, you have no resources! Owning a horse ranch takes a lot of money! You have to buy land. You have to pay for the original breeding stock . . . and later you'll have to pay large stud fees. There's no way you could ever do it! So, if you will rewrite this paper with a more realistic goal, I'll reconsider your grade."

Monty went home and asked his father, "What should I do?" His father said, "Son, you have to make up your own mind on this. I think it is a very important decision for you."

Finally, after sitting with it for a week, Monty turned in the same paper making no changes at all. Only across the top of the first page in large red letters he wrote, "You can keep the F, and I'll keep my dream."

Today, Monty lives in his four-thousand-square-foot house in the middle of his two-hundred-acre horse ranch where he often has children come to learn about horses. And he has that school paper framed over the fireplace! Some time ago, that same school teacher brought thirty kids to camp out on his ranch for a week. Upon leaving, he looked at Monty and said, "I stole a lot of kid's dreams, they gave up too easily. Fortunately, your dream crystallized. You made it happen."[7]

When John finished telling us the story of Monty Roberts, he said, "When someone shares their dream with you, it is the center of their soul. Do everything in your power to come alongside them and help them reach their dream."

If one advances confidently in the direction of his dreams, and endeavors to live the life which he has imagined, he will meet with a success unexpected in common hours. —HENRY DAVID THOREAU

WHAT'S MAKING YOU BUSY?

Be careful how you live. Don't live like fools, but like those who are wise. Make the most of every opportunity in these evil days. Don't act thoughtlessly, but understand what the Lord wants you to do. EPHESIANS 5:15-17

PHYSICIAN LARRY DOSSEY coined the term "time sickness" in 1982 to describe the obsessive belief that "time is getting away, that there isn't enough of it, and that you must pedal faster and faster to keep up."[8] By that definition, we're almost all time sick. Who among us isn't busy and in a rush?

When we were first married and living in Pasadena, we attended the same church as Dr. James Dobson. One Sunday morning he made a guest appearance in our newlywed class, and in the context of his lesson, he said something that got the full attention of every neophyte in the room: "Overcommitment and exhaustion are the most insidious and pervasive marriage killers you will ever encounter as a couple." We've never forgotten that. In fact, we've been working at guarding against busyness ever since. Once you realize the potential harm busyness can have on your marriage, you become more conscious of how much or how little time you have together each day.

No matter how much time stealing, time stretching, and time bending we attempt, we always find ourselves up against a certain mathematical law: Thirty-two hours' worth of tasks can't be crammed into a twenty-four-hour day. So we are busy. Nobody's disputing that fact.

The real question is, How busy are you? We take that back. The real question—the one upon which this chapter hinges—is, What are you busy doing?[9]

When the fire of prayer goes out, the barrenness of busyness takes over.
—GEORGE CAREY

BECOMING BETTER FRIENDS

There are "friends" who destroy each other, but a real friend sticks closer than a brother.

PROVERBS 18:24

"IT IS NOT A LACK OF LOVE," said Friedrich Nietzsche, "but a lack of friendship that makes unhappy marriages." We tend to agree. And so do a lot of other social scientists. In fact, world-renowned marriage researcher John Gottman, of the University of Washington, told us one day over lunch: "Happy marriages are based on a deep friendship."

And get this, Gallup's research indicates that a couple's friendship quality could account for 70 percent of overall marital satisfaction. In fact, the emotional intimacy that a married couple shares is said to be five times more important than their physical intimacy.

So how do you become better friends? Barbara Brown Taylor, a professor at Piedmont College in rural Georgia, knows. "My husband, Edward," she writes, "is devoted to hawks and especially to the golden eagles that are returning to our part of Georgia. Driving down the highway with him can be a test of nerves as he cranes over the steering wheel to peer at the wing feathers of a particularly large bird." Her husband, like any bird enthusiast, wants to know: is it an eagle or just a turkey vulture? In fact, he has to know, even if it means weaving down the road or running off it from time to time. "My view," she continues, "is a bit different: 'Keep your eyes on the road!' I yell at him. 'Who cares what it is? I'll buy you a bird book; I'll even buy you a bird—just watch where you're going.'"

A couple of summers ago, Barbara's and Edward's schedules kept them apart for two months, and she thought she'd get a break from hawks. "Instead I began to see them everywhere," she says, "looping through the air, spiraling in rising thermals, hunkered down in the tops of trees. Seeing them, really seeing them for the first time in my life, I understood that I was not seeing them with my own eyes but with Edward's eyes. He was not there, so I was seeing them for him."

Barbara couldn't wait to connect with her husband and tell him of the hawks she'd seen. Her story illustrates perfectly that stepping into your partner's shoes makes you better friends.[10]

> *To the world you may be just one person, but to one person you may be the world.*
> —BRANDI SNYDER

FROM GENERATION TO GENERATION

Ruth [said], "Wherever you go, I will go; wherever you live, I will live. Your people will be my people, and your God will be my God." RUTH 1:16

WHAT DO YOU KNOW about your grandparents' marriage? your great grandparents' marriage? Of course you know plenty about your mom and dad's relationship. After all, it was your model for marriage growing up. Whether it was happy or sad, or nearly nonexistent, you observed it up close and personal.

All of us take something from the previous generation's example of marriage into our own. It's inevitable. We may even resist some aspect of our parents' marriages and then find ourselves repeating the very same thing. We psychologists call that an introject—it's kind of like getting injected with ways of being from our families of origin. And this process can offer both good and bad character qualities. But make no mistake; we are all inextricably linked to our family's lineages.

Consider this telling poem about the passage of time through the generations:

When I was a little lad, my old Grandfather said
That none should wind the clock but he, and so, at time for bed
He'd fumble for the curious key kept high upon the shelf
And set aside that little task entirely for himself.
In time, Grandfather passed away, and so that duty fell
Unto my Father, who performed the weekly custom well.
He held that clocks were not to be by careless persons wound
And he alone should turn the key or move the hands around.
I envied him that little task, and wished that I might be
The one entrusted with the turning of the key;
But year by year the clock was his exclusive bit of care
Until the day the angels came and smoothed his silver hair.
Today the task is mine to do, like those who've gone before.
I am a jealous guardian of that round and glassy door.
And 'til, at my chamber door, God's messenger shall knock
To me alone shall be reserved the right to wind the clock.[11]

From generation to generation, whether we know it or not, we are handed responsibilities and qualities that keep the customs going. So take a moment to explore what you brought into your marriage from your bloodline. Simply talking about this "relational inheritance" will make you more conscious of it and shed light on your current conditions.

What character qualities were handed off to you by your parents and grandparents? Consider your family's positive qualities as well as inevitable shortcomings. If you were to diagram a family tree of strengths and weaknesses, what would yours look like?

A family is . . . a place where principles are hammered and honed on the anvil of everyday living. —CHARLES R. SWINDOLL

SEX: A GIFT FROM ON HIGH?

God blessed them and said, "Be fruitful and increase in number and fill the water in the seas, and let the birds increase on the earth." GENESIS 1:22, NIV

WHY DID GOD CREATE SEX? Procreation is the obvious answer. God clearly gave us sex to make babies (see Genesis 1:28). But he also had something more in mind. God wants us to take pleasure in physical intimacy. If you don't believe me, read the Old Testament Song of Songs. It is replete with erotic metaphors and sexual excitement. And consider the fact that unlike most animals that mate only during the female's fertile period, God created us to continually enjoy physical intimacies within marriage.

You don't have to be a Bible scholar or decipher metaphors in this message: "The husband should fulfill his wife's sexual needs, and the wife should fulfill her husband's needs. The wife gives authority over her body to her husband, and the husband gives authority over his body to his wife. Do not deprive each other" (1 Corinthians 7:3-5).

As one of my seminary professors once said after reading this passage aloud in class, "The Bible is clear as it can be—it says if you are married, 'Do it!'" He was making his point emphatically because people outside the church (and some deeply religious people) think of God as the great spoilsport of human sexuality, not as its inventor. But truth be told, physical intimacy is a gift from on high.

What is basic is the enriching of their relationship itself through their repeated "knowing" of each other as persons who belong to each other exclusively and without reserve. —J. I. PACKER

LOOKING FOR GOLD

Though you lie down among the sheepfolds, you will be like the wings of a dove covered with silver, And her feathers with yellow gold. PSALM 68:13, NKJV

AT ONE TIME ANDREW CARNEGIE was the wealthiest man in America. He came to America from his native Scotland when he was a small boy, did a variety of odd jobs, and eventually ended up as the largest steel manufacturer in the United States. At one time he had forty-three millionaires working for him. In those days a millionaire was a rare person; conservatively speaking, a million dollars in his day would be equivalent to at least twenty million dollars today.

A reporter asked Carnegie how he had hired forty-three millionaires. Carnegie responded that those men had not been millionaires when they started working for him but had become millionaires as a result.

The reporter's next question was, "How did you develop these men to become so valuable to you that you have paid them this much money?" Carnegie replied that men are developed the same way gold is mined. When gold is mined, several tons of dirt must be moved to get an ounce of gold; but one doesn't go into the mine looking for dirt—one goes in looking for the gold.[12]

That aim is exactly the way spouses develop a positive and healthy relationship. Unhealthy couples see only the dirt—the flaws, warts, and blemishes. If you want a great relationship, look for the gold in each other, the good not the bad. As with everything else in life, the more good qualities we look for in each other, the more good qualities we are going to find. In fact, why don't you take this opportunity to name one specific quality you see in your spouse right now?

Truth is obtained like gold, not by letting it grow bigger, but by washing off from it everything that isn't gold. —LEO TOLSTOY

EXPLORING YOUR DARK SIDE

When you fast, don't make it obvious, as the hypocrites do, for they try to look miserable and disheveled so people will admire them for their fasting. I tell you the truth, that is the only reward they will ever get. MATTHEW 6:16

HAVE YOU EVER BEEN SURPRISED by someone's description of you? Maybe they said you were outgoing when you thought of yourself as shy. Or perhaps they said you were insensitive when you thought you were compassionate. When a surprising description emerges, it almost always gives one pause. It may also give us a glimpse into an aspect of ourselves we've never acknowledged.

We may be hard driving, self-righteous, a tightwad, defensive, have unrealistic goals, an insatiable need for recognition, a preoccupation with appearance, or any number of other things. The list of unhealthy traits we don't see in ourselves is endless.

But is that so bad? Truth be told, everyone has tendencies toward meanness, selfishness, envy, materialism, cruelty, dishonesty, lust, and irresponsibility. In fact, the more of these miserable parts we have, the stronger our potential for spiritual sensitivity is. Why? Because our character is hammered out, not in the absence of negative traits, but because of them. For example, your struggle to overcome selfishness will make your generous spirit, once honed, far more prized, meaningful, and valuable than if it had come more easily or more naturally to you. There is no virtue in not acting on a desire that doesn't exist.

Yet so many people, especially some well-intentioned religious folks, work diligently to block out or bury their baser parts. They operate under the false assumption that if they ignore such bad tendencies, their dark sides will disappear. Spiritually healthy people take a different approach. They come to terms with the rotten parts of their nature, eventually learn why they have them, and most importantly, they learn how to subdue, control, and even transform them by giving them over to God.

We know this is a heavy topic, but we want to pose a simple two-part question: What is one of the traits in your dark side that you'd be willing to acknowledge to your partner right now, and what's one thing you can do today that will help you improve it?

> *The worst lies are the lies we tell ourselves. We live in denial of what we do, even what we think. We do this because we're afraid. We fear we will not find love, and when we find it we fear we'll lose it. We fear that if we do not have love we will be unhappy.*
> —RICHARD BACH

FINDING SAFE HARBOR AT HOME

Encourage one another daily, as long as it is called Today, so that none of you may be hardened by sin's deceitfulness. HEBREWS 3:13, NIV

ON A RECENT SUMMER TRIP TO the New England coast, we discovered a little lighthouse that has been a source of encouragement to many lonely sailors over the years. Minot's Ledge Light, near Scituate, Massachusetts, was first lit on November 15, 1860. Its cost of $300,000 made it the most expensive lighthouse ever constructed in the United States at that time. Its special encouragement to sailors comes in the fact that it signals nautical code, a 1-4-3 flashing cycle, to spell "I love you." Wives in this sailing town originated this message to encourage their husbands out at sea and remind them how much they were loved.

Several years ago the Coast Guard decided to upgrade the light by replacing the old equipment. They announced that for technical reasons the new machines would be unable to flash the "I love you" message. Both the people of Scituate and the sailors protested. The Coast Guard finally weakened. The old equipment, noticeably out of date, was reinstalled and remains in Scituate to faithfully send its encouraging message to the sailing husbands.

Every spouse—sailor or not—needs an encouraging word. More than that, we need a marriage that serves as a kind of safe harbor, a place where we can count on being encouraged and loved. Is your marriage such a place? Do you "encourage one another daily"?

It is astonishing how little one feels alone when one loves. —JOHN BULWER

MAKING TIME FOR YOUR CLOSEST FRIEND

Can two people walk together without agreeing on the direction? AMOS 3:3

WE HAD JUST FINISHED speaking to a group of students at a retreat center in Kentucky and had returned to our room when we heard a loud knock at the door. "Monty Lobb?!" I exclaimed. We couldn't believe it. Monty had driven four hours from Cincinnati and tracked us down without directions or an address.

"I knew I could find you," he said with a big bear hug. "I heard you were near Wilmore, and I just had to see you." We talked and laughed for about an hour and a half, then Monty had to drive another four hours home. He was teaching Sunday school the next morning at his church back in Cincinnati.

Few actions speak more loudly about the value of a good friend than making time for the relationship. Why? Because few people invest the time required to keep friendships alive. Friends can sometimes forget to phone, fail to write, ignore important events, stand each other up, and let each other down. Some try to gloss over the cause of an ill-fated friendship by saying nothing could be done to save it. They blame its demise on busy schedules, pressing deadlines, or geographical distance. But we all know that most failing friendships suffer from only one ailment: neglect.

It's no wonder that "making time" ranks high on the list of our survey of what matters most in a good friend. So many of us juggle so many things, it's easy for friendship to take a back seat—even when that friend is our spouse. In fact, if we don't prioritize friendship with our spouse, we're prone to take that friendship for granted.

But here's news that will encourage you to put your spouse (and your friends) back at the top of your priority list. A growing body of recent research says ignoring friendship not only diminishes your quality of life but could also be a health hazard. Close friendships act as an ounce of prevention, bolstering the immune system and reducing the risk of illnesses like colds, flu, and perhaps even heart disease and other serious disorders. That makes maintaining friendships a health must, right up there with exercising and eating right.

> *Don't walk in front of me; I may not follow. Don't walk behind me; I may not lead. Just walk beside me and be my friend.* —**ALBERT CAMUS**

KEEPING THE SABBATH HOLY

Come, let us worship and bow down. Let us kneel before the LORD our maker.

PSALM 95:6

A FRIEND OF OURS TOLD US A funny story about two guys who were fishing fanatics. On a recent Sunday morning they arose at 4 a.m. and drove more than a hundred miles into the mountains, expecting to catch trout in their favorite secluded stream. They kept its location secret for years. After they'd hiked two miles in from the road, they saw that rains farther upstream had produced silt that muddied the waters and made fishing impractical. Their enthusiasm was dampened, and they aborted the expedition. In their disgust one said to the other, "You might as well have stayed home and gone to church."

His companion retorted with a straight face, "Oh, I can't go to church anyhow; my wife is sick."

The church where we worship is a place of support and spiritual refueling. Singing hymns, learning from Scripture, worshipping God, and meeting with friends who share our spiritual quest is comforting and inspiring. Worshipping together buoys our relationship and makes the week ahead more meaningful.

How we choose to incorporate the church into our marriage is critically important to our relationship. Paul recognized the idea of the church as being God's family when he said we are "members of God's family" (Ephesians 2:19). When Jesus taught his disciples to pray, he did not say, "My Father"; he said, "Our Father" (Matthew 6:9). We cannot live the Christian life in isolation. Even a couple needs a community of worship.

The perfect church service would be one we were almost unaware of; our attention would have been on God. —C. S. LEWIS

LOVE WILL KEEP YOU SAFE

May the LORD bless you and keep you. NUMBERS 6:24, NCV

YOU WOULD THINK our two young boys, ten and five at the time, would have been more impressed. Here we were, on a beautiful sunny day, standing on the steps outside Mirabell Palace in Salzburg, Austria—the exact spot where Julie Andrews filmed the memorable "Do-Re-Mi" scene with the von Trapp children in the celebrated film *The Sound of Music*.

"Boys," I (Leslie) said with excitement, "do you remember that scene? Remember how they all jumped on these steps and—"

"Are we going to see the fort?" John, our oldest, interrupted just as I was about to break into song.

"Yea," little Jackson chimed in. "I want to see the fort."

"Can we go to the fort now?" John asked again.

I suppose you can hardly blame them. Salzburg Fortress towers over Mozart's city. This imposing structure is unmistakable. And to little boys who love the thought of being knights in armor with drawn swords, it's simply irresistible. So we put our singing voices on hold and hummed "Climb Every Mountain" as we took the inclined railway up the steep hill to tour the great fortress and see all the weapons and armory that fascinate little boys.

It's worth noting that throughout its long history, the thousand-year-old fortress with spectacular views of the city and the snow-capped Alps has never been captured or successfully besieged by its enemies. Which is exactly the point. A fortress, after all, is designed to keep you safe and out of harm's way.

And in a very real sense, your love for each other is meant to do the same thing. When you keep your love alive, your love keeps you safe—safe from the squabbles that inevitably attack every unsuspecting couple; safe from the polarizing opinions that try to pull you apart; safe from the inexplicable moments that make you wonder why you chose to be with each other in the first place.

The word "keep," when used as a noun, is actually the strong central tower of a fortress. The keep is the most defended area of a castle, containing the most important items for surviving during a siege. That's why Christians around the world often conclude their worship service by singing the benediction: "May the LORD bless you and keep you" (Numbers 6:24, NCV). [13]

} *Chains do not hold a marriage together. It is threads, hundreds of tiny threads which sew people together through the years.* —SIMONE SIGNORET

THREE WORDS THAT NEVER GROW OLD

If I could speak all the languages of earth and of angels, but didn't love others, I would only be a noisy gong or a clanging cymbal. 1 CORINTHIANS 13:1

EMILY SAT IN OUR OFFICE WEEPING. She had come for counseling on her own, without telling her husband. "I am so hungry for affection," she confided in us. "We have been married for twenty-five years, and I know he is capable of tenderness. He shows it to the dog. But . . ." Emily's voice broke down, and her tears began to flow. She reached for a tissue and quietly said, "I'd just like to hear him say, 'I love you.'"

Three simple words. So critical to marriage. We take these tender words for granted sometimes, but we have never known anyone who got tired of hearing "I love you" . . . before leaving the house in the morning . . . in a quick message on the answering machine . . . while working in the garden . . . before dozing off in bed. These little words are like nutrients to a marriage. Without a consistent dose of verbal expression, without saying and hearing those words, the soul of a marriage withers.

Think about it. We have over six hundred thousand words in the English language and more synonyms per word than are found in any other language. However, we have only one word with which to express all the various shadings of love. Deficient as English is in this respect, we long to hear the familiar words "I love you."

Again and again, your spouse needs to hear those words. And it is just as important for you to say them. I (Les) need to say, "I love you," as much as Leslie needs to hear it. The poet W. H. Auden remarked, "We must love each other or die!" He was surely right. A marriage cannot survive without verbal expressions of love. So pray that the Lord will make your love for each other strong and overflowing.[14]

The most important things are the hardest to say, because words diminish them.
—STEPHEN KING

NOVEMBER 20

HEALTHY HUMILITY IS A PRELUDE TO THANKSGIVING

The LORD has told you what is good, and this is what he requires of you: to do what is right, to love mercy, and to walk humbly with your God. MICAH 6:8

IN NIKOS KAZANTZAKIS'S NOVEL *Christ Recrucified*, there is a scene in which four village men confess their sins to one another in the presence of the pope. One of the men, Michelis, cries out in bloated humility, "How can God let us live on the earth? Why doesn't he kill us to purify creation?"

"Because, Michelis," the pope answered, "God is a potter; he works in mud."[15]

Whether you see it the same way or not, the point is that humility is lowly. And that's where God meets us—in the places where we are humble. That's where we become malleable. Humility is the opposite of pride, of course. Pride is riddled with self-doubt that's desperate to deny any weakness. So it swings the heart's pendulum of self-assessment toward feelings of superiority. Humility does the opposite. Well, not quite. Healthy humility is not about feeling inferior.

There are two kinds of humility: true and false.

True humility is grounded in a sense of dignity and self-worth. In other words, it seeks an accurate inventory of both strengths and weaknesses. When it receives a compliment, it doesn't deflect it with self-effacement and demure posturing. That's the approach of false humility, which is built on self-deprecation. False humility clumsily rejects its own gifts, talents, and accomplishments out of hand. "Oh, I had nothing to do with it," false humility says in response to a compliment for hard work.

False humility's self-appraisal is just as unhelpful and distorted as pride's. While pride takes the position of superiority, false humility takes inferiority as its stance. Both are unrealistic. Neither is healthy.

So how would you measure your personal barometer of false humility? Are you taking an accurate inventory of both your strengths and weaknesses? What situations can tempt you to respond with false humility? Are you willing to discuss them with your partner? How would your marriage grow by an increase in true humility?

The goal is a truly humble heart that recognizes both positive attributes as well as inadequacies. It's a heart that shines a light on its dark corners and confesses its neediness—of others and of God. By the way, it's also the perfect prelude to a grateful heart on Thanksgiving.

Humility is often a false front we employ to gain power over others.
—**FRANÇOIS DE LA ROCHEFOUCAULD**

HOME FOR THE HOLIDAYS

Devote yourselves to prayer with an alert mind and a thankful heart. COLOSSIANS 4:2

MAYBE YOU'VE HEARD or read this story before:

> An elderly man in Phoenix called his son in New York saying, "I hate to ruin your day, but I have to tell you that your mother and I are divorcing; forty-five years of misery is enough."
>
> "Pop, what are you talking about?" the son shouted in surprise.
>
> "We can't stand the sight of each other any longer," the old man said. "We're sick of each other, and I'm sick of talking about this, so you call your sister in Chicago and tell her," and he hung up.
>
> Upset, the son called his sister, who couldn't believe what she was hearing. "What, they're getting a divorce? I'll take care of this!" she shouted.
>
> She called Phoenix and said, "Daddy, you're not getting divorced. Don't do a thing until I get there. I'm calling my brother back, and we'll both be there tomorrow," and hung up.
>
> The old man hung up his phone, too, and turned to his wife. ""Okay, they're coming for Thanksgiving. You think of something for Christmas."[16]

We may chuckle at this story, but the truth is that many of us have a tough time getting together as a family around this time of year. For innumerable reasons, the family is more fragmented these days than ever before. So if you're not going to be with your extended family during this season, don't let it stop you from expressing your appreciation for them.

And if for some reason a rift is keeping you from connecting, try a little humble pie with your turkey dinner. Why? Because as Henry Ward Beecher put it, "Pride slays thanksgiving, but a humble mind is the soil out of which thanks naturally grow. A proud man is seldom a grateful man, for he never thinks he gets as much as he deserves."

Not what we say about our blessings, but how we use them, is the true measure of our thanksgiving. —W. T. PURKISER

THANK YOU

Be thankful in all circumstances, for this is God's will for you who belong to Christ Jesus.

1 THESSALONIANS 5:18

"THANKS," SAID LES.

I had just handed him a stack of mail I picked up at his office. "You bet," I replied without giving it a second thought.

"No, I mean it—thank you," Les said with all seriousness. "It was really thoughtful of you to pick up my mail and bring it home. You didn't have to do it, and I appreciate it."

It's always nice to be around somebody who's grateful. Cicero, the Roman philosopher, said, "Gratitude is not only the greatest of virtues, but the parent of all the others." When a person is grateful—when he or she has an attitude of gratitude—he or she becomes a better person.

Saying "thank you" tends to diminish over the years of marriage as we take each other more for granted. One group of social scientists discovered that the phrases *shhh*, and *what's on* are more common in most homes than *thank you*.

Scripture abounds with encouragement to be thankful: "Let the peace of Christ rule in your hearts, since as members of one body you were called to peace. And be thankful" (Colossians 3:15, NIV). "Giving thanks to the Father, who has qualified you to share in the inheritance of the saints in the kingdom of light" (Colossians 1:12, NIV). "Be anxious for nothing, but in everything by prayer and supplication, with thanksgiving, let your requests be made known to God" (Philippians 4:6, NASB). The apostle Paul advised the church at Thessalonica: "Give thanks in all circumstances, for this is God's will for you in Christ Jesus" (1Thessalonians 5:18, NIV). Scripture also tells us that thankfulness is a prerequisite for worship: "Enter into His gates with thanksgiving, and into His courts with praise. Be thankful." (Psalm 100:4, NKJV).

So keep the attitude of gratitude alive in your marriage. Cultivate it by looking for things to appreciate in your partner each day. After all, gratitude really is the parent of all virtues.[17]

 } *Silent gratitude isn't much use to anyone.* —G. B. STERN

THE BUTTERFLY EFFECT

Whoever wants to be a leader among you must be your servant, and whoever wants to be first among you must be the slave of everyone else. For even the Son of Man came not to be served but to serve others and to give his life as a ransom for many. MARK 10:43-45

PERHAPS YOU'VE HEARD or read about the theory that says a butterfly's wings fluttering can affect weather patterns thousands of miles away.

> On an ordinary winter day in 1961, an MIT meteorologist named Edward Lorenz ran some routine experiments and found some unusual results. Lorenz discovered that seemingly tiny and insignificant changes in his data could produce huge differences in the final result. At first, Lorenz and other scientists in the field of chaos theory called this "the sensitive dependence on initial data." Fortunately, later on Lorenz used a simpler term—"the butterfly effect." In 1972, Lorenz presented a scientific paper entitled "Predictability: Does the Flap of a Butterfly's Wings in Brazil Set Off a Tornado in Texas?" According to Lorenz's theory, the butterfly's wing flapping doesn't actually cause a tornado, but it can start a chain reaction leading to giant changes in worldwide weather patterns. In other words, even tiny, insignificant movements or actions can produce huge changes that affect millions of people.[18]

The Bible often describes a similar "butterfly effect" for the spiritual life. According to Jesus, the spiritual butterfly effect occurs when we do acts of service. We know of nothing else that can cultivate intimacy for a couple more than reaching out to the world as a team—even in small ways. Doing good for others as a couple creates a surprisingly powerful effect on your marriage. It helps you transcend yourselves and become part of something larger.

God is committed to one major objective: helping us conform to the image of his Son (see Philippians 2:5-11). And his Son, Scripture says, "came not to be served but to serve" (Mark 10:45). It is as straightforward as that. God wants us to be a giving people. Philippians 2:4 says, "Don't look out only for your own interests, but take an interest in others, too." Galatians 5:13 says, "Serve one another in love."

Marriage is a great means to becoming more like Christ. Paul says to "motivate one another to acts of love and good works" (Hebrews 10:24). Marriage helps us do that, and when we join our efforts in service together, we are doubly blessed.

There are literally hundreds of ways to incorporate shared service into your marriage—offering hospitality in your home, volunteering at a shelter, sponsoring a needy child, working in the church nursery. The key is to find something that fits your personal style together. And when you do, your marriage will create a butterfly effect of service.

The highest form of worship is the worship of unselfish Christian service. The greatest form of praise is the sound of consecrated feet seeking out the lost and helpless.
—BILLY GRAHAM

HOW TO WIN LOVE AND INFLUENCE YOUR PARTNER

Understand this, my dear brothers and sisters: You must all be quick to listen [and] slow to speak. JAMES 1:19

A POOR FARMER'S BOY WAS born on this day in 1888 in Maryville, Missouri. As a teen he awoke every day at 4 a.m. to milk his parents' cows. He managed to obtain an education at a small college in Warrensburg and shortly thereafter landed a job selling soap and bacon. He earned enough money to follow his dream of moving to New York. Unfortunately, the money dried up and he became nearly broke, living at the YMCA. But he persuaded the manager at the Y to allow him to offer a class on public speaking. That class evolved into a course that more than 8 million people have completed.

In 1937, he published the grandfather of all people-skills books, and it was an overnight hit, eventually selling 15 million copies. *How to Win Friends and Influence People* by Dale Carnegie is just as useful today as it was when it was first published, because Dale Carnegie had an understanding of human nature that will never be outdated. The skills he teaches in this classic book are undergirded by a pervasive principle: people are craving to be known and appreciated.

We are not talking about throwaway questions like "How about those Red Sox?" or "Can you believe this weather?" though they certainly have their place. Quality questions are intentionally designed to open up a person's spirit. They invite vulnerability, but are not invasive. They are personal, but respect privacy. They are asked out of genuine interest, but never blunt. A quality question conveys kindness, warmth, concern, and interest. It is couched in affirmation and appreciation.

But don't think this simple skill of asking heartfelt questions is only for "winning friends." It's just as important within your relationship with each other. Happy couples make a habit out of asking each other good questions.[19]

 The royal road to a person's heart is to talk to him about the things he or she treasures most. —DALE CARNEGIE

GIVING THANKS FOR MARRIAGE MENTORS

Is not wisdom found among the aged? Does not long life bring understanding?

JOB 12:12, NIV

CHAIM POTOK'S NOVEL *The Chosen* tells the story of a young boy born to a Hasidic rabbi. As the boy matures, his father recognizes that his child is especially clever and gifted, if not already a little arrogant and impatient. Knowing that his boy was likely to become the rabbi of his people, the father makes a mysterious and difficult decision not to speak to the boy. He raises the boy in a house without the comfort of a speaking relationship. As the story draws to a close, Potok reveals that the father has chosen this unconventional path of parenthood with the boy because he wanted to create in him the capacity for understanding and compassion. He wanted him to minister from a heart that knows pain and can feel the pain of others. The father feared that his son's analytic brilliance and arrogance would rob him of the capacity to love.

The father in Potok's novel intuitively understood how keen analytic abilities, unsoftened by emotional tenderness, lead to manipulation rather than ministry, how they lead to control rather than compassion. You may not agree with this rabbi's methods, but it is difficult to dispute his insight.

The story of this powerful novel has reminded us as a couple to consider the "wisdom found among the aged." God's wisdom often comes from those who have traveled the path before us.

For this reason, we recommend that you take inventory today of the couples in your life who have ministered to your marriage. It doesn't matter whether they are formal mentoring relationships or informal friendships with seasoned couples. All of us, if we've been married long enough, have looked to wiser, more experienced couples who have traveled the marriage road before us and are willing to let us learn from them. Who comes to mind when you think of these kinds of relationships? And what can you do, in practical terms, to thank them? Perhaps you'd want to jot them a little note of appreciation and thanksgiving. It doesn't take much to let them know you don't take them for granted.[20]

The years teach much which the days never know. —RALPH WALDO EMERSON

NOTHING BUT THE BLOOD OF JESUS

You know that God paid a ransom to save you from the empty life you inherited from your ancestors. And the ransom he paid was not mere gold or silver. It was the precious blood of Christ, the sinless, spotless Lamb of God. 1 PETER 1:18-19

EVERY ONCE IN A WHILE we'll be watching the nightly news in our home and hear about a tragedy that compels our attention. It could be something on the global scale, like a massive hurricane, or on a more localized level, such as a house fire. Whatever the sad story, we will sometimes ponder out loud together what we would do in such a circumstance.

That was the case some years ago when we heard the news of a terrible terrorist attack in Mumbai, India. Do you remember the story? On November 26, 2008, a gang stormed the Taj Mahal hotel, shooting people randomly. In the aftermath, two hundred people were dead.

A reporter on the scene interviewed a number of guests who were at the hotel that evening, but one interview stood out. The guest described how he and his friends were eating dinner when they were startled to hear gunshots. Someone grabbed him and pulled him under the table. The assassins came striding through the restaurant, shooting at will, until everyone had been killed. Or so they thought. Miraculously, this man survived. The interviewer asked the guest how he had lived when everyone else at his table had been killed. The man replied, "I suppose because I was covered in someone else's blood and they took me for dead."

In his book *Has Christianity Failed You?*, author Ravi Zacharias uses this story to illustrate the sufficiency of Christ's death for our sin. It's a powerful illustration. One that every believer should ponder. Even as husband and wife, consider God's gift through Jesus Christ to each of you.

We recently read these relevant words from nineteenth-century British preacher Charles Spurgeon:

> *Remember, sinner, it is not thy hold of Christ that saves thee—it is Christ; it is not thy joy in Christ that saves thee—it is Christ; it is not even faith in Christ, though that is the instrument—it is Christ's blood and merits; therefore, look not to thy hope, but to Christ, the source of thy hope; look not to thy faith, but to Christ, the author and finisher of thy faith; and if thou doest that, ten thousand devils cannot throw thee down.*

Spurgeon would have appreciated the modern-day metaphor of Mumbai. It illustrates the unfathomable gift of God's gift to us. Because Christ paid the penalty for our sin—because we are covered in the blood of his sacrifice—we may have eternal life

This is faith: a renouncing of everything we are apt to call our own and relying wholly upon the blood, righteousness, and intercession of Jesus. —JOHN NEWTON

A GRATEFUL HEART

This is the day the LORD has made. We will rejoice and be glad in it. PSALM 118:24

SCIENTISTS ARE LATECOMERS to the concept of gratitude. Research psychologists have tended to look down their noses at gratitude as little more than a question of having good manners and remembering to say thank you. But that's changing. New gratitude experiments by social scientists seem to be popping up across university campuses.

Consider one of the most revealing experiments to date. Robert Emmons, a professor of psychology at the University of California, Davis, and psychology professor Michael McCullough of Southern Methodist University in Dallas, Texas, took three groups of volunteers and randomly assigned them to focus on one of three things each week: hassles, things for which they were grateful, and ordinary life events.

The first group concentrated on everything that went wrong or that irritated them. The second group honed in on situations they felt enhanced their lives, such as, "My husband is so kind and caring—I'm lucky to have him." The third group recalled recent everyday events, such as, "I went shoe shopping."

The results: The people who focused on gratitude were happier by far. They saw their lives in favorable terms. They reported positive feelings, fewer negative complaints, and they even reported experiencing better health (fewer headaches and colds). They also offered more grace to others and did more loving things for people. Those who were grateful quite simply enjoyed a higher quality of life because they had found the secret to surrender.

Dr. Emmons was surprised. He found that this is not just something that makes people happy, like positive thinking. A feeling of gratitude really gets people to do something, to become more pro-social, more compassionate. Such was not the case in either of the other two groups.[21]

The bottom line is that your life is never more full—and your marriage more fulfilling—than when you are joyfully surrendered and conscious of your blessings. Husbands and wives who feel grateful for each other and for the blessings around them are more likely to feel loved as well as do loving things. What are you grateful for today?

If you concentrate on finding whatever is good in every situation, you will discover that your life will suddenly be filled with gratitude, a feeling that nurtures the soul.
—HAROLD KUSHNER

A FIRST-CLASS BEDTIME

People who work hard sleep well, whether they eat little or much. But the rich seldom get a good night's sleep. ECCLESIASTES 5:12

A FEW YEARS AGO I (LES) HAD an abundance of air miles that were going to expire if I didn't use them. Short on time but not wanting to waste them, I asked my dad if he'd like to fly first class to Rome, Italy, with me for four days. "Here's the deal," I told him. "I'll pay for the airline, if you want to pick up the hotel." Seemed like a pretty good deal to me! Truthfully, Dad jumped at the chance and we had a terrific trip. Since Dad had been to Rome before, he knew just where we should go. We visited all the traditional landmarks, and through a friend of a friend we even attended a service with the pope at St. Peter's Basilica. It was a fantastic trip. The only downside was flying first class.

Don't get me wrong, I'm not complaining. It's just that it has made all my other air travel seem so shoddy. The flight attendants didn't serve the airline food I'm accustomed to. It was elegant cuisine that seemed to have no end. After the fresh fruit and cheese plate, they brought the salad, followed by hot soup, delicious breads, and a mouth-watering entrée. For dessert? Hot fudge sundaes! We couldn't believe it. Flying two thousand feet above the earth somewhere over the Atlantic Ocean eating ice cream. It was too much. To top it all off, they brought out a gold foil box of chocolates to nibble on while we watched the movie we selected for our individual screens. After the feast, the real benefit of flying first class kicked in. Our chairs reclined. Not just a little—into a full-fledged bed with a privacy curtain that encircled it. It was like a mini apartment on the plane. To amend the old airline commercial a bit, "It's the only way to sleep while you fly."

However, the experience doesn't hold a candle to sleeping with my spouse in our own bed. For most happy couples, their shared bed is one of the safest places on earth. It's where intimacy—both physical and emotional—reaches its highest pitch. It's where conversations go on even after the lights go off.

While many couples too often take this safe place for granted, we want you to give it some conscious thought today—especially on these wintery nights. What do you enjoy most about sharing your bed with your partner, about the ritual of relating under covers (and don't think of this as a setup to just say "sex")? Focus on the first-class feeling of sleeping with your soul mate, sharing pillow talk that's sweeter than a box of chocolates.

Good night, good night! Parting is such sweet sorrow that I shall say good night till it be morrow. —WILLIAM SHAKESPEARE

PILLOW TALK

Each day the LORD pours his unfailing love upon me, and through each night I sing his songs, praying to God who gives me life. PSALM 42:8

I (LESLIE) WAS HAVING A sleepless night—an evening cup of coffee, my ill husband's coughing and restlessness, and details about an upcoming trip were keeping me hopelessly awake. Even after I slipped into the guest bedroom, I still had trouble. Finally, at 3:15 a.m., I crawled back into my own bed, next to a now half-awake husband. "Can I do anything to help you sleep?" he whispered with a groggy voice.

I couldn't believe it. Les was having a miserable night himself and still wanted to know if he could do anything to help me sleep better. I suppose I would have done the same thing. And my guess is you would do the same for your spouse. Why? Because we all know how valuable a good night's sleep is.

Poet William Wordsworth, in "To Sleep," describes the agony of attempting to get a good night's sleep:

> *A flock of sheep that leisurely pass by*
> *One after one; the sound of rain, and bees*
> *Murmuring; the fall of rivers, winds and seas,*
> *Smooth fields, white sheets of water, and pure sky—*
> *I've thought of all by turns, and still I lie*
> *Sleepless. . . .*

We all need sleep. It's not a luxury. It is as important as breathing or eating. In fact, it might surprise you to know that people can survive longer without food than they can without sleep. If you don't have enough sleep, you not only make more mistakes, but your thinking becomes muddled. You become more irritable. You become sluggish. And if that weren't enough, you increase your odds for becoming sick. We even age more quickly and gain weight more easily. Experts tell us we require about eight hours to function at our best. Yet one-third of adults report they normally sleep less than six and a half hours a night. And even those hours are not always restful.

Sleep plays such an important, yet unrecognized, role in your married life (especially during the busy Christmas season). So this topic deserves some serious pillow talk, even tonight. What can you do to help one another become better sleepers? As you help each other become more rested, you and your relationship will operate at the optimum level. Think of all the needless conflicts you can avoid by being rested!

Here are a few suggestions from the sleep experts to get you started: get to bed at the same time each night, exercise at some point in the day, avoid snacking late at night, and give each other a gentle back rub before dozing off. Be intentional about your sleep. Your marriage will thank you later.

People who say they sleep like a baby usually don't have one. —LEO J. BURKE

THE NEED FOR GREED?

True godliness with contentment is itself great wealth. . . . People who long to be rich fall into temptation and are trapped by many foolish and harmful desires that plunge them into ruin and destruction. 1 TIMOTHY 6:6, 9

THE TREASURE OF THE SIERRA MADRE is the story of three down-on-their-luck prospectors and their search for gold in Mexico. At one point in their search, the prospectors are joined by a fourth man who is soon killed in a shootout with bandits. The other three approach the body, which is propped up against a large rock. They decide to find out who the man was.

They remove the dead man's wallet and some papers. "His name is James Cody; Dallas, Texas. There's a letter from Dallas too. Must be his home," one of the men says, and shows the others a photo of a woman and starts reading.

> *Dear Jim: Your letter just arrived. It was such a relief to get word after so many months of silence. Little Jimmy is fine, but he misses his daddy almost as much as I do. He keeps asking, "When's Daddy coming home?" You say if you do not make a real find this time, you will never go again. I cannot begin to tell you how my heart rejoices at those words. Now I feel free to tell you, I've never thought that any material treasure, no matter how great, is worth the pain of these long separations.*
>
> *I do hope that you are back for the harvest. Of course, I'm hoping that you will at last strike it rich. It is high time for luck to start smiling upon you. But just in case she doesn't, remember, we've already found life's real treasure.*
>
> *Forever yours,*
> *Callie*

Nothing pulls us further away from our true treasure than insatiable greed. Jim certainly had a fine wife in Callie, but he felt compelled to once again leave home in search of more fortune. It's a common trap, even today. The desire to "strike it rich" has come between many a husband and wife. Sure, we don't go off to cash in on an actual gold rush these days, but we do go off to put in more hours at something that keeps us away from each other, all for more money. When we let greed get hold of our hearts, we often miss the richness, the fortune that we already have in each other. So the next time you find yourself trading in time together for a "great opportunity" or for more cold cash, consider the plight of ol' Jim and how money-hungry ways caused him to miss out on the true treasure of his marriage.

One of the weaknesses of our age is our apparent inability to distinguish our needs from our greeds. —**DON ROBINSON**

THE RIDE OF A LIFETIME

Faith is the confidence that what we hope for will actually happen; it gives us assurance about things we cannot see. HEBREWS 11:1

IT WAS AN ORDINARY THURSDAY EVENING on December 1, 1955, in an unhurried southern town. But what was about to happen that evening would change nothing less than the history of an entire country. A frail, middle-aged woman made a decision that few would have imagined in those days and in that place. After completing her workday as a tailor's assistant at a Montgomery department store, Rosa Parks stepped onto the Cleveland Avenue bus to go home—just as she had done on countless other evenings. She paid her fare and found a seat as the bus lumbered on to make two or three stops until it ended up in front of the Empire Movie Theater. More passengers entered the bus at this stop. They filled the empty seats until one man, who happened to be white, was left standing in the aisle. That's when the bus driver asked the four black passengers on Rosa's row to move and give the man a seat. Three of them got up. But not Rosa. She made a decision to just sit there.

Unthinkably, the bus driver warned Rosa that he would have her arrested if she didn't move. It was the law. "Well, you can do that," Rosa replied, but she stayed put. And so did the bus. Two police officers arrived in their squad car in no time and carted Rosa off to jail.

Rosa hadn't planned to make a point that evening, but her decision ignited the entire civil-rights movement. Word of this little lady's decision spread like proverbial wildfire throughout Montgomery and beyond. The result? A little more than a year later, the United States Supreme Court finally ruled that the segregation of buses was illegal.

Talk about making a difference! And it all started with a decision. Our question for you today is, What decision would change everything for the better in your marriage? If today was to serve as a monumental day in the history of your relationship because the two of you made a decision, what would it be?

To accept the status quo is to resign yourself from making a difference. Why settle for the status quo in your marriage? Sometimes all it takes is one decision to change everything.

I have learned over the years that when one's mind is made up, this diminishes fear; knowing what must be done does away with fear. —ROSA PARKS

CHOOSING YOUR MIND-SET

Lead me by your truth and teach me, for you are the God who saves me. All day long I put my hope in you. PSALM 25:5

YOU'VE SEEN IT IN THE MOVIES. The weary desert traveler, barely putting one foot in front of the other as he trudges over the sand dunes. It's not long before he begins to see distant and flickering sources of water. But do they exist? Is his mind playing tricks on him? Perhaps it's just a mirage.

A similar scene, minus the sand, is sometimes played out in our marriages. We cultivate a mind-set that causes us to literally see things that aren't there. For example, some time ago I was convinced Leslie had borrowed a key I keep tucked away in one of my desk drawers. It opens an outside storage room and is rarely used. But on this particular day I couldn't find the key. It wasn't in its place.

"Leslie," I asked, "did you take the key to the storage room?"

Before she answered I was certain she had. But she denied it. "No," she replied. "I haven't touched it." But because I take special care to place the key in the back of my lower left-hand drawer, I was certain I did not remove it. If it was gone, it had to be her. But during the entire afternoon everything she did seemed suspicious—the tone of her voice, her gestures. I was convinced she had taken the key and either lost it or forgot. By the look in her eye, I sensed that even she was uncertain.

My mind-set changed in an instant, however, when that evening I found the key in the pocket of my jacket. I'd left it there from a previous trip to the storage room and had forgotten. Still, my mind was made up. *I couldn't have lost the key because I'm so conscientious,* I said to myself. That's the power of a mind-set. It will cause to you read facial expressions inaccurately, and you'll conjure a scenario that doesn't exist.

One of the reasons some people can't find a solution to their problems is because they aren't looking for one. They've developed a mind-set, in fact, that filters them out.

Husbands and wives around the world are divided into two camps when it comes to their attitudes: those who have a positive mind-set and those who have a negative mind-set. The negative person defends his attitudes, while the positive person looks beyond the current state of affairs and sees people and situations in terms of possibilities. The choice is theirs, or should we say, yours.

We don't see things as they are, we see them as we are. —ANAÏS NIN

GIVING OURSELVES

God loved the world so much that he gave his one and only Son. JOHN 3:16

DID YOU KNOW THAT TODAY, December 3, is recognized as International Day of Persons with Disabilities? It began in 1992 when it was promoted by the United Nations. But long before that, there was a man named Jean Vanier who was recognizing people with disabilities in ways few of us ever consider.

In 1964, after publishing his doctoral thesis on Aristotle and securing a teaching position at the University of Toronto, Jean Vanier became aware of the plight of thousands of people institutionalized with developmental disabilities. In a dramatic move, he gave up the security of his job and joined a community for men with mental disabilities. The change was transforming for Vanier, and it eventually led him to establish L'Arche (French for Noah's Ark), small communities where people with developmental disabilities, volunteers, and a sprinkling of staff live together. "When you start living with people with disabilities," he says, "you begin to discover a whole lot of things about yourself." He learned that to "be human is to be bonded together, each with our own weaknesses and strengths, because we need each other."[2]

Here's Vanier's take on unconditional love between a husband and a wife:

> *I know a man who lives in Paris. His wife has Alzheimer's. He was an important businessman—his life filled with busyness. But he said that when his wife fell sick, "I just couldn't put her into an institution, so I kept her. I fed her. I bathed her." I went to Paris to visit them, and this businessman who had been very busy all his life said, "I have changed. I have become more human." I got a letter from him recently. He said that in the middle of the night his wife woke him up. She came out of the fog for a moment, and she said, "Darling, I just want to say thank you for all you're doing for me." Then she fell back into the fog. He told me, "I wept and I wept."[3]*

Sometimes Christ calls us to love when we don't seem to get love in return. And in marriage, we are sometimes called to love our spouse in the fog of not only a disability, but a weary spirit, a weak body, a stressed mind, or spiritual immaturity. As we love each other in these tough times, we may receive only fleeting glimpses of gratitude. But just as Jesus has loved us in the midst of our spiritual confusion, so we try our best to love, and in the process we learn how much we need each other.

To give and not expect return, that is what lies at the heart of love. —OSCAR WILDE

OWNING YOUR PIECE OF THE MARRIAGE PIE

For we are each responsible for our own conduct. GALATIANS 6:5

IN 1990 UNIVERSITY OF COLORADO football coach Bill McCartney founded Promise Keepers, a ministry dedicated to building men of integrity. At the time, he truly believed that his marriage to Lyndi was just fine. But it wasn't. In spite of his professional success and being the head of a major ministry, his marriage was not what it appeared. "It may sound unbelievable," he writes in his book *Sold Out*, "but while Promise Keepers was spiritually inspiring to my core, my hard-charging approach to the ministry was distracting me from being in the truest sense, a promise keeper to my own family."[4]

How could this be? McCartney points to two events. One was a Promise Keepers rally where men were told to write down the number their wives would give their marriages if rating them on a scale of one to ten. He had to admit with embarrassment to the other men on the platform that Lyndi would probably only give their marriage a six.

Another eye-opener occurred in the fall of 1994 when McCartney heard a speaker make this pointed statement: "If you want to know about a man's character, then look into the face of his wife. Whatever he has invested in or withheld from her will be reflected in her countenance." Something clicked in McCartney. As he puts it, he escorted his "wounded wife" out of the parking lot determined to rebuild his marriage, even if it would require drastic measures. And it did. He announced his retirement from the University of Colorado in order to spend time with Lyndi. He gave up the ten years remaining on his $350,000-a-year contract. *Sports Illustrated* called it "un-American." McCartney called it taking responsibility for the state of his marriage.

Of course, taking responsibility for your marriage doesn't require anything as dramatic as quitting your job, but it can be just as scary."[5] In the short run, it is far easier to avoid responsibility for our problems by blaming someone else. But admitting mistakes and owning up to our part of the problem is the single most powerful predictor of turning something bad into something good, "for we are each responsible for our own conduct." Talk to God today about how taking responsibility may be just the change your marriage is looking for.

 Our greatest fear is not that we will discover that we are inadequate, but that we will discover that we are powerful beyond measure. —NELSON MANDELA

REAL LOVE

Love never fails. 1 CORINTHIANS 13:8, NIV

"REAL ISN'T HOW YOU ARE MADE. It's a thing that happens to you," said the toy horse. "When a child loves you for a long, long time, not just to play with, but really loves you, then you become Real."

This old toy horse in Margery Williams's classic children's book, *The Velveteen Rabbit*, squarely identifies the fact that we are most real when we are most known and loved. It's synergistic: The more real we become, the more love we experience. And the more love we experience, the more real we become.

The toy rabbit didn't know real rabbits existed. He thought they were all stuffed with sawdust like himself. "And he understood that sawdust was quite out-of-date and should never be mentioned in modern circles." The rabbit kept authenticity at bay through his fear of being found out. He never wanted to risk being really known. And yet authenticity is the only way to be loved.

That's the irony. We fear that being known will lead to rejection. It will get our vulnerable hearts kicked across the floor. But it is only by being known that our hearts are truly loved.

C. S. Lewis, as he so often does, puts his finger on a truth that resonates:

> To love at all is to be vulnerable. Love anything, and your heart will certainly be wrung and possibly be broken. If you want to make sure of keeping your heart intact, you must give your heart to no one, not even to an animal. Wrap it carefully round with hobbies and little luxuries; avoid all entanglements; lock it up safe in the casket or coffin of your selfishness. But in that casket—safe, dark, motionless, airless— it will change. It will not be broken; it will become unbreakable, impenetrable irredeemable. . . . The only place outside Heaven where you can be perfectly safe from all the dangers and perturbations of love is Hell.[6]

Nobody wants a hard-boiled heart. And yet each time we pass up an opportunity to be known by our spouse, we face a greater danger than having our heart being rejected. We risk a hardened heart that even guards against the risk of love. And for a marriage to be truly healthy and thriving—for both partners—each partner much take the risks of being known and of being a safe place to be known.

I love thee to the depth and breadth and height my soul can reach.
—ELIZABETH BARRETT BROWNING

THE FORGIVING GIFT

When you are praying, first forgive anyone you are holding a grudge against, so that your Father in heaven will forgive your sins, too. MARK 11:25

"WHERE'S MY WHITE SHIRT you said you'd pick up from the cleaners?" says the husband.

"I never said I'd get your shirt."

"I can't believe you."

"Don't pass the blame to me. It's your shirt."

"Yes, but I asked you last night to pick it up for me. Why didn't you?"

"You're crazy. We hardly even talked last night because you were at the game with Rick. Remember?"

"Oh, I get it. You didn't pick up my shirt because you're mad about me going to the game."

"Wait a second. Who's the one who gets mad if I'm not home to make dinner every night?"

This inane dialogue bleats on and on until, at last, one partner says, "I'm sorry. Will you forgive me?" In the daily grind that is sometimes marriage, forgiveness keeps it moving forward.

But for some agonizing couples, a devastating hurt—one that was completely undeserved and goes against God's moral grain—is calling on forgiveness to do much more than that. Sometimes in a good marriage a pain of betrayal has cut so deeply that forgiveness is the only thing between this couple and their demise. It is their last hope for keeping them from their finale. Can it do so? Is it fair to ask so much of forgiveness? Yes, indeed. It is the very thing forgiveness was designed to do, to heal the deepest wounds of a human heart.

Untold marriages have been saved by little more than forgiveness. Just ask Gordon MacDonald, former pastor of Trinity Baptist Church in New York City. "I had horribly offended God and those whom I loved the most," he writes. "They had every right to turn their backs on me and hold me hostage to anger."[7] His betrayal of his wife brought their marriage to the ragged edge of its darkest abyss and the only thing that kept them from tumbling in was his humble repentance and his wife's brave forgiveness.[8]

The most creative power in the soul of any marriage is the power to heal the hurts it didn't deserve. It is what allows transformation in the guilty party and healing in the person who has been wronged.[9]

Love is an act of endless forgiveness, a tender look which becomes a habit.
—PETER USTINOV

AN ABIDING DETERMINATION

A man who makes a vow to the LORD or makes a pledge under oath must never break it. He must do exactly what he said he would do. NUMBERS 30:2

"FOR BETTER OR FOR WORSE, for richer or poorer, in sickness and in health, until death do us part." Just words. A mere phrase, really. You hear them at every wedding. Are you impressed? Probably not. It's one thing to say these words; it's another to keep them. Let's face it, it's a covenant that bears out only over the course of a lifetime. And half the time it doesn't.

We had assembled a small panel of marriage experts to interview in an auditorium of nearly two hundred college students studying marriage at our university. None of these experts had a PhD. They'd never published scholarly articles or anything else related to marriage. We don't even know if they'd ever read a single article on matrimony. All we knew is that these couples were experts by virtue of the longevity of their relationships. Elvin and Lois, married seventy-two years. Ken and Mable, sixty-eight years. Eldon and Dotty, seventy.

"Did you know marriages could last so long?" we asked our students in opening the floor for their questions. They sat in awe of these affectionate couples, like they were viewing a rare curiosity that belongs in a museum. One student raised his hand to break the ice: "If you combine the number of years each of these couples have been married, it comes to 210." Students chuckled, but they got deadly quiet when the next student asked, "What has kept you together all these years?" Elvin was the first one to speak up. "An abiding determination to do so," he said. The rest of the panel nodded in agreement.

The "till death do us part" of marriage is not an ideal. It is a reality that is ensured by an unswerving commitment—a willful agreement to keep love alive. And, no matter how long a couple has been married, it may be the most effective tool good marriages use in battling bad things. Without commitment and the trust it engenders, marriage would have no hope of enduring.[10]

Marriage is a commitment—a decision to do, all through life, that which will express love for one's spouse. —HERMAN H. KIEVAL

THE GIFT OF TRUST

The LORD is good, a strong refuge when trouble comes. He is close to those who trust in him. NAHUM 1:7

IN THE 2010 VANCOUVER OLYMPICS the Netherlands' superstar skater Sven Kramer learned a heart-wrenching lesson in trust. In the Olympic finals for the 10,000-meter race, he skated the 25 times around the rink so well that he set an Olympic record. He finished a full 4 seconds ahead of the second-place skater. He was thrilled. The week before he had won gold in the 5,000 meter race. Now he had won a second Olympic gold medal, and done that representing a country that adores speed skating. He was a national hero!

But some of that glory quickly evaporated. Moments after Kramer crossed the finish line, his coach, a former Olympian himself, approached him and broke the unthinkable news. Kramer had been disqualified from the race. With eight laps to go, he had changed lanes improperly. What made this disqualification so bitter for Kramer was that he had changed lanes for only one reason: his coach had told him to change lanes. In other words, he had no plans to change lanes until his coach called out for him to change.

In a situation when a split-second decision had to be made, Kramer trusted his coach, and it cost him an Olympic gold medal. Kramer, of course, was not the only one to suffer an emotional blow. The coach later said it was "the worst moment in my career." He said, "Sven was right. I was wrong." No doubt he will reflect on what happened for the rest of his life.

What do you do when you fail someone else's trust? What do you do when someone fails your trust and costs you plenty? What happens to trust in a relationship after a costly failure?

The next day Sven Kramer told the media that he had forgiven his coach, and they would continue working together. Kramer said, "The past few years have been too good. We have won so much together. You can't just throw that away."[11]

Every couple can learn from Kramer's forgiveness. After all, trust begins to crumble in a marriage most often when little promises are broken. When little deceptions are discovered. And the tragedy of most seemingly insignificant experiences of deception is that they mushroom and ultimately create a cloud of distrust that hovers over a relationship. That's why the author of Nahum reminds us that God cares for those who trust in him.

Trust is built on integrity. Without it, Scripture says, we will be despised and destroyed (see Psalm 5:6). Integrity means telling the truth, keeping our promises, doing what we said we would do, choosing to be accountable, and taking as our motto, *semper fidelis*—the promise to be always faithful.

The gift of trust is rare. But doesn't your marriage deserve it?

 To be trusted is a greater compliment than to be loved. —GEORGE MACDONALD

GOD IS LOVE

I am convinced that nothing can ever separate us from God's love. Neither death nor life, neither angels nor demons, neither our fears for today nor our worries about tomorrow— not even the powers of hell can separate us from God's love. ROMANS 8:38

ON A TRIP TO LONDON with two other couples, we thought it only fitting that we take the opportunity to see the long-standing musical production of Charles Dickens's story of Oliver Twist. In the opening scene, destitute boys in a London orphanage are hovering over a miserable meal of gruel. Meanwhile, the family and friends of the orphanage's manager are enjoying heaping platters of succulent fowl and tasty vegetables in an adjoining dining room that the boys can see. Although the paint is peeling on the stark gray wall behind the rough tables where the boys are sitting, a huge motto is visible: GOD IS LOVE.

The audience is left to wonder whether the ragged, coughing urchins ever notice the dusty sign, let alone comprehend its meaning. But in reality God's love is not part of a theatrical backdrop. It is not meant to have a paradoxical place on stage. God's love has been real since the beginning of time, when the Lord laid the foundations of the earth.

How you perceive God's love shapes your love for each other. God's love is self-sacrificing (John 15:13), compelling (2 Corinthians 5:14, NIV), and unchangeable (John 13:1, NKJV). Those qualities are what make it perfect.

The late Ruth Bell Graham once wrote, "When I stop to think of all that love should be—accepting, forgiving, supporting, strengthening—God is all that and more. He is perfect love." And when Ruth Graham felt that her love for her husband, Billy, did not measure up to such divine standards, "At that moment Romans 8:31-39 comes into my consciousness, and I am surrounded again by an awareness of God's love. He loves me in spite of me!"[12]

If the GOD IS LOVE sign had the audacity to cling to the scaly wall in Oliver's dreadful orphanage, it can surely abide in the hearts of a husband and wife who care for each other.

Though our feelings come and go, [God's] love for us does not. —C. S. LEWIS

MAKING A CHOICE

If the godly give in to the wicked, it's like polluting a fountain or muddying a spring.

PROVERBS 25:26

LISTEN TO THESE WORDS: "We stand at the crossroads, each minute, each hour, each day, making choices. We choose the thoughts we allow ourselves to think, the passions we allow ourselves to feel, and the actions we allow ourselves to perform. Each choice is made in the context of whatever value system we've selected to govern our lives. In selecting that value system, we are, in a very real way, making the most important choice we will ever make."[13] Benjamin Franklin said this, and his words have more wisdom for married couples than he probably ever knew.

We have a friend who says the quality of a couple's marriage can basically be measured by the quality of their choices together. We tend to agree. Good choices keep a couple moving in the right direction. Bad choices steer them toward the rocks. And every day in every marriage, choices are made that lead couples to better places, and choices are made that serve as a detour.

It is difficult to exaggerate the power of our choices. Even the small choices we make determine how the future will treat us. We often use the legendary story of a man in the railroad station in St. Louis to illustrate the point. He accidentally moved a small piece of railroad track just three inches. As a result, the train that was supposed to arrive in Newark, New Jersey, ended up in a station in New Orleans, Louisiana, some thirteen hundred miles away from its intended destination. Apocryphal or not, the illustration makes it clear: we choose our destiny. And the small choices matter.

That's why unhealthy choices are one of the leading causes of difficulty in marriage. Here are a few examples of bad choices good couples make:

A wife who chooses to keep information from her husband about the money she spent with a girlfriend on a recent shopping spree.

A husband who knows his work schedule is interfering with his marriage, yet chooses to work at the same pace because his job "demands it."

A wife who chooses to use sex with her husband as a reward system rather than an expression of passion.

A husband who chooses to keep his wife in the dark about the debt that is accruing on their credit cards.

Regardless of how insignificant a choice may seem at the moment, it is bound to direct our steps toward something that either enriches or diminishes our relationships. Marriage is filled with hundreds of crossroads each week, and when we choose the road less traveled, we are choosing to build a stronger marriage.[14]

 Two roads diverged in a wood, and I—I took the one less traveled by, and that has made all the difference. —**ROBERT FROST**

HAPPILY EVER AFTER?

A worthy wife is a crown for her husband, but a disgraceful woman is like cancer in his bones. PROVERBS 12:4

LIKE NEARLY ALL THE WORLD, we watched the highlights of the royal wedding on April 29, 2011, when Prince William married Catherine Middleton. And in the seemingly endless hours of news coverage about the royal nuptials, we were reminded of a different royal drama occurring in the 1930s. At the time, the world's most eligible bachelor, the Prince of Wales, was still unmarried at age forty-one. He seemed incapable of pulling the proverbial trigger. But when the man that would be king came to a decision, it was a big one.

On December 11, 1936, in a radio broadcast heard by millions, the newly proclaimed king announced the unthinkable. "I have found it impossible to carry the heavy burden of responsibility and to discharge my duties as king as I would wish to do," he said, "without the help and support of the woman I love." That woman, Wallis Simpson, was a twice-divorced American.

It never occurred to Wallis that Edward would exchange the monarchy for marriage. By many accounts, she never really wanted to marry the king. She was content with the status quo and had in mind, according to Donald Spoto, author of *The Decline and Fall of the House of Windsor*, being a royal mistress. Besides, as head of the Church of England, the king is forbidden to marry a divorcée. But this didn't stop Edward from declaring, "The throne means nothing to me without Wallis beside me."

The couple married six months later before only sixteen guests. The life that followed was empty. They lived in voluntary exile in Paris. "You have no idea how hard it is to live out a great romance," Wallis told a friend.[15]

Fairy tale romance is just that—a fairy tale, not reality. King Solomon, of noble lineage himself, surely understood the heartache of trying to live a storybook existence. Faraway castles, beguiling jewels, and even surrendering the throne for love are only an illusion of real-life romance. A husband's true crown, according to this Proverb, is "a worthy wife." This is the only authentic and healthy way to live out a great romance. "Charm is deceptive, and beauty does not last; but a woman who fears the LORD will be greatly praised" (Proverbs 31:30). Fearing the Lord—it is a phrase that appears numerous times throughout the Bible. It means showing reverence for our maker and being in awe of God. It means loving God.

Fearing the Lord and living with godliness from day to day is the only authentic and healthy way to live out a great romance.

The fairy tale is irresponsible; it is frankly imaginary, and its purpose is to gratify wishes, "as a dream doth flatter." —SUSANNE K. LANGER

HOLDING ON TO I LOVE YOU

And may the Lord make you increase and abound in love for one another.

1 THESSALONIANS 3:12

IN EARLY DECEMBER 2006, a local news story broke in our part of the country and grabbed everyone's attention. Forty-eight-year-old landscape architect Kelly James and two of his friends had set out to climb Mount Hood near Portland, Oregon. They had been caught by a sudden blizzard after reaching the summit of the mountain, and they were forced to take shelter in a snow cave. Kelly was able to use his cell phone to call his family and tell them what was going on, but the storm was too severe for rescue workers to attempt a search. All three hikers eventually perished.

Kelly's widow, Karen, did an interview with Katie Couric on the *CBS Evening News*, during which Couric asked her if she was angry with her husband for choosing to climb in the first place. She replied, "I'm not angry. I'm really sad our journey is over for a while, and I miss him terribly. But he loved life so much, and he taught me how to love. He taught me how to live. And I don't know how you can be angry at someone who loved their family, who loved God . . . and gave back so much more than he took." [16]

When asked how her husband would like to be remembered, Karen referred to his faith in Jesus: "Kelly had this little ornament, and he's had it since he was little. It's a manger. It's just this little plastic thing. And it's always the tradition that [our son] Jack and Kelly put it on the tree together. And so I said this Christmas, 'We're going to put that ornament on the tree.' And one of the things that we really understand about Christmas is that little baby born in a barn is the reason our family has so much strength now. And that is really important to Kelly."

Impressed by the strength of Karen's faith, Couric asked if the family's confidence in God had been tested by her husband's death. "No, it was never tested," Karen answered. "I remember one time we were watching TV, and Kelly said to me, 'I can't wait to go to heaven.' And I said, 'What?' We were watching some show that had nothing to do with it. And he said, 'Yeah, that's going to be really cool.' And I said, 'Can you hold off? Can we wait?' But he wasn't scared. And so those conversations are what I hold on to."

Finally, when asked by Couric if there were any lessons that could be learned from her husband's tragedy, Karen replied, "I've told a colleague of mine that men should hold their wives really, really tight, because you don't know when our journey's going to end. My journey ended with an 'I love you.' And . . . for others, if their journey ends with an 'I love you,' it's a lot to hold on to."

So, God forbid, if tragedy were to strike your marriage, as it did for Kelly and Karen James, would you have enough "I love yous" to hold on to?

Faith is the art of holding on to things your reason once accepted, despite your changing moods. —**C. S. LEWIS**

THE LONG CONVERSATION

Let everything you say be good and helpful, so that your words will be an encouragement to those who hear them. EPHESIANS 4:29

THE MONKS AT A REMOTE monastery deep in the woods followed a rigid vow of silence. Their vow could only be broken once a year—on Christmas—by one monk. That monk could speak only one sentence. One Christmas, Brother Thomas had his turn to speak and said, "I love the delightful mashed potatoes we have every year with the Christmas roast!" Then he sat down. Silence ensued for 365 days.

The next Christmas, Brother Michael got his turn and said, "I think the mashed potatoes are lumpy, and I truly despise them!" Once again, silence ensued for 365 days.

The following Christmas, Brother Paul rose and said, "I am fed up with this constant bickering!"

We chuckle, but truth is that some couples can carry on a conflict that lasts nearly as long. In our book *Love Talk* we devote an entire chapter to "When Not to Talk." It may seem a bit unorthodox that in a communication book we are telling our readers to stop talking, but let's be honest: Some conversations simply don't need to take place. They waste our time.

If you've been telling your husband for eight years to not put his jacket on the back of the dining room chair and he's still doing it, or you've been arguing for four summers about whether or not to buy an expensive barbeque grill, it might be time to take a permanent break from the conversation. At some point you've got to realize that talking is not going to provide the solution. You might simply have to agree to disagree. You may be able to work out a compromise that will at least partly satisfy you both. Or maybe you agree to table all discussion on the matter for, say, the next six months.

If your conversations are getting you nowhere, give it a rest and reclaim the time you've been wasting on them. Of course, in some cases there are actions you can take that do speak louder than words. If you've asked, cajoled, threatened, and analyzed your man on the subject of not hanging up his coat in the closet, and he keeps promising to do so but never does, you have a couple of options. (A) You could decide to hang it up for him and say no more about it. Or (B) You could leave it there and say nothing. The only option not available to you is to keep talking about it.

The bottom line is that you need to give up the conversations you keep having that grind both of you down and steal precious time from talks that could be much more meaningful. So take a moment to identify what one of those "long conversations" might be for each of you.[17]

Marriage is one long conversation, chequered by disputes. —ROBERT LOUIS STEVENSON

THE CHRISTMAS STORY

As he considered this, an angel of the Lord appeared to him in a dream. "Joseph, son of David," the angel said, "do not be afraid to take Mary as your wife. For the child within her was conceived by the Holy Spirit. And she will have a son, and you are to name him Jesus." MATTHEW 1:20-21

WE MUST HAVE FORTY OR FIFTY BIBLES. They are of all sizes and colors and in all kinds of versions—the King James, the New King James, the Good News, the New American Standard, the Amplified, the *Living Bible*, the *Message*, the New International Version, the New Revised Standard Bible, the New Living, and on and on. And then we have the workbook editions, the pocket editions, the illustrated editions, and the devotional editions. Some are old, some new. Many were gifts on various occasions. Most of these, most of the time, however, sit on a shelf in our study at home.[18]

But there are two Bibles—our personal Bibles—that are very different. Les's Bible is a black leather edition with study help and fancy thumb indentions for quick reference. These days, however, he's just as likely to read from an electronic edition on his smartphone or tablet, where he can quickly compare various translations.

Leslie's Bible, on the other hand, has a more personal feel. Its light brown leather cover, because of wear, is no longer affixed to the spine. Les gave it to me on December 14, 1979—our first Christmas as a dating couple. How can I remember the date all these years later? Because the inscription, penned in Les's teenage handwriting, is still clearly visible. And it's from this Bible that, around this time of year, we traditionally read Matthew's biblical account of the birth of Christ (Matthew 1:18–2:23). For us, there is something about reading it from this particular Bible that joins our spirits as we celebrate this special time of year.

How about you? Do the two of you ever read the biblical account of Christ's birth together? If not, we suggest you give it a try this year. You just may start a new and meaningful Christmas tradition.

The event of Christ is the only event in human history that promises relocation and centering, meaning and purpose. This promise and its fulfillment evoke passionate and heartfelt praise and thanks, especially for those aware of their own brokenness and the healing which Christ brings into their lives. —ROBERT WEBBER

A CHRISTMAS LIGHT IN THE DARKNESS

The people who sat in darkness have seen a great light. And for those who lived in the land where death casts its shadow, a light has shined. MATTHEW 4:16

IT WAS HER FIRST CHRISTMAS ALONE. Her husband had died of cancer just a few months earlier. Feeling terribly lonely, the elderly woman decided she was in no mood to decorate for Christmas.

A few days before Christmas, a delivery boy with a box arrived at her door. He said, "Mrs. Thornhope?" She nodded. He said, "Would you sign here?" She invited him to come in out of the snow and closed the door to get away from the cold.

She signed the paper and said, "What's in the box?" The young man laughed as he opened up the flap to reveal a little puppy. The delivery boy picked up the squirming bundle of fur and explained, "This is for you, ma'am. He's six weeks old, completely housebroken." The young puppy began to wiggle in happiness at being released from the box.

"Who sent this?" Mrs. Thornhope asked.

The young man set the animal down and handed her an envelope and said, "It's all explained here in this envelope, ma'am. The dog was bought last July while its mother was still pregnant. It was meant to be a Christmas gift to you."

She again asked, "Who sent me this puppy?"

As the young man turned to leave, he said, "Your husband, ma'am. Merry Christmas."

Her husband had written the letter three weeks before he died and left it with the kennel owners to be delivered with the puppy as his last Christmas gift to his wife. The letter was full of love and encouragement to be strong. He vowed that he was waiting for the day when she would join him. He wanted this little dog to keep her company until then.

She wiped away the tears, put the letter down, and picked up the puppy. She heard from the radio in the kitchen the strains of "Joy to the World." Suddenly she felt peace washing over her. Her heart felt a joy and a wonder greater than the grief and loneliness she'd been suffering.

She decided to decorate her home for Christmas after all.

God has a way of sending a signal of light to remind us that life is stronger than death. Light is more powerful than darkness.

You can't have light without a dark to stick it in. —ARLO GUTHRIE

LOVE MEANS WHAT?

Pride ends in humiliation, while humility brings honor. PROVERBS 29:23

ON DECEMBER 16, 1970, a drama premiered in movie theaters across the country and became a staggering commercial success. To this day it is considered one of the most romantic of all time by the American Film Institute.

> *It's the story of Oliver Barrett, who comes from a wealthy family and a line of well-respected Harvard University graduates. At the Radcliff library, Oliver meets and falls in love with Jennifer Cavelleri, a working-class, quick-witted student. Upon graduation the two marry, against the wishes of Oliver's father, who severs ties with his son.*
>
> *Without his father's financial support, the couple struggles to pay Oliver's way through Harvard Law School, but they get by and he eventually graduates and takes a position in a respectable New York law firm. With Oliver's new income, the pair of twenty-four-year-olds decides to have a child. After failing, they consult a medical specialist, who after repeated tests, informs Oliver that Jenny is ill and will soon die.*
>
> *With their days together numbered, Jenny begins costly cancer therapy, and Oliver soon becomes unable to afford the multiplying hospital expenses. Desperate, he seeks financial relief from his father. When the senior Barrett asks if he needs the money because he got some girl "in trouble," Oliver says yes instead of telling his father the truth about Jenny's condition.*
>
> *From her hospital bed, Jenny speaks with her father about funeral arrangements, then asks for Oliver. She tells him to avoid blaming himself and asks him to embrace her tightly before she dies. They lie together on the hospital bed.*
>
> *When Mr. Barrett realizes that Jenny is ill and that his son borrowed the money for her, he immediately sets out for New York. By the time he reaches the hospital, Jenny is dead. Mr. Barrett apologizes to his son, who replies with something Jenny once told him: "Love means never having to say you're sorry."[19]*

The movie was *Love Story,* and the line became etched in public memory. But to this day it baffles nearly everyone who hears it. All these years later, even the actors who played the starring roles, Ryan O'Neal and Ali MacGraw, say it doesn't ring true.

Truth is, love means having to say you're sorry quite often. Why? Because sorrow is the humble admission of making a mistake—and we all make mistakes. Whenever we apologize we must first set aside our pride. Genuine sorrow is based on humility. There is no way around it. Paul understood this when he said, "Knowledge puffs up, but love builds up" (1 Corinthians 8:1, NIV). Perhaps he was echoing the wisdom of Proverbs: "Pride leads to disgrace, but with humility comes wisdom" (11:2; see also Proverbs 29:23).

Do you want to write your own love story? Be sure to generously interject these two humble words into your dialogue: I'm sorry.

 Love means having to say you're sorry every fifteen minutes. —JOHN LENNON

SPACES IN OUR TOGETHERNESS?

Work hard so you can present yourself to God and receive his approval. Be a good worker, one who does not need to be ashamed and who correctly explains the word of truth.

2 TIMOTHY 2:15

EVER FEEL LIKE YOU'RE living under scrutiny and surveillance—in your own home? After all, marriage is the closest bond that is possible between two people. Legally, socially, emotionally, physically, there is no other means of getting closer to another human being. Our desire for this extraordinary closeness propels us into matrimony. We sometimes call this kind of intimacy the rocket fuel of marriage. It enables couples to transcend themselves and explore the universe of love.

Eventually, however, seasoned couples also discover that such closeness can be exhausting. Intimacy, it seems, leaves nowhere to hide. That's what Robert Louis Stevenson is getting at when he says that marriage willfully introduces a witness into our lives. It causes us to submit to the humility of being known in all our phoniness and pride, in all our frailty and the blackness of our sin. And who cares, really, to be known that well by another person?

Shortly after we were married and living in Los Angeles, our friend James Scott Smith gave us a collector's edition of poetry by Khalil Gibran. In it we found the famous words Gibran penned concerning the invasion of intimacy in marriage. So many years later in our own marriage, these words now make so much more sense.

Let there be spaces in your togetherness,
And let the winds of the heavens dance between you.
Love one another, but make not a bond of love:
Let it rather be a moving sea between the shores of your souls,
Fill each other's cup but drink not from one cup.
Give one another of your bread but eat not from the same loaf.
Sing and dance together and be joyous, but let
*   each one of you be alone,*
Even as the strings of a lute are alone though they
*   quiver with the same music.*[20]

We'll say it again. Marriage is the closest bond that is possible between two people. And the price marriage puts on intimacy is to be in the spotlight of our spouse. That's why having spaces in our togetherness becomes important.[21]

Love is missing someone whenever you're apart, but somehow feeling warm inside because you're close in heart. —KAY KNUDSEN

A GIFT FROM THE HEART

In the sixth month, God sent the angel Gabriel to Nazareth, a town in Galilee, to a virgin pledged to be married to a man named Joseph, a descendant of David. The virgin's name was Mary. The angel went to her and said, "Greetings, you who are highly favored! The Lord is with you." LUKE 1:26-28, NIV

THE ILLUSTRATIONS OFFERED on PreachingToday.com include the following story of one couple's gift of encouragement at Christmastime:

> *Every December since 1992, Morrill Worcester, owner of one of the world's largest holiday wreath companies, has taken time in the midst of his busiest season to haul a truckload of wreaths to the Arlington National Cemetery. Morrill and his band of volunteers spend a day laying wreaths on the graves of over 5,000 soldiers as part of the Wreaths Across America program.*
>
> *Worcester, 56, started the program when one of his warehouses called to report an overproduction of several thousand wreaths. He said: "Well, I'm not just gonna throw them away. That's when I thought of Arlington." He called Washington and asked for permission to lay his wreaths. To his surprise, he got it.*
>
> *"When people hear about what we're doing, they want to know if I'm a veteran," Morrill said on the Wreaths Across America website. "I'm not. But I make it my business never to forget." His wife, Karen, agrees: "We want to honor the veterans, and we do it with the products we make ourselves. We're like the Little Drummer Boy. He had his drum; we have our wreaths."*
>
> *For Morrill and Karen, the program is a way to give back. Christmas wreaths had made them rich. Through Wreaths Across America, they feel they are reclaiming the true meaning of a wreath, showing it as something more than a glitzy holiday ornament: "We wanted to get back to the simple idea of what a wreath represents— respect, honor, and victory."[22]*

Morrill and Karen remind us all that Christmas is not about what we find under the tree. It's about giving back. Christmas, as someone has said, is when God came down the stairs of heaven with a baby in his arms. That gift of love is what the wonder of Christmas is all about. And that's the gift we can give, as a couple, in some meaningful way to our own community. It may not be as dramatic as five thousand wreaths. But a gift of love from the heart can be even more meaningful.

Probably the reason we all go so haywire at Christmas time with the endless unrestrained and often silly buying of gifts is that we don't quite know how to put our love into words. —**HARLAN MILLER**

THE QUIET INVASION

The Word became human and made his home among us. He was full of unfailing love and faithfulness. JOHN 1:14

IN THE FAITH, author Charles Colson makes a comparison between the Normandy invasion on D-day, 1944, and the way God "invaded" the world in the birth of his Son.

> *In one sense, the great invasions of history are analogous to the way in which God, in the great cosmic struggle between good and evil, chose to deal with Satan's rule over the earth—He invaded. But not with massive logistical support and huge armies; rather, in a way that confounded and perplexed the wisdom of humanity.*
>
> *It was a quiet invasion. Few people understood what was happening. Mary, the mother of Jesus, knew that she was with child, but she also knew that she had never been with a man, not even Joseph, to whom she was engaged. She had learned of her pregnancy and what was to be a virgin birth when an angel told her that she was pregnant with the Son of God.*
>
> *For many, including Joseph, the doctrine of the Virgin Birth is hard to accept. But the God who could speak the universe into being, who could create human life, could certainly choose to make himself known by the power of the Holy Spirit through a virgin. . . .*
>
> *Most of the people in Palestine at the time of Jesus' birth were expecting a Messianic invasion like we saw at D-day—conquerors in armor bringing a sword to set the people free from oppression.*
>
> *Jesus only added to the bewilderment of the people who knew him when he announced: "The time has come. . . . The kingdom of God is near. Repent and believe the good news" (Mark 1:15). This was the time the Jews had awaited for so long? Liberation? And who was this ordinary Nazarene carpenter to say he was bringing in the Kingdom of God?[23]*

In just six days we'll celebrate the quiet invasion of God on Christmas Day. While it may perplex and confound the human mind, it can still permeate the human heart and free us from oppression. What aspect of this quiet invasion, what freedom that it brings, are you hoping to see in your married life this week?

I am not alone at all, I thought. I was never alone at all. And that, of course, is the message of Christmas. We are never alone. Not when the night is darkest, the wind coldest, the world seemingly most indifferent. For this is still the time God chooses.
—**TAYLOR CALDWELL**

TWO TREES FOR CHRISTMAS?

When Joseph woke up, he did as the angel of the Lord commanded and took Mary as his wife. MATTHEW 1:24

MIKE ROYKO WAS A POPULAR newspaper columnist in Chicago for more than thirty years. Like many columnists Royko created fictitious mouthpieces with whom he could "converse," the most famous being Slats Grobnik, the epitome of the working class Polish Chicagoan.

In one column, Royko tells the story of how every December, Slats Grobnik would sell Christmas trees in Chicago. And one year, so the story goes, he met a couple that was on the hunt for just the right tree:

> *The guy was skinny with a big bulging Adam's apple and a small, receding chin. She was kind of pretty. But the two of them were wearing ragged clothes that looked like they'd come from the Salvation Army store. They didn't have much, it was clear. Grobnik walked along with them as they found most of the trees in his collection far too expensive.*
>
> *Eventually, they settled on a Scotch pine that was okay on one side, but pretty bare on the other. And then, a little further along, they picked up another tree that was hardly any better—full on one side, Charlie-Brown-scraggly on the other.*
>
> *A few days later, Slats was out walking on the street when he happened to glance up through a picture window into a ground-floor apartment where he saw an absolutely spectacular tree. It was beautiful—full and thick and luscious. Then he was shocked as he saw come into the window view the couple that he'd sold the lousy trees to.*
>
> *Curiosity got the best of him, so he went up to the door, knocked, and started up a conversation. He had to know where they had gotten that beautiful tree. They told him how they'd come home with the two scraggly trees he'd sold and worked them together where the branches were thin. It had been difficult to get the branches interlaced; they had to use wire to bind the two trunks together. But with time and effort and the grace of God, they found a way to overlap the branches. The trees were now so thick and rich you could not even see the wires.*
>
> *"So that's the secret," said Grobnik. "You take two trees that aren't perfect, that might even be homely, that maybe nobody else would want, but if you put them together just right, then sometimes you can make something really beautiful."*[24]

You don't have to be a poet or a psychologist to see the analogy of this story. The beauty of marriage is achieved when two imperfect people come together and commit themselves to each other and to God.

 } *There has been only one Christmas—the rest are anniversaries.* —W. J. CAMERON

HOW TO BE FULLY PRESENT
THIS CHRISTMAS

From his abundance we have all received one gracious blessing after another. JOHN 1:16

IF YOU WERE TO DROP BY our home some evening in the days leading up to Christmas, you might find us huddled in the living room with popcorn and blankets watching one of the predictable classics. In fact, most years we'll watch at least portions of *A Christmas Story*. And invariably, as a particular scene is about to unfold, we'll start saying something along the lines of, "Oh, no! Here it comes!" It's where the kids are gathered at a school playground on a snowy day and one child tells a story about a kid who got his tongue stuck to the flagpole. On a triple-dog-dare, one of the children, Flick, agrees to put his tongue on the flagpole, and it actually sticks. Flick screams, "Stuck! Stuck! Stuck!" All the children abandon Flick, retreating into the warm classroom.

As class resumes, the teacher realizes Flick is missing. She asks where he is, but no one confesses. Finally, one girl points out the window. The teacher recoils in horror as she sees Flick's tongue frozen to the pole.

After help from the firemen and police, Flick somberly walks into the room with a bandaged tongue, and the teacher addresses the class with a shaming tone: "Now, I know that some of you put Flick up to this, but he has refused to say who. But those who did it know their blame, and I'm sure that the guilt you feel is far worse than any punishment you might receive. Now don't you feel terrible? Don't you feel remorse for what you've done? That's all I'm going to say about poor Flick."

Still, no one confesses. Everyone sits silently, but we hear Ralphie (the main character) as he silently muses: *Adults loved to say stuff like that, but kids knew better. Kids knew darn well it was always better not to get caught.*

Truth be told, most adults feel the same way. Why confess, we reason, if no one will know otherwise? The reason is that confessing our regret brings a tremendous release, especially when it involved something we did or said that hurt the person we love. Confession empowers us to move beyond our past and live fully in the present. And isn't that what you want for you and your relationship this Christmas?

Christmas was on its way. Lovely, glorious, beautiful Christmas, upon which the entire kid year revolved. —**RALPHIE IN** *A CHRISTMAS STORY*

A CHRISTMAS COMMUNION

I pass on to you what I received from the Lord himself. On the night when he was betrayed, the Lord Jesus took some bread and gave thanks to God for it. Then he broke it in pieces and said, "This is my body, which is given for you." 1 CORINTHIANS 11:23-24

LAST CHRISTMAS WE DIDN'T have many presents under the tree, and that was the result of a conscious decision. We decided as a family that we would forgo a lot of the gift giving and, instead, have one big gift that we'd enjoy together—a trip to China. And we had a wonderful journey with lots of memories and hundreds of photographs.

In preparation for our trip, we watched several documentaries on the country and, among other things, learned about China's Cultural Revolution. It was a time when Christians were often sentenced to hard labor in prison camps. They weren't allowed to express their faith in any way. But for one dedicated man, Christmas was not complete without Communion. The significance of Jesus' birth and death made celebrating the Lord's Supper on a cold Christmas Day in China worth the risk.

It was 1961 when the prisoners were working around rice paddies in zero-degree temperatures and the wind was howling over the frozen ground. This man approached his supervisor and asked for some time off from work since it was Christmas. The guard gave him permission but warned him to beware of the warden. The old man found a deep ditch, out of sight, and built a small fire, where he began to celebrate Christmas.

A few minutes later the friendly guard saw the warden headed straight for them. He hurried over to warn the old prisoner, just in time to see him sipping something from a chipped cup and eating a bite of bread.

When the warden arrived, all he saw was a small fire with the prisoner and guard huddled over it. But the prisoner had completed his Christmas celebration, not with a banquet or with sweets, but with a cold cup and a cold crust—with Communion. His celebration of Christmas demanded Communion.

The birth of God's Son would leave us cold, if not for the death of Jesus, enfolding us in the warm glow of his mercy. Our celebration of his birth needs to be wrapped in the swaddling clothes of God's grace. Our awe at Advent is not just that he came at all, but that he came to be crucified.

 Thus may we abide in union with each other and the Lord, and possess, in sweet communion, joys which earth cannot afford. —JOHN NEWTON

IS THIS ALL THERE IS?

Suddenly, the angel was joined by a vast host of others—the armies of heaven—praising God and saying, "Glory to God in highest heaven, and peace on earth to those with whom God is pleased." LUKE 2:13-14

PASTOR MARK BUCHANAN LIVES with his wife and three children on Vancouver Island, British Columbia. He's also the author of a book, *Things Unseen*, whose goal is to help you to be of more earthly good by becoming more heavenly minded. And he points out how we all continually live for the "Next Thing"—the next item on our checklist that gets us excited. He says this can become so obsessive "that we lose the capacity to enjoy and to be thankful for what we have right now." It's a message that is particularly poignant during this Christmas season. Pastor Buchanan writes:

> *I saw this close-up . . . when my children first got to that age when the essence of Christmas becomes The Day of Getting. There were mounds of gifts beneath our tree, and our son led the way in that favorite childhood (and, more subtly, adult) game, How Many Are for Me? But the telling moment came Christmas morning when the gifts were handed out. The children ripped through them, shredding and scattering the wrappings like jungle plants before a well-wielded machete.*
>
> *Each gift was beautiful: an intricately laced dress Grandma Christie had sewn, an exquisitely detailed model car Uncle Bob had found at a specialty store on Robson Street in Vancouver, a finely bound and gorgeously illustrated collection of children's classics Aunt Leslie had sent. The children looked at each gift briefly, their interest quickly fading, and then put it aside to move on to the Next Thing. When the ransacking was finished, my son, standing amid a tumultuous sea of boxes and bright crumpled paper and exotic trappings, asked plaintively, "Is this all there is?"*[25]

Using this all-too-familiar Christmas scene, Buchanan shows how we too often forget to treasure and to savor. As he says, "The pressure of constant wanting dissipates all gratitude."[26] And isn't that true? That's why savoring and treasuring are so vital during this holy week when we celebrate Christmas together.

By the way, Buchanan makes an important and somewhat surprising point here. He states that God made us this way. God gave us this yearning and hunger to find the "next thing." It's a restlessness and a yearning that he says is healthy and God-given. The issue is not the wanting that tarnishes the season. It's the unbridled wanting that's misplaced, that's set on the wrong thing, that leads to disappointment. As we said, his message is to help us become more heavenly minded to be of more earthly good.

So how can you, in this important season, remember to treasure and savor each other as a couple?

"Maybe Christmas," he thought, "doesn't come from a store. Maybe Christmas . . . perhaps . . . means a little bit more!" —DR. SEUSS

WHAT'S YOUR TRADITION?

The Lord himself will give you the sign. Look! The virgin will conceive a child! She will give birth to a son and will call him Immanuel (which means "God is with us").

ISAIAH 7:14

DO YOU OPEN YOUR Christmas presents tonight or tomorrow morning? Les says, tongue in cheek, that "true Christians open presents on Christmas Eve." Of course, he thinks that's the way to celebrate because that's what his family did growing up. I, on the other hand, grew up in a home where we always opened our gifts on Christmas morning. I still recall the excitement of waking up early and rushing downstairs to let the excitement begin.

So what's our pattern in the home we created together? We open our gifts on Christmas Eve. Chalk one up for Les! Actually, it was a mutual decision, and after all these years I can't imagine changing this tradition. We love it. The evening typically begins with an evening service at our church that involves singing some of the most sacred of Christmas hymns, followed by a scrumptious holiday dinner. Then we gather around the tree and distribute the gifts one by one.

Now, if you happen to be newly married, you're likely still working out your traditions, but you'll soon have them. And like a groove that we feel was made just for us, we all seem to find our own traditions that work in our home. Sometimes the traditions begin very early on. Consider Pastor Rick Warren, author of *The Purpose of Christmas*. When he was just three years old, he asked his mom why they celebrated Christmas. She explained that Christmas is a celebration of Jesus' birthday. In a burst of preschooler inspiration, Rick concluded with a child's logic that they should have a birthday party— with cake, Kool-Aid, and singing happy birthday to Jesus. And that's what they did.

That little party began a tradition in the Warren family that has lasted over five decades. Every Christmas Eve they have angel food cake, complete with candles. But that's not all. Besides singing carols and reading the Christmas story from the Bible, each family member takes a turn sharing his or her answers to two personal questions: "What, from the past year, are you thankful to God for?" and "Since it's Jesus' birthday, what gift will you give him this next year?"

According to Pastor Warren, these two simple questions have prompted some of the most profound and moving moments in their marriage and family's history. They might be two questions we could all make a tradition of starting this evening.

Unless we make Christmas an occasion to share our blessings, all the snow in Alaska won't make it "white." —BING CROSBY

READING THE CHRISTMAS STORY

Joseph named him Jesus. MATTHEW 1:25

IN HER BOOK *AMAZING GRACE*, the writer and poet Kathleen Norris shares what she calls "the scariest story" she's ever heard about the Bible. Norris and her husband were visiting a man named Arlo, a rugged, self-made man who was facing terminal cancer. During their visit, Arlo started talking about his grandfather, a sincere Christian. The grandfather gave Arlo and his bride a wedding present: an expensive leather Bible with their names printed in gold lettering. Arlo left it in the box and never opened it. But for months afterwards his grandfather kept asking if he liked the Bible. Arlo told Norris, "The wife had written a nice thank-you note, and we'd thanked him in person, but some-how he couldn't let it lie, he always had to ask about it."

Finally, Arlo grew curious enough to open the Bible. "The joke was on me," Arlo said. "I finally took that Bible out of the closet, and I found that granddad had placed a twenty-dollar bill at the beginning of the Book of Genesis, and at the beginning of every book . . . over thirteen hundred dollars in all. And he knew I'd never find it."[27]

Sometimes even those of us who rely on God's Holy Word on a regular basis can become a tad like Arlo when it comes to reading the Christmas story. After all, we've likely read it countless times. But during these days of celebrating the birth of Jesus, we miss out on a reward if we don't do our best to read it for the first time all over again. So take a moment right now, to do just that:

> *This is how Jesus the Messiah was born. His mother, Mary, was engaged to be married to Joseph. But before the marriage took place, while she was still a virgin, she became pregnant through the power of the Holy Spirit. Joseph, her fiancé, was a good man and did not want to disgrace her publicly, so he decided to break the engagement quietly.*
>
> *As he considered this, an angel of the Lord appeared to him in a dream. "Joseph, son of David," the angel said, "do not be afraid to take Mary as your wife. For the child within her was conceived by the Holy Spirit. And she will have a son, and you are to name him Jesus, for he will save his people from their sins."*
>
> *All of this occurred to fulfill the Lord's message through his prophet: "Look! The virgin will conceive a child! She will give birth to a son, and they will call him Immanuel, which means 'God is with us.'"*
>
> *When Joseph woke up, he did as the angel of the Lord commanded and took Mary as his wife. But he did not have sexual relations with her until her son was born. And Joseph named him Jesus. (Matthew 1:18-25)*

You can never truly enjoy Christmas until you can look up into the Father's face and tell him you have received his Christmas gift. —JOHN R. RICE

JESUS CALLING

God showed how much he loved us by sending his one and only Son into the world so that we might have eternal life through him. 1 JOHN 4:9

AUTHOR DOUG MENDENHALL shares a brief parable that seems appropriate on the day after Christmas.[28] It starts with Jesus calling from a convenience store off the interstate and asking if he can spend a day or so with Doug and his wife:

> *I must have gotten that Bambi-in-headlights look, because my wife hissed, "What is it? What's wrong? Who is that?"*
>
> *So I covered the receiver and told her Jesus was going to arrive in eight minutes, and she ran out of the room and started giving guidance to the kids—in that effective way that Marine drill instructors give guidance to recruits. . . .*
>
> *My mind was already racing with what needed to be done in the next eight—no seven—minutes so Jesus wouldn't think we were reprobate loser slobs.*

Medenhall goes on to say he turned off the TV in his den, as well as the one in their bedroom. He continues:

> *My wife had already thinned out the magazines that had been accumulating on the coffee table. She put* Christianity Today *on top for a good first impression. Five minutes to go.*
>
> *I looked out the front window, but the yard actually looked great thanks to my long, hard work, so I let it go. What could I improve in four minutes anyway?*
>
> *I did notice the mail had come, so I ran out to grab it. Mostly it was Netflix envelopes and a bunch of catalogs tied into recent purchases, so I stuffed it back in the box. Jesus doesn't need to get the wrong idea—three minutes from now—about how much online shopping we do.*
>
> *I ran back in and picked up a bunch of shoes left by the door. Tried to stuff them in the front closet, but it was overflowing with heavy coats and work coats and snow coats and pretty coats and raincoats and extra coats. We live in the South; why'd we buy so many coats? I squeezed the shoes in with two minutes to go.*
>
> *I plumped up sofa pillows, my wife tossed dishes into the sink, I scolded the kids, and she shooed the dog. With one minute left I realized something important: Getting ready for a visit from Jesus is not an eight-minute job.*
>
> *Then the doorbell rang.*

Mendenhall calls this piece "Getting Prepared for the Arrival of Jesus." So on this day after Christmas, we pose this question: What would the two of you do to prepare if Jesus called and asked if he could spend a day or two with you at your home?

> *Trumpets! Lightning! The earth trembles! But into the Virgin's womb thou didst descent with noiseless tread.* —AGATHIAS SCHOLASTICUS

GETTING OUT OF THE NEGATIVE RUT

Love each other with genuine affection, and take delight in honoring each other.

ROMANS 12:10

WE HAD A SPEAKING ENGAGEMENT in British Columbia recently. And it wasn't in the great city of Vancouver. We were in the back country. Deep in the woods. We flew by seaplane from downtown Seattle into some of the prettiest scenery you can imagine. Snow-capped mountains and lush valleys with breathtaking waterfalls. And we hit it at just the right time. It was a pristine summer day.

People joke that in the Canadian northlands there are just two seasons, winter and July. And it's more than a joke. When the back roads begin to thaw, they become so muddy that vehicles going into the backwoods country leave deep ruts that become frozen once winter returns. For those entering this primitive area during the cold months, there is a sign that reads, "Driver, please choose carefully which rut you drive in, because you'll be in it for the next twenty miles."

We've thought about putting a similar sign outside of a church following a wedding ceremony for the newlywed couple. Something like, "Beware, your attitudes are so habit forming they become like frozen ruts, and you could easily find yourselves in them twenty years down the road."

Of course, it's a message for more than new couples. Even after years of marriage, our frozen ruts can get the best of us. So why not resolve to make this coming year the year that you get out of a negative attitude rut? Can you think of something in your attitudes that you'd like to change? The more specific you are the better.

It takes serious effort to change these negative thinking patterns, so we urge you to give yourself and your partner grace along the way. And ask for help when you need a boost. If your attitude change isn't as quick or as consistent as you'd like, go easy on yourself. Remember that each new day presents another opportunity to start fresh. And each day you make this effort to improve your attitude brings you closer to the marriage you desire.[29]

"It's snowing still," said Eeyore gloomily. . . . "However," he said, brightening up a little, "we haven't had an earthquake lately." —A. A. MILNE

THE PASSING
YEARS OF MATRIMONY

Those who trust in the LORD will find new strength. ISAIAH 40:31

IN 1941, AN ENGAGED COUPLE, Violet Bailey and Samuel Booth, were walking leisurely through the English countryside. A diamond engagement ring—Violet's most treasured possession—sparkled on her finger.

But, as can happen with couples, something was said that hurt the other's feelings and an argument ensued, then escalated. Violet became so angry that she pulled the diamond ring from her finger and hurled the treasured possession with all her might into the field. The ring sailed through the air, fell to the ground, and under the grass, making it impossible to find.

When Violet and Samuel eventually made up, they were desperate to recover the lost ring, but never did.

They were married two months later. They had a child and eventually a grandson. Part of their family lore was the story of the lost engagement ring. It was told and retold. Everyone knew about it even decades later.

Violet and Samuel grew old together, and in 1993 Samuel died. Fifteen years passed, but the ring was not forgotten. One day Violet's grandson, playing around with a metal detector, thought that maybe it could help him find his grandmother's ring. He went to the field where Violet had tossed her treasured possession sixty-seven years earlier. He turned on the machine and began to crisscross the field, waving the detector over the grass. After two hours of searching, he found what he was looking for.

With immense joy and pride, the grandson placed the diamond ring into the hand of his astonished grandmother. The treasured possession had finally come home.[30]

Can you imagine finally discovering what you've been hoping to find for more than six decades? The story, of course, is bittersweet. Although the ring was found, Samuel didn't get to finally place that lost ring on Violet's finger. Violet found what she was looking for, but most would say it was too late.

Don't let the same thing happen in your marriage. We're not talking about losing a ring, of course. We're talking about something far more precious. We're talking about losing days that turn into years when you don't keep the gift of your marriage in sight.[31]

Don't be fooled by the calendar. There are only as many days in the year as you make use of. —CHARLES RICHARDS

ANOTHER YEAR BITES THE DUST

Be careful how you life. Don't live like fools, but like those who are wise. Make the most of every opportunity. EPHESIANS 5:15-16

BELIEVE IT OR NOT, there's a website that allows you to enter your birth date and gender so that you can discover how much time you have left. Yikes! Known as the "Death Clock," it will instantly calculate the day you would die according to projections for the average life span. If you were born on March 16, 1969, and are male, it says you'll have until December 26, 2042, based on an average life span. It'll also tell you that this is just 1.4 billion seconds away. Kind of crazy, don't you think? The site's slogan is "The Internet's friendly reminder that life is slipping away."

It doesn't get much more macabre than that, but it's right. Time is slipping away. And as the year is coming to a close in this last month, there's nothing like a startling in-your-face reminder like this website to make you take notice of time's quick passage. And the older you get, the more you notice how fleeting it is. Each year seems to move more quickly than the last. When we were children, time sometimes felt like it was standing still, didn't it? But no longer.

It may not be the most pleasant of thoughts, but an occasional reminder that our time on this planet is finite can awaken our appreciation for each and every moment we have. After all, nothing you can do will stop the march of time, but you can do plenty to make sure the time you have left is not wasted. You can begin by paying attention to what makes your time on this earth so valuable. And, of course, your relationships are at the top of the list. You may enjoy your home, your vacations, your work, or any other good fortunes, but everyone agrees that it is your relationships that give life meaning and fulfillment—especially your relationship with your soul mate.

So, as morbid as it might first seem, consider the days that you are likely to have left in this earthly life. Give serious thought to how you want to spend the days that stretch before you. Do you really have time to fuss and fight? Do you want to spend your time bellyaching and moaning? Do you want to give your very best at the office and only have what's left over at home? Of course not. Nobody does.

We're all bound to have our share of conflict and busyness, but why let negativity steal the precious moments you have together? Instead, consider how you can curb whatever it is that tends to take time away from what you want most in your relationship and in this life you share together. Don't allow another year to bite the dust without squeezing the very life out of it.

The years shall run like rabbits. —W. H. AUDEN

RESOLVING TOGETHER

"I know the plans I have for you," says the LORD. *"They are plans for good and not for disaster, to give you a future and a hope."* JEREMIAH 29:11

JEAN NIDETCH WAS OVERWEIGHT in high school and became obese in her twenties and thirties, despite trying all kinds of diet regimens. But in 1961, at age 38, Jean gained a new insight. While she often started a new diet with a lot of inspiration and optimism, she would eventually lose her motivation. So she decided she would lose weight with her friends. She invited them to start the diet with her and then meet in each other's homes each week to weigh in, literally, and then encourage and support one another's efforts while keeping each other accountable. They would experience it together.

Out of those first meetings in Queens, New York, grew a company that is known worldwide: Weight Watchers. Nidetch's idea was simple: If you're going to stay motivated in your efforts to lose weight, you need peer support.

Eventually Nidetch, who'd lost seventy-two pounds, rented office space and started leading groups across New York City. Today, Weight Watchers International is a billion-dollar enterprise with exercise programs, cookbooks, portion-controlled food products, and a magazine. Nidetch retired in 1984, leaving behind a legacy that has saved the lives of literally millions of men and women. As the company's current CEO, Dave Kirchhoff notes, "Though the science of weight loss has evolved over the years, the core of Jean's program—support and accountability—has remained constant."[32]

In this last week of the year we want to leave you with a meditation on the concept of support and accountability. Why? Because if you are like most people, you are contemplating a resolution or two about now. "Every New Year, I resolve to streamline my body, be more sensitive to others, and be more productive. And every year, my resolutions fail." We hear something to this effect from dozens of people in our counseling office about the time March rolls around each year. In fact, in one poll, taken by *Newsweek*, only 22 percent of respondents believed they would actually stand by their resolutions for a complete year.

So how can you resolve to do something for your marriage and stick with it? We've got some good news: Couples who make resolutions together for the good of their marriage are far more likely to make their resolutions last than those making resolutions on their own.

"Teamwork wins goals," notes Terry D. Hargrave, a professor of marriage and family therapy at Fuller Theological Seminary. "If a resolution is as good for your spouse as it is for you—bet on success with the resolution and a sweeter marriage." Why? Because you have a built-in support system for making the same resolutions work. You each have a cheerleader in one another.

> *Make your resolutions so clear and firm that nothing can lure you from your chosen path.* —GRENVILLE KLEISER

YOUR TOP-TEN LIST

May the LORD bless you and protect you. May the LORD smile on you and be gracious to you. May the LORD show you his favor and give you his peace. NUMBERS 6:24-26

SHORTLY AFTER GRADUATING from college and before we got married a month later in 1984, Les gave me a gift I never even imagined. Without telling me, Les had saved every ticket stub and every memento from every date we had ever been on and organized them in a book where he recorded a few thoughts and recollections of each date. I was speechless. It started with our first date at a Kansas City Royals game. It included our date to an art museum, to the zoo, to concerts. They were all there. He didn't miss one. Needless to say, I was impressed. You see, we dated for seven years before we got married. Looking back, it's tough to believe that we dated for so long. Les collected and reflected all on his own for seven years and then presented me with three volumes of priceless memories.

I can't count how many times we have gone through the pages of these books and recalled details of dates that would have been lost forever if he hadn't taken the time to preserve them. Each page of this treasure evokes specific feelings and memories and joins our spirits together.

A few years back, Les started a journal that now rivals the dating records. And on the eve of most New Year's celebrations, we steal away and review the past 365 days to come up with a list.

Celebrating our wedding anniversary at Snoqualmi Lodge makes the list. So does a cookout on the Oregon coast with Kevin and Kathy. Les achieving his promotion at the university makes the list too. As does walking the Freedom Trail in Boston and eating brunch at the Parker House Hotel. Our Jackson losing his first tooth while we were hiking in Yellowstone and his older brother John leading his school in Boy Scout flag salute makes the list as well.

We've been making a list of the top ten highlights of our years together since 1997. I suppose we've always reminisced about our times together, but not until '97 did we begin to take it seriously and actually review our year and write down our highlights. Now, with several years of this ritual under our belt, we've got to say these lists are a true treasure to us. As you close out the year, you might want to make a list of your top ten. It is sure to bring you to a vantage point where you will breathe deeply and take in a sweeping view of all that's blessed your lives together.

History is a hill or high point of vantage, from which alone men see the town in which they live or the age in which they are living. —G. K. CHESTERTON

NOTES

January

1. *Campus Life* 53, no. 9
2. Joe Posnanski, "Part Ii: Made to Last," SI Vault online, August 23, 2010.
3. Martin Seligman, *Authentic Happiness* (New York: Free Press, 2002), 90.
4. Joie Davidow, *Marked for Life: A Story of Disguise, Discovery, and Redemption* (New York: Harmony Books, 2003), 12.
5. Chelsea J. Carter, "Teacher's Lesson Echoes across Years via Internet Chain Letter," *The Topeka Capital-Journal* online, http://cjonline.com/stories/020799/new_teacher.shtml.
6. Robert Ajemian, "Interview with Frank Reed: Terror and Tedium," Time.com, http://www.time.com/time/magazine/article/0,9171,970999,00.html.
7. Bill Gaither and Jerry B. Jenkins, *I Almost Missed the Sunset: My Perspectives on Life and Music* (Nashville: Thomas Nelson, 1992).
8. Jack Canfield and Mark Victor Hansen, *Chicken Soup for the Soul: 101 Stories to Open the Heart and Rekindle the Spirit* (Deerfield Beach, FL: Health Communications, 1993), 207.
9. Philip McFarland, *Hawthorne in Concord* (New York: Grove Press, 2005), 87.
10. James Patterson and Peter Kim, *The Day America Told the Truth: What People Really Believe about Everything That Really Matters* (New York: Prentice Hall Press, 1991).

February

1. Cathy Lynn Grossman, "Couples Take Their Vows in a New Direction," *USA Today*, May 30, 2001.
2. Fred Smith, "The Care and Feeding of Critics," http://www.ctlibrary.com/lebooks/libraryofleadershipdevelopment/conflictreconciliation/lldev01-25.html.
3. "What Life?," Bible.org, http://bible.org/illustration/what-life.
4. Belden Lane, "Rabbinical Stories," *Christian Century* 98 (December 16, 1981): 41.
5. *Leadership*, October 1, 1981, http://www.christianitytoday.com/le/1989/fall/89l4097.html.
6. Carl Honoré, *In Praise of Slowness: Challenging the Cult of Speed* (New York: HarperCollins, 2004), 168.
7. E. J. Langer and J. Rodin, "The Effects of Choice and Enhanced Personal Responsibility for the Age: A Field Experiment in an Institutional Setting," *Journal of Personality and Social Psychology* 34 (1976): 191–198.

8. J. H. Johnson and I. G. Sarason, "Life Stress, Depression and Anxiety: Internal-External Control as a Moderator Variable," *Journal of Psychosomatic Research* 22 (1978): 205–208.

9. Associated Press, "Kidney Saves Marriage," Foxnews.com, May 6, 2007.

10. Mark Trahant, "Native News: 'Somehow,'" in *American Indian Nations: Yesterday, Today, and Tomorrow*, ed. George Horse Capture (Plymouth, UK: Altamira Press, 2007), 151.

March

1. "Robert McQuilken," YouTube video, 2:11, posted by "tkdmaster001," February 1, 2007, http://www.youtube.com/watch?v=f6pX1phIqug&feature=player_embedded#at=99.

2. Robertson McQuilkin, *A Promise Kept: The Story of an Unforgettable Love* (Carol Stream: Tyndale House, 1998), 23.

3. Associated Press, "Naked Man Hides in Plane Wheel Well at L.A. Airport," *USA Today*, November 4, 2004, http://www.usatoday.com/travel/news/2004-11-04-lax-naked_x.htm.

4. Lorne Peasland, "Beating the Effects of Stress—Part 1," StatsSheet.com, http://www.statssheet.com/articles/article16434.html.

5. G. E. Schwartz, "Psychophysiology of Imagery and Healing: A Systems Perspective," in *Imagination and Healing*, ed. Anees A. Sheikh (Farmingdale, NY: Baywood, 1984), 51–67.

6. Jeanne Achterberg, *Imagery in Healing: Shamanism and Modern Medicine* (Boston: New Science Library, 1985).

7. Eugene H. Peterson, *Subversive Spirituality* (Grand Rapids: Eerdmans, 1997), 237.

8. Dennis Waitley, *Seeds of Greatness: The Ten Best-Kept Secrets of Total Success* (New York: Simon & Schuster, 1983), 43.

9. Marcus Buckingham and Donald O. Clifton, *Now, Discover Your Strengths* (New York: Free Press, 2001), 21.

10. M. Voboril, "A Weighty Issue: Empathy Suit Shows Medical Personnel What It's Like to Be Obese," *Newsday*, April 16, 2000, B03.

11. Jo-Ellan Dimitrius and Mark Mazzarella, *Reading People: How to Understand People and Predict Their Behavior—Anytime, Anyplace* (New York: Ballantine, 1999), 7.

12. Robert Rosenthal, Judith Hall, M. Robin DiMatteo, Peter L. Rogers, and Dane Archer, *Sensitivity to Nonverbal Communication: The PONS Test* (Baltimore: Johns Hopkins University Press, 1979); see also Robert Rosenthal and Ralph L. Rosnow, *Essentials of Behavioral Research: Methods and Data Analysis* (New York: McGrawHill, 1991).

13. Maggie Scarf, *Intimate Worlds: Life Inside the Family* (New York: Random House, 1995).

14. Robert J. Sternberg, *Why Smart People Can Be So Stupid* (New Haven: Yale University Press, 2002).

April

1. Brent Kelly, "Chi Chi's Golf Games You Gotta Play," review of *Chi Chi's Golf Games You Gotta Play: Shots and Side Bets to Outscore and Outshark Your Opponents*, by Chi Chi Rodriguez and John Anderson, About.com, http://golf.about.com/od/equipment reviews/fr/chichigames.htm.

2. M. Craig Barnes, "Easter in an Age of Terror," *Christianity Today*, April 1, 2002.

3. Adapted from Les and Leslie Parrott, "Talking to Yourself," *Marriage Partnership* (Fall 2004).

4. Mark Galli, "The Good Friday Life," *Christianity Today*, April 4, 2007.

5. Anna Muoio, "My Greatest Lesson," *Fast Company*, May 31, 1998, http://www.fast company.com/magazine/15/one.html#.

6. Steven D. Levitt and Stephen J. Dubner, *Freakonomics: A Rogue Economist Explores the Hidden Side of Everything* (New York: William Morrow, 2006), 239.

7. Focus on the Family letter, September 1992, 14, quoted in "Burnout," *Sermon Illustrations*, http://www.sermonillustrations.com/a-z/b/burnout.htm.

8. James Pennebaker, *Writing to Heal* (Oakland, CA: New Harbinger Publications, 2004).

9. Bjorn Carey, "Ant School: The First Formal Classroom Found in Nature," Foxnews.com, January 13, 2006.

May

1. Adapted from Les Parrott, *You're Stronger Than You Think* (Carol Stream, IL: Tyndale House, 2012).

2. Adapted from Les Parrott, *High-Maintenance Relationships* (Carol Stream, IL: Tyndale House, 1996), 2–3.

3. John Ortberg, "Ruthlessly Eliminate Hurry," *Christianity Today*, July 4, 2002, http://www.christianitytoday.com/le/currenttrendscolumns/leadershipweekly /cln20704.html.

4. John Maxwell and Les Parrott, *25 Ways to Win with People: How to Make Others Feel Like a Million Bucks* (Nashville: Thomas Nelson, 2005), 71.

5. Based on a true story submitted by Pam Hoepner to *Reader's Digest*, July 1998, quoted in Gary Thomas, *Sacred Marriage: What If God Designed Marriage to Make Us Holy More Than to Make Us Happy* (Grand Rapids: Zondervan, 2000), 154.

6. Laura Rowley, "Stay Married, Get Rich," *Money & Happiness Blog*, January 27, 2006, http://www.moneyandhappiness.com/blog/?p=426.

7. *Up*, directed by Pete Docter and Bob Peterson (Emeryville, CA: Pixar Animation Studios, 2009).

8. Marilyn Wellemeyer, "The Class the Dollars Fell On," *Fortune*, May 1974.

9. Gail Sheehy, *Pathfinders: Overcoming the Crises of Adult Life and Finding Your Own Path to Well-Being* (New York: Morrow, 1981).

10. Adapted from Les and Leslie Parrott, *L.O.V.E.: Putting Your Love Styles to Work for You* (Grand Rapids: Zondervan, 2009).

11. Adapted from Les and Leslie Parrott, *L.O.V.E.: Putting Your Love Styles to Work for You* (Grand Rapids: Zondervan, 2009).

12. Adi Ignatius, "The HBR Interview: 'We Had To Own the Mistakes': An Interview with Howard Schultz," *Harvard Business Review*, July–August 2010, http://hbr.org/2010/07 /the-hbr-interview-we-had-to-own-the-mistakes/ar/1#.

13. Les and Leslie Parrott, *The Complete Guide to Marriage Mentoring* (Grand Rapids: Zondervan, 2005), 139.

June

1. Larry Chang, ed., *Wisdom for the Soul: Five Millennia of Prescriptions for Spiritual Healing* (Washington, DC: Gnosophia, 2006), 70.

2. Charles R. Swindoll, *Strengthening Your Grip: Essentials in an Aimless World* (Waco, TX: Word Books, Inc., 1982), paraphrasing a statement originally made

by W. C. Fields. Quoted in Barbara Johnson, *Splashes of Joy in the Cesspool of Life* (Nashville: W Publishing Group, 1992), 19.

3. Maxwell and Parrott, *25 Ways to Win with People*, 36–37.

4. Philip Yancey, *Rumors of Another World* (Grand Rapids: Zondervan, 2003). Also adapted from Yancey, "Holy Sex," *Christianity Today*, October 1, 2003.

5. Skye Jethani, "The Discipline of Communal Examination," *PreachingToday.com*, February 2010, http://www.preachingtoday.com/sermons/sermons/2010/february /disciplinecommexam.html.

6. Patrick Swayze and Lisa Niemi, *The Time of My Life* (New York: Atria, 2010), 4.

7. J. Krueger and R. A. Mueller, "Unskilled, Unaware, or Both?: The Better-Than-Average Heuristic and Statistical Regression Predict Errors in Estimates of Own Performance," *Journal of Personality and Social Psychology* 82 (2002): 180–188.

8. Dietrich Bonhoeffer, *Letters and Papers from Prison* (New York: Touchstone, 1997), 43.

9. Adapted from James Michener, *The World Is My Home: A Memoir* (New York: Random House, 1991), 484–86.

10. D. Kahneman, A. B. Drueger, D. Schlade, N. Schwartz, and A. Stone, "A Survey Method for Characterizing Daily Life Experience: The Day Reconstruction Method," *Science* 306 no. 5702 (December 3, 2004): 1776–1780.

11. Dick Peterson, "Living with an Intruder," *Marriage Partnership* (Fall 2007), 18–19.

12. Taken from Les and Leslie Parrott, *Meditations on Proverbs for Couples* (Grand Rapids: Zondervan, 1997), 67–68.

13. Taken from Parrott, *Meditations on Proverbs for Couples*, 73–74.

14. Honoré, *In Praise of Slowness*, 71.

July

1. Garrison Keillor, *We Are Still Married: Stories and Letters* (New York: Penguin, 1990).

2. Frederick Buechner, *Whistling in the Dark: A Doubter's Dictionary* (New York: HarperOne, 1993), 86–87.

3. Nancy Guthrie, *Holding On to Hope: A Pathway through Suffering to the Heart of God* (Carol Stream, IL: Tyndale, 2006).

4. *Shrek 2*, directed by Andrew Adamson and Kelly Asbury (Universal City, CA: DreamWorks Studios, 2004).

5. Janine Pouliot, "The Secret to Feeling Closer," *Ladies Home Journal*, January 2005, 32.

6. George Lewis, "Are Ya Kidding Me?! No Complaints for 21 Days," MSNBC, March 6, 2007, http://today.msnbc.msn.com/id/17362505/ns/today/.

7. Tony Campolo, "If I Should Wake before I Die" (sermon, *30 Good Minutes*, April 25, 1993, http://www.csec.org/csec/sermon/campolo_3627.htm).

8. Tom Hennen, *Crawling out the Window* (Black Hat Press, 1998).

August

1. Dini von Mueffling, *The 50 Most Romantic Things Ever Done* (Grove Press, 2001), 1.

2. Dr. Harold McNabb, "Wait for It" (sermon, West Shore Presbyterian Church, Victoria, British Columbia, May 4, 2008, http://www.islandnet.com/~ws_pres/sermon/yeara08 /wait.html).

3. Adapted from Les Parrott, *You're Stronger Than You Think* (Carol Stream, IL: Tyndale House, 2012).

4. Ken Sutterfield, *The Power of an Encouraging Word: Planting the Seeds of Kindness to Reap a World in Bloom* (Green Forest, AR: New Leaf Press, 1997).

5. Martin E. P. Seligman, *Learned Optimism: A Leading Expert on Motivation Demonstrates That Optimism Is Essential for a Good and Successful Life—and Shows You How to Acquire It* (New York: Knopf, 1991).

6. Marlo Thomas, *The Right Words at the Right Time* (New York: Atria, 2002), 104–106.

7. Adapted from Les and Leslie Parrott, *Getting Ready for the Wedding* (Grand Rapids: Zondervan, 1998), 150.

8. John Mossman, Associated Press, August 11, 2002. This illustration was found at http://www.preachingtoday.com/search/?query=sosa&searcharea=illustrations &type=.

9. J. W. Schooler, D. Gerhard, and E. F. Loftus, "Qualities of the Unreal," *Journal of Experimental Psychology: Learning, Memory, and Cognition* 12 (1986): 171–181.

10. Maynard Good Stoddard, "Billy Graham: The World Is His Pulpit," *The Saturday Evening Post*, March 1, 1986, http://www.highbeam.com/doc/1G1-4151300.html.

11. Norman Cousins, *Anatomy of an Illness as Perceived by the Patient: Reflections on Healing and Regeneration* (New York: W. W. Norton, 1979).

12. Adapted from Les and Leslie Parrott, *The Love List: Eight Little Things That Make a Big Difference in Your Marriage* (Grand Rapids: Zondervan, 2002), 42–43.

13. Charles W. Colson, "Redeeming the Time," *Jubilee* (February 1991).

14. Quoted in "To Illustrate . . . ," *Leadership*, July 1, 1986, http://www.christianitytoday .com/le/1986/summer/86l3038.html?start=1.

15. Parrott, *Meditations on Proverbs for Couples*, 107.

16. Adapted from Les and Leslie Parrott, *Becoming Soul Mates: Cultivating Spiritual Intimacy in the Early Years of Marriage* (Grand Rapids: Zondervan, 1995), 221–222.

17. Quoted in Michael Kilian, "He Looked to Me Like a God," *Chicago Tribune*, April 30, 1995.

18. Bernie Siegel, *Peace, Love and Healing: Bodymind Communication and the Path of Self-Healing: An Exploration* (New York: Harper and Row, 1989), 245–46.

19. Parrott, *Meditations on Proverbs for Couples*, 88.

20. Parrott, *Getting Ready for the Wedding*, 18–19.

21. Adapted from Les and Leslie Parrott, *When Bad Things Happen to Good Marriages: How to Stay Together When Life Pulls You Apart* (Grand Rapids: Zondervan, 2001), 164.

22. Adapted from Leslie Parrott, "May 13," *Daily Seeds from Women Who Walk in Faith* (Chicago: Moody Bible Institute, 2008).

September

1. John C. Maxwell, *Today Matters: 12 Daily Practices to Guarantee Tomorrow's Success* (New York: Hachette, 2004), 10.

2. Rico Tice, "What Shall I Do with Jesus?" Sermon at All Souls Church, Langham Place, London, www.preachingtoday.com/illustrations/2011/july/7071811.html.

3. "Hours Available for Leisure Per Week," http://www.marketingcharts.com/television /us-leisure-time-plummets-20-in-2008-hits-new-low-7470/harris-interactive-harris-poll -hours-available-leisure-week-december-2008jpg.

4. Gordon MacDonald, *Ordering Your Private World* (Nashville: Nelson, 2003), 39.

5. Adapted from "Stand and Deliver: Leading Through Hardship" an illustration from the film of the same name.

6. http://www.menningerclinic.com/about/early-history.htm.
7. Shane Claiborne, *The Irresistible Revolution: Living as an Ordinary Radical* (Grand Rapids, MI: Zondervan, 2006), 167–68.
8. http://preacherstudy.com/members/heart.html.
9. John Ortberg in the sermon "Guide," *PreachingToday.com*, posted 10/26/2009, http://www.preachingtoday.com/illustrations/2009/october/3102609.html.
10. Adapted from Parrott, *Meditations on Proverbs for Couples*, 40.
11. The Bohemian Comedian, "Top Cheating Songs of All Time," *The Kabosh*, April 7, 2010, http://thekabosh.wordpress.com/2010/04/07/top-cheating-songs-of-all-time-musical-musings-on-infidelity/.
12. Brendan I. Kroerner, "Secret of AA: After 75 Years, We Don't Know How It Works," *Wired*, June 23, 2010.
13. Taken from Les and Leslie Parrott, *Trading Places: The Best Move You'll Ever Make in Your Marriage* (Grand Rapids: Zondervan, 2008), 55–56.
14. Taken from Les Parrott and Neil Clark Warren, "Discovering Your Blind Spots" in *Love the Life You Live: 3 Secrets to Feeling Good—Deep Down in Your Soul* (Carol Stream, IL: Tyndale, 2004), 11.
15. Daniel Goleman, *Working with Emotional Intelligence* (New York: Bantam, 1998).

October
1. Michael Hodgin, *1001 More Humorous Illustrations for Public Speaking: Fresh, Timely, and Compelling Illustrations for Preachers, Teachers, and Speakers* (Grand Rapids: Zondervan, 2004), 152.
2. Samantha Miller, "Sitting Pretty," *People* (December 13, 1999): 228. See also http://www.people.com/people/archive/article/0,,20130067,00.html.
3. Maxwell and Parrott, *25 Ways to Win with People*, 27.
4. Mary O'Brien, MD, *Successful Aging* (Concord, CA: Biomed General, 2005).
5. M. W. McCall and M. Lombardo, *Off the Track: Why and How Successful Executives Get Derailed, Technical Report No. 21* (Greensboro, NC: Center for Creative Leadership, 1987).
6. Richard Boyatzis, *The Competent Manager: A Model for Effective Performance* (New York: John Wiley and Sons, 1982). Commentary and reference from Goleman, *Working with Emotional Intelligence*, 64.
7. Gordon MacDonald, "The Volcanic Spirit," *LeadershipJournal.net*, April 21, 2010.
8. Kirkpatrick Sale, *Christopher Columbus and the Conquest of Paradise* (London: Tauris Parke, 2006), 60.
9. "I'm Drawing God!," *Jokes Lab Magazine*, March 31, 2009, http://jokeslab.com/mag/I-m-Drawing-God.html.
10. Sheri and Bob Stritof, "Marital Sex Statistics," *About.com Guides*, http://marriage.about.com/cs/sexualstatistics/a/sexstatistics.htm
11. "Being in Love Eases the Pain," *New Scientist* (October 15, 2010), http://www.newscientist.com/article/dn19593-being-in-love-eases-the-pain.html.
12. "John Keats," *Wikipedia*, last modified June 14, 2011, http://en.wikipedia.org/wiki/John_Keats.
13. Tracie White, "Love Takes Up Where Pain Leaves Off, Brain Study Shows," *Inside Stanford Medicine* (October 13, 2010), http://med.stanford.edu/ism/2010/october/love.html.
14. Malcolm Gladwell, *The Tipping Point: How Little Things Can Make a Big Difference* (New York: Little, Brown, 2002), 165.

15. Ibid.

16. Les and Leslie Parrott, "Time to Slow Down," *Focus on the Family New Zealand*, http://www.focus.org.nz/default.aspx?go=article&aid=593.

17. "The Sound of Slow," *PreachingToday.com*, http://www.preachingtoday.com/illustrations/1998/april/2714/html.

18. "A Little Light Humour!," Histon Salvation Army Church, Cambridgeshire, UK, http://www.histonsalvationarmy.co.uk/2009/index.php?option=com_content&view=article&id=100:a-little-light-humour&catid=15:church-news&Itemid=35.

19. Taken from Parrott, *L.O.V.E.*, 67.

20. James Bryan Smith, *The Good and Beautiful God: Falling in Love with the God Jesus Knows* (Downers Grove, IL: InterVarsity Press, 2009), 162.

21. The illustration of Susan is taken from Parrott, *Becoming Soul Mates*, 65–66.

22. This devotional is taken from Les and Leslie Parrott, "Busyness: The Modern Disease," *eH Advice*, http://advice.eharmony.ca/about-you/mind-body-and-spirit/busyness-the-modern-disease.

23. Parrott, *Becoming Soul Mates*, 205.

24. Ron Vample, "'Avoid Death' Is Wacky Warning Winner," *USA Today* (December 12, 2007), http://www.usatoday.com/money/2007-12-12-wacky-warnings_N.htm.

25. Ann Landers, "A Woman of Letters," interview by Norma Libman, *Chicago Tribune* (October 7, 1990), http://articles.chicagotribune.com/1990-10-07/features/9003260428_1_fax-machines-readers-dear-abby/5.

26. Charles Colson, "Barbarians in the Parlor," *CWC Jubilee* (May 1988), http://www.thepointradio.org/search-library/search?view=searchdetail&id=1284.

27. Les and Leslie Parrott, "Revealing the Real You," *Stronger Families*, December 30, 2010, www.strongerfamilies.org/revealing-the-real-you/.

28. Paul Tournier, *To Understand Each Other* (Louisville: Westminster John Knox, 1967), 60–61.

November

1. "'Open Range': God Patiently Waits," *PreachingToday.com*, http://www.preachingtoday.com/search/?query=open+range&searcharea=illustrations&type=.

2. Hilary Stout, "Family Dinners Improve Kids' Health, Grades; How Not to Dread Them," *Wall Street Journal* (November 11, 2004); see also http://lists101.his.com/pipermail/smartmarriages/2004-November/002463.html.

3. Hillary Stout, "Family Dinners."

4. "A Little Boy Named Timmy," *Jokes and Riddles for Christian Teens* (blog), August 4, 2009, http://humorforteens.com/2009/08/04/august-4th-of-2009.aspx.

5. Adapted from Les Parrott, *Crazy Good Sex: Putting to Bed the Myths Men Have about Sex* (Grand Rapids: Zondervan, 2009), 46–47.

6. Les Parrott III, *High-Maintenance Relationships: How to Handle Impossible People* (Carol Stream: Tyndale, 1996), 89–90.

7. Jack Canfield and Mark Victor Hansen, *Chicken Soup for the Soul* (Deerfield Beach, FL: Health Communications, 2003), 64–65.

8. Larry Dossey, *Space, Time, and Medicine* (Boston: Shambhala Publications, 1982).

9. Les and Leslie Parrott, *Your Time-Starved Marriage: How to Stay Connected at the Speed of Life* (Grand Rapids: Zondervan, 2006), 33.

10. Parrott, *Trading Places*, 46–47.
11. Edgar A. Guest and W. T. Benda, "Winding the Clock," in *All That Matters* (Chicago, Reilly & Lee, 1922), 70–71.
12. Taken from John Maxwell, *Developing the Leader Within You* (Nashville: Nelson, 1993), 132.
13. This devotional is taken from Parrott, *L.O.V.E.*, 9–10.
14. Taken from Parrott, *Becoming Soul Mates*, 132–33.
15. Rick Ezell, *The Seven Sins of Highly Defective People* (Grand Rapids: Kregel, 2003), 27–28.
16. Joseph F. Sica, *Embracing Change: 10 Ways to Grow Spiritually and Emotionally* (Mystic, CT: Twenty-Third Publications, 2003), 48.
17. Adapted from Parrott, *Becoming Soul Mates*, 188–189.
18. Kenneth Chang, "Edward N. Lorenz, a Meteorologist and a Father of Chaos Theory, Dies at 90," NewYorkTimes.com, April 17, 2008.
19. Adapted from Les Parrott and Neil Clark Warren, *Love the Life You Live: 3 Secrets to Feeling Good—Deep Down in Your Soul* (Carol Stream: Tyndale, 2003), 165–66.
20. Adapted from Parrott, *Becoming Soul Mates*, 148–49.
21. R. A. Emmons and M. E. McCullough, "Counting Blessings Versus Burdens: Experimental Studies of Gratitude and Subjective Well-Being in Daily Life," *Journal of Personality and Social Psychology* 84 (2003): 377–389. See also Robert Emmons's wonderful book *Thanks: How the New Science of Gratitude Can Make You Happier* (New York: Houghton Mifflin, 2009).

December
1. Adapted from Les and Leslie Parrott, *I Love You More: How Everyday Problems Can Strengthen Your Marriage* (Grand Rapids: Zondervan, 2005), 59.
2. "John Vanier, Founder of L' Arche," *L' Arche.org*, http://www.larche.org/jean-vanier -founder-of-l-arche.en-gb.23.13.content.htm.
3. Stanley Hauerwas and Jean Vanier, *Living Gently in a Violent World: The Prophetic Witness of Weakness* (Downers Grove, IL: InterVarsity, 2008), 66.
4. Parrott, *When Bad Things Happen to Good Marriages*, 134.
5. Adapted from Parrott, *When Bad Things Happen to Good Marriages*, 135.
6. C. S. Lewis, *The Four Loves* (Orlando, FL: Harcourt Brace, 1960), 121.
7. Gordon MacDonald, "How to Experience Forgiveness from the Heart," *Christian Herald* (March/April 1991): 19.
8. When forgiving a moral wrong in marriage, most of us need to remember that forgiveness is like grief. You can be healed of pain and anger, but a memory might make the scar break open. The important thing is not to have forgiven, but to be in the process of forgiving.
9. This devotional is adapted from Les and Leslie Parrott, *When Bad Things Happen to Good Marriages* (Grand Rapids, MI: Zondervan, 2001), 142–43.
10. This devotional is taken from Les and Leslie Parrott, "Five Traits of a Good Marriage: Commitment: Living the Love You Promise," *Family Minute*, http://www.familyminute .com/article/five-traits-of-a-good-marriage#commitment.
11. Craig Brian Larson, "Confused Coach Costs Dutch Skater Olympic Gold," *Preaching Today*, http://www.preachingtoday.com/search/?query=sven+kramer&searcharea= illustrations&type=.
12. Quoted in Les and Leslie Parrott, *Becoming Soul Mates: 52 Meditations to Bring Joy to Your Marriage* (Grand Rapids: Zondervan, 1995), 198.

13. Benjamin Franklin, "Franklin's Formula for Successful Living — Number Three," in Benjamin Franklin's *The Art of Virtue: His Formula for Successful Living*, ed. George L. Rogers (Eden Prairie, Minn.: Acorn Publications, 1986), 88.

14. Adapted from Les and Leslie Parrott, *When Bad Things Happen to Good Marriages* (Grand Rapids: Zondervan, 2001), 43–44.

15. "King Edward VIII and Wallis Simpson," *People* vol. 45, no. 6 (February 12, 1996), http://www.people.com/people/archive/article/0,,20102762,00.html.

16. "Climber's Widow Tells Her Story," *CBS Evening News*, December 21, 2006.

17. Portions of this devotional are adapted from Les and Leslie Parrott, *Love Talk: Speak Each Other's Language Like You Never Have Before* (Grand Rapids: Zondervan, 2004), 139.

18. Parrott, *Becoming Soul Mates*, 111.

19. *Love Story* synopsis is taken from www.imdb.com/title/tt0066011/synopsis.

20. Kahlil Gibran, *The Prophet* (New York: Alfred A Knopf, 1955) 15–16.

21. Adapted from Les and Leslie Parrott, *When Bad Things Happen to Good Marriages* (Grand Rapids: Zondervan, 2001), 51–54.

22. Rick Hampson, "Gift of Wreaths Touches Nation," *USA Today* (December 15, 2006): 1A.

23. Charles Colson and Harold Fickett, *The Faith: What Christians Believe, Why They Believe It, and Why It Matters* (Grand Rapids: Zondervan, 2008), 84.

24. Mike Royko, "A Lovely Couple, Bound with Love," *Chicago Tribune* (December 24, 1995): 3, quoted in Daniel Meyer, "For Better but Worse," *Preaching Today Audio*, issue 280.

25. Mark Buchanan, *Things Unseen: Living in Light of Forever* (Sisters, OR: Multnomah, 2006), 50–51.

26. Buchanan, *Things Unseen*, 50.

27. Kathleen Norris, *Amazing Grace: A Vocabulary of Faith* (New York: Riverhead, 1998), 95.

28. Doug Mendenhall, "Getting Prepared for the Arrival of Jesus," *Abilene Reporter News*, September 24, 2009.

29. Adapted from Les and Leslie Parrott, *When Bad Things Happen to Good Marriages* (Grand Rapids: Zondervan, 2001).

30. "It Wasn't All Bad," *The Week* (February 15, 2008): 4.

31. Adapted from Les and Leslie Parrott, *L.O.V.E.: Putting Your Love Styles to Work for You* (Grand Rapids: Zondervan, 2009).

32. "New Year's Resolutions and the Importance of Community," *PreachingToday.com*, http://www.preachingtoday.com/illustrations/2009/December/5122109.html.

Do-able. Daily. Devotions.

START ANY DAY THE ONE YEAR WAY.

Do-able.
Every One Year book is designed for people who live busy, active lives. Just pick one up and start on today's date.

Daily.
Daily routine doesn't have to be drudgery. One Year devotionals help you form positive habits that connect you to what's most important.

Devotions.
Discover a natural rhythm for drawing near to God in an extremely personal way. One Year devotionals provide daily focus essential to your spiritual growth.

For Women

The One Year® Devotions for Women on the Go

The One Year® Devotions for Women

The One Year® Devotions for Moms

The One Year® Women of the Bible

The One Year® Coffee with God

For Women
(continued)

The One Year®
Devotional of Joy
and Laughter

For Men

The One Year®
Devotions for
Men on the Go

The One Year®
Devotions for
Men

For Families

The One Year®
Family
Devotions, Vol. 1

For Couples

The One Year®
Devotions for
Couples

The One Year®
Love Language
Minute Devotional

The One Year®
Love Talk
Devotional for
Couples

For Teens

The One Year®
Devos for Teens

The One Year®
Devos for Sports
Fans

For Personal Growth

The One Year®
Walk with God
Devotional

The One Year®
At His Feet
Devotional

The One Year®
Daily Insights
with Zig Ziglar

For Bible Study

The One Year®
Praying through
the Bible

The One Year®
Through the
Bible Devotional

It's convenient and easy to grow with
God the One Year way.

CP0145

The Perfect Gift

THOUGHTFUL. PRACTICAL. AFFORDABLE.

The One Year Mini for Women helps women connect with God through several Scripture verses and a devotional thought. Perfect for use anytime and anywhere between regular devotion times. Hardcover.

The One Year Mini for Students offers students from high school through college a quick devotional connection with God anytime and anywhere. Stay grounded through the ups and downs of a busy student lifestyle. Hardcover.

The One Year Mini for Men helps men connect with God anytime, anywhere between their regular devotion times through Scripture quotations and a related devotional thought. Hardcover.

CP0161